I, Maya Plisetskaya

I, Maya Plisetskaya

Maya Plisetskaya

Translated by Antonina W. Bouis

Foreword by Tim Scholl

Yale University Press   New Haven & London

Designed by Rebecca Gibb and set in Fournier type by Tseng Information Systems, Inc., Durham, North Carolina. Printed in the United States of America by R. R. Donnelley, Harrisonburg, Virginia.

Library of Congress Cataloging-in-Publication Data
Pliseëtìskaëïa, Maæiëïa Mikhaæilovna, 1925–
[ëÌìA, Maæiëïa Pliseëtìskaëïa — English]
I, Maya Plisetskaya / Maya Plisetskaya ; translated by Antonina W. Bouis ;
foreword by Tim Scholl.
p. cm.
ISBN 0–300–08857–4 (alk. paper)
1. Pliseëtìskaëïa, Maæiëïa Mikhaæilovna, 1925–   2. Ballerinas — Soviet Union —
Biography.   I. Title.
GV1785.P55 A3   2001
792.8′028′092 — dc21
2001002490

A catalogue record for this book is available from the British Library.

The paper in this book meets the guidelines for permanence and durability of the Committee on Production Guidelines for Book Longevity of the Council on Library Resources.

10   9   8   7   6   5   4   3   2

For Shchedrin

Contents

Contents

Contents

Foreword

Tim Scholl

Like opera enthusiasts who recognize a singer's voice by its timbre or vibrato, dance-goers identify their favorites by idiosyncrasies of phrasing or line. Yet this relatively intimate knowledge of the workings of a dancer's body may be all that is known about the dancer after decades on the stage. We rarely hear one speak.

Ballet has been called a mute art, but Maya Plisetskaya, one of its greatest practitioners, was never quiet. The de facto prima ballerina of the Bolshoi Ballet from Galina Ulanova's retirement in 1960 until her own belated departure from the Bolshoi stage in 1990, Plisetskaya was one of the few international celebrities the Soviet Union produced. She appeared in art films, documentaries, and frequently on television; she barnstormed first Russia's theaters, then the world's. Yet her path to stardom was littered with obstacles, and the difficulties she faced—especially in the early stage of her career—became known to her Russian fans through the intricate, unofficial network of gossip that thrived everywhere information was controlled. In a society where the personal was hardly public, legends grew up around Plisetskaya in the absence of fact. Today, nearly six decades after her career began, she remains a public persona.

Much of Plisetskaya's uniqueness and appeal to the Russian fans lay in her ability to straddle several spheres of Soviet life without belonging entirely to any one category. A Bolshoi star rumored to be a rebel, Plisetskaya was also the wife of a famous composer yet remained truest to her own career. She was the prima ballerina who could not tour with her company, the anti-Soviet who would not emigrate.

The contradictions that characterize Plisetskaya's autobiography began at home. Her mother's enormous family occupied a myriad of positions in the theater world. They were dancers, actors, and designers; her mother was a silent film star. Her aunt and uncle, Asaf and Sulamif Messerer, were lead dancers in the Bolshoi Ballet and People's Artists. Yet it took only one "infamous" relative to demonstrate the hazards of family connections in Stalin's Russia and negate any assistance Plisetskaya's famous relatives might have given her. Plisetskaya's father was a rising apparatchik in the Soviet coal industry when he was summoned to Moscow in 1935 and summarily purged. The dancer's mother was subsequently sent to a camp for "enemies of the people" (in this case, the wives of arrested husbands). In a paradox typical of the freakish absurdity of the Stalin era, Asaf and Sulamif were decorated on the occasion of the twentieth anniversary of the Great October Revolution as their sister waited in the Gulag.

The "thaw" and de-Stalinization of the Khrushchev years did little to erase these permanent blots in Plisetskaya's file: stains she was forced to recall on every application to travel abroad throughout her long career. And each of those forms required her to declare her Jewish nationality, another reproach to the Party.

Plisetskaya's decidedly mixed political pedigree, her lack of interest in Party matters, and her "political immaturity" (as the entire issue was conveniently cast) meant that the West would make its acquaintance with the Bolshoi's brightest star only belatedly. Born in 1925, Plisetskaya joined the Bolshoi in 1943 and rose to prominence almost immediately, but she was not allowed to tour with her troupe until 1959. Up to that time, Plisetskaya was told she was needed at home: there was always one more *Swan Lake* to dance—for Stalin, Mao, Ribbentrop, Tito, and other luminaries of the totalitarian world.

The Bolshoi Ballet that Plisetskaya finally joined on tour took the West by storm. The company had developed an energetic, impetuous style quite unlike the careful academicism of Leningrad's Kirov Ballet or the restrained dance classicism the West then knew. The Bolshoi had served as Russia's second dance theater from the time of the tsars, but Soviet centralization demanded that the dance capital accompany the seat of government to Moscow, and the Bolshoi began, in Plisetskaya's phrase, to "gather its muses" from Leningrad: Marina Semyonova moved to Moscow in 1930, Ulanova and Leonid Lavrovsky arrived in 1944.

Plisetskaya's brush with Leningrad classicism — mostly in the person of legendary pedagogue Agrippina Vaganova — was a fleeting one. But Plisetskaya compensated for her lack of first-rate training and coaching by developing an individual, iconoclastic style that capitalized on her electrifying stage presence, a daring rarely seen on ballet stages today, and a jump of almost masculine power. Her very personal style was angular, dramatic, and theatrical, exploiting the gifts that everyone in her mother's family seemed to possess. Plisetskaya's body scarcely resembled that of the interwar ideal, yet the fluidity and force with which she presented it made an asset of its singularity. Those who saw Plisetskaya's first performances in the West still speak of her ability to wrap the theater in her gaze, to convey powerful emotions in terse gestures. She redefined the role of Odette/Odile for good, and made Fokine's *Dying Swan* her own.

At nearly the same time that she began to travel with her company, Plisetskaya began to explore a new, more contemporary repertory in such ballets as *Spartacus, The Legend of Love,* and *The Stone Flower.* The long, angular lines of those suffering heroines suited her body and temperament perfectly and marked a sharp departure from the more compact figures and purer academic technique that still characterized Leningrad's dancers. More important, the passionate, powerful heroines Plisetskaya created in these roles reflected the new, overtly dramatic style of ballet the Bolshoi was then developing, and the larger-than-life quality she brought to the Bolshoi became the company's trademark. Much as Plisetskaya herself had done, the new Bolshoi melded bravura dancing with melodrama, putting pyrotechnics and histrionics ahead of academic technique.

With her status at the Bolshoi now firmly established, Plisetskaya longed to work with the leading European choreographers of the day. Yet her collaborations with Roland Petit and Maurice Béjart became possible only in the 1970s, her fourth decade on the stage. By that time, her frequent work abroad had raised yet another contradiction. Though she toured extensively in the years of the famous ballet defections (Rudolf Nureyev, Natalia Makarova, Mikhail Baryshnikov, and Plisetskaya's own partner, Alexander Godunov) Plisetskaya always returned to Russia.

Plisetskaya's memoirs help to explain some of the paradoxes her life embraced while they shed light on an even greater enigma: the Soviet Union's curious relationship with its artists. Plisetskaya's position — at least by the 1960s — was an elevated one in the peculiar hierarchy of a classless society. Yet the humiliations she and other artists endured at the hands of government handlers and arts bureaucrats challenge popular notions of the privileged lives of Soviet artists. Always forced to beg—to travel, to prepare new works, to be paid fairly—Plisetskaya and her colleagues more closely resembled Russian serf artists of the eighteenth century than cultural workers in a modern socialist state.

Had Plisetskaya only dancing to think about, her memoirs might focus narrowly on the preparation of roles or her philosophy of Fokine's *Swan*. They might read like a recitation of premieres and parties. But Plisetskaya was rarely left in peace to prepare her roles. More often she was forced to negotiate the indignities of a communal apartment or the inhumanity of KGB handlers anxious to ensure the isolation of Soviet artists abroad. Plisetskaya's account of her dancing life includes scenes quite unimaginable to her Western colleagues: pleading with the Ministry of Culture to let the show go on, or dancing for the Cheka, who had imprisoned her parents.

Plisetskaya also documents the rapid changes occurring in Soviet society in the post-Stalin years. Where attendance at an embassy party would have ensured a trip to the KGB in Stalin's day, in Khrushchev's a fledgling social scene had sprung up, and dancers were expected to grace embassy soirées. The bureaucrats made other demands in exchange for an artist's limited autonomy. One of the Party's more outlandish notions of service to the state involved Plisetskaya's curious friendship with Robert Kennedy, which the KGB hoped to foster as a means of furthering political goals.

It comes as no surprise that Plisetskaya is still fighting as she ends her memoirs. If Soviet power and the KGB ceased to be worthy opponents, much of the system they put in place remained. The names (and sometimes, the allegiances) of many of the bureaucrats have changed but not their investment in the status quo, still anathema to Plisetskaya, who danced a gala to mark her half-century in the theater as Moscow's White House burned.

As the Soviet Union and its symbols recede farther into the past, other memoirs and accounts of life on and off the Bolshoi stage will undoubtedly appear. Less courageous dancers may feel freer, some day, to write truthful accounts of their time in the theater. Given her persistence, courage, and candor, it is probably no surprise that Plisetskaya was the first to have her say.

Preface

I wrote this book by myself. And therefore it took a long time.

Over the years of my career tons of untruths were written about me. They'd start out with something true, then switch to a half-truth, and end up with incredible nonsense and lies. I was lucky if it wasn't meant maliciously.

My first desire was to restore the truth. The truth of my own life. And through my life to tell how ballet artists lived in the first socialist nation. In a country that was "ahead of the entire planet" in the dance business.

But how to start? Where?

I began with what I had recorded onto eleven tapes. It was all confused, without any chronology. A journalist I knew started turning my tapes into a book. My book. He needed three months for that. He wrote a lot; it was wordy and pompous. And it seemed to me, with false wisdom. All from the point of view of a girl named Margarita. He had decided on this approach, which he thought incredibly good, from a passing remark on the tape that as a child I had liked that name.

Perhaps it wasn't at all bad. But the red-haired girl called Margarita had nothing to do with me, my feelings, my soul, the essence of my character. The only things we had in common were appearance and events. No, that wasn't my book.

I rejected it. The journalist was unbearably hurt. We argued. If at first you don't succeed . . .

The next journalist–co-writer took the conversational dialogue route. His questions — my answers. Some of it was interesting. But it was clearly plagiaristic — copying the format of the conversation between Stravinsky and Robert Craft. I've read their book.

When I was in Paris visiting Galina Vishnevskaya on the avenue Georges-Mandel, I started interrogating my hospitable hostess and old friend: who had helped her on her book, *Galina?* I liked the book very much; I had brought its first Russian edition to Moscow to lend to friends. Back then that was risky, since *Galina* was on the Sheremetyevo Airport customs officials' "anti-Soviet literature" list: Vishnevskaya really let the Soviet regime have it. If the guardians of Soviet ideology had found *Galina* in my suitcase, there would have been trouble.

Galya raised her voice. It rang with determination. "No one helped me. I wrote it myself. And you should write your own book too. By yourself. I started by looking for helpers, too, but they were useless. It was a mess. Write it yourself!"

"But how is that done? Where do you start?"

"Did you keep a diary?"

"Yes. My whole life. Even now."

"Then what more do you need? Sit down and write! Start. Don't put it off. It'll take a long time if you do it yourself. It took me four years."

Well, this was good advice. I had to heed it.

But it had always seemed to me that books were written by people who were absolutely extraordinary. Supersmart. Superscholarly. And here was a ballerina picking up the pen. It remanded me of an old joke. When a huge ship, practically the *Titanic*, sank in the ocean, only two passengers survived, because they could float: a government minister, because he was a such a big turd, and a ballerina, because she was an airhead.

And then another impetus. One of Shirley MacLaine's publishers called from London — she had given him my number — and in barbaric Russian told me that he was interested in my memoirs.

"I haven't even started my book."

"Shirley said your memoirs were finished."

"The ones the journalist wrote for me are no good. I have to write the book myself."

"Well, then, sorry. Good luck. Write."

And that's when I started writing.

I wrote for three years, less three months. Not three months, but three years! But in those three years the most incredible events took place in my country.

When I began my first chapters, in February 1991, perestroika was still limping along. Censorship still put on the squeeze, the "united, mighty Soviet Union" still existed. The flag, the seal, the anthem. The first president, the first First Lady, and so on . . . Whenever I called a spade a spade, to be honest, I shivered inside: they won't print this, they'll be afraid, they'll make me soften it and fix it up. But I wrote it anyway.

The book was born right on the cusp of the eras. What yesterday had been bold, and even unmentionable, became old news in an instant, in just one day. It was like some sort of competition to see who could damn the formerly all-powerful organizations and mighty rulers most fiercely. A new political correctness began, one of permitted boldness.

I couldn't keep up with these newly hatched iconoclasts. "We reject the old world." In fact, they were rejecting it *once again!*

More power to you, honest people, go forth and reject . . .

But nothing ages faster than things that are truly bold. And by the final chapters of my book I sensed clearly that the correctness had changed again, and a new wind was blowing. People were sick of politics. They were bored to death by cursing and muckraking. They were tired of reading about the misdeeds and vileness of the Bolsheviks. So perhaps, in view of the situation, I should bypass all the interventions by the KGB into my life? And write only about art? Only about ballet?

No, I won't change anything. I won't touch things up. They way it was written is the way I'll leave it. And you, the reader, can make allowances for the wild changes of those three unusual years in the life of our country.

I planned the book for a local, Russian audience. But I was also thinking about a far-away Western audience. The far-away ones who know very little about the byways, the delirious fantasies, the masquerades of our strange, incredible, and unbelievable former Soviet life. There are some things that Russian readers understand perfectly well, better than I. And they can fill in the gaps vividly. Well, then, skip those pages, my former countrymen—move along. But those are the very things that are of interest to the far-away readers. I can't write two books!

Another thing. I bring up events that are quite recent, which are fresh in the memory. Reading about them today is probably like watching a recording of yesterday's hockey game, when you already know who won. But what if you read about it years later? A lot of people will have forgotten. And I'll remind them. I was a participant.

Finally, people close to me in those three years, about whom I wrote in the present tense, have gone into the past. My mother died. Asaf Messerer is gone . . .

But I'm not going to change tenses. Everything that was in the present, I'll save.

So, off you go, readers. Godspeed!

7 February 1994. Madrid

Chapter One

The Dacha and Sretenka Street

Many books begin with ruminations about one's earliest memories. Who remembered earlier, who started later. Should I look for another beginning?

I began walking at eight months. This I don't remember. But my numerous relatives were thrilled by my early mobility. And their delight was the start of my self-awareness.

My grandmother died in the summer of 1929. I remember her passing very clearly and distinctly. Our family rented a dacha, a summer house, near Moscow. And Grandmother, already looking waxy and haggard, spent long hours on an incongruous, nickel-plated bed in the large meadow in front of the house. A Chinese doctor was treating her. He would come to the house in a theatrically broad-brimmed black hat and make mysterious motions over Grandmother.

That summer heaven sent me my first ballet message. Behind the plank fence, listing in places in the thick grass, stood a dark, boarded-up dacha. It belonged to the dancer Mikhail Mordkin, Anna Pavlova's partner. By that memorable summer he had already moved to the West, but his sister lived in a small outbuilding, kept an eye on the dacha, and grew aromatic Russian flowers. Their intoxicating smell remains in my memory to this day.

I was a willful child, and they called me *neslukh*, the "not-listener." Impressed by an old postcard that I had seen with sailboats, I sent my first pair of sandals sailing downstream. Mother agonized: children's shoes were impossible to get then. You had to run all over Moscow searching. "Hard times, hard times," Mother repeated to herself. And I still keep hearing that to this day — hard times, hard times. My poor country.

I played with a paper fastener until it got stuck up my nose. Mama took me to the village doctor in the cart of a talkative peasant. The doctor relieved my discomfort instantly.

I couldn't stand my loving relatives, who seemed to be in a conspiracy to pinch my right cheek. They always fussed about how much I had grown since the last time. And I also hated going to bed and being forced to eat the milk noodles those same relatives stuffed me with, insisting that they would make me big and strong. Once they stuffed me until I threw up. Ever since, I shudder if I even hear the words.

In Moscow we lived on Sretenka Street, number 23, apartment 3, on the top floor, the third. All threes. It belonged to my grandfather, Mikhail Borisovich Messerer, a dentist. It had eight rooms. They were all along one side, and their unwashed windows faced Rozhdestvensky Boulevard. A narrow corridor along the other side led to a smelly kitchen, whose single window revealed a filthy courtyard filled with plywood crates. The rooms were divided among Grandfather's grown children, except for the very last one, which was occupied by the virtuoso pianist Alexander Tsfasman. He had graduated from the Moscow Conservatory with a medal, but he went crazy for jazz, which was just becoming popular then, and forgot about classical music. Tsfasman was a great lover, in Gogol's phrase, "of strawberries." Adoring females were always making their way down the long corridor to his door. The dim lighting helped; the single source of light was a bare, fly-specked bulb on the cracked ceiling — an ordinary fixture once known as "Ilyich's bulb" (electricity was for a time represented as a gift from the great Vladimir Ilyich Lenin himself).

A restless child, I would wander along the corridor, where I ran into the visiting ladies. To keep me from spilling the beans, our neighbor entered into hushed dialogues with me: "Mayechka, which one do you like better — the brunette or the blonde?"

"The blonde, the blonde," I would say without hesitation.

I always preferred the light-haired ones.

The first door from the stairs was Grandfather's dentistry office. It was cold, with crooked floorboards, an ancient, sagging glassed-in case for his instruments, and the leading character—the drill. Leaning over his patient's open mouth, Grandfather would press his foot on the worn metal pedal. It turned a wheel with a strap that kept slipping, interrupting the session.

The focal point of the office was a cast-iron Napoleon on a horse. This was in keeping with the solemnity of the moment, as if to remind the patient, Bear in mind—we are all mortal!

A large colored engraving, framed in glass, hung on the wall. It depicted a woman's head with a heavy bun at her nape. The poor woman's cheek was open and the viewer could see all thirty-two of her teeth, plus the inner anatomy of the face all the way to the ear. This was surrealism, to use today's terminology, worthy of the brush of Salvador Dalí. I saw something similar a few years ago at the Dalí Museum, which rises like eggshells to meet the southern Spanish sky of Figueras, close to where Dalí was born. But back then I had no idea of the scandalous artist's existence. I was simply afraid to be alone in Grandfather's office.

The apartment had no bathroom. Actually, there was one, but we didn't use it for bathing. Our nanny, Varya, and Kuzma, her mighty, mustachioed janitor husband, lived there. Washing was always a problem. The water would be heated on the kerosene, or Primus, stove, until it reached the proper temperature, a long, boring time to wait. The kitchen faucet was messy in some way and splashed the whole kitchen with icy water. To restrain it, we blocked the flow with an old sign, its enamel peeling, that advertised, "Dentist Messerer; Soldiers free." It had hung by the front door since before the war of 1914.

Another detail from Grandfather's apartment sticks in my mind. In the room next to the office, in a dark wooden frame, hung a clumsy copy of the famous painting *The Princess Tarakanova*.* Water poured into the prison window and mice raced around the bed on which the countess stood in a lovely, theatrical pose and a low-cut velvet dress. She was in a near-faint, her hair tumbling about her shoulders. I was afraid of that painting too. And I felt very sorry for the princess.

In my most difficult days, when the KGB decided to consider me a British spy and a car with three burly men followed me around Moscow and stood round the clock beneath my windows on Shchepkinsky Passage, I recalled that paint-

---

*Princess Tarakanova claimed to be the heir to the throne, alleging that she was the daughter of Empress Elizaveta Petrovna. She died in 1775 in prison. K. D. Flavitsky's painting (1864) inaccurately depicts her dying in the flood of 1777.

ing. Poor Countess Tarakanova. In impotent rage and pain caused by absurdity, lies, betrayal, and idiocy, I wanted to dance a ballet that would let me share my bitterness.

Many years later I told Roland Petit about my tormented dreams.

Chapter Two

What I Was Like at Five

What was I like at five?

Carrot-red hair with a light blue bow, my face covered in freckles, green eyes, and white lashes. My legs were strong and my thighs taut. As a baby, I would pull myself up and sit back down, holding onto the cold, crooked bar of the crib, in rhythm to the raspy voice of Nanny Varya (the one who lived in our bathroom):

I'm small and neat
And what's on me, sticks to me.

I wouldn't be surprised if the days I spent doing those exercises strengthened my legs. Once out of the cradle, I ran on tiptoe, making holes in my shoes. I didn't know the meaning of tired. Putting me to bed was a major production.

For some reason I liked the name Margarita. "What's your name, little girl?" always got "Margarita" for an answer from me. I liked going to the market. It was located near the Sukharev Tower. It was blown up when I was three, but I remember it. Loud women in white kerchiefs crowded the market. They offered the appetizing wares in shrill voices. The Soviet system had not yet made peasants forget how to tend cows in those days. My job—this was a sort of game with my mother—was to taste the butter and pick the best. The sellers were amused by me. Red-haired, giggly, with wild eyes, and overjoyed with life. And the butter was delicious.

None of the childhood diseases missed me. Even in good health, I was no angel. In sickness I was unbearable. But I was patient and put up with pain heroically. Even today, I am stoic when faced with huge hypodermics, spinals, electric shock, chiropractic torture, or wrenching deep-tissue massage — the everyday elements of the ballet life (since no one has managed to avoid injuries yet!).

I naively loved Delibes's waltz from *Coppélia*. On holidays a cadet band played it on Sretensky Boulevard — out of tune but with feeling. That fall, on a walk with my nanny, I suddenly heard the familiar waltz coming from a black loudspeaker hanging from a wooden post. I pulled my hand from Nanny's tight hold and unexpectedly — even for me — started to dance. Improvising. A crowd gathered; a few loafers. Nanny was furious, but I didn't listen. This short story may sound saccharine and artificial, but it did happen. It's the truth. If, fifty or sixty years from now, somebody ever decides to do a movie about my vain and restless life, I beg the directors to leave out this episode.

My mother was a film actress. She had graduated from the film institute. Catercorner from our house was a movie theater, displaying a gigantic — as it seemed to me then — poster of my mother in the silent film *The Leper*. I watched the film with my mother in that theater. I wept and sobbed loudly when my mother was trampled by horses. She sat next to me, comforting me, saying, "I'm here, I'm fine, I'm right here with you." Angrily, I pulled my hand away from her, furious that she was interfering with my crying.

In order to tame me, they sent me to kindergarten. It was situated in the present Moscow City Council building, through a side entrance. The building was shorter then. They say it was built up on the orders of Stalin. My life in a collective was brief. Everything in me, in my nature, resisted "socializing." They tried to turn us into little Leninists, October brats, constantly delighting in our "happy childhood." I ran away at the first opportunity. It took me an hour and a half to get home.

Soviet people are brought up to have a phony, hypocritical interest in children. A long line of slow-moving buses on the highway. Barely moving. Each has a cardboard sign: "Caution, Children." Police car in front, police car in back. Headlights on. As you have already guessed, I'm talking about today. But at the same time, at the height of radiation danger in Kiev from the Chernobyl accident, on the third and fourth days, the Pioneers* spent hours on Kreshchatik Street

---

*Soviet Scouts.

with bare heads in the blazing sun, rehearsing with their red flags for the happy May Day parade. And the smug minister of health — without even a stutter — lied on T.V., saying there was no danger. The children were not threatened. This murderous hypocrisy was born in the years of my childhood. I had to protect myself from all these hypocrites as I made my way home, and I did it by pretending to be with an adult passerby: I'm not alone. I found my house. Everyone was in a panic. The school had called, worried that the child was missing. After my little revolution, they stopped taking me to the Moscow Council kindergarten.

I had my first trip to the theater when I was five. The play was called *Don't Joke with Love*. I don't remember the author; you can't expect that from a little girl. It was a drama, with no music. Or dancing. But I left the theater thrilled to my soul. Long after the performance, I dreamt of that slender, beautiful woman in the long, slinky black dress. She stood down front in a spotlight, in front of the curtain, listening to a conversation she was not supposed to hear. For a good week I was insane, making noise, playing out all the parts. My favorite was the woman in black. By the end of the week, my family's patience had ended. Papa smacked me on the behind. I took umbrage.

The next morning at breakfast, I would not talk. Father was upset. "Mayechka, you're not mad, are you? Forgive me, it was just a joke. I love you."

"Don't joke with love," I replied dramatically, striking the pose of the woman in black.

Chapter Three

Relatives

When I married the composer Rodion Shchedrin on October 2, 1958, Lilya Yuryevna Brik,* who was our neighbor at 12, Kutuzovsky Prospect, said to him, half-jokingly, "I like your choice. But Maya has one major flaw. She has too many relatives all over the place." And it's true, God did not stint on relatives for me.

Who makes up my family?

The head of the family was my grandfather, Moscow dentist Mikhail Borisovich Messerer. This is the second mention of his name and profession, because I remember his personality, and I know it would have pleased him. He was from Lithuania and he was a graduate of Vilna† University. The family language was Lithuanian. He moved to Moscow — with the whole household — in 1907. Six of his children, including my mother, were born in Vilna.

Grandfather was not tall. Thick, Brezhnev-like eyebrows, a massive nose, round bald head, well-fed, if not fat. He walked with dignity, playfully waving his carved stick with a figured top, which he rarely failed to use. He had much to be proud of. His fillings held a long time. Mother still has three, and she's almost

---

*The wife of literary theorist Osip Brik and lover of the poet Vladimir Mayakovsky. Alexander Rodchenko immortalized Brik's image in his photographs.
† Now Vilnius.

ninety. His other pastime was making children. When they were ready, he had to name them. And that called for the third love of his life—the Bible. From two marriages he had twelve children. They were all given a legacy of sonorous biblical names. In our suspicious Soviet life these names brought only cares and woes. But they have the sound of poetry, you must agree:

Pnina

Azarii

Mattanii

Rakhil

Asaf

Elisheva

Sulamif

Emanuil

Aminadav

Erella . . .

There were two more men's names that were so complex that I can't remember them; don't judge me harshly. I listed them by age.

Pnina. She died of encephalitis at nine. Grandfather couldn't forget her, and I heard about her throughout my childhood. A picture of a skinny, long-nosed girl hung over Grandfather's bed. Grandfather insisted that she was a born beauty.

Azarii. He took a stage name and became Azarii Azarin. He was a talented dramatic actor and teacher, one of the first to get the title of Honored Artist of the Republic, back in 1929.

He had worked with Konstantin Stanislavsky, Vladimir Nemirovich-Danchenko, Yevgeny Vakhtangov, Vsevelod Meyerhold. He was also a close friend of Mikhail Chekhov's. Their correspondence is a family heirloom. Just before his death he auditioned for the role of Lenin in the film *Lenin in October.* Backlit, there was something about him that reminded one of a monument to the unforgettable leader. I can say that with certainty, since such statues of Lenin flooded the squares and culs-de-sac of our huge land. Azarii was stocky, round-headed, and totally bald. In 1937, after the stress of both the closing of the second Moscow Art Theater, where he worked, and my father's arrest, he died suddenly of a heart attack.

Mattanii. A year younger than Azarii, he also took the surname Azarin. He was a professor of economics. His first wife, Mariana, wrote a hysterical political denunciation of him in 1938 (out of jealousy), and he was given eight years. First they tortured him horribly, then made him stand up for three days. His legs swelled unbelievably. They threatened that if he did not confess his anti-

Communist activities and turn in his co-conspirators, they would send him to the "Lefortovo meat grinder." No one came out of there alive. But he held out.

After the tortures, he was sent to a camp in Solikamsk. The famous actor Alexei Dikii was there; after he was freed he joined the Maly Theater, played Stalin in the movies, and was awarded the Stalin Prize to wear in his lapel. (There were fates like that, too.) At the camp they organized a theater for inmates, and that saved their lives. Mattanii came back from prison camp in shattered health. He had water on the lungs, and his heart was diseased. He died soon afterward.

At home in Moscow, in Shchedrin's study, a death mask of Beethoven hangs on the wall. Every time I see it I shudder. How it resembles Mattanii's face! And both men died at the same age — fifty-seven.

Rakhil. My mother. Not tall, round-faced, well-proportioned. With huge brown eyes and a button nose. Black, raven-glistening hair, always neatly parted in the middle and held at the nape with complex pins. Straight legs and small feet, but not ballet legs. There was something of ancient Persian miniatures about her. I think that's why she was offered film parts playing Uzbek women.

She spent a short time, four or five years, in sentimental silent films, playing a dozen roles. The cast lists called her Ra Messerer. Life was very hard for her. She had worked as a film actress, a telephone operator, a receptionist in a hospital, and an extra in amateur theater.

You couldn't call her a fashion-plate. For years she wore the same dress. I remember her in all the summer months in a blue chiffon outfit. She had one preoccupation: relatives. Relatives near and far. All relatives had to live amicably, help one another, dance with one another, and even, if necessary, sing with one another. She caught the bug from Grandfather, who fell into raptures whenever he saw Asaf and Sulamif dancing together. My father, like me to this day, found her relativomania annoying.

Mother's personality was soft and hard, kind and stubborn. When she was arrested in 1938 and they demanded that she sign a statement saying her husband was a spy, traitor, subversive, criminal, conspirator against Stalin, and so on, and so on, she simply refused. A heroic act in those days.

She was given eight years in prison.

Asaf. He, of course, belongs on the Mount Olympus of ballet. A brilliant dancer, he was the source of many technical tricks and pioneered a virtuoso style of solo male classical dance. An outstanding teacher — his class heals legs. I would hurry to his class almost every morning of my conscious ballet life. His students included Galina Ulanova, Vladimir Vasiliev, Ekaterina Maximova . . .

Not many people know that he started studying ballet late, only at sixteen, and at eighteen he was taken into the troupe of the Bolshoi. That means something.

He is a quiet, steady, and friendly man, who would not harm a fly. But when he explodes in anger, he can say something really stupid.

Everyone loves him at the theater.*

Elisheva. Simplified to Elizaveta. Elya. She was unlucky. Everything went wrong. She played professionally and vividly on the stages of the dramatic theaters of Yuri Zavadsky and Ermolovsky. The KGB tried to get her to snitch on her fellow artists, and when she refused, bawling, they threw her out of the theater. She got back through a lawsuit. But the newly appointed director was given orders to get rid of her. This happened four times. The courts, the rehiring and refiring, the courts . . . She suffered, heart-breakingly, and, harassed and stressed, died of cancer of the esophagus.

Sulamif. Mita for short. My relationship with her is the most complicated. It will take an effort to be objective. I promise to try.

Miniature, dark-haired, mercurial. Squints when she laughs and pleats her face like a harmonica. Loud-voiced, argumentative with people, impatient. She would make a poor hunter.

As a ballerina she had technique and pushiness (in life, she was pushy too) and could take a lot; she danced almost the entire repertoire at the Bolshoi. But she had no sense of line. She did a lot of good for people but then tormented them afterward, demanding an incommensurate price for the kindness. That's why people avoided her—a nagging person elicits nothing but bitterness.

I lived at Mita's after Mother was imprisoned. And I adored her. No less than my mother, and sometimes it seemed, even more. But in payment for her kindness, she humiliated me painfully, every day, every day. And my love gradually went away. She was the one who forced me to stop loving her. She didn't manage it right away. But once she did, it was gone forever.

Mita sadistically stung me with reproaches: you eat my bread, you sleep on my bed, you wear my clothes. Once, when I couldn't take it anymore, I wrote to my mother in exile in Chimkent, like Chekhov's Vanka Zhukov.† I had even sealed the letter. Mita sensed that she had gone overboard and gave me a little tenderness. I immediately forgave everything and tore up the letter.

---

* Asaf Messerer died in Moscow in 1992.

† In Chekhov's short story, the unhappy Vanka sends a letter to his grandfather addressed "To grandfather, in the country."

The crowning demand was that I dance *Swan Lake* with her son, who had just graduated from the choreographic school. The whole school heard that Misha would have his debut at the Bolshoi Theater as Siegfried with Plisetskaya. My confusion and meek objections were cut off with, "You owe me everything. Do you mean that I was wrong to help your mother and to save you when they came to take you away to the orphanage?" My brother Alexander spent all the years of Mother's prison living at Asaf's house. And not once did Asaf or his wife, the artist Anel Sudakevich, reproach him for anything.

In 1979, when the Bolshoi was touring Japan, Sulamif and her son applied to the American Embassy for political asylum. They stayed in the West.

Once the political climate in Russia had changed, my would-be partner, my blood relative, Cousin Misha Messerer, came to Moscow and sued me in a Moscow court to get back a garage that had once belonged to him and Mita. He sued without even talking to me. How fiery was his thirst for revenge for my refusal to dance with him a thousand years ago.

Emanuil. The shyest and best-looking of the Messerer brothers and sisters. Nature gave him a charming, flirtatious birthmark on his cheek, like a French marquis. Everyone adored him for his quiet ways. Nulya had nothing to do with the arts; he was a construction engineer.

In 1941, at the start of the war, the Germans bombed Moscow. When there were air raids people would go down into the metros and bomb shelters. The authorities made residents take turns holding watch on the rooftops, to put out firebombs if the Germans started dropping them. (The magazines kept running a photo of young Dmitri Shostakovich on the roof of the conservatory, where he taught, in a fireman's helmet with an extinguisher in his hands.) One fatal day it was Nulya's turn. A firebomb hit the building, and Emanuil died at twenty-five. His younger brother Aminadav looked for him in the smoking ruins and found a hand, which he recognized.

Aminadav. The smallest, of subtle make-up. He looks like Asaf, and they are often taken for each other, but he does not dance; he's an electrical engineer. A man filled with compassion for everyone. He spent half his life in long lines for bread, sugar, milk, kefir, and potatoes. Then he carried the food round to his relatives. He cooked lunches for them, brought doctors, fixed the plumbing and the locks.

The Soviet regime pushed him around. He is meek and mild man. His wife left him because he was never home because of his philanthropy.

Erella. I know nothing about her. Grandfather was very old when his second wife, Raisa, had a baby girl. In 1942 Mikhail Borisovich Messerer died near Kuibyshev,* where he'd been evacuated. He was seventy-six, Erella was two.

No information about my distant relatives ever reached me. I know only that they lived in Lithuania. Mother's grandmother on the maternal side — Krevitskaya or Kravitskaya, no one remembers now — spent most of her life in district courtrooms. She would walk twenty kilometers into town to attend trials. The courtroom dramas were her theater. Family legend holds that she pitied the condemned, brought them food, suffered along with them, calling out from the crowd. It was her passion. No one stopped her.

Now about my father.

I inherited his looks. He was a good height and well-proportioned. On the thin side: sinewy, slender. The forelock that always fell onto his face had a reddish tint. His gray-green eyes — mine are an exact copy — looked at you attentively and warily. Even I remember seeing the spark of merriment begin to vanish from his eyes — terrible times had come. Old friends still called him by his student nickname, Veselovsky, from *vesely*, "cheerful." They remembered him as the merrymaker, leader of pranks, card player, and gambling billiards player. He was not the only one who had his spine broken, fate crushed, personality changed, life taken away by the Soviet system.

Father was born in the quiet city of Gomel, filled with apple trees and dust. The Plisetskys come the Belorussian regions of quiet beauty that brings a lump to your throat. He was born at the beginning of the century, in 1901. In 1918, as a seventeen-year-old teenager, he signed up with the Communists, joined the Party. Like all Don Quixotes of that wild year, he fiercely believed in the bookish concept of making all humanity happy, making it unselfish and full of brotherly love — a concept that every young man today realizes is absurd. About ten years before perestroika, which loosened tongues, I told an old musician in the West who hated everything paired with the word *Soviet*, "My father was an honest Communist." His gaze measured me with icy sympathy. If there ever were honest Communists, they were single-minded, naive Don Quixotes. Father paid in full for his trust and dreams. In 1938 the Cheka[†] executed him, at the age of thirty-seven, and during the Khrushchev "thaw" they rehabilitated him, "for lack of criminal charges." What a banal, clichéd story!

His older brother, Lester, had much more foresight at sixteen; he did not fill

*Now Samara, Russia.
† Predecessor of the KGB (as was the NKVD, below).

his head with fluffy Marxist theories about saving humanity. A few years before the stormy petrel of bloody revolution flew overhead, he had saved money for a passport and steamship ticket by picking Gomel's abundant apples and safely reached New York. He cobbled together some capital in America's food industry, got himself a family, and presented me with two cousins in faraway America — Stanley and Emmanuel. These family ties were added to the charges against my idealistic father in the nocturnal torture and interrogations in the cellars of Lubyanka Prison, and against my bewildered mother with a seven-month-old infant in the cell of Butyrka Prison with its weeping, wailing women, and against me, banned, not allowed to travel abroad and trying to knock on any official's door to simply ask, What for? I did not know then that Stanley (Plisetsky, Americanized to Plesent) had risen to the high levels of President John F. Kennedy's circle, as a counselor on legal issues. And what better way for the octopus of American imperialism to find out the secrets of the dressing rooms of the Bolshoi but from me? The secret meanings of each door, the quota of ballet slippers for each performance, the schedule of rehearsals?

It's easy to joke about it now. Back then it wasn't funny.

Father's older brother, without realizing it, committed another grave sin against his Russian relatives. In 1934, a few months before Stalin's Jesuitical murderer of Leningrad Party boss Sergei Kirov, Lester came to visit Moscow. He clearly relished the role of rich transatlantic uncle. Our pathetic Moscow life elicited condescending skepticism. Father, to hold his head up a bit, took the traveler to our cooperative dacha in Zagoryanka, outside Moscow. The two-room wooden house under the canopy of intoxicating linden trees seemed like royal luxury to our family. Some closed-faced, grim travelers in the crowded commuter train listened to the snatches of conversation between the two brothers. Father, as I clearly understand now, had to have been aware of the danger from "connections with foreigners," but he did not want to act like a coward. That was in his character.

"Relatives abroad," as they were listed in endless questionnaires and applications, were a great mistake. Everyone tried to cover up their existence; those who were too late or too brave were severely punished. It was only in the years of Khrushchev's "thaw" that distant relatives appeared, like mushrooms after rain. The conductor Yuri Fayer, who had successfully posed as an orphan to his Party comrades, suddenly found a brother, Myron, across the ocean. The actress Alla Tarasova, faithful daughter of the Communist Party, recalled a brother in Paris. A whole pile of people had been forgotten. (I use the word *pile* advisedly.)

Yet here was a fraternal American walking around openly in Moscow in 1934. And after his departure, when the Plisetskys finally breathed a sigh of relief, the naive brother who had understood nothing, heard nothing, and seen nothing started sending his father and sisters loving letters. A sudden rush of nostalgia, perhaps? That was fun for the censors.

Father's mother, two sister — Liza and Many — and his younger brother, Volodya, were living in Leningrad. Their fates were difficult and sad.

I loved Volodya. He was handsome, fecklessly bold, and marvelously athletic. A professional acrobat and actor, he was in the show of the famous popular singer Klavdia Shulzhenko. His act was called Trio Castelio, and their tricks became classics. Volodya ended up at the front in the first days of the war. As an athlete, he was sent to the parachute paratrooper division. On December 31, 1941, his birthday (he was two years younger than Father), Volodya was shot at close range by Germans when he landed in his parachute.

The two sisters would see more suffering. Mania's husband, Ilya Levitsky, was an important engineer in Leningrad, but thanks to political denunciations he served two long prison terms. When he was released — alive for a second time — he headed straight for the steambaths. And he died there. On his first day of joyful freedom.

Liza's twenty-year-old son, Mark Ezersky, was killed early in the war. He died, as we later learned, a hero's death. After the victory, an obelisk was erected to mark the site of his death. Liza wasn't allowed to go to her son's grave for a long time. She had a weak heart. But With her mother's stubbornness, Liza sneaked out of the house and went there, and her heart gave out.

This was the effect of the Stalin era on my relatives on my father's side, even though they had not signed up to be Communists. Undoubtedly, the older brother's Russian trip and his love of correspondence were used by the NKVD and pulled out of their fat "personal files" at every crossroads in their lives.

The scale of the challenge to the authorities created by the tourist trip of the older brother from America may be easier to understand if I mention that the children and grandchildren of my Leningrad aunts fled in every direction when my American cousin showed up in his father's footsteps during the stagnant Brezhnev era. (The one shining light was my Leningrad cousin Era Ezerskaya, Liza's daughter. A beautiful, fearless, sympathetic, and pure soul.)

After all the tragic disappearances, the Plisetskys, sobered by fear, stopped responding to the letters with bright American stamps and lost track of the Plesent family in New York.

It was only in 1959, after my letter to Khrushchev finally reached him, that the head of the KGB, A. N. Shalepin, received me pompously in his frightening, cold office on Lubyanka Square.

"Your uncle died on April 7, 1955, in New York. His two sons live there with their families. If they wish to meet with you, well, we won't forbid it. It's your business. Don't be afraid."

"How did they learn all that?" flashed through my mind. "Were they watching them, did they attend the funeral?"

But I certainly do not want to reduce the tragedy of my family to one uncle with an American passport in the pocket of his checked tweed jacket. It was a complex of circumstances and dirty politics.

Later I will describe more fully the arrest and killing of my father. But now I want to go to the next chapter.

Chapter Four

Spitzbergen

Father worked for Arktikugl (Arctic Coal). In 1932 Otto Yulyevich Shmidt—a kind of Bolshevik enlightener with a beard bigger than Marx's (Lenin called him a "great bumbler," which saved him from Stalin's bloodthirsty paws)—appointed Father general consul to Spitzbergen* and chief of the coal mines there.

The whole family set off for the end of the world. Father, Mother, my eight-month-old brother Alexander, and me. It was a very long journey, with stops and awkward changes in various countries. Ordinary people didn't fly in airplanes yet. The train traveled to Berlin via Warsaw, where mother and I met on the platform with Grandmother's sister, who had made the voyage from the distant Lithuanian provinces just to see us. Father and the baby stayed on the train. "You've lost weight," I commented loudly and tactlessly, taking Mother's aunt for my grandmother.

Mother's endless love for all her relatives flowed so strongly that our train left without us. The three of us cackled and rushed around the platform. Luckily, a local train on the next track was headed in the right direction. Mother and I jumped up on the step at the last second. The train was moving.

The car was a bright red with mysterious Latin letters in the center. Next to

* An island off the coast of Norway, above the Arctic Circle.

us—the car did not have reserved seats—were a multitude of dolled-up, semi-beautiful women with a supercilious and viperous demeanor. I was offended that these blond women were so bad-tempered. They certainly weren't civil. And when Mother and I returned from the toilet for a minute, we found a buxom lady spread out, sleeping languorously on our bench. She didn't respond to our meek entreaties, so we stood beside her throughout the trip.

We caught up with Father. He was furious, but controlled himself. We were abroad, and here . . . What the hell were we doing?

Then came Berlin. Two years later—in 1934—I would make that long trip again, and we would spend a few days in Berlin once more. On that second trip my eyes were filled with the swastika armbands on the storm troopers' uniforms. Naturally, my childhood impressions of Berlin were profound. The gray, hulking houses, the screaming neatness of the lawns, the severe streets washed by large foaming mops, the alien slabs of the high curbstones, and the trouser-skirts of polished, fashionable women. It was all new to me. Later, I saw lots of films showing the Berlin of that period. It was like that, but not quite. There was always something missing. Those images remain embedded in my memory forever.

My new meeting with Berlin in 1951 at a youth festival was a striking contrast. Horrid ruins gaped everywhere. There was no city. And I had an acute memory of its former power and threatening majesty.

From Berlin we took a comfortable train through Denmark into Norway. A giant ferry swallowed our train as if it were nothing. It was like Ershov's story where Chudo-Yudo the Whale swallows up ships with passengers and, when commanded with magic words by the Ivan the Fool, returns them safely.

In Oslo we disembarked onto a small, clean square in front of the train station on a bright, pretty day with blinding sunlight. The capital of Norway has remained in my memory as a cheerful, multicolored, sunny city. We stopped by the windows of a small and cozy shop. The plump owner, seeing our obvious interest, beckoned to Mama and me to enter its door, with its jangling tiny bell.

Beyond the door were untold riches. All out of wool. Colorful warm dresses, wide skirts, playful mittens, suits threaded with gold and silver, fluffy sweaters, and purses knit with strange stitches. It took my breath away. Mama went over her crumpled notes, counting her pitiful allowance of hard currency. There was enough for one child's suit. She didn't buy anything for herself. The owner, touched by our poverty, gave me a present—a tiny porcelain tea set, for playing house with dolls. God only knows how, but I still have it. It's in the dining room of our Moscow apartment.

From Oslo our journey continued by ship to Barentsburg. Look at a globe, reader, to see how long we had to sail. We were taken by the Soviet icebreaker *Krasin*, which made that polar marathon twice a year. According to the calendar, it was summer, but there were terrible storms for the two weeks of our journey. I don't know what magnitude—nine, ten, eleven, or twelve. But they turned my soul inside out. Our simple things, packed in a few worn suitcases, never stood still. Gogol wrote about flying coffins; our suitcases had wings.

No one even stuck a nose outside the cabins. I kept trying to see something through the round, cloudy porthole. But I never saw anything besides endless huge waves. The captain gave Father an ancient record player with a wind-up handle to while away the time. The captain had only one record—excerpts from the opera *Carmen*. Holding down the record player, which kept trying to fly away, we listened to Bizet's melodies a hundred times. Decades later, rehearsing *Carmen Suite*, my memory added the howling stormy wind and the smack of furious waves against the ship.

The first thing I saw when the icebreaker dropped anchor was an endless, completely vertical, wooden staircase going up the side of a hill. The ladder led to a white-and-blue house at the top. Norwegians lived there. We were given space in the house of the Soviet colony, at the edge of the town. After that came the mountains.

We had two rooms. In one a strong electric light burned constantly throughout the winter, to represent the sky. In the endless black polar nights a person really misses the sun. I am writing these lines in Nerja, in Andalusia, in the fantastic Spanish South, where in February almonds flower intoxicatingly and the white sun blinds the eyes. Shchedrin is writing a piano concerto on commission from Steinway. Once again I am surrounded by mountains, but these are so different. How marvelous your planet Earth is, oh Lord!

Summer has a different value beyond the Arctic Circle. You are twice, three times as glad to see everything. When dwarf lilac flowers appear on the moss, my delight took my breath away. Once in the mossy flowerbeds I found a wounded albatross. For five days I brought it food, and on the sixth I found it dead. Everything was special. The rainbow over the mountains—I wanted to touch it, caress it, it seemed so close, so pretty, so definite in its colors: truly the blue was like a cornflower, the red like blood, the orange like a fruit, the green like grass in June near Moscow. And the gorgeous northern lights. Six months of darkness is hard. But the polar day is endless joy. Six months of light.

What there was in great surplus in Spitzbergen was snow. Clean, white, crystal, glowing snow. I never got off my skis. With no sense of time, I flew down until late at night, made my way back up, and flew down once more from the eccentrically uneven hills. There was no possibility of getting me back in the house. I had often heard the word *Grumant* — the island's second largest city — and it had captured my imagination. I decided to walk there on my skis. And I went. I walked a long time. The snow poured down. A wall of snow. I couldn't see in front of my face. Just a solid mass of snow.

My parents noticed I was gone. Mother worked as a telephone operator in Spitzbergen, and she raised the alarm quickly. They sent out skiers and a trained dog. I had gotten tired and decided to rest, sitting down on my skis. The snow began transforming me into Hans Christian Andersen's maiden. I got sleepy and fell into a sweet dream. My rescuer, the wonderful sheepdog Yak (I would remember the name if you woke me in the middle of the night), dug me out of the snowdrift and pulled me by the collar to the men. Thus I was born a second time.

I also remember the Spitzbergen winds. They could knock a person down, and he would be swept over by snow. On squall days, people walked in chains, holding hands, twenty to twenty-five people. The walked slowly, as if across a snow swamp.

I remember the weather and landscape better than the people. They all looked alike to me because of their many layers of warm clothing, and the winds battered their faces into one type. People came to work in the polar mines because they need the high salary. As they used to say, a long ruble. Not everyone would travel to those distant cold regions, to spend day after day underground in the light of carbide lamps, breathing coal dust. They came with their wives, and some brought their children, too.

And that meant there was enough "living material" for putting on amateur productions. Without bringing in outsiders — anyway, there was nobody outside besides bears and albatrosses — the Barentsburgers managed to do a performance of Alexander Dargomyzhsky's opera *Rusalka*. The role of the little mermaid, who speaks the famous Pushkin lines, "But what is money, I know not," was given to me. I don't know whether it was our traditional Soviet sucking-up — Father was the consul, after all — or because I truly was artistic. With no false modesty I can say that I was. So even if they were sucking up, they didn't go wrong. I played my tiny part with flair. Miraculously, a faded photo of the cast survived. I am among them. When Pierre Cardin was preparing my book of photos, he picked that snapshot, despite its terrible physical shape. One can trust Cardin's taste. It was my first public appearance on the stage.

I also encountered humanity's meaningless cruelty in Barentsburg. In the spring a cute polar bear floated over to the wharf on an ice floe. Near the opened water, on a wooden platform, were several barrels of pickled apples. As if we were at the Moscow zoo, the bear deftly scooped up the tasty treats from the barrel. From the top of the ladder, a group of us kids watched, mesmerized. The bear was graceful, with a long pink tongue and red eyes, not at all big, apparently not adult. Suddenly a shot rang out, and the bear fell dead in the water, its lifeless body forming a bloody circle. Where did the nasty man with the gun come from, and why did he shoot the cub? What for? Did he begrudge it the apples?

As long as I'm on apples, let me tell you about when the Norwegian authorities sent Father a Christmas present. A crate of oranges. Father, without letting me enjoy the fruit, which was rarely seen in Northern regions, gave orders to bring the package down to the miners' cafeteria. Mother agonized: Your own child needs vitamins, and you send it all down to the cafeteria. Father gave Mother such a hard look that she stopped in mid-word.

The larger of our two rooms had a glass cabinet filled with lovely Palekh boxes.* For the two years we lived there I nagged Father to let me have one for my games. "They're not mine," he would explain patiently. "They're state property." I write these two tiny details not to show my father as a hero and altruist. It's just that his behavior was so unlike the behavior of today's Partycrats, who steal and grab whatever isn't tied down. State property, cooperative, gifts, they take everything that's richer, sweeter, dearer. Unfortunately, to my great, enormous regret, he believed in a Communist utopia. He believed that you could make an equal sign between the words *mine* and *ours*. He did not or could not see that there were a million light years between *mine* and *ours*. That the Communist concept is hostile and repugnant to human nature. That it is flagrantly antibiological!

In the early days of an unbearably cold December in 1934, at the back of the stage of the miners' clubhouse, lost in the snows of Spitzbergen, hung a portrait of Kirov, painted by a miner's hand, and draped in black crepe. Kirov had been killed in Leningrad. There was a rally of the entire Soviet colony, as befitted such an event.

Father's deputy Pikel gave a fiery speech in voice hoarse with excitement. He was considered the best orator in Barentsburg. In 1937 Pikel was one of the main defendants in yet another vicious Stalin show trial. And he was executed.

Only now, toward the end of my life, have I begun to see a terrible pattern. Pikel had been a secretary of Trotsky's. Everything, however peripherally or di-

---

*Lacquer boxes pointed with Russian folk or fairytale scenes, in the manner of the artists of the town of Palekh.

rectly involved with the name Trotsky, was destroyed by Stalin with bloody fire. Father had been friends with Pikel all his life. Mother often told me how loyal a friend Father had been. When Pikel ended up without work and in political disfavor, Father took his old friend to Spitzbergen as his deputy. Before Spitzbergen, Pikel was director of the Tairov Chamber Theater. The destruction of the talented theater was, I fear, also tied to Pikel's political legacy. Meyerhold's death suggests the same name to me: Trotsky. Meyerhold had dedicated one of his plays to Trotsky and that rankled with the ruthless, vengeful, treacherous Stalin.

Had Father known, did he have a sense of foreboding, did he have fears, did he push away his doomed thoughts that the price of his loyalty would be his life? Taking Pikel to Spitzbergen had been a deadly risk. Alas, the disaster came to pass. As soon as the waters were navigable, two detectives came on the *Krasin* — for Father! Whoever sent them had no sense of humor. For their names sounded like something from a provincial vaudeville show: Rogozhin and Rogozhan. Later, their names appeared in Father's case as prosecution witnesses. And I came across those two names in the second paper on the rehabilitation of M. E. Plisetsky — "executed through false denunciation." But that was in 1989. Back then, in Barentsburg, I was friends with their sweet Pioneer daughters.

And I also remember Pikel in Moscow. Before Spitzbergen. At his house, in the circle of his festive family. His plump, giggling wife, who later repeated her husband's martyred death. I remember their dazzling New Year's tree, dressed to the hilt. The branches were weighed down by the sparkling ornaments, and I asked ecstatically, "May I smash a ball?"

"You may," Pikel replied insouciantly. With a squeal, I smashed a big silver ball on the floor.

And in 1937–38 Stalin smashed both Pikel and my father.

Chapter Five

I Study Ballet

Let me return to the summer of 1934.

After two years of winter on Spitzbergen, Father was given a vacation. A long, wearying journey across all of Europe brought our family back to Moscow. This was when the visit from the nostalgic American uncle occurred that I've already described. But one of the family's main concerns was that they had decided to send me to the Moscow Choreographic School, the ballet school, if I passed the entrance exams. My success in *Rusalka* had played an important part in my parents' decision—and I drove them crazy every day, dancing, playacting, making noise, as if our little apartment in Barentsburg were a stage.

On a rainy June morning (or was it late May?), Mita took me to the ballet exam. I was dressed all in white for such a solemn occasion: a white Viscose dress, white socks, and a big white bow, ironed carefully, pinned to my red braids. Alas, there weren't any appropriate shoes in my wardrobe — everyday brown flat sandals marred my matrimonial look.

The ballet boom had not yet swept the country. Now, everyone wants to be Anna Pavlova, impersonate the muse Terpsichore, dance *Swan Lake* at the Bolshoi for the American president, and tour the world. No one wants to sign up at the Three Mountains Manufacturing Plant or the Ilyich Factory. No, no, they want the stage.

But in those "Stakhanovite" years, everyone dreamed of soaring like red-starred Stalinist falcons into the sky, drifting their way to the Pole, setting records for flights marked out by the dry, paralyzed hand of the leader, landing on broken ice, drowning with the crew of the *Cheluskin*, only to report, "mission of the Homeland completed, dear Comrade Stalin."

Judge for yourselves. All the children of Party leaders were pilots. They participated in all the air parades at Tushino; they were in the front ranks of the fighters for the classiest Lenin rubbish. Both of Stalin's sons—Yakov and Vasily—flew professionally. Mikoyan's children flew. Frunze's children flew. The fame of pilot Chkalov eclipsed that of Alexander the Great, Napoleon, and Tamerlane; it was beginning to rival the sacred reputation of the divine leader himself. Actually, according to recently unearthed documents, that may have cost the talented ace his life. Stalin preferred to praise the dead. I'm writing this for my Western readers, since my countrymen have known it since before they read their first primer.

The places where our dictators educate their offspring offer an infallible guide to the times, its mores and values. Suddenly long lines of armored ZILs and Chaikas* drive down Frunzenskaya Street, which now houses the ballet school with its mirrored practice rooms. A seditious thought buzzes. Did they move the ballet school from the corner of Pushechnaya and Neglinnaya to Frunzenskaya so that the huge state cars could park more easily in the parking lots (planned even before the building went up)? So that the leaders' tiny daughters and granddaughters who slip out of those limousines could more easily reach the private office of the smiling, welcoming director, to leave their fancy coats there?

And my exam? In 1934 there were few applicants. Maybe thirty, if my memory serves. But not a thousand like today. An applicant needed to have the right physical attributes, good health, musicality—definitely!—and a sense of rhythm. We walked *en dansant* to the music, the tempo constantly changing, to see if the body heard the changes. Natural artistry was particularly valued. My fate was decided by the simple curtsy I made before the admissions commission.

(Let me switch—parenthetically—to today. In July 1991 the king of Spain, Juan Carlos I, bestowed Spain's highest honor upon me. Now I am Excelentísima Doña Maya. Well-trained courtiers, following court etiquette, plied me with preliminary questions: Would I be making a speech of gratitude? I promised, "My speech will be a curtsy."

They agreed, hesitantly. I kept my word. All the television news programs

*Limousines.

for several days "quoted" my speech; they kept showing my dancing bow to the king, Queen Sofia, and high society.)

The admissions committee was headed by the director of the school, Victor Alexandrovich Semenov, a former premier dancer of the Maryinsky Theater. He was married to a young star of the Vaganova School's first graduating class, Marina Semenova (Semenova was also her maiden name) and had moved with her to Moscow.

In 1976 I was in America and visited the legendary Olga Spessivtzeva in a home for aged performers near New York (all such visits were made in anxious secrecy, to be kept out of reports of the KGB informers who accompanied us in droves).

Spessivtzeva was abashedly quiet, ashamed of her less-than-free situation. She asked me only one question in her pure voice, not at all elderly, and accent-free, "Is Vitya Semenov still alive?" The shadow of some secret crossed her noble face, framed by her neatly combed gray hair, parted in the middle as it appeared in all her stage photos.*

Well, "Vitya Semenov," after my curtsy, personally took what is now called a individualistic decision: "This girl we'll take."

My fate was decided. I started studying ballet.

Nowadays we have lost much of the natural element in choosing our professions, including dancing. A child's body tells the experienced eye the potential of the dancing form and the future changes clever nature will make in it, as well as the answer to the eternal question of whether to be a dancer. But nowadays, before the entrance exams parents perform all sorts of tortures on their child's body, forcing the child to demonstrate super turn out, super flexibility, super stretch to the commission. They hire private trainers and coaches, attend gymnastics classes and pools. The child comes to the exams prepared but exhausted. All the unnatural forcing of the body, especially in childhood, come back to haunt the adult. By forty, the "forced dancers" become lame invalids who walk with canes. Perhaps I'm old-fashioned. But I prefer natural selection to diligence and effort.

I was put in Yevgenia Ivanovna Dolinskaya's class. Writing her name makes me feel warm and happy. It is fortunate when the first teacher elicits a child's curiosity and interest. Unlike children today, we did not know a thing, none of the basics. Not first through fifth position, not pliés, not preparation. Dolinskaya gave us all that patiently. We did all our exercises facing the ballet barre. The

---

*Spessivtzeva died on the Tolstoy Farm in upstate New York in 1991.

entire first course. Of course, it was boring and dreary. We wanted to dance right away, not study. But Moscow wasn't built in a day.

Dolinskaya played the piano well. Later, when she staged small ballets for us, she often sat at the piano and made the musical phrases clear. In the past she had been a soloist at the Bolshoi in character parts. She was artistic, attractive, but a bit too bulky. The Lord had given her a lot of patience; I can't remember a single occasion when she blew up, or reacted harshly to someone's slowness or lack of comprehension. I consider that one of her virtues.

She liked me. She used me in all her sweet, unpretentious choreographic miniatures. I danced a Russian peasant woman to the music of Knipper's *Polushko-pole*. I wore a long, patterned *sarafan*, a head scarf with a bit of a visor, and cloth boots made to look like box leather. I reveled in keeping the simple beat, gesticulating, flirting, and winking, which made our school audience laugh.

Another of Dolinskaya's numbers was set to Tchaikovsky's *Serenade*. Later I heard the music in Balanchine's great work, and it brought back my ballet childhood and the sweet soul of Yevgenia Ivanovna. Dolinskaya had four girls, including me, in the number. We danced in the kingdom of an abstract pastoral as graceful, mythological shepherdesses bathed in the sun and sky, catching floating butterflies.

Dolinskaya yearned to do more choreography, and her school productions helped her move on to more serious works, but she was never allowed to do a full-scale ballet. Put simply, they didn't let her, though for many, many years the Bolshoi used a *Swan Lake* (the old *Lake,* as we called it) with Act I choreographed by Dolinskaya. She took part in opera premieres as well, staging the dances and pantomimes. To this day, her pastoral is used in the Bolshoi's production of *Queen of Spades*. She also staged the dances in *Rusalka*. By the way, my second *Rusalka* — on the Second Stage of the Bolshoi, when I was definitely a soloist among the corps de ballet water plants at the bottom of the river — was staged by Yevgenia Ivanovna.

But the main success of Dolinskaya's choreography I shared with Lyonya Shvachkin in a saucy number *à la russe:* "In a small village Vanka lived, Vanka fell in love with Tanka." Shvachkin had an artistic gift and humorous manner, and we took delight in competing with each other, kicking up fancy figures, making faces, flirting, rhythmically cracking sunflower seeds and spitting out the shells, pretending to be shy.

But I'm getting ahead of myself. That was in my third year.

I must mention my first meeting in my first class with Leonid Veniaminovich Yakobson. I worked with him — sporadically, alas — my entire life. I consider that a gift from the gods. Later I will write about Yakobson in greater detail. But now, just about our first meeting.

Leonid Veniaminovich took me for his number *Disarmament Conference*. I can't remember the music for the life of me. But this is how the dance went. Ten or twelve dancers, like the U.N. of those years. Every dancer represented a different country. I remember Volodya Levashyov, who danced a stupid English lord in a top hat. I got the part of a Chinaman. I was shorter than the others. I came out from the wings in a pointy straw hat in a series of Yakobson's glissades. I was afraid all the time, swiveling my head and narrowing my eyes. I ended up hiding under a chair. This was supposed to depict the useless ruler of China, Generalissimo Chiang Kai-Shek. How small and ridiculous he was. There has been a lot of water under the bridge since then, but the world is still disarming and disarming, conferences are convened and ended, and it looks as if this will continue until our planet is blown up.

Besides ballet, we were also taught common sense and the usual subjects: Russian, arithmetic, geography, history, music, and French. As I wrote that last word, my hand trembled. It takes some doing to teach and study a language so that I ended up not knowing a thing. Neither to speak nor to comprehend — even though the professional ballet terminology is based on French. If I were to teach a dance class on Mars, I could do it with fifteen to twenty French expressions. As for music lessons, I peaked at Beethoven's piano piece *Für Elise*. That I learned solidly. I can play it even today.

The first year was very brief for me. Father's vacation ended; in fact, he had extended it. We had to return to Spitzbergen. The question of what to do about me was discussed at length. They came to the decision that we would all go back to Barentsburg before the sailing season ended. There was no one to leave me with in Moscow. Mita and Asaf were on an extended tour, and the school didn't have a dormitory in those days.

Once again, suitcase, trains, Berlin, German lawns, ferry, seasickness, boundless high waves, snow, plank stairs, albatrosses, cold, and wind.

Chapter Six

Back in School and Father's Arrest

I'm not going to describe Spitzbergen a second time. Enough. Nothing had changed. There was more snow this time, and we had moved to a larger apartment.

The polar night was insufferably long this time. The main event was the public memorial service for Sergei Kirov. I still raced around on skis. Upset my parents. My father was becoming more irritable and grumpy. Something was bothering him.

Sometimes I dreamed about the crowded but welcoming building of the choreography school on Pushechnaya Street. Blue-eyed Muza Fedyaeva, giggly Atochka Ivanova, Tanya Lankovits concentrating on her arabesques, slant-eyed half-breed Nadya Maltseva . . . I was bringing them a bulky jar filled with Spitzbergian sea monsters in formaldehyde. That would amaze them. My leg muscles twitched in my sleep like a puppy's. My body remembered Dolinskaya's lessons.

I missed dance after all: the scraped and thoroughly washed classroom floor, the sweaty rehearsal barre, the ancient mirror with cracked corners in which you could judge and adjust your first poses, the bitter odor of a room filled with overheated people.

By spring, seeing my longing, Father decided to send me with someone on the first icebreaker to the mainland, to Moscow. So I discovered a new way from Spitzbergen to the mainland via Murmansk.

My companion was the bookkeeper, sick with scurvy, whose work with the miners' salaries had brought him to nervous exhaustion. His surname was appropriate — Zolotoi, or Golden. I don't know whether it was my nastiness and sarcasm or whether he had really lost his mind, but the bookkeeper counted all the time. His lips formed a column of figures.

I tormented him cruelly on board ship. I hid, vanished, was found, and disappeared again . . . He lost what little health he had dealing with me.

I was too late for the end of the school year. And in the second year, we had a new teacher. Elizaveta Pavlovna Gerdt took Dolinskaya's class. I studied with her for six years.

Elizaveta Pavlovna was the daughter of Pavel Andreyevich Gerdt, soloist of His Imperial Majesty. If E. P. is to be believed, he was the only one with that title at the Maryinsky Theater. If you translate it into Soviet terms it would be something like Hero of Socialist Labor. The Russian emperor also gave him a fabulous pension — 800 gold rubles a year. Not bad. Today's rulers have adopted the royal family's interest in ballet folk, but without the pensions. And they have their own ideas about ballet subtleties.

Legend has it that Alexandra Fedorovna Romanova, the Russian empress, left her box noisily and wrathfully when Vaslav Nijinsky appeared onstage at the Maryinsky in silk tights that hugged his masculine body too tightly.* Every fashion-plate wears tights like that on the street today. But today's rulers continue the habit of knowing what is good and what is bad in ballet, what is allowed and what isn't.

So, back to my teacher, E. P. Gerdt. Her mother was a Maryinsky ballerina, Shaposhnikova. "Ballet on all sides," she would say. She hated Soviet power fiercely but quietly. She always responded the same way, hiding the real reason, to my permanent, tricky question, Why didn't you leave in 1917? "There wasn't room for me in Siloti's sleigh." †

For a long time the conductor Alexander Gauk was E. P.'s husband, and she moved from Leningrad to Moscow with him. They were both quiet, noble, polite. But one day Gauk suddenly developed a passion for Galina Ulanova and accidentally ended up as her tenant for a while. E. P., thinking fast, cut her wrists.

---

*The origins of this famous theatrical scandal are generally attributed to the empress mother, Maria Fedorovna, not the empress.

† Alexander Siloti was a Bolshoi conductor who emigrated during the Revolution.

She was revived, and the timid Gauk returned home quickly to the old stall. You couldn't indulge all your Freudian inclinations under Stalin.

But I keep going off on tangents. What kind of a teacher was she? It's hard to say: Should I soften the edges, be mealy-mouthed, or should I tell the truth, bringing down thunder and lightning on my head once again? She was a nice woman. Steady, not rancorous, good-natured. Life brought her in contact with brilliant people — Rachmaninoff, Siloti, Glazunov, Kuprin, Karsavina, Korovin, Klemperer, Blok. What more could you ask? And talking with her was always interesting and amusing.

But she knew little about ballet, or to be kinder about it, she didn't understand it fully. That's how it seemed to me after I had tasted the sharp clarity of Vaganova's school. Both women had come out of the Maryinsky, both had gone through the same training, both had studied with the same teacher, both had breathed the same magical air of the northern capital, both lived only for ballet. But nature had not endowed Gerdt with analytical wisdom or professional vision. She could see that this was right and that was wrong, but she couldn't explain or teach how and why, she couldn't "write the prescription." She always made the right diagnosis, but she had no idea how to treat the patient.

"You're hanging on the barre like wet laundry on the line." But what are you supposed to do to stop hanging?

Vaganova would have said, quite prosaically, "Move your hand forward." And the ballerina would achieve equilibrium as if with the wave of a magic wand.

That's schooling. With a simple phrase, mysterious for an outsider, you can put things in their place. Here's a tiny example. Vaganova liked to say, "Squeeze your rear end around an imaginary fifteen-kopeck piece through the whole class, so that it doesn't fall."

And a ballerina learned for life to keep her rear end pulled together, not flabby. And that gives you the proper carriage, correct position of the pelvis and the spine. Vaganova had a hawk's precise eye. Gerdt didn't.

I heard the story of how, at the turn of the century, Pierina Legnani, for the first time in Russia, finished the coda of *Cinderella* with thirty-two fouettés. The Petersburg dancers watching from the wings dropped their jaws. They had never seen that trick. The next morning the classes were filled with people trying to do at least three or four. And falling. By the way, it was E. P. herself who told me this story; she got it from her father, Pavel Andreyevich, who had been one of the characters in those distant and confusing days of the Russian state. And then came Vaganova. She went to the middle of the room, stood in fourth position, whispered to herself, "She did it this way," and right off the bat did all thirty-two, one after another.*

All my life I suffered for my lack of professional classical schooling, which I did not get properly as a child. I knew some things, others I stole, some I figured out for myself, took advice, blundered through. And it was all haphazard, random. If only someone had explained it all when I was ten or twelve!

A few years ago, for an important birthday, Japanese television prepared a sweet color film of my recent performances. They sent me a video cassette in Moscow. I watched it and groaned with satisfaction. Then I angrily told Shchedrin, "I think I've finally learned to dance."

And I was telling the truth. But it was late, damn it!

I know that Shchedrin had similar experience, in composing, with his conservatory professor Shaporin. He also wasted a lot of time reinventing the wheel. But you can't go back and redo your life.

Here's another funny thing about Elizaveta Pavlovna. Very few people know this. Once, Shchedrin and I had been visiting Shostakovich at his dacha in Zhukovka, and as we were leaving, and I was pulling on my coat, Dmitri Dmitrievich asked me ironically, "And how is my dear Elizaveta Pavlovna doing?"

"All right."

"Do you know that I left the manuscripts of my symphonies — the Fourth, Fifth, and Sixth — with her and Gauk for safekeeping, and she lost them."

"How can that be?"

"Well, it just happened . . ."

The next morning, I attacked Elizaveta Pavlovna. "Is it true what Shostakovich said?"

"Yes," E. P. babbled in her phony, little-girl voice. "Alexander Vasilyevich and I were evacuated to the Caucasus at the start of the war. I put Mitya's music in my sturdiest suitcase along with my best shoes. They were wonderful shoes, brand new. In all the bustle at the Kursky Station, I turned away for a second and some bandit took away the suitcase with my shoes. It was awful. Mitya's manuscripts were in there, too."

---

*It was Legnani who introduced the thirty-two fouettés to Russia in 1893, but Imperial Ballet ballerina Mathilde Kchessinska mastered the trick long before Vaganova. That Vaganova was credited with this innovation in Soviet times testifies to both the near-complete obliteration of Kchessinska's name in the Soviet Union (she had been the lover of Nicholas II) and the mythology created around Vaganova's.

The originals of Shostakovich's symphonies were lost forever. That is Elizaveta Pavlovna's crime before the history of music.

There were so many of us studying together, about twenty-five to thirty, boys and girls. Together. I'm recalling them now. Neli Shaburova, Lida Menshova, Vera Logvina, Tata Cheremshanskaya, Ida Sonina, Prushinskaya, Kholshchevnikova, Erik Volodin, May Vlasov, Yuri Sobolev, Malyshev, Berkovich, Vdovchenko, Kalinin, Pavel Getling, German Munster. Every name has its own story. A large segment of my female classmates went into the Bolshoi's corps de ballet. Of the boys, many were killed in the war, and the ones with German surnames were exiled. None of them became dancers. Erik Volodin was an exception; he did become a soloist and did dozens of character roles. Lida Menshova, with her beautiful and aristocratic features, ended up playing queens, willful princesses, and matrons. Muza Fedyaeva did some solo parts. Competently. But all of us lacked a real "school."

The fates of our teachers were not happy, either. My dear "unfortunates," as the playwright Ostrovsky put it. Althuasen and Kheister, the teachers of geography and physics, died. Boris Alexeyevich Nurik, who tried to pound the four rules of arithmetic into our heads, died under strange circumstances on the street.

Now I will move on to sad and terrible pages.

In the summer of 1935 Father was summoned to Moscow. I met my parents and my four-year-old brother, Ala, at the Kazan Station, packed with angry, grim people. So much sorrow and so many tears were seen in those nightmare years by the square outside that station, which was blasphemously and cheerfully called Komsomol Square.* Three of Moscow's main stations had been there forever: Kazan, Yaroslavl, and Leningrad, but the great architects Ton, Shchusev, and Shekhtel had never imagined the innumerable Russian lives that would be ruined inside their creations or on those platforms open to the sky.

Father was withdrawn and gray, immersed in something I could not know. I do not want to portray myself now as a Wunderkind who understood what was going on in my penitentiary of a country. The most perspicacious adults did not understand it. The only one who did was the paranoid Stalin, as he carried out his bloody evil.

They played out the script page by page. They called Father back unexpectedly. But not to punish him. On the contrary, they gave him a new apartment. The gave him an important post in Arktikugl management. A personal car was

---

*Komsomol was the Communist Youth League.

one of the perks, a black Emka. It came with a neatly dressed, attentive — very attentive — chauffeur. My father was praised in a decree of the people's commissar of the coal industry. But why was he so unhappy then? What sense of foreboding did he have?

The new apartment seemed strange to me, even after the bohemian atmosphere of our crowded life on Sretenka. It was located in Gagarin Alley, no. 3/8, in an old two-story wooden house. We lived on the second floor, up a creaky staircase. The stairs let us know a guest was coming long before there was a knock at the door.

Our apartment was sort of separate but also communal at the same time. We were given two rooms, a dining room and a bedroom. But the way to two other "separate" apartments was through our dining room. People had to go through our dining room to get to their apartments. Everyone watched everyone else. Vigilantly. Willy-nilly. Greeted one another a hundred times a day. By the way, both neighboring families followed Father's tragic path just a little later.

Father spent days at a time at work while Mother took care of my brother. I made the trip to school on Pushechnaya Street every day, an easy ride on the metro. Gagarin Alley was right opposite the Palace of Congresses metro station. Nothing came of the Bolsheviks' grandiose plans for their palace with a huge Lenin at the top. Just a metro stop and some postage stamps. In too much of a hurry to study the ground, which proved unsuitable for the foundation, they had blown up the ancient and lovely cathedral of Christ the Savior in vain. Now the site holds the Moscow pool, where the workers of Moscow and the region rinse their weary bodies. But the evaporation from the huge heated pool is the last thing all the Rembrandts and Rubenses in the Pushkin Museum across the street really need.* (How bitter I am! I surprise even myself!)

One evening Father came home earlier than usual. And without eating, he lay down on the bed, still fully dressed. He lay motionless, for an eternity, his long arms behind his head, staring at the ceiling. There was a cold, oppressive silence. I went over and sat on the edge of the bed.

"Are you sick, Papa?"

"I was thrown out of the Party, daughter."

Who threw him out? For what? Why? What was this party? Why was it tormenting my father? He was a good man.

---

* After the collapse of the Soviet Union, history reversed itself once again: the Cathedral of Christ the Savior has been rebuilt.

That night my parents whispered. You couldn't speak out loud—there were ears everywhere.

And then came the presentation of the great Stalin Constitution, which, as people know, was written by Nikolai Bukharin.* The whole family, along with our neighbors, listened to the leader's speech from the Bolshoi Theater (you can't escape the Bolshoi). This was already December 1936. Stalin spoke in his hard Georgian accent, unhurriedly, dragging out the words (he was in no rush) almost syllable by syllable. The audience, in raptures, applauded for a long time. Our black old radio had trouble with applause. It crackled and sizzled and sparked. No one said a single word, not the neighbors, not us.

The car with its fastidious driver stopped coming for Father in the morning. He stayed at home. He rarely shaved. He spent hours in bed. He didn't answer questions. Didn't eat. He was haggard and black. They fired him from work.

The telephone, which used to ring nonstop, especially at night, fell silent. No one came to see us anymore. Father had the plague. They were afraid of him.

A few days before May 1 father was summoned somewhere. He came back overjoyed and looking younger.

"I have guest tickets to the Kremlin tribune. Mayechka, we're going to go to Red Square on May 1, for the parade."

I trumpeted through my fist. Hurray! What dress should I wear? Mother began making me something eclectic but formal.

It happened on April 30, 1937. At dawn, a few hours before May 1, early in the morning. Around five, the stairs creaked beneath the leaden weight of sudden steps. They had come to arrest Father. These predawn arrests have been described often in literature, shown in films and onstage. But believe me, living through one is very frightening. Strangers. Roughness. The search. The whole house upside down. My mother, unkempt, pregnant with a big belly, weeping and clutching. My little brother screaming, rudely awakened. My father, white as snow, dressing with trembling hands. He was embarrassed. The neighbors' faces were remote. The witness, the blowsy janitor Varvara, with a cigarette between her lips, didn't miss a chance to suck up to the authorities: "Can't wait for all of you bastards to be shot, you enemies of the people!" And I—eleven years old, skinny, scared, not understanding what was going on, my childish head filled with arabesques and attitudes. I had tried on my new dress ten times before the mirror, and I had been prepared to put it on just three or four hours later to go to

---

*A high-ranking Politburo member and leader of the rightist opposition to Stalin who was purged in a famous show trial in 1938.

Red Square. I hoped that this wouldn't last more than a few days, when life would go back to normal. And my father tried to console me, whispering, "Everything will be fine . . ."

The last thing I heard my father say before the door shut behind him forever was, "Thank God, they'll settle this at last."

Now, whenever I happen to pass that ill-starred corner house on Gagarin, I feel a chill. The sense of horror never leaves me. The house, as opposed to its residents, survived very well.

Chapter Seven

My Mother Disappears

The apartment in Gagarinsky (Gagarin Alley) and the wooden house in Zaroyanka were not confiscated right away. They did that later. Mother suffered, begging in the waiting rooms of the NKVD; relatives clucked. But quietly. The neighbors shunned us. Varvara, the janitor, was angrily silent. I continued my daily trips on the subway named for yet another Stalin bandit, Lazar Kaganovich, to my ballet school. Mornings there, evenings back.

Fortunately for me, the attitude at school did not change toward me. I was not the only one engulfed by grief. Many in my class had lost their parents in the same sweet Stalinist manner.

The father of Atochka (a diminutive of Artemia) Ivanova lost his life publicly. He was a participant — a victim — in the Zinoviev show trial. His surname Ivanov, the most common in Russia, appeared in newspaper lists of alleged conspirators at the end of the blacklist. Intentionally, I think. To hint that the conspiracy was massive and therefore all the more dangerous. Be vigilant, Soviet people!

The father of another Maya, Kholshchevnikova, simply vanished, like a rock in water. Also on an early, predawn morn.

The father of Galya Prushinskaya followed the Dantesque circles of my father. He had also been called to Moscow and praised. "Ten years without the right to correspondence." That was what my mother was also told in response to her persistent, hopeless questions . . .

But there were pupils in the class whose relatives stood on the other side of the barricades. Not the ones who were judged but who judged, who executed the sentences of the "extraordinary troikas." My classmate Valya Bolotova proudly informed the class that her uncle had sat in the back of a truck the night before on top of the body of Georgy Pyatakov.* Served him right! The corpses of executed people were delivered by night to secret pit graves.

Why were we left in the school and not kicked out? Why were we later accepted at the Bolshoi Theater, the imperial theater? I never once asked myself or my relatives that question. My peers well remember Stalin saying in one of his speeches that "the son does not answer for his father." But the children did answer—and how! Now we know the stories of the younger Yakirs, Tukhachevskys, Rykovs, Bukharins, Uboreviches, and Kosiorovs. And I heard a few things from some of the survivors personally. But the children of not-so-famous people were left alone. Weren't touched. We were on view all the time but not touched. We were already in the palms of their hands. The personnel files were updated annually, even two or three times a year. And you can't hide in a file. Where is your father, where is your mother, when was he born, where does he work, under what statute was he arrested, in what year? Over my lifetime I filled in thousands of these forms. Before every trip. Every single one, readers. And the questions were always the same: father, mother, date of birth, place of employment, what statute for arrest?

Nevertheless, I am grateful to the fates. I studied what I loved. I danced in grown-up ballets. I went out onto the magical stage of the Bolshoi. To the music of a marvelous orchestra. Dances were created for me. I had a clean bed. I did not starve. The label "daughter of an enemy of the people" did not ruin my life's calling. I avoided the hell of a Soviet orphanage, where they wanted to put me. I was saved by Mita. I did not end up in Vorkuta, Auschwitz, or Magadan.† They tormented me, but they didn't kill me. Didn't burn me in Dachau.

My knowledge of the ballet grew.

I am trying to remember. But what had happened? Every day the class, every day plié, tendu, rond de jambe, grand battement, fondu, the rattle of the piano,

---

*Old Bolshevik economist who was purged by Stalin.
† Vorkuta and Magadan were forced-labor camps in the Soviet Gulag.

sweat, toes rubbed raw. Arithmetic, geography, French under an evil spell, zoology. The daily grind.

In the third year new subjects appeared, which I liked. Character dance and historical dance. They were taught by two great beauties, Bolshoi ballerinas: Nadya Kapustina and Margarita Vasilyevna Vasilyeva. The character dances included Spanish, Gypsy, Russian, Hungarian, and the mazurka. I had trouble with the Gypsy dance but the Spanish worked. My sources for *Carmen, Don Quixote, Laurencia,* and my present feckless life in Spain go back that far. The historical dancing was so far from everything around us, it was like a vacation from worry.

I studiously attended all the dress rehearsals at the Bolshoi, both ballet and opera. That was a good tradition: playing one dress rehearsal for the insiders — the school, the costume workshops, the pensioners. The artists knew that the audience was composed of colleagues, and they were relaxed, playing for joy and inspiration.

Back then, the children danced in the theater's repertory. We learned great things from that experience. I danced the Breadcrumb Fairy in *Sleeping Beauty,* flowers in Rimsky-Korsakov's *Snegurochka,* and the cat in *The Little Stork.*

In the summer they took us to Pioneer camp, the whole bunch of us. There, it was morning exercises, line up, flag-raising ceremony, heart-rending bugles, brave counselors, reports, evening campfires. We were Pioneers. Sort of like the Hitler Youth. Disciplined, sowing loyalty to the Homeland.

My mother began selling off things to live on. One by one. She had been in her seventh month when they took away Father. While I was marching to the bouncy tunes of Isaak Dunaevsky at summer camp, Mother gave birth in July to my younger brother. She lost her milk. She was in constant need of money.

In early March 1938 (I don't remember the exact date), Mita was dancing in *Sleeping Beauty.* It would be easy enough to check the program in the theater archives. I did not attend all my aunt's performances, but Mother and I planned to go to this one. We decided to buy flowers. Or rather, to get some. It wasn't easy finding flowers in spring in Moscow then.

And there we were at home, in the entry of the apartment on Gagarinsky, with flowers in hand. Now I struggle to remember how I ended up that evening at the theater all alone. Without Mother. With a big bouquet of Crimean mimosas. It's a total blank. I have this stupid ability to be so lost in my own thoughts that I don't notice anything going on around me. I don't like this habit of mine. But that's what happened that March evening.

The performance was coming to an end, bows, applause. But where's Mother? We had been together.

I went with the flowers to Mita's house to congratulate her. She lived nearby, behind the theater in Shchepkinsky Passage, in a building that belonged to the Bolshoi, where I would later live for many years in a large communal apartment.

Mita took the flowers and regarded me closely with her dark, serious eyes. And unexpectedly, she asked me to stay the night. She gave me some ridiculous story about Mother having been called out suddenly to see Father and rushing off, straight from the theater, without waiting for the end of the ballet, to catch a night train. Naturally, I believed her. I'm very trusting to this day. At the age of twelve, you'll believe any story.

And so I moved in with Mita. I did not understand that Mother was in prison. That she had also been arrested. Also at the most unexpected, inappropriate hour. Have people come up with an appropriate hour for arrests? They have for executions, I think.

For a long time I did not understand that the telegrams "from Mother" were sent by Mita from the main post office on Myasnitskaya (already renamed for Kirov, just like the theater; it was all intertwined). I swear that it was much, much later when I realized that the repulsive, short-haired women (who stank so terribly that we had to open all the windows after their visits) who interrogated me so closely and suspiciously about Mother and Mita were from the orphanage, where they were planning to send me, the homeless orphan, daughter of an "enemy of the people."

The apartment on Gagarinsky was sealed and then confiscated with all our simple worldly goods. My wedding outfit was gone — dress, socks, ribbons, sandals. How did those killers divide up the things, furniture, shoes, pots and pans of their victims? At night, at dawn, or in broad daylight? Did their fat wives squeeze into other people's used clothing, or did they drag everything to the flea market?

For several long years I did not know the whole truth about my parents. It was clear to me about other people — things were bad. But for me, things had to turn out well, there had to be a happy ending. Mother and Father, all dressed up, healthy, beautiful, laughing, would appear in Mita's crowded room on Shchepkinsky, embrace me, and be happy.

My paternal grandmother, Babulya, was also sent forged letters by her daughters, my father's sisters. The letters were allegedly from her son, Misha, saying things like, "Dear Mama, everything is fine. I'll be back soon and I'll come visit you in Leningrad. How are you?"

Just think how many holy deceits were perpetrated then in our miserable, god-forsaken, blood-covered Russia.

Chapter Eight

Chimkent

I would like to talk about *Sleeping Beauty* and *Swan Lake*, how I could toss off grands battements, and my handsome partners. But no matter what end of my childhood I look at, it all turns to politics, to the Stalin terror.

I learned about my mother's bitter odyssey only later. She was incarcerated in Butyrki Prison with a newborn infant. Butyrki loomed near the center of Moscow. People walked past the grim edifice cautiously. To this day, the prison has not been torn down, and its narrow barred windows squint menacingly at passersby — you'll need me yet again, don't bet you won't, oh, decent people. That horrible word *Butyrki* won't be forgotten for centuries.

Father was no longer alive. He had been executed by firing squad on January 7, 1938. The family learned the date only in 1989 from a piece of paper clipped to a terse official document about his posthumous rehabilitation.

But the investigators behaved as if Father were alive during Mother's interrogation. It was all in the present tense. Mother held her ground. She did not shudder, did not panic, was stubborn. She had the right character for that. I've already written about that. She did not admit anything, did not sign anything, did not confess to anything. She was given eight years in prison.

She was sent from the prison for wives of "enemies of the people" by stages to Siberia. "By stages" meant a cattle car with a tiny, hand-sized barred window for ventilation. The prisoners were sorted. Mother ended up in a large group of "criminals" with infants. I can imagine it even without her telling me — children's wails, the smells, a real hell. The car was stuffed, there was nowhere to sit or turn. The train crawled along for days. They stopped at all stations. The guards clanged the locks. A whispered rumor traveled through the car that they were being taken to Akmolinsk Oblast (province) in Kazakhstan. But she could not believe that they were all widows.

Mother pushed her way to the window. In her fist she clutched a tiny note written on a scrap of newspaper with a matchstick, with Mita's address and four more words: "taken camp Akmolinsk Oblast." At a deserted crossing where the train halted briefly, Mother saw a young, severe-looking woman in a padded jacket with a railroad flag. Their eyes met. Mother flicked the crumpled note at the woman's feet. The crossing guard did not react. As if she had not noticed. The train started.

Thanks and glory to you, kind people. You were always there in those hard years. By unknown channels the letter — a scream — reached the recipient. Whether it was the simple woman herself or someone close to her, pure and honest railroad workers, but from hand to hand — and believe me, in 1938 this was a heroic act — Mother's tearful scribbles got here. That meant that people did not believe in "wreckers" and "saboteurs," in "agents of foreign intelligence," or "murderers." They believed in kindness, help, and sympathy.

I am writing these pages in Spain. I live here now. I am writing at the beach, in a small town called Herradura, 60 kilometers from Malaga. Near Africa. I am sitting in the Bueno, a cozy café on Andrés Segovia embankment, right on the seashore, having just put away a plate of tender calamari with Shchedrin. This morning that delicacy was calmly swimming around in the Mediterranean Sea, suspecting nothing. How tricky and unpredictable life can be. How far, how immeasurably far is the distance between Mother's prison cattle car and the Andalusian beach in the hot southern sun. But let me return to Moscow in the fall of 1938.

Russia always respected a person with a medal. I know this from the short stories of my favorite writer, Nikolai Leskov. In "Product of Nature," Leskov made a profound statement: If I had a real order instead of a clip, I could whip everyone in Russia personally. (I'm quoting from memory; you can't find a copy of Leskov for love or money in Herradura.) And both Asaf and Mita had just been given awards for creative achievements. For the twentieth anniversary of the immortal October Revolution. Asaf got the Order of Labor of the Red Banner and Mita the Mark of Honor. In those years there were not many orders. Not like today, when everyone is a medal-bearer, with a chestful of ribbons. So they both pinned their orders on their chest and plunged into saving their sister. They pounded on every door, wrote tons of pleas. And they got what they wanted. Mother was transferred from the camp to "free living" in the area. This reduction in regimen came just in time. In the Gulag, Mother had been forced to carry heavy burdens, push immovable wheelbarrows, and she had a bad hernia.

Mita came to the camp commander to get her sister, wearing her magic-wand order in her buttonhole. She charmed him and made him fall in love with her. At least, that is her version of the salvation trip. There were six thousand women ("enemies of the people") behind barbed wire — it was a women's camp for wives of arrested husbands. Armed with court documents, she moved Mother and the baby to the nearest town, a shabby Kazakh place called Chimkent.

Now I can recount the rest of this sad tale in the first person. At the end of summer 1939 — I had summer vacation — I was granted permission by the authorities to visit my mother.

Mita, using her medal-holder's certificate, got me a rail ticket. And I went off on my own, heading south this time.

In those years the whole country was on wheels. Train stations and trains were filled with people. You couldn't get near the ticket office. Marathon train journeys of several days' duration — say Moscow–Vladivostok and back, Vladivostok–Moscow — saved quite a few lives. The older brother of yet another of my girlfriends, a Komsomol activist, traveled around like that for almost two years. On his parent's money. And he survived. The wave of Yezhov's* executions had ebbed a bit, and he returned home untouched. But not everyone was so lucky. The Cheka's pincers had a strong grip, and in the majority of cases, these trips merely put off the inevitable, inexorable end.

I got on the train with my small bag of underwear and a bit of food for Mother. The trip would be a long one. My family had given me some money, too. It was sewn into a canvas bag that hung from my neck on a ribbon under my clothes. Watch out for crooks, my aunt had warned. The train was not an express, but the mail train. It stopped at length at every dinky station. It seemed strange, but people everywhere were selling all sorts of things. There were buckets of apples. On faded newspapers lay roasted chickens and bricks of pork fat, brown jugs of fresh milk, jostled, heaped sacks of sunflower seeds, and piles of pumpkins.

---

* Nikolai Yezhov was head of the Commission for Party Control and People's Commissar of the USSR in the 1930s and thus responsible for many of the purges. He himself was executed in 1940.

As soon as we entered Kazakhstan, the sellers' hands held camel wool and dried fruits and raisins; small mountains of melons stood nearby. Where has all that bounty gone? My poor country is so impoverished now, the long years of the irrational Bolshevik experiment have brought it to this. You can't even find a dried-up sandwich.

Mother met me at the station. I saw her big, bewildered eyes right away, scanning the row of braking railroad cars. She had grown thinner and older, her hair touched with gray. Her experiences had left their mark. We had not seen each other almost a year and half . . . Leaping down from the steps before the train came to a halt, I flung my arms around her neck. And hung on. We were both crying. People at the station began staring at us.

What was the city of Chimkent? Dust to the skies, to the very sun, one-story mudbrick houses, and donkeys, the main form of city transport. My mother had found a haven in a tiny shed for chickens, with a dirt floor, basically a chicken coop, which a kindly, talkative Bukhara Jew called Isaac rented to her out of the kindness of his heart for a small fee. He had a one-room white house, a hard-scrabble garden, and an obese, silent, almost mute, wife, Iofa, and a tiny child, Yakov, who was always up to his ears in filth. Isaac, as befits a learned Jew, asked everyone about everything. In this case, I think, without any prompting from the NKVD, simply out of inborn curiosity. Where was Father, why was he arrested, how long had Mama been married, why was I so skinny, did I eat fruit, how many days was I on the train from Moscow, was it stuffy on board, what were the conductors carrying, did anyone sit with me along the way, had I been to the Mausoleum, what can you buy in Moscow stores, had I ever seen Stalin?

Mother, in order to live, gave dance lessons at some club. She showed me the Dance of the Four Cygnets. Her experience in silent Uzbek films had come in handy. She had not studied dance when she was free, but she had attended performances at the Bolshoi often, and she remembered quite a bit. My baby brother had started walking and looked just like a midget Kazakh. The skullcap suited his dusky features. The flies, which had the city of Chimkent under siege, tormented him. He used a wet towel to get his fatal revenge, knocking the tin tooth mug from the low shelf onto the dirt floor each time. The 3-meters-square room was no place for such battles.

I went with Mother to the police precinct, where she had to check in twice a month. She had to appear in person before the keepers of law and order. Otherwise, how would they know whether she had run away?

There were a lot of members of the intelligentsia settled in the city. Doctors, engineers, writers, teachers. It was all mixed up. A mishmash. And somehow it seemed that this was the way things should be, completely in order. I didn't quite understand why Mother was there, whether she was an exile or free, why she had to check in, why she wouldn't come back to Moscow, since Father would return.

One unbearably hot night I had trouble sleeping. The flies were eating me alive. I slept fitfully, waking and then falling back into a troubled sleep. My baby brother started crying. Mother jumped up from her cot and began to rock him, humming softly. I fell back asleep. I don't know how much time passed. But I woke up abruptly and saw my mother sharply outlined against the window, brandishing her fist at someone and muttering something.

"What's the matter, Mama?"

"Sleep, darling, sleep."

They organized amateur concerts in the summer garden, late at night. That year the heat was absolutely intolerable. There were exiles on the stage and in the audience. Amusing one another. I danced in one of the concerts. Mother insisted that I appear in public: You're losing your form and you'll be afraid of audiences. Don't forget you must become a good dancer. You have talent.

A downcast exile played a potpourri from Tchaikovsky ballets for me. I improvised, getting on toe, bending my torso, doing a series of arabesques. A vague precursor of the future *Dying Swan*, but in the exiled Chimkent version, to accordion music. I was a hit, but a rather large woman began to shout from the front row during the applause. I heard her say, "She's a visitor. Don't let her dance. She's a professional ballerina."

Her daughter was dancing in the concert. Also with a ruined life, a vanished father. And the woman, jealous, wanted success for her daughter alone. People are always people. Forever. That's why communism is abstract nonsense.

The twenty days allowed me by the authorities came to an end. I had to return to Moscow. Mother, upset and lifeless, my baby brother suddenly serious, the entire family of genial Isaac (fat Iofa seemed to have water in her mouth again and didn't say a single word), and Mother's hopeless ballet students saw me off at the dusty, filthy, Chimkent station, full of vicious flies. I traveled back with a full pack of Central Asian delicacies. I had melons, watermelons, wool, and rosy apples. The leader of all the peoples had not managed to cut off family ties, the need of people for one another, or the lovely ordinariness of human socializing. I was going back to ballet.

Chapter Nine

Concert for the Cheka

Moscow greeted me with dreary autumnal frosts. The train arrived in the pale dawn, and Mother's brother Nodya, who could not get a sleepy porter's attention, had to haul all the packages, boxes, and marvels of Kazakh flora by himself.

I was living at Mita's again, and my brother Alexander was with Asaf. On Mondays — the traditional day off at the Bolshoi and the ballet school — I went to see my middle bother. He was growing up with Boris, the son of Asaf and Anel Sudakevich. (Boris Messerer is now a famous theater designer. It was he who created the wonderful sets for *Carmen Suite,* which were successfully repeated in numerous productions around the world.) Back then Anel, who feared treacherous colds more than anything else in the world, dressed both boys in a good hundred pieces of clothing, and the two of them, sweaty and barely able to move, went with me to the Central Movie Theater on Pushkin Square. The American film *The Great Waltz,* about Johann Strauss, creator of the classic Viennese waltz, was playing there. The film played a long time. Every Monday Alik and I, and perhaps Boris as well, stared for the umpteenth time at the laughing, happy, snow-white face of the "Hollywood star," Miliza Korjus. We knew the subtitles by heart. The film was the peak of perfection as far as I was concerned. Everyone has "the movie" of his childhood. Mine was *The Great Waltz.*

In 1966 when I was appearing at the Shriner Auditorium in Los Angeles, I was visited backstage by a tall, heavy woman whose face reminded me of something. My God, it was Miliza Korjus. My childhood idol. And the idol rushed to me and unleashed a squall of compliments in good Russian. I responded with my own squall. And so we stood there, praising each other, for a good fifteen minutes.

Miliza had not known that Stalin, who had always had a soft spot for plump singing women, adored *The Great Waltz* no less than I. What a surprise: our tastes corresponded. The leader gave orders to distribute *The Great Waltz* on Soviet screens. Let the subjects of his empire enjoy a Hollywood product, forgetting for a moment the imperialists and their conspiracies. Let them relish the loveliness of his overseas passion to the sounds of Strauss melodies.

Miliza and I became friends. She was born in Kiev, where she spent her child-hood. Many different types of blood were mixed in her, apparently, but the source of her culture was Slavic. What a strange world. Half of Hollywood speaks Russian. Right up until her sudden death, she tried to see every one of my perfor-mances. She would react wildly, shouting "Bravo" — I could recognize her silver voice among the roar of the crowd of ballet lovers crowded around the stage. She would be the last to leave. And she never did fully believe me when I told her that she had been an inaccessible goddess for an entire nation, a beautiful extra-terrestrial, a ray of happiness in the hardest years of the slave state. I can picture her unbelieving, kind, lovely face touched by damned age. I truly dreamed about you, Miliza!

But the movie ran for only ninety minutes. The early Moscow twilight gath-ered outside the theater. Soviet life went on.

We began rehearsals at school for an important concert that really did threaten to become extraordinary. It was going to be at the club of the NKVD. Think of that hell, reader: the ballet school and the NKVD together. Why did the secret police have a desire to see the young ballet sprouts, the sixth- and seventh-class students of E. P. Gerdt? One can only imagine. But I didn't give it any thought then. All the participants worked very hard to prepare.

E. P. had always believed in my abilities. She entrusted May Vlasov and me with the main parts of Act 3 of *Paquita*. That is, I was to dance Paquita herself. That was the first part of the evening. The second consisted of solo numbers from all sorts of things. Besides my own Rachmaninoff "Melody," which was choreographed for me and upperclassman Slava Golubin by Alexei Chichinadze, I recall the effective Ravel waltz, choreographed by Leonid Yakobson. It was danced, and danced brilliantly, by my classmate Muza Fedyaeva. (For more than two decades, Chichinadze was artistic director of the Stanislavsky Theater. He danced in Vladimir Burmeister's *Swan Lake* with me.)

The NKVD was a powerful and wealthy organization. Just think of all the things they stole, confiscating them from the people. But they didn't have enough money for an orchestra. We all danced to piano accompaniment by our best school pianist, Ekaterina Shlikhting, thin as a museum skeleton.

Everyone did their best to stand out before that blood-curdling audience. When I took my bows I tried to make out the faces of the people in the auditorium. Were they really people? Were the ones who had come up the creaking stairs on Gagarinsky, rummaged in our closets, rifled Father's bookshelves, and shoved him into the Black Maria sitting there applauding? Or the ones who conveyed Mother to Kazakhstan and still, twice monthly, verified her presence at the police station in dusty Chimkent?

Chapter Ten

Tchaikovsky's Impromptu

Mother was released in April 1941, and she finally returned to Moscow with my little brother. There were two months left before the start of the war. The whole family was waiting for her on the platform of Kazan Station, from which she had left all those years ago. A sea of tears was shed. Hugging until we were dizzy. No end to the joy. They had released her early. The efforts had paid off!

I was preparing for the next performance. I wanted to show my mother that I had not wasted my time, that I had progressed. Mother, switching swiftly from her travels, started asking me about my ballet studies, what new works I had learned.

Her last year in Chimkent had not been easy. On one of her visits to the police, to check in, she was sent to a back room on some technicality. An imposing and pleasant-looking man awaited her. He asked about her health, her children, how the daughter who had visited her was doing. Mother sensed something wrong. She bristled like a hedgehog. The conversation was banal. "You must help us, it is important to report on the moods and conversations of those around you, what the exiled parents of your ballet students at the club think, who visits your landlord Isaac." She was supposed to do this in written form, in ballpoint pen, neatly and clearly. Simply put, they wanted her to be a snitch.

They couldn't break Mother in Butyrki Prison, where they didn't understand her innate stubbornness, and certainly the pleasant fellow got an implacable refusal. No matter what he threatened, her categorical response was, "You can shoot me and my children, but I won't do that." When recruiters came up against such steadfastness they either quickly dispatched the person or gave up. But the process lasted for several months, and it took its toll on Mother's nerves.

An admirer appeared. Later, she figured out he was from the KGB. This was an approach from the other end, a different scenario. The newly created Romeo, also an exile, naturally, was passionate and chatty. He brought flowers (on an expense account perhaps?). He wanted to marry her and adopt all three of us. "Your husband, unfortunately, is no longer alive. I love you madly, I saw all your films when I was free. You are the love of my life. And the children need a father." Mother sent him packing. She did not want to believe that Father had been killed. She waited for him in Chimkent and later in Moscow. She waited her whole life. Like Grieg's Solveig. She jumped every time there was an unexpected peal of the doorbell, ring of the phone, or unfamiliar voice in the front hall. She never saw him again.

I wonder if I exaggerate the drama of my family? Whether I'm overdoing the shades of black in my narrative? But it all happened. It's all true. That's how we lived. And suffered. It left scars on my heart. I don't want to smooth the sharp angles or hide the nasty details. This is how my generation lived. I am its child. No better, no worse. Judge those who "sowed" the mores of the times.

The school was preparing for its graduation concert. For the first time this would be accompanied by the Bolshoi orchestra and held on the stage of its second theater. Before, these concerts had been held inside the school. The innovation was a fortunate one. The date was set: June 21, 1941, a Sunday. The main performers were those graduating that year. It was a strong group: the beauty Inna Zubkovskaya, a future prima of the Kirov Ballet, Violetta Prokhorova (who took the name Elvin when she married), Nelya Kuznetsova, Golubin, Levashyov. I don't want to get sidetracked from the story of that memorable evening, but I will run ahead a bit. Violetta Prokhorova was smarter than the rest (her forebears were famous industrialists in Russia). Right after the war, in 1945, she married an Englishman and moved to the West. Nelya Kuznetsova followed in her footsteps but was too slow: the Iron Curtain rang down. She had to move from the Bolshoi to the Stanislavsky Theater, and her mother, an usher, also lost her job at the State Academic Bolshoi Theater. Nelya's American went back alone. You have to fall in love at the right time and not hesitate.

The concert had three sections. The younger students also danced, to make a full program. I danced the Tchaikovsky *Impromptu* in Yakobson's staging. The pas de trois was a very successful piece of choreography. My partners were Shvachkin and Evdokimov.

It's hopeless trying to describe dance. But I'll try. It was all Yakobsonian. Classical and yet not. Shvachkin and Evdokimov were satyrs, and I was the nymph. The satyrs, as is their wont, moved on imaginary hooves. They carried equally imaginary panpipes. They played them, barely touching their lips. That was the dance. The nymph was naughty, tugging at the satyrs' beards, slipping out of their grasp, swaying in fragile bends. Believe me, it was a poetic number.

I've stopped writing, in order to sit, eyes shut, and recall that little ballet. Some things float up in my memory, some are gone forever. What a miracle the mechanism of human memory is. I'm often asked, "How do you remember all the moves and their order?" How do readers and actors remember poems, verse, hundreds of pages of prose text, roles, and monologues? How do musicians remember entire symphonies, sonatas? How do physicists keep strings of mind-bending formulas and ten-figure numbers in their heads? I cannot explain how the body remembers the most complex choreographic text. There are times when you can keep an entire ballet with all its performers in your head for years. And sometimes you struggle to remember when the left goes, the left arm, the elbow in a variation you danced only yesterday. It's like a telephone number you've dialed a hundred times which suddenly is erased from your memory and you can't think of it no matter how hard you try. Explain to us, wise men, what memory is.

The three of us adored the Yakobson number, and we worked hard in rehearsals. When we did the run-through to piano accompaniment at school and our audience consisted of teachers and a few pupils who had looked in, we got applause. My patient piano teacher, the kind Yurchenko, forgave me my horrible laziness and came over with tears in her eyes to give me a sincere kiss. Vera Vasilyeva, the wife of Kasyan Yaroslavich Goleizovsky, the great choreographer and great martyr (I will write about my meetings with him later and in detail), was moved by the dance. So many, many years later at my jubilee evening she added to her congratulations, "The best dancing you did in your life was Yakobson's *Impromptu* at school. I never liked you better." (By the way, Vasilyeva was a marvelous dancer and lived a long, martyred life with Goleizovsky. She did a moving first performance in Moscow of Maria in *The Fountain of Bakhchisarai*. She was refined musically. And she was memorable looking: her legs were a copy of Anna Pavlova's, and her face a twin of Greta Garbo's.)

Leonid Lavrovsky's *Walpurgisnacht* to music by Gounod is well known. And truly, it is a successful piece. But it would not have existed had not Yakobson done the Tchaikovsky *Impromptu*. I can see the influence with great clarity.

The Moscow audience was delighted by the number. Perhaps it was—dare I say it?—the concert's high point. We bowed endlessly. Mother was in the audience, and I saw her happy eyes glowing in the first row of the parterre boxes. She was seeing me after our long separation on the stage of the second theater of the Bolshoi to the strains of the orchestra, conducted inspiredly by Yuri Fayer. He truly was incomparable. The audience applauded wildly, and we kept bowing and bowing, coming out from the curtain onto the ramp. She was happy. Asaf, when he congratulated me, made a mocking face: "You bowed like an audience favorite—you should be more modest."

It is too late for modesty when the audience has accepted you and rewarded you for your successful work. It may have been that night that I first understood the higher value of bows. The ritual is very important. To this day I believe that the bows are a component of the performance. The audience must take away not only impressions of the dance but of the entire image of the dancer, a vignette framed by the grateful response to the audience for its recognition. The audience should get to keep the comet's tail. Forgive my bold comparison.

In Yakobson's *Impromptu* I tasted for the first time the love of an audience and joy of success, the intoxicating roar of clapping hands, the thrill of the first reading. But I also noticed the mean squint of envy in some eyes. I have lived with that my whole life.

Now, from the distance of the years I have lived, I see that the memorable evening on the stage of the Bolshoi's Second Stage was particularly significant for me. That day I left my meek ballet childhood for an independent, adult, risky— but beautiful—professional life in ballet.

At dawn the next day, war broke out.

Chapter Eleven

The War

I remember the first day of the war very well.*

People huddled in the streets around loudspeakers broadcasting heroic music and giving the latest news. In some areas the trolleys stopped running because large groups of people were walking along the tracks toward the center of the city. Faces reflected anxiety and tension. Some were drunk. Even the most feckless realized that the business of war was killing people. And who lived and who died was the business of fate. Only now are the true figures being published on the victims of the terrible clash of two mighty nations. And here's one that stunned me: 97 percent of my countrymen born in 1923, two years before me, were killed or missing. Only 3 percent survived.

I was naive, even though deep inside I felt a sinking sensation. We assured ourselves that the war would be over quickly. Two or three months. Well, not longer than the one with Finland. Mita's husband, Boris Kuznetsov, was grim. He predicted the worst. But he did that only at home, among the family, which, besides Mita and me, included my mother. I forgot to mention that after Chim-

---

*Germany invaded its former ally the Soviet Union on June 22, 1941, which for Russians marks the beginning of the Great Patriotic War.

kent she had also moved in with my aunt, setting up her folding bed right by the door at night. My younger brother slept on it, too, with Mother. The middle one — Alik — still lived at Asaf's.

Air raids started, and the sound of howling sirens returned to our lives. The Germans bombed Moscow at night. The whole city was plunged in blackest darkness. They painted the Kremlin, Red Square, and the Bolshoi Theater. Camouflage. Protective zeppelins floated in the sky — traps for German bombers. Paper strips were glued criss-cross over windows. Actually, I don't know why I'm describing this. There are many documentary shots of all that.

In the theater and school we learned to decline a new noun: *evacuation*. Where you would be sent, when, with or without your family. Mita worked up a sweat to be the first to learn the secret of our destination. She was always ahead of the curve and did not want to spoil her reputation this time either.

One September evening she came home triumphantly: "The theater is going to Sverdlovsk. So-and-so told me in secret" — she lowered her voice to a whisper — "and he knows all."

How she managed to get hold of four tickets (two children's) for seats on the Moscow–Sverdlovsk train I'll never know. But get them she did. Mother, my two brothers, and I were on the road again . . . Setting out from Kazan Station, yet again. We managed to leave Moscow in late September, long before — in terms of those days — the panic of October 17, 1941, when the Germans were at the gate of Moscow.

The train trip and life in Sverdlovsk were torture. But the whole country was suffering, so I'm not complaining.

In Sverdlovsk we were put up in the apartment of Paduchev, an engineer. I remember his name. In that crowded, three-room apartment, the Party Executive Committee placed yet another family from the Ukraine. Four women, four generations. A great-grandmother, grandmother, mother, and seven-year-old daughter. The engineer — a kind and timid man — huddled with his family of five in the third, far room. So we lived like this: 4 × 4 × 6, almost like a soccer formation.

But that wasn't the limit. One morning two more were squeezed into Paduchev's apartment. The engineer's uncle and his two-ton wife. They were also from Moscow and also evacuated "by luck." You'll find it hard to believe, but we lived in peace, helping one another, holding places in kilometer-long lines, lending little loaves of bread or a three-ruble note until payday.

With great difficulty, Mother got a job as a registrar at the clinic. I remember her behind an unpainted wooden window in a white coat. From there she gave me "strategic" orders: which line to get into and which coupon to tear off from our ration cards.

I spent long hours in lines, hearing sad, touching war stories and incredible life stories. I made friends with evacuees like myself. There were widows by then, with death notices from the war office, silently standing in line like charred black statues with sunken eyes.

There were lines for everything. Without exception. People, stood, stood, and stood, begging leave to go off for a bit, coming back and standing some more, complaining, grumbling, and worrying when the numbers were called out. The woman with the loudest voice called out the three- and four-digit numbers. The line responded in hoarse, trembling tones: 276—here; 277—here; 265—went off somewhere. Cross her off!

We wrote our numbers on our hands, licking the stub of what we called a chemical pencil. You couldn't wash off the number for weeks. That was one thing we knew how to make—those permanent marking pencils. The numbers for various lines got all mixed up on your hand, which was for yesterday, which for today.

And my patient, meek fellow countrymen and women still stand in lines in the large and small cities of a once rich and now ruined, bankrupt country.

There's one line I remember acutely. In the middle of summer in the courtyard of a grocery store, they unloaded crates of apples from a truck. The apples were green and stunted. But a crowd formed instantly. No one had seen apples since the war started. Under a barrage of rude shouts, the crowd formed a convoluted, very long line, about five kilometers in length. I was comparatively close to the beginning. But I didn't get any apples. There weren't enough. Never again in my life did I ever want an apple as much as I did then. I've seen many delicious varieties since, but I can't forget those Sverdlovsk wartime apples.

Winters in Sverdlovsk are fierce. After the Spitzbergen blizzards, my body refused to accept any more cold. A polar explorer once said that man can get used to anything except the cold. That's true. And how could you in a cloth coat that barely covered the knees? My feet got desperately chilled from standing in lines for hours. Ballet was forgotten.

I found support in going to the theater. In Sverdlovsk during that war year, there was a pretty good troupe at the opera and ballet theater. I remember Meyerbeer's *Huguenots* and the only production in the country of Asafyev's ballet *Sulamif,* based on the Kuprin book. Sulamif was danced by the aristocratic and attractive Nina Mladzinskaya, perfectly formed from head to foot, a Vaganova student. Her husband had also been a victim of the terror of 1937, while Mladzinskaya herself, after prison, labor camp, and Siberian exile, had miraculously ended up at the Sverdlovsk theater. This time her divine beauty helped her. She had started out brilliantly in Leningrad, and I have no doubt that she would have been a prima at her dear old Maryinsky Theater. But her fate had been dashed.

I also liked the operetta company in Sverdlovsk, considered to this day the best in the Soviet Union. They did the entire Kálmán repertoire — *Czardas Princess, Countess Maritza,* and so on.

You may ask how I got to the theater. Long lines and the cheapest balcony seat. Tickets were incredibly inexpensive. In fact, until quite recently, front-row seats at the Bolshoi were only 3 rubles 50 kopecks. When tomatoes at the markets were 10–15 rubles a kilogram. So there's the choice. Have a salad of green market tomatoes — or go to the Bolshoi four times. In Sverdlovsk I chose food for the soul.

Mita's forecasts were wrong. The Bolshoi was evacuated to Kuibyshev, and the ballet school went to a small town, Vasilsursk, on the Volga. This accidental mistake cost me dearly. An entire year, from fifteen and a half to sixteen and a half, I spent without working at ballet. That was my year for standing in line. Gradually I was overtaken by panic. Another year like that and I could kiss ballet goodbye.

I noticed an item in the paper that said that the remaining members of the troupe in Moscow had given a premiere on the stage of the Bolshoi's Second Stage. The Bolshoi itself was closed. Then we heard that part of the school had remained behind, too. Studies continued. It was like a bolt of electricity. I had to go to Moscow. Like Chekhov's three sisters, I kept repeating to myself, "To Moscow, to Moscow, to Moscow . . ." But how? You needed a special pass. We had no influential friends. Going to offices trying to explain why and what for would be a waste of time. Who would listen to some girl about ballet, training, physical conditioning, teachers?

I decided to take a desperate step — to make my way into Moscow illegally. Mother was in a panic and tried to talk me out of it. "They'll pick you up and arrest you."

"Let them!" I responded. "Time's running out, I'm exhausted, wooden, stiff."

It wasn't easy getting a train ticket. It was expensive, and we had almost no money. And you couldn't buy one without a pass. The hand of Providence led me the chess player Rokhlin, who offered to help. He was married to the ballerina

Valentina Lopukhina, who would extend a helping hand to me a few years later, too. Both are no longer with us. But I remember the kindness of your family, such responsible, wonderful people.

The train took five days from Sverdlovsk. The whole time I pondered whether to get out at the stop before Moscow and walk the rest of the way. Or to risk it all, counting on the crowds to conceal me. I repeat, I had no pass allowing me into Moscow. I decided to take the gamble. And I won. I attached myself to a limping old man, carrying his bag, which pleased him greatly, and his sincere attention helped me slip past the military patrol at the station doors. I played the part of teenager with elderly invalid with great success. And—I was in Moscow.

Taking several trolleys, I reached Mita's apartment on Shchepkinsky Passage. I knew that Mita had not left Moscow with the theater. But I had been unable to let her know that I was trying to get back to the capital. I appeared out of the blue.

Luckily, Mita herself opened the door. She clasped her hands. Where did you come from? After greetings and hugs, my eyes fell on the loaf of white bread, the kind we call French for some reason, on the round dining table. I was starving. My stomach churned and I felt nauseated. I hadn't seen French bread in so long I had forgotten that it existed.

"Are we allowed to eat it?"

Mita's eyes filled with tears.

We talked all night and in the morning we went to the school building on Pushechnaya. My heart was beating as if I had just completed a difficult solo variation. It was about to burst. People were happy to see me. No one asked how I had returned to a closed city, whether I had a pass, whether Mother was with me.

Maria Mikhailovna Leontyeva (E. P. Gerdt had been evacuated) taught the final, graduating class. She was also a former dancer of the Maryinsky Theater. As I write, I am amazed to see that all my sources lie in St. Petersburg, even though by birth and character I am a true Muscovite. Maria Mikhailovna agreed to take me in, not worried about my lost year.

"You'll have to work like the devil to make up for lost time. Your gifts will help you. I believe in you. Get back in shape!"

I attacked my work fiercely. I liked being at the barre, doing my assigned combinations, seeing myself in the mirror. I had grown taller over the year in Sverdlovsk, but I had grown gaunt. No one would think I was over fourteen.

Leontyeva was a placid, attentive teacher. She knew my family history and showed me warmth and compassion. On the Maryinsky stage, M. M. had danced every solo part — duos, trios, every solo fairy. She knew her ballet, and her tenacious gaze caught all our mistakes. A particular concern of hers was that the back be professionally straight. M. M. had a deep voice; she was a chain smoker. Her hair was always neatly, smoothly dressed, and she was pulled together and calm.

I worked with Leontyeva for more than six months. Graduation exams were coming up. Naturally, we couldn't even consider a stage or an orchestra. We were supposed to dance in Room 6 — the largest — each doing a solo variation, and also show ourselves in the general class. M. M. and I prepared the variation of the Queen of the Dryads from *Don Quixote.*

The examination day came. It was late March 1943. The war continued. Mother was still in Sverdlovsk. Everyone was expecting the second front to open. They blamed the Allies for delaying. They were pleased by reports from Informburo* about cities won back from the Germans. They listened to Levitan's resonant voice on the radio reading decrees from the Supreme Commander.

A lot of people crowded into Room 6. But it was nothing special. The commission sat at a narrow table, familiar faces, tendu, battements, center, leaps, fingers . . . It was all extremely businesslike, without flowers or ovations. We all knew that we would be accepted into the theater. The troupe that remained in Moscow needed more people. But we were still nervous; how can you dance without that?

My turn came. My variation. I was strung tight as a bow. Ready. And suddenly I heard the wrong music. The pianist got the order of variations mixed up. I did not budge. "Not my music" played on diligently and passionately. I stood there. There was a stir in Room 6. Leontyeva stopped the concertmaster with an imperious cry.

"Play the Dryad. Plisetskaya is dancing the leader."

Everything went smoothly. I passed the exam. I got an "A." School was behind me. The war went on. But now, I was faced my own war. For my place in life.

---

*The state war news agency.

Chapter Twelve

My First Year at the Bolshoi Theater

When I was taken into the ballet company, the Bolshoi Theater had just returned from Kuibyshev (now renamed Samara, its original name), and Marina Semyonova and Olga Lepeshinskaya reigned supreme on the stage. Sulamif Messerer, Sofia Golovkina, and Irina Tikhomirnova were the grand duchesses. They divided the ballet repertoire among them. The sun was setting on the careers of Viktorina Kriger, Lyubov Bank, Anastasia Abramova, and Lyubov Podgoretskaya, who were dancing out their last days. They no longer danced the premieres. The leading male dancers were Alexei Ermolayev, Asaf Messerer, Mikhail Gabovich, Alexander Rudenko, and Yuri Kondratov.

The repertoire consisted of the usual titles known the world over. Shall I name them? *Swan Lake, The Nutcracker, Sleeping Beauty, Don Quixote, Coppélia* . . . A famous Russian nineteenth-century author once remarked in a fit of temper, "What I love about the ballet is its constancy" (I'm quoting from memory).* I've spent nearly fifty years onstage, and the repertoire — *The Nutcracker, Don Quixote, Swan Lake, Sleeping Beauty* — hasn't changed.

---

* Mikhail Saltykov-Shchedrin wrote his famous tirade on the Russian ballet's inherent conservatism in 1863.

I was offered the lowest possible salary: 600 rubles, a sum which lost a zero during the first postwar devaluation and became 60 rubles.

The arrival of a new dancer is always disruptive. No one wants to move over to make room for others. Moreover, Asaf Messerer, who simultaneously occupied the throne of artistic director of the ballet and danced during the war years, was my uncle. He was overly fussy about his scruples and considered it improper to promote his own niece. As scrupulous as he was, he nonetheless vigorously promoted his wife, Irina Tikhomirnova (scenes reminiscent of the storming of the fortress of Izmail awaited him at home if he didn't). So I was immediately embroiled in family strife. During my last year at the choreographic school, there were precious few performers — remember that most of the company was evacuated — and I danced solo parts on the stage of the Bolshoi's second theater. I danced the pas de trois and one of the prospective brides in *Swan Lake,* the pas de trois from Alexander Gorsky's old *Little Humpbacked Horse,* and two of Kitri's friends in *Don Quixote.*

The first time I saw my name, Plisetskaya, listed with the names of other artists (I was already a dancer in the company) was as one of the eight nymphs in the Polish act of the opera *Ivan Susanin.* Written in blue ink, it was posted with all sorts of other notices near the ballet office, on a soiled bulletin board which informed performers of their assigned parts in the repertoire but also about more imperative matters: when the obligatory political hour was held; when ration cards for shoes and food items were issued and the gifts from Roosevelt (canned goods, candy bars) distributed; when assembly for the November parade, costume fittings in the theater's workshops and the local Party committee meetings were scheduled . . .

I was chagrined. My conversation with Asaf was brief.

"I've never danced in the corps de ballet."

"You will now."

This is how my life at the Bolshoi Theater began.

I could not disobey, but I could protest and I did. I danced on demi-pointe instead of on toe, I danced without makeup, I didn't warm up before performances. Asaf himself danced the Satyr with Lepeshinskaya. During the performances, all eight of us rhythmically sang along quietly, but audibly, as we danced, "Little bitty Asaf, listen as we all laugh," to the tune of Glinka's waltz. I wasn't the only one who was taking her revenge.

In order to stay in condition, I began performing at many concerts and "made the rounds" of all the concert and club stages of Moscow, where I could dance to my heart's content. *The Dying Swan,* Gluck's "Melody," Rachmaninoff's "Elegy." My partners were Vyacheslav Golubin and Yuri Kondratov. The pay was meager, and the Philharmonic box office took months to disburse it. Yet I had to dress myself, eat, and help my brothers.

Concert performances were the main source of income for the entire world of performing artists. Stars of great eminence — Kozlovsky, Maksakova, Lemeshev, Nortsov of the Moscow Art Theater, Kachalov, Androvskaya, Yanshin, Moskvin, Zharov of the Maly Theater, Khenkin of the Theater of Satire, Tatiana Bakh, the prima of the Moscow operetta — performed at concerts alongside newcomers.

Of my colleagues, I remember Ekaterina Geltser particularly well. Although she no longer performed onstage at the Bolshoi, she continued to dance at concerts until she was eighty. She was extraordinarily colorful. Her hats were provocative — she wore them at such a radical angle that you couldn't tell whether she had a second eye. She pinned her Lenin decoration to the lapel of her gray Persian lamb coat so that, in her words, the boys wouldn't run whooping after her on the streets. She used to submit a photo of herself in tutu and feathers from *Swan Lake* to the passport section of the police department. She would ask me in her low, acerbic voice, "My child, where do you get that red strepticide to dye your hair?" When I answered, "I don't dye my hair, Ekaterina Vasilyevna, I really am a redhead. It's my natural color," she would get angry and reply, "Do you know who you're lying to?"

Concerts were rushed and bustling, but sweet. Everyone arrived in a rush, all in a lather — they'd nervously hurry the emcee — they had to make it to the next concert. I was a complete stranger, and they kept shuffling my number to the end of the program. My legs would cool down. At one of my first such performances, the emcee, whose name I don't recall now, kept asking us our names backstage.

"So it's Maya Plisetskaya and Vyacheslav Golubin in Rachmaninoff's 'Melody.' Is that correct?"

Naturally, he introduced us as Maya Golubina and Vyacheslav Plisetsky, just like the old theater joke.

The stages were cramped, narrow, and dimly lit; they lacked depth and had slippery, uneven floors. In Gluck's "Melody," where the ballerina constantly soars as she is lifted high up by her partner, the surprised audience kept losing sight of me because I was completely obscured by the damaged stage lights, which were modestly draped with rags hung from a valance.

But the audiences were wonderful. Badly washed and poorly dressed, they lived off ration cards, exchanging them for food and material goods, but they were hungry for the minutest display of artistic expression from the shabby, crudely built stage. These were the concerts that saw the Swan's first encores. The audience liked me. I was always a great success, and they applauded warmly for a long time. I was soon getting many invitations from concert organizers. I, too, began rushing around, performing at three or four concerts on my evenings off from the Bolshoi. I had just enough time to take off my fluffy white tutu and pull felt boots over my ballet tights. It was wintertime, and I would tie a warm scarf of coarse wool over my swan feathers and rush madly to the next concert. In sports lingo, I scored a lot of points at these concerts, not to mention gaining a lot of experience.

But I'll get back to the Bolshoi Theater. A small ray of light flashed on my horizon. A noisy campaign "to promote youth" was launched to celebrate yet another Komsomol anniversary — I think it was the twenty-fifth one, although even then I made a muddle of numbers like these. They crowed pompously about it up one street and down the other. Could the theater have remained uninvolved? I was also promoted.

I quickly grasped the "jumping" mazurka in *Chopiniana* in two rehearsals with the rehearsal coach, A. Monakhov a stern and bushy-browed former dancer from Leningrad (who acquired his bearing from dancing kings and influential vassals in the ballet). And I danced it with thundering success. Nature had not passed me over when it came to jumps, and I flew across the stage in three jetés. That's how Fokine choreographed it, and that's how all ballerinas perform it. But I deliberately tried to hover in the air for a moment at the top of each leap, and the audience responded enthusiastically. Each leap was accompanied by a crescendo of applause. I myself couldn't have imagined that the audience would take such a liking to this little trick. It really was a great success. The subsequent *Chopinianas* were attended by some balletomanes who came to see "Plisetskaya" dance in them. I could hold my head up now.

During the second or third performance, while I was taking my bows, I spotted Agrippina Yakovlevna Vaganova in the dark arch of the director's box. She had just returned to Moscow and was seriously considering "employment opportuni-ties" at the Bolshoi. Our meetings and, alas, my all-too-brief work with Vaganova turned all my ideas about the technique and principles of dance upside down. Not continuing lessons with her is a wound that has never healed. She was not compliant by nature and soon returned to Perm (sorry, that is, Perm-Molotov-Perm, the names of ancient cities which were renamed in honor of the deceased or perpetually and "selflessly laboring" leaders). And like every wound which makes itself felt in bad weather, at every difficult point in my professional life, appropriate or not, or when I simply can't sleep at night, I still reproach myself for not having the determination to follow her to work with her on *Swan Lake*. I remember her exact words, "Come visit me and we'll do a *Lake* to make the devils turn green." Marina Semyonova, when she was so inclined, would repeat the reproach, "Go see her, because she's going to die, and then you'll never forgive yourself." And I really haven't forgiven myself to this day.

Now everything in sequence. After *Chopiniana*, Agrippina Yakovlevna came up onstage. I'd obviously caught her eye. The next day she set up a rehearsal with me. We went through the entire mazurka from the first movement straight through to the end. She literally "gilded" several sequences, changing angles of the turns and head and hand positions. She wove the transition from one movement to the next together logically, making the mesh of the steps oh, so comfortable. She directed my attention to the ultimate importance of initiating the movement. The start of each movement has to be beautiful and imperceptible, I remember her saying to me. She didn't actually say it, so much as show it to me, using gestures from the universal language of ballet, understood only by members of its guild. She focused my attention precisely on the places where I faltered. It was all right to the point—hit the bull's eye. It's very difficult to explain to the uninitiated reader what stunning results can be achieved with just a few words or a simple gesture. After the rehearsal with Vaganova I changed, I was unrecognizable . . .

Monakhov took offense. The usual backstage battle of egos. To top it off, I signed the performance sign-in sheet incorrectly and in the wrong place, and Konovalov, the assistant director, a little man who obliged the mighty of the world, wrote a report about me. I was a transgressor. Explanations didn't help matters: the Komsomol office also intended to "eradicate irresponsibility," and made an example of their victims. And so I wound up on that shabby bulletin board next to the ballet office again. The ballet office was then located on the first floor, and everyone who walked by could see my disgrace, my first conflict with the authorities. This "public hanging" on the bulletin board deprived me of my gift from Roosevelt, which is the way errant ballerinas were punished in those days. I'm speaking about a minor punishment. But at that time, I certainly could have used the canned meat and wool skirt. My political unreliability dated from that announcement.

A strict seniority reigned in the theater. A place in the sun, that is, a small dressing table with locking drawers to keep ballet slippers, leotards and tights, tunics, ribbons, leg warmers, and makeup, was allocated with exaggerated care. If it was your first year in the theater, you had to run to the fourth floor. The venerated stars had spaces in the cramped dressing rooms near the boxes at stage level.

All that racing up and down the steep and drafty staircases between the floors couldn't have been more damaging. The galloping up and down wrecked my knee. I realized that I had to secure a place for myself by whatever means possible near the stage-level boxes. (Let me parenthetically remark that two narrow, unreliable elevators served the entire theater; nine to eleven people would cram into each of them instead of the permissible maximum of six, which caused the elevators to come to a grinding halt and be under constant repair.)

A good soul did turn up—there's not a village in existence without its holy man. Our soloist, Valya Lopukhina, a fair-haired, affable woman with beautiful legs, well-trained by Vaganova,* and a high instep, curved like an arch, suggested that I use the two drawers on the right side of her dressing table. Another reason why I'm going into such particulars is that I sat at this three-sided mirror for forty-six years and because there are some amusing details associated with it.

Once a month each space was allocated a piece of household soap that reeked of dog and a pair of pink silk tights that tore like spider webs. For performances, a whitish cotton piqué towel along with a portion of lignin makeup remover was doled out. Each towel had two fat letters—a B and an A—embroidered in acrid orange threads. Kidding around, we decided they stood for Big Ass. In fact, it was something totally unimpressive—Bolshoi Artists.

By the end of my first theater season, my uncle Asaf had become kinder. For concerts he choreographed a waltz based on Godard's music for Rudenko and me. This was a solid number, a true concert piece that the public liked.

As happens routinely in the theater, ballerinas got sick one after another, and there was no one to dance in *The Nutcracker*, which Vasily Vainonen originally staged for the Second Stage. Asaf suggested that I learn the role of Masha in the shortest imaginable time. Aglow with happiness, I agreed. I had an indescribable love for Tchaikovsky's *Nutcracker* music then, and I still do. It sparkles with beauty, a mischievous smile, the glow of theater footlights. Vaganova couldn't come to the rehearsals—stricken by a cold, she stayed home. All we did was discuss the plan of the proposed work on the phone.

I rehearsed with Elizaveta Pavlovna Gerdt. I already knew the pas de deux from the second act, having danced it for my graduation. I liked the rest of the part and memorized it with lightning speed.

Vaganova didn't come to the theater until the last rehearsal. There was never

*Vaganova's famous "Pas de Diane," from *Esmeralda*, was created for Lopukhina.

any love lost between Vaganova and Gerdt. Agrippina Yakovlevna sat through almost to the end of the rehearsal. But after some inconsequential remark by Gerdt, she couldn't restrain herself and made a quiet, apparently unkind rejoinder. Elizaveta Pavlovna blushed bright red. So nothing ever came of our rehearsing together. But I did get to dance *The Nutcracker*. (My partner was Alexander Tsarman, a unique and experienced dancer. In *Swan Lake*, for example, he would variously dance the pas de trois, Siegfried, and the clown from one performance to the next. Tsarman played the piano well, and after he retired, he directed ballet performances for many years. And he did it very reliably.)

Since I've recalled Ekaterina Vasilyevna Geltser, it would be a sin not to recall my impressions about the prima donnas of the Bolshoi Ballet of that time.

I used to rush over to see Marina Semyonova perform while I was still a girl. Our class worshiped her. But it was love at a distance. Upon closer inspection, she appeared rather plump, with a small, well-placed head and the strong torso of a woman from the times of Parasha Zhemchugova's serf theater. Naturally, I had never in my life seen either the serf theater or Parasha Zhemchugova herself. I hadn't even seen a lithograph of her, but in my imagination, I had always associated Semyonova with that distant page of Russian theater history. She was a serf but had a regal bearing. Our directors were asleep on the job; she's the one who should have played the role of Catherine the Great. There was something foxlike in her face, something unkind; she seldom smiled but used to reward people with a squeamish squint of her eyes. The darkness in her face I read as the reflection of the recent dismal events in her life: in 1938 Karakhan, the Soviet ambassador to Turkey, who was her husband at the time, was arrested and executed while she was held under house arrest.

Her dancing was dazzling.

Her large, excellent, steely legs, impeccably trained by Vaganova, turned, held, and spun her sculpted body wonderfully. Semyonova was Vaganova's first graduate, and her teacher revealed to Marina all the technical laws of dance that she knew. Semyonova once asked me many years later, "Have you ever noticed that I can't do a plié and that my arms are rather short?" I was surprised. "It's all Agrippina's work." Semyonova had a hypnotic presence on the stage. When she appeared onstage, no one else existed. But she was quarrelsome and cunning, not gentle. She got lazy early, skipped class, warmed up before performances in the shower instead of at the barre, and put on weight. But I managed to catch her enchanting performances.

Lepeshinskaya, on the other hand, was not my ideal at all. She had no height, her arms and legs were short, and her head always reminded me of a mask some-one would wear to a Mardi Gras carnival. Her tiny fingers didn't improve the proportions of her body either. Fully aware of this, she never failed to hold a the-atrical prop in her hands onstage — an umbrella, a fan, handkerchief, flowers. In short, her physical qualities differed from my idea of beauty in a woman's body in ballet. But she did possess passion, ambition, fearlessness, and dynamic turns. She would throw herself from a long running start into a fish dive right into her partner's arms. Pyotr Andreyevich Gusev and Yuri Kondratov, who took turns performing Moszkowski's striking waltz with her, were the perfect strong, re-liable partners for her. They caught her without a single miss. The public liked Lepeshinskaya's prettiness and joie de vivre. However, I won't hide the fact that the latter seemed unnatural to me.

She was a noisy social activist, a most energetic, tireless member of the Com-munist Party, who was involved with all its offices, committees, and presidiums. Olga Vasilyevna didn't pass up a single opportunity to stride up to the rostrum and vociferously declare her membership in the Bolshevik Party for the thou-sandth time and teach everyone a thing or two "in light of the most recent Party decisions."

She was also the wife of a general. Her husband was the terrifying Cheka gen-eral Raikhman, who was part of Lavrenty Beria's inner circle. He came to a bad end, as is fitting — he was sent to prison. But she wasn't in widow's weeds for long. The next one wearing a general's tunic was Antonov, a white-haired, baro-nial army general and head of the General Staff of the USSR. She was justifiably feared in the theater world, and in spite of the smile which she lavished, with-out exaggeration, upon everyone, people stopped in mid-sentence and lowered their voices when she appeared. Especially when she picked up the telephone receiver in the crowded director's box and in her distinct, clear voice demanded of the invisible person on the other end of the line, "Hello, is this the Kremlin?"

Sofia Nikolayevna Golovkina was another devotee of influential generals. She, too, was vociferously involved in social activism and also favored the Bol-shevik Party with her membership.

She couldn't dance at all. She would wobble doing pirouettes and chaînés but didn't fall over. It was like the Leaning Tower of Pisa. She possessed neither spirit nor brilliance. She used her lips to assist her as she danced, as if chewing gum. (This was even before Americans had invented the stuff.) Her performances reeked of boredom and mediocrity. Audiences languished and applauded spar-ingly. In her younger days, she had gotten herself promoted to soloist by sharing a connubial bed with the venerable ballet master Fyodor Lopukhov, who had been the head of the Bolshoi Ballet for a short period before the war. Their marriage was brief, but the spicy aspersions Golovkina cast at Komsomol meetings left a certain mark on the history of the Moscow ballet . . .

To jump ahead a bit, when she ended her dancing career with a disastrous *Don Quixote* (oh, how sweet it is to tell the uninformed afterward that you retired just in time!), she had the sense to push her way into pedagogy. That's when her name cropped up more and more often in the newspapers. "A once famous ballerina passes on her experience," "Young people study with renowned dancers." "A green light for young people."

But these young people weren't just ordinary kids, young people off the street. It turns out — God help us! — that the children and grandchildren of the mighty of this world were the ones blessed at birth with a special talent for ballet. They could be very useful. You need a new building? Here's one with a greenhouse and exercise rooms! And a pool, of course. And convenient driveways for black armored ZIL and Chaika limousines.

I could cover two or three pages with the family names of our leaders, ministers, and deputies who patronized the school. Here are the most resounding: Ekaterina Furtseva, Yuri Andropov, Ustinov, Andrei Gromyko, Ryzhkov, Alexei Kosygin, Nikolai Tikhonov, Chairman of the Soviet of Ministers, Chief Procurator Rekunkov, and dare I say it — Mikhail Gorbachev . . . Raisa Gorbachev herself graced this temple to the Soviet Terpsichore and subsidized the school theater without hesitation.

Naive readers, don't get the impression that being the director of a choreographic school is all just celebrations and brilliant meetings with foreign heathen leaders. What to do with the progeny of those whom our system pitilessly pushed off the Kremlin walls into the backwoods of vegetative retirement during some routine historical plenum of the Central Committee? Seize the moment! Slam the oak door to my director's office (which undisciplined parents turned into a shabby changing room)! Slam it right in the face (tenderly gazed upon by the amicable teaching staff) of the conceited, spoiled child who falsely and self-importantly imagines herself Pavlova or himself Nijinsky! But I'm running far ahead of myself into the future . . .

Viktorina Kriger lived only for the ballet. Thin, wiry, and angular, she seemed to be charged with electricity. However, she didn't like to miss all sorts of meetings either, because she, too, was a red-card-carrying Communist Party member. One might suppose that she became a Communist out of fear, in order to offset her German ancestry and the piety which permeated everything about her. She and Geltser, just like my teacher Gerdt, were descendants of Russified German families.

During my first season, she danced the role of the fairy Carabosse ecstatically, without sparing her toes. She didn't do anything half-heartedly even at rehearsals — she gave her all. Among ourselves we nicknamed her Viktorina Steel Toe. She was of indeterminate age, but always heavily perfumed and carefully coiffed, as if she had just gotten out of a hairdresser's chair. I got into harmless conflicts with her because of my touchy nature, but she was uncommonly forgiving and was favorably disposed toward me professionally right from the start.

Her religiosity was intensified by panicky superstition. An amateur fortune teller had predicted that she would meet her death in an elevator. From that time on, she assiduously avoided elevators and always climbed the highest staircases on foot, which, according to present-day research, greatly enhanced her health. If you heard the sound of heels echoing from the stairwell somewhere up on the fifth tier, you could be sure that it was Kriger.

The fortune-teller's competence was discredited. Viktorina Vladimirovna lived to the age of eighty-five and died in bed. I consider her Stepmother in Prokofiev's *Cinderella* her highest achievement. She imbued this role with brilliance and humor.

Tusya (diminutive of Anastasia) Abramova was feminine and easily amused. Pretty, radiant, with big eyes. Now as I sort through the ballerinas of that time in my mind, I realize that many of them were real beauties. Lyubov Bank, for example, looked like a marble cameo. I don't mean to say that fine, attractive ballerinas have become extinct. Maybe it's nostalgia that's getting to me, but it seems to me that a certain breed has disappeared from the theater.

Some soloists left no artistic trace in my memory; but then our paths rarely crossed.

In 1942 a new director came to the ballet. He was in charge for nearly a quarter of a century. Like many directors, Leonid Mikhailovich Lavrovsky came to Moscow from Leningrad.* His wife, the spirited ballerina Elena Chikvaidze, also arrived with him.

Galina Ulanova joined the theater at almost the same time. She was married to the Moscow conductor Yuri Zavadsky, and evacuated to Alma Aty along with his theater, the Mossoviet.

The end of the war was drawing near. Stalin's red mustache twitched in the

---

* All the Bolshoi Ballet's directors came from Leningrad (St. Petersburg) in the Soviet era.

darkness of the armored state box during one of the ballet performances. A deluge of bodyguards in civilian clothes, as alike as peas in a pod, flooded the theater and stood, shifting their weight from foot to foot, vigilantly scrutinizing everyone from head to toe, as if to prove we weren't imagining things . . .

The capital city was gathering its muses.

Chapter Thirteen

The Apartment on Shchepkinsky Passage

And so I graduated from the ballet school in 1943, was accepted into the Bolshoi Theater, danced a few noticeable parts, and received my first award. I was given a room 10 meters square in a communal apartment, in a building owned by the Bolshoi Theater at No. 8 Shchepkinsky Passage. The name Shchepkinsky is derived not from the word *shchepka* (wood chip) but from the name Shchepkin, a well-known nineteenth-century actor of the Maly Theater.

There are three theaters on Theater Square in the heart of Moscow — the Bolshoi, the Maly, and the Central Children's Theater. I know of no other place in the world where there are three theaters located on a single city square. It used to be called Theater Square until it was renamed Sverdlov Square, a name that is just as ludicrous as the name Kirov Ballet.*

My renowned apartment building was located on the other side of the famous quartet of horses drawing Apollo's chariot. At night after performances cumbersome, dusty, stinking stage props were brought in and out of this narrow passage with a crashing din that the quiet of the night amplified. Trucks rumbled. Armchairs, tables, trees and doors, walls, windows, staircases and vases, chande-

---

*Yakov Sverdlov was the first Soviet president, Sergei Kirov the Communist Party boss of Leningrad.

liers, balconies, and sphinxes were hurled about, to the sound of colorful curses. This went on every night until about three or four in the morning. That's when I learned to manage without sleep!

My room was tucked away in a large, endless communal apartment, located on the second floor of the three-story building. (There was a construction office on the first floor, the second and third floors were set aside for performing artists. A theater dining hall is located there now). Seven doors opened out onto a long ugly hallway, but there were nine rooms. Twenty-two people lived in the apartment. A single toilet served all of them; they locked it with a simple nail bent into a hook. And there was a single kitchen in which humpbacked, roughly planked tables of varying heights were pushed together — each family had its own table. There were four gas burners, and you had to patiently wait your turn to cook soup or boil water in the kettle. There was also only one bathtub, used according to a strict schedule. Fortunately, the theater was just across the way, a minute-and-a-half walk from the house. Impatient tenants would run over to the Bolshoi to take a leak.

There were two rooms hidden behind the first door. The singer Borovskaya, a first-class coloratura soprano, lived there. She had a husband, a maid named Katya, and a Chekhovian lapdog named Umka. She vocalized in the morning, and the entire apartment knew her vocal exercises by heart.

The Borovskys lived a rich life. They had St. Petersburg furniture, an antique chandelier with candelabras, stern portraits in thick frames of rich mahogany, and a card table with a light with an enormous red-lace shade hanging above it. To me this seemed the height of chic. Borovskaya used to sing in the Maryinsky Theater, then she was invited to Moscow. The government capital drew the best talents like a magnet. She sang Verdi's Gilda especially well, but her appearance, alas, had gone downhill; something about her reminded me of a dachshund.

Three of the Chelnokovs lived in the next room. God only knows how they wound up in the Bolshoi's building. The head of the family was a pilot who, at the end of the war, would fly to Berlin on bombing missions. My ballet girlfriends perceived the aura of a hero around him. His wife languished waiting for him, moaning and groaning, while his son Seryozhka drank — serenely, though a great deal.

Nina Cherkasskaya, a dancer in the corps de ballet, occupied the third room. All her physical qualities contradicted the idea of ballet — thick, crooked legs, a feeble body, a parrot's-beak nose — but she worked in the ballet theater her whole life. All sorts of things were possible in ballet in those days. Her husband, Vasya, also drank, and he, too, drank a lot. He loved to whisper complaints to the neighbors in the kitchen about the injustices of life after he'd had a few. He'd been through the war, but instead of gratitude he was being forced to work in a place that didn't suit him. When the mood struck him, he even hinted that he had refused to be a stool pigeon . . . Nina also had a pockmarked maid named Nyura and three sluggish, obese, neutered cats. They all slept in one room.

In the next room — the fourth one — lived Pyotr Andreyevich Gusev, a well-known ballet dancer, teacher, former director of our ballet school, and chore-ographer (at the end of his life he even acted the part of Marius Petipa in a film). Later he was also artistic director of the Bolshoi Ballet. I remember him kindly — he was the one who invited Vakhtang Chabukiani to choreograph *Laurencia*. (I also had some bright days. There is a film entitled *Masters of the Russian Ballet*, in which Gusev dances the part of Giray in *The Fountain of Bakhchisarai* and I dance Zarema.) His wife, Varya Volkova, danced in the corps de ballet and was beauti-ful but a little blind and deaf. She constantly asked everybody about everything in our dim kitchen, blackened by smoke from frying potatoes, thereby causing a lot of confusion in our collective life. A nanny would come over with her daugh-ter to the Gusevs during the day to look after little redheaded Tanya Guseva. All her childrearing efforts also took place in the kitchen. The nanny taught Tanya good manners, scaring her away from her favorite place in the hallway, where she had gotten into the habit of sitting on her potty. Gusev himself used to make wisecracks and kept the kitchen rolling in laughter.

Next to them lived my aunt Mita and her husband, Boris Kuznetsov, professor and doctor of some technical science or other. He was reserved, taciturn, and blindingly handsome. Had he been born in Hollywood, he would have eclipsed Robert Taylor.

Fedotov, the dramatic tenor, and his family lived in the two corner rooms facing noisy Pyotrovka Street. He sang all the leading parts in classical operas and sang them well. But he was fat and paunchy, as is customary in the world of tenors even today. His wife was German and taught German in school. Dur-ing the war she passed herself off as Estonian, since all Germans were sent to Siberia as a precaution. It wasn't difficult to do because their maid Alma actu-ally was Estonian. Alma spoke Russian atrociously. She earnestly warned chil-dren inclined toward hygiene, "Without mama's question, you can't go bath, because one man went bath, he went bath and drownded." A saucepan to her was *yakobchena*, which meant *zakopchennaya* (blackened with smoke). Whereas we, mistaken ones, thought that the saucepan belonged to Yakobson, who was a frequent guest at the Gusevs'.

The Fedotovs' son Rudik inflicted great suffering. He was forcibly and agonizingly taught music. Every damned day for years he practiced the same piece, stumbling over the same passage. I could hear Rudik's piece so clearly through the thin, slightly listing wall, that I had the impression he was accompanying Borovskaya right in my room. But the worst misfortune befell us when his singing lessons began. He had no natural singing voice whatsoever. What the tenants heard was deafening, hysterical shrieking. Fortunately, this ordeal came to an end one day: Rudik became passionately interested in film. His multiple wives did not hang around long. They didn't fancy his voice either. But they frequently added their own noise to all the discordant sounds of our apartment. The majority of the tenants of No. 23 later moved to the first postwar cooperative theater house on Gorky Street. As fate would have it, in 1963 my husband and I bought Borovskaya's three-room cooperative apartment from her and still occupy it to this day. The conductor Kirill Kondrashin rented it before we purchased it.

The sound recording of our daily life would be incomplete in my narrative if all this were not permeated with the incessant, shrill ringing of the only telephone—a single phone for all of us!—which was screwed to the wall in the hallway. The people who called us had no sense of time. There were phone calls in the dead of night and in the earliest part of the morning. We were informed about the minutest details of each other's lives.

There were also guests who visited. Sometimes, rushing through the hallway, I would stumble upon the writers Leonov, Kataev, Vishnevsky, Kirsanov (the latter carried off two volumes of my collected works of Pushkin, which I regret to this day), the satirist Laskin, the violinist Madatov, film director Roman Karmen, the pianist Emil Gilels . . .

The neighbor's lively, resilient son drove back and forth, day and night, like one possessed, in the hallway on his homemade bicycle, often knocking down lingering tenants who were shuttling between the kitchen and their rooms. Pyotr Gusev, who loved his sleep, would dash out into the hallway from time to time and demand quiet in a tense, quavering voice. The boy was proud and responded to Gusev's outbursts with leaflets, which he slipped under the tenants' doors: "Petie's an old fart . . ."

I lived in this apartment until 1955, when I was given No. 24, conductor Fayer's two-room apartment, on the same staircase landing.

Chapter Fourteen

Mastering the ABCs of the Theater

Lavrovsky began with *Giselle*.

The Adolphe Adam ballet ran in Leningrad for a long time; it was just premiering on the Moscow stage. Lavrovsky set *Giselle* on Galina Sergeyevna Ulanova, who had joined the theater, as I already mentioned, at almost the same time as he did.

I first saw Ulanova in 1939. Hitler's minister Joachim von Ribbentrop had arrived in Moscow to sign the ill-fated Nonaggression Pact. We have regaled distinguished guests with the ballet throughout our history. Come to think of it, we still do to this day. Whatever else is lousy, we say, our ballet's always in great shape. There were no superstars in Moscow at that time. Semyonova was still considered the wife of an "enemy of the people" and thus couldn't be allowed to take part in the celebration of Soviet-German friendship. One of our high-ranking officials conceived the great idea of summoning Ulanova, with her perpetual partner Sergeyev, from Leningrad. Even officials can sometimes come up with bright ideas.

Galina Sergeyevna and I were often put at odds with one another. We were compared, informed on, and gossiped about. I'd like to faithfully recall my first impression of her.

Her lines amazed me. She had no equal in this regard. It was as if her arabesques were sketched in with a finely sharpened pencil. She had remarkably well-trained feet. This caught my attention. She seemed to speak softly with them. Her arms fit well into ideally drawn poses. The sense that she constantly observed herself from the side never left me. Everything had been carefully thought out and had a completeness about it. The difference between the Leningrad and Moscow schools was strikingly apparent. She didn't "fudge" anything even once during the entire performance. Moscow dancers permitted themselves such liberties constantly — it was, frankly speaking, par for the course.

I preferred her "white" act.* Her Odette. The "gentleness" of this character was closer to her nature than the self-assurance and demonic character of the evil sorcerer's daughter. (Though she did look good in the severe black lacquered wig. Wigs rarely look good on anyone, but they suited Ulanova's facial type.) To me she lacked style and range in the "black" act, and distinctness from the white swan. There wasn't enough contrast. It was clear to me that one ballerina was dancing both parts. Later on, when I danced the part, I tried to make myself unrecognizable to the audience. At least for the first two or four minutes. But I'm not going to find fault with Ulanova for being herself.

The performances was also memorable for their atmosphere. I managed to get a ticket in the dress circle. Ribbentrop was sitting in the Tsar's Box (we use the old-style name to this day for the theater's central box), very close to my seat. He was upright and of good breeding, and his hair was gray. The large ring he wore sparkled so brightly that it was blinding. About a thousand carats! Placing his long-fingered hands on the edge of the box in the manner of a lord, he deliberately caught the light with his marvelous jewel. Whatever happened to this ring when he was hanged in Nuremberg? But at that time, still alive and powerful, he attentively and graciously gazed upon the stage and applauded Ulanova unstintingly.

My second impression of Ulanova is from 1940 during the "Ten-Day Celebration of Leningrad Art" in Moscow. Bolshevik leaders loved these ten-day window-dressing showcases; it was they who probably invented them for humanity. Would a Frenchman have liked to attend a glorious "Ten Days of Marseilles Art" at the Opera in Paris or a Parisian show in Marseilles? This kind of ostentatious spectacle corresponded to the falsehood of our entire national life. The tables in the movie *Cossacks of the Kuban* were piled high with food, while daily existence meant half-starvation, filth, darkness, vodka. The friendship of

---

*The white swan in *Swan Lake*.

nations, the friendship of nations was extolled, but the reality was knifings, slaughter, and racism.

But there was a certain benefit to this ceremonial display of art. These displays mobilized creative people to the maximum. They all pushed themselves to the breaking point (otherwise, if you weren't careful, you'd miss out on that little decoration or wouldn't get invited to the final gala banquet). Now here's where you'd forget everything that ailed you. The temperature might be 42 degrees Celsius (108 degrees Fahrenheit), but you had to dance, flutter about, and smile. Besides, these ten-day affairs brought all the best performing artists together.

I still see before my eyes the fireworks of the Leningrad Ballet, which I had occasion to see that last year before the war.

Moscow was seeing *Romeo and Juliet* for the first time. Ulanova danced Juliet. That evening was a real artistic sensation for Muscovites. The whole cast was strong, but Ulanova stood out.

Going to the performance, I had expected to see another warhorse, although word of incalculable praise for the production reached even my schoolgirl's ears. But what I saw moved me profoundly.

There was much in it that was new and uncommon, in the ballerina's role, most of all. Nowhere did Ulanova move from a telling of the story to the series of movements familiar to every ballet student — plié, passé, à la second, changé to an arabesque . . . Naturally, all these movements were there, but I didn't notice them. She conveyed the drama of Shakespeare's play beyond the language of ballet. Whose achievement was this? The producers, Prokofiev, the splendid training of Vaganova's school, or Galina Sergeyevna herself? All of these contributed, but I think that the deciding factor was a gift from the heavens.

These are my first impressions of Ulanova. Later on I'll talk about her in more detail.

Now back to *Giselle*.

Lavrovsky arranged reviews of his new troupe. He would diligently come to our morning classes, look each of us over with his small, piercing eyes. He was always buttoned up and neat, freshly shaved, and impeccably dressed. Sitting with his back to the enormous ballet mirror, he would sometimes cast angry, sidelong looks at the pianist, who flubbed his notes because of the new boss's presence. And we got to see the neatly trimmed back of Lavrovsky's head in the mirror's reflection.

He didn't have any problems with Giselle herself or with Albrecht. When Ulanova joined the theater, she chose as her partner Mikhail Gabovich, an elegant dancer onstage, and a handsome, responsive, sympathetic man in real life.

(Incidentally, an intriguing detail. Before I was even born, when Gabovich was baptized in the Russian Orthodox faith in the church near the Sretensky Gate, my uncle Asaf offered Gabovich safe haven in my grandfather's apartment on Sretenskaya Street. Gabovich's father, a zealous believer in Judaism, had driven the heretic from his home. His godmother and godfather—Gorshkova and Ivan Smoltsov—were also ballet people.

In the first panic-filled days of the war, when the war commissions indiscriminately recruited and sent everyone they could to the front—which merely increased the number of dead—Gabovich boldly came to the defense of many dancers. Yuri Gofman, who later became one of the Bolshoi's premier dancers, related to me how stunned he was when Gabovich, dressed in a heavy woolen civilian coat, appeared on the edge of a trench at the front to help him. In the first years of the war, Gabovich bore the burden of the ballet's directorship of the Second Stage. We must keep alive the memory of such noble acts.)

Lavrovsky assigned the roles of the two Wilis to me and Lyalya Vanke. We resembled one another somewhat—oval faces, elongated bodies. Later our paths diverged, and she danced the Capulet mother in all the performances in which I danced Juliet. In *Giselle* each of us had to do a small variation. I prepared my variation with Vaganova. She showed me a particular way of doing a renversé, and I stole all the applause. If you coordinate your body in the right way, you can do just about anything well: we are ignorant and do too much intuitively.

Lavrovsky was pleased with us. At least that's what we both decided. For me, the Wili was sort of my own original study, a sketch for Myrtha (the Queen of the Wilis), the part I dreamt about. But first I must tell about my last lessons with Vaganova.

For a time she gave a class which I diligently attended. I say "for a time," because soon thereafter, Agrippina Yakovlevna had a falling out with Lavrovsky, with whom she had been at loggerheads in Leningrad. After Vaganova left Moscow, we exchanged insignificant conversation about the weather and mutual inquiries about health during our rare, short meetings. Although I did go to her brilliant class again while I was in Leningrad in 1951, it turned out to be her last one. I was dancing *Swan Lake* at the Maryinsky then, and Vaganova came to the theater. She came over to see me during both intermissions, gave me some advice about something, and invited me to her class the following morning. There I heard her lips pronounce the highest praise, "Not too bad."

Everyone in class was genuinely afraid of her. She was demanding and merciless, but they hung on her every word and followed her every instruction. Everyone valued their lessons with her. Agrippina Yakovlevna had a slight lisp and used to brand ballerinas with nicknames that, to use Gogol's phrase, "followed them to posterity and thereafter."

She called me the "red crow." Red, because I was a redhead, and crow because I missed some of her combinations in class. And she had to repeat them for me, which she loathed doing. I know that my innate lack of attention and focus can irritate anyone. But the fact that Vaganova reconciled herself to it—and did not raise her voice—was really astonishing. Valya Lopukhina, who was so sisterly in sharing her place in the dressing room, once remarked, "Grushka treats you in an unprecedented way, she would have dismissed anyone else from her class long ago."

I saw Myrtha as an otherworldly figure from the spirit realm. I had no desire to dance her as a "cemetery manager" or as a managing director charged with reviving the Wilis. She was not to be lively and ordinary. She was to emanate icy coldness and horror to the audience. When I was a child, my aunt Elya read me the story of the Venus de l'Ille. How a marble statue which was standing in an old palace park fell in love with a young man. Although he was engaged to a young woman his own age, as a joke he slipped the engagement ring on the marble statue's finger. Naturally, everything came to a bad end. Something like Pushkin's "The Stone Guest" in reverse. But the story etched itself deeply into my memory. And dancing the part of the marble goddess appealed to me. And that is how I created Myrtha. "Created her" doesn't mean that I willfully changed dance steps. But I tried to imbue each step with my own distinct meaning. All the arabesques, the port de bras, with regal grandeur, significance, sorcery, mystery, and secrecy.

Myrtha served as the basis for my encounter with Ulanova as an artist. I now saw her in terms of the space onstage. I could now judge from the short range, not the viewer's seat.

G. S. succeeded in becoming a ghost in the second act. The expression of her eyes, her mime, her gestures were all disembodied. When I was absorbed by the action, it would begin to seem at times that it wasn't Ulanova at all but the hovering corpse of a dead woman who had come alive through the magic of sorcery. Her feet didn't seem to touch the ground.

(I'll remark parenthetically that I overheard the following "insiders'" conversation. Someone was enumerating G. S.'s flaws: her extension was not big, nor was her jump; she was turned in, and so was her technique. And suddenly Semyonova, who was herself a virulent and annihilating critic of art but fair when it came to an objective evaluation, retorted, "Galka is light, and that, too, is technique.")

Lightness onstage is a rare gift. You do always hear the clunking of ballet shoes on the stage floor. I noticed that Ulanova always danced the second act of *Giselle* in soft shoes in order to prevent the slightest distraction from her image. At one rehearsal she addressed Fayer, the conductor, across the orchestra pit in her soft voice, "Take out the drum at the end of my variation. It bothers me." But the point, for me, is neither the shoes nor the drum. Throughout the performance, it seemed that she touched the floor less frequently than mortals are permitted by Newton's law of gravity.

Lavrovsky, for reasons I don't understand, put me onstage as Myrtha only during performances in which Ulanova danced. I never had anything to do with other Giselles. I liked this. But I myself never had the occasion to dance the part of Giselle, perhaps the only one of the main roles in the classical repertoire I didn't do.

I have been endlessly asked why I didn't dance Giselle. I haven't been able to come up with a convincing answer yet. Most likely, if I had really wanted to, I could have done it, but something in me opposed it, resisted, argued with it. Somehow it just didn't work out.

The next ballet was *Raymonda*. But it didn't happen instantly, not right away. There was the mundane routine, there were classes, rehearsals, performances, disappointments, there was life in the theater. I'd like to recall, and it might be interesting from today's heights to recall, how I mastered the ABCs of the Bolshoi Theater.

I got a raise in the middle of my second season. My salary was originally 600 rubles, and it now rose to a whole thousand (again, I want to remind you that during the devaluation one zero was removed, making it 100 rubles!). I really did dance a great deal. In addition to what I've already mentioned, there were also the Lilac Fairy and Violante in *Sleeping Beauty*, the Queen of the Dryads in *Don Quixote*, the dance with bells in the *Fountain of Bakhchisarai*, which the choreographer Rostislav Zakharov created for me. And there was Prokofiev's *Cinderella*, in which I was the first to dance "Autumn," also choreographed by Zakharov.

The theater went into a white heat before the premiere of *Cinderella*. The music, heard on the planet for the first time, was unusual. The orchestra musicians, either because they were lazy or because they had been ruined by Marxist dogma (which held that music belonged to the people), nearly mutinied against Prokofiev. Earlier, his scores had been simplified and rearranged within the theater. *Romeo and Juliet*, now included in every musical textbook, is a classic example. It was reworked by an orchestra musician, Boris Pogrebov, for sluggish and deaf dancers. "Louder, louder, we can't hear anything, why so soft?" they squealed from the stage.

Prokofiev came to all the rehearsals, and maintained a polite and cultured silence as his cheek muscles twitched. I felt sorry for him. It probably wasn't easy to endure it all. As for me, I was drawn to *Cinderella*. In the music of "Autumn" I heard melancholy, the rustle of dying leaves driven by the wind, and the damp, cold rain. Much later on, *Cinderella* brought me together with Rodion Shchedrin.

A tape recorder, a great rarity in those days, appeared in the apartment of my friends, Lilya Yuryevna Brik and Vasily Abgarovich Katanyan. It was a rarity in those times. Katanyan began to collect a small audio library of recordings of the voices of the house's friends. Nature, thank God, endowed me with a good musical ear and memory. And I sang practically the entire *Cinderella* to the Briks for their home library of recordings. Just for the fun of it. Shchedrin and I weren't acquainted yet, but he, too, was a frequent guest of the old Moscow house on Staropeskovsky Passage. Fourth floor, no elevator. They had him listen to my "choreographic" singing—I sang the Pogrebov drums (Pogrebov was the orchestra drummer) and the ringing flutes and Prokofiev's captivating, tart melodies. The Briks said that my singing stunned Shchedrin. Well, and . . .

The second reason for the anticipated thunderstorm of the premiere was the perpetual question of who was going to dance in the first performance. Ulanova and Lepeshinskaya rehearsed for it. Semyonova wasn't allowed near it. Ulanova had talent on her side. The management favored Lepeshinskaya. Ulanova won. She danced the premiere. And Shostakovich wrote a laudatory review of *Cinderella* in which he even mentioned me. It's all history now.

Ulanova and Lepeshinskaya were changing in the spacious dressing room near the stage boxes. Tina Galetskaya, Chidson, Lyulya Cherkasova, and Elena Mikhailovna Ilyushchenko also shared it. Around the theater, this dressing room was called the "vipers' pit." The gossip was malicious and merciless.

I rehearsed several of my parts with Ilyushchenko (incidentally, she was the wife of the well-known film director Sergei Yutkevich), and as I walked in after her, I would hear some memorable one-liners. At the door, just before walking out of the dressing room, she said to the remaining women, "Don't get it confused now—I had four husbands and eleven abortions." Two dancers who were squabbling about who had the right to the leading male soloist were told, "Don't make a big fuss, girls, we're all family here." When it was noted that Lepeshinskaya had begun visiting a certain "distinguished" house, Galetskaya said to her,

"What's this, Lyolya, you've gotten into the habit of coming up to the top floor of our house? That's where the flying ace Yumashev lives."

"He's also a painter, and he's painting my portrait."

"We modeled for him, too" Ilyushchenko replied.

But Ulanova always kept silent. She knew how to keep quiet. She knew better than anyone that silence was golden.

I was a witness of the following incident during the Leningrad Ten-Day Celebration. A few days before the opening, something brought Galina Sergeyevna to the choreographic school on Pushechnaya Street. A flock of my friends and I were talking on the staircase, which was crowded with chirping schoolchildren. It was recess. Ulanova came through the heavy front door, which pale children, exhausted by their studies, had to strain their guts to push open. She wore a gray fox-fur coat. It was a cold spring. We stopped speaking in mid-sentence.

She climbed the stairs to our sullen custodian Kuzma's domain and went to check her coat. Nothing doing. The vigilant guard, vastly overstuffed with Soviet radio broadcasts and newspaper reports of Stalinist hysteria about the spies lying in wait for us on every corner, grabbed the "stranger" by the sleeve. "Where are you going, my dear citizeness?" Anyone else would have immediately revealed her name. More than that, they would have flaunted a name like Ulanova with pleasure. But G. S. didn't rush into an unfair fight; she stepped back and froze in her tracks. Someone came to the rescue and loudly defended her, chiding the negligent guard for his choreographic ignorance . . .

But back to the Bolshoi Theater.

The director's box was the center of the universe. You could only get to it through the director's entrance—No. 16. Performers did not leave their coats there, though, even though the cloakroom was comfortable and spacious . . . "For those who are a bit cleaner, Sir," as Gogol's character Osip used to say.

There were two marble staircases. With two carpet runners, as is customary here. In those Stalinist times, there wasn't a speck of dust on them. Nowadays there's always a mass of fresh muddy tracks on them. The upper staircase led to the directors' offices. The lower one led the intimidated visitor to a box lined in patterned red satin. Inside were several armchairs with gilded arms. A marble table with a silver swan which had survived intact for centuries. In the corner a marble fireplace with a mirror. On it a gilded inlaid clock with a secret chime which had also stood there for many centuries and was impossibly heavy. (But it didn't remain there. Just recently someone managed to steal it. I can't figure out how the thief pulled it off. Only the three legendary bogatyrs* would have had the strength to lift this clock and carry it all the way through the theater.) A small toilet right behind an elegantly camouflaged door. In case someone couldn't bear it any longer— "Those who are a bit cleaner . . ."

In the days that I'm recalling, certain people in civilian clothes moved around the box slowly like silent, Giselle-like ghosts. The ushers on duty were dressed in Bolshoi Theater uniforms, but they were all from the same institution. Security. The KGB. After all, this was the imperial theater!

It was always a little terrifying to go in there. You felt penetrated, transparent.

Serafima Yakovlevna Kovalyova, a smart, plump, focused woman, was the secretary of the director's box. She fit the ceremonial nature of the environment perfectly. She held that position for more than a quarter of a century and knew everyone and everything. Nowadays it's called a computer. She loved home-cooked meals. She wasn't supposed to leave her combat post for long, but No. 8 Shchepkinsky was just a stone's throw away. The conductor Fayer was kind and hospitable to all powerful persons who lived there. No wonder he was always humming, "I love the management."

Each entrance had its designated function, too. Nowadays everything has changed: enter and exit where you please, whichever is most convenient. But in those days, each person had walk in through his own door. There you were a familiar face; the watchful old codgers knew you. "Hello, Maya Mikhailovna," they'd say, yet still stare at your theater pass with its glorious Soviet coat of arms and compare your photo with your living face. Yes, it's her, all right. Pass through, please. Everything was very polite, and the pace was measured and unhurried.

The war ended in victory.

The buttons of military uniforms gleamed in the auditorium. Being a civilian was somewhat shameful. Many women performers tried to keep up with the times. Some of them, having left their prewar husbands, ran like mad to marry generals. Alla Tarasova, an actress of the Moscow Art Theater, Stalin's favorite on the dramatic stage, left the great Ivan Moskvin because she no longer needed him. Now she appeared at Kremlin receptions with the gallant pilot General Alexander Semyonovich (who came up to her shoulder in height). At the Bolshoi there was a headlong rush to hunt down generals, whoever had more stars

*Mythic Russian folk heroes.

on their shoulder boards. And at our entrance, No. 21, generals' trouser stripes flitted, and their boots, polished to gleaming, sang like nightingales. You had to keep up with fashion—our generalissimo, according to eyewitness accounts, loved to make his new chrome-tanned leather boots squeak.

And I began rehearsing *Raymonda*. I was still a virgin and had other things on my mind besides generals. *Raymonda* was tough going, but more about that in the next chapter.

Chapter Fifteen

Raymonda

When I set out to write this book, the first thing I did was to carefully read my skimpy notes from those years. I began jotting things down after Ulanova made a casual remark about taking notes on all the performances in which she danced. And so I, too, noted down nearly everything I did. Except, of course, when I was too lazy. I'd emphasize many things differently today, focus on other things. But the notes were of invaluable help to me. They show much bitterness, many absurdities of the time, and many callous, vile people. My climb up the theatrical ladder was a difficult one, and I got painfully bashed from all sides. But what I achieved is all the more precious.

The war ended. Gun salutes. Crowds. Joy. Tears. The last year of the war, the Komsomol office often sent me, along with many other theater artists, to perform at military hospitals. I never refused. Like everyone else, without exception— I underline *without exception*—I was a member of the Komsomol. You became a member of the Komsomol at age fourteen. Automatically. We all took part in this simple initiation ritual, which took place in the ballet school. We swore that we would "loyally serve our Homeland," "further the Communist future with our labor," and "fulfill the plans of the Party." And so everyone fulfilled them as best they could . . .

But I always gave my all at these hospital concerts, with total sincerity and warmth. The faces of the wounded young men, wrapped in soiled bandages, were pure, defenseless, open to the world. They took in everything that we danced, played, and sang for them as seriously and enthusiastically as if Chaliapin and Galli-Curci were singing for them, Pavlova and Nijinsky were dancing for them, and Liszt and Paganini were playing for them. And the questioning expression in their eyes always troubled me. I felt sorry for those boys.

Raymonda came my way, as they say, by accident. Yet another noisy campaign "promoting youth" forced the theater management to add my name to the list of those performing Glazunov's ballet. The premiere had already taken place. I rushed to catch up.

For my partners Lavrovsky chose Alexander Rudenko as Jean de Brienne and Pyotr Gusev as Abderkhman. Elizaveta Pavlovna Gerdt was the rehearsal coach. She had once danced Raymonda herself and remembered the entire ballerina role. This was not surprising, since Glazunov had been a little in love with Elizaveta Pavlovna, had sent her flowers and taken her for troika rides under a bear rug with Gypsies around frosty St. Petersburg. Slightly embarrassed, she claimed that Glazunov wrote and dedicated the pizzicato variation in the second act to her. But rehearsals with her were boring. Her remarks were beside the point. "Don't stick out your tongue, adjust your ribbon . . ." If it weren't for Gusev's advice, which angered E. P., I would have danced the entire ballet with my spine hunched. Whereas Raymonda's regal bearing must dazzle from her first entrance onstage until the end of the performance. Absolutely.

Gusev rehearsed splendidly. He offered to make several lifts more elaborate and more contemporary. I was enthusiastic. Suddenly, during a difficult turn, Gusev nearly dropped me on the floor and fell down, howling. He literally howled like an animal. His ankle and hip convulsed in spasms. The rehearsal ended.

"My dear girl, this could also happen during a performance. I'll let you down. That would mean shame, humiliation. Get another partner."

That is how Gusev left the stage.

It's easy to say, "Get another . . ." The chief choreographer assigns partners. The boss. Just go and try to ask for what you want!

At this point, to my chagrin, I have to fit another character into the plot of my story.

Shashkin was the manager of the ballet troupe. Comrade Shashkin, Sergei Vladimirovich. He was one of many in the throng of unprincipled, shifty bureaucrats — grab 'em but you'll never hang onto 'em because they'll slip away — spawned by the Soviet system. If you can't do your job, become a manager.

Party-style. He had a Party membership card in his pocket as big as a flaming heart.

He began as a dancer in the corps de ballet, but he had no talent. He was square, heavy, and short, with a big head and a nose half the size of his head. Yet no single meeting went by without one of his enthusiastic speeches. Shashkin's zeal did not go unnoticed. He was promoted to a managerial position. The manager of the ballet troupe. Having attained significant power, he bullied us until he was sated. Later on he worked as the deputy director of Gosconcert*—and left bad memories there, too.

He perceived my request to change partners as a personal whim. This is how he set Lavrovsky against me, which he always did with cunning "trustworthiness." "Let Gusev rest up in bed and get well, then you'll start up the rehearsals again." The gap lasted for a long time, interminably long. That's how it seemed to me then. Only when Gusev moved to Leningrad did Lavrovsky assign Alexei Ermolayev to be my partner. Rehearsals began again. But a lot of time had been lost.

I don't want to settle any accounts with anybody on the pages of my life story. But I'm not going to wink at the intrigues of nameless ill-wishers. Each one had a given name, a family name, and a bureaucrat's cushy chair. I never had an out-and-out fist fight with Shashkin, but he inflicted unmerciful torment on me with hundreds of imperceptible dirty tricks. Sometimes I would have to replace some ballerina after she had learned a small but difficult part, and so rehearsals for *Raymonda* would go by the wayside; other times, the pianists would be busy all week—again *Raymonda* would be shunted aside; or we'd have to get jostled around for three hours in a bus to go perform in a semi-amateur manager's concert for "village laborers," and my rehearsals would be shelved again.

I have racked my brains trying to figure out why he took such a dislike to me, what it was in me that provoked such hostility. It wasn't because of personal incompatibility or a difference of taste. There's no doubt in my mind that he was carrying out someone else's ill will. I was shaken and felt an invisible spider web starting to entangle me during those stressful months.

Suddenly a passionate admirer of my talent appeared. Her name was Polya, even though her passport, which I once happened to see, said Tamara. She constantly cleaned my room on Shchepkinsky Passage, scrubbed the faded floor, sorted through my things in the closet, cooked dinner, washed the dishes . . . She

*The state concert agency, which booked artists and arranged tours.

absolutely refused to take any money for her work—it was all for the love of art. And, naturally, she cross-examined me about politics, my family, people close to me . . . I kept silent. She disappeared just as suddenly as she had appeared. Without a trace.

About fifteen years later at a reception at one of the foreign embassies, I felt someone's piercing look on me. I turned around sharply and my eyes met those of that wayward Polya-Tamara, who had washed my floor on Shchepkinsky. She was shapely, well-coiffed, and elegantly dressed. We greeted each other. But she walked away. I never ran into her again.

Tata Cheremshanskaya, a classmate of mine whose existence I had completely forgotten, paid me an unannounced visit without a warning phone call, saying that she had remembered me for no particular reason. And she also cross-examined me: what did I know of my father's fate, how was my mother, did I hold a grudge, what was my mood? And then she disappeared. For good, too . . .

But I'll get back to the rehearsals. Ermolayev was very different from Gusev. He calculated the audience's reaction ahead of time and chose the most striking angle for each pose vis-à-vis the audience. He hypercritically rehearsed himself and his partner, as if observing from the side. He immersed himself in the music. But we worked passionately and harmoniously together.

Rudenko, on the other hand, was a slacker; he would get lazy. He was always late for rehearsals. Then he would tediously explain for ten minutes who had detained him and where. He would repent sincerely. Then he would start warming up listlessly. Then begin mumbling again. It was impossible to catch the drift of what he was saying. I would get nervous. Even unflappable Elizaveta Pavlovna would lose patience, "Come on now, Sasha, get going . . ."

Fayer conducted *Raymonda;* he conducted most of the ballets. Perhaps he wouldn't have inspired wild ovations on the concert-hall stage, but Fayer was an expert when it came to ballet. He always came to the piano rehearsals, watched the tempos, and could prompt dancers on combinations they had forgotten. He had an incomparable musical memory. He conducted all the ballets by heart, without scores. Including *Raymonda*. It was his memory that helped him at the end of his artistic path, when he went completely blind. He passionately conducted both the classics and the new ballets of Prokofiev and Aram Khachaturian at that time, snuffling loudly across the entire auditorium. He loved to move slowly around backstage like a turtle, arms wide open, with his guides leading him. The guides were always female and very pretty. Hearing the staccato tapping of heels, Fayer always tried to thoroughly grope the approaching body. He would invariably recognize who it was by her body, although he would excitedly ask, "Who are you, who's this?" as he held his prey tightly. Then he would call her by name and set her free.

The day of the long-awaited premiere arrived. Elizaveta Pavlovna was in a severe black dress with a pearl necklace, the hunched-over, high-cheekboned Gauk in the arch of the director's box beside her. Fayer solemnly floated to the conductor's stand from his dressing room. Ermolayev checked his hawklike poses for the hundredth time. Rudenko muttered something to the stage director. I stuck my pink shoes in the rosin box by the first wing and tied my ribbons tightly. Shashkin's barrellike shadow flitted by. Lavrovsky, impeccably dressed, like an English dandy, kissed me on the cheek and wished me success.

Music.

Raymonda's entrance onstage . . .

My *Raymonda* debut was a sensational success, rare for a nonpremiere performance. It's fair of me to say this since six stills from *Raymonda* appeared in the magazine *Ogonyok* on the same page as reports about the victories of Moscow's Dynamo soccer team over in England and portraits of the great Bobrov, Beskov, Khomich, Seminchastny. The seventh photo was a ridiculous one of me in real life, embarrassed and half-smiling. "Photo by G. Kapustyanskaya." And a small item about the appearance of a new ballerina in the Bolshoi Theater troupe. I was happy as a child. A week later, the mailman delivered heaps of different-colored envelopes with letters to Shchepkinsky Passage addressed to me. People were offering me their hands and hearts in marriage, confessing they were in love with me, asking for loans, explaining that they were relatives. It seems I'd become famous.

Chapter Sixteen

Swan Lake

I'm coming up to *Swan Lake*. This Tchaikovsky ballet played a central role in my life. I danced it more than eight hundred times. And I danced it for thirty years: from 1947 to 1977. The dates are like the birth and death dates on a tombstone. Thirty years is an entire lifetime.

The most memorable cities in which I performed in *Swan Lake* are Moscow, New York, Kharkov, Paris, Leningrad, Buenos Aires, Minsk, Helsinki, Kiev, London, Odessa, Milan, Riga, Washington, Ufa, Rome, Sofia, Tokyo, Vancouver, Munich, Tbilisi, Baku, Erevan, Montreal, Cologne, Warsaw, Los Angeles, Sidney, Melbourne, Philadelphia, Budapest, Cairo, Mexico City, San Francisco, Seattle, Berlin, Detroit, Prague, Belgrade, Pittsburgh, Tashkent, Chicago, Kazan, Toronto, Osaka, Bucharest, Lima, Beijing.

I danced three versions, three productions of *Swan Lake* at the Bolshoi Theater. Also Burgmeister's version at the Stanislavsky Theater, Berezov's variation at Milan's La Scala, and Vakhtang Chabukiani's Tbilisi production . . .

The hard-of-hearing choreographer Julius Reisinger commissioned the diligent Pyotr Ilyich Tchaikovsky to write a ton of music for future use, for two full-length ballets (the first production of *Swan Lake,* as everyone knows, was a failure and was dropped from the repertory). Now, following Gogol's example, every choreographer wants to display what a "smart fellow" he is and reshuffles the sequences of the dance numbers. And since there's such an abundance of them, he reinstates cuts, drops entire musical episodes, slashes into the real body of the work, abridges, extends, enlarges, modifies, changes fast tempos into slow ones and vice versa . . . A real disaster. Is Pyotr Ilyich turning in his grave or has he given up on these ignoramuses?

Nonetheless, the main dance episodes — the "black" and "white" pas de deux, the brides scene, the pas de trois, the three swans, the Dance of the Four Cygnets — are lifted straight from the brilliant predecessors Marius Petipa, Alexander Gorsky, or Lev Ivanov. "Personal vision" extends no further than pretentious novelties added to the simple plot. Yet you get to see your name writ large, splashed across the entire city: so-and-so's production, with all kinds of conceivable and inconceivable titles; the long-deceased Petipa, Gorsky, and Ivanov are forgotten — with no feelings of remorse. None of the erudite ballet critics will come to the defense of these long-dead men, no one's conscience bothers him — "our sense of shame was removed like an appendix" (Andrei Voznesensky). And the ballet troupe is so intimidated by its little dictator, its little Napoleon, that it doesn't speak up even if the impostor passes off the music as his own. Open your mouth and you won't get to go on tour abroad. You'll have to stay home. Everybody got smart, kept quiet.

I could be reproached for dancing versions of *Swan Lake* that were not to my liking. For not proudly refusing. But we performers slavishly depend on the choreographer's decree. For us, the head choreographer is first and foremost a boss, and a creator only secondarily. God the Father, God the Son, God the Holy Ghost. All rebellions against the leader ended in your expulsion from the everyday core repertory. A ballerina without practice and without the barre loses her form with lightning speed. It means death.

But I've digressed.

I used to consider *Swan Lake* every ballerina's touchstone, and I still do: you can't hide anything or hide behind anything in that ballet. Everything's in plain view: two characterizations (incidentally, at one time the "white" and "black" acts were danced by two different ballerinas), the entire palette of colors and technical challenges, the art of transformation, the dramatic quality of the finale. The ballet demands the full output of all your physical and spiritual strength. You can't dance *Swan Lake* "half-leggedly," without giving it your all. Every time I danced this ballet, I felt drained, turned inside out. It would take two or three days to recover my strength.

It's interesting for me to recall how I worked on my first *Swan Lake*. Here are short excerpts from my journals dating from 1946–47.

September 6, 1946. I'd very much like to dance *Swan Lake*, but Lavrovsky says that I won't be able to portray the cunning seductress Odile.

October 4. I started rehearsing with Gerdt anyway. Preobrazhensky is the Prince.

November 5. Lavrovsky still isn't giving me *Swan Lake*. Says I have to grow up first!

. . . And we began again on January 20, 1947, and stopped until March.

Finally, on April 13, there was a preliminary run-through in the second auditorium.

On April 27, 1947 I danced my premiere *Swan Lake*. It was a matinee performance. I couldn't believe that I was dancing, that my dream was coming true. All the performers applauded me after each act onstage.

I'm leaving out all the intrigues, big and small, that Shashkin created, all his machinations (I will, for the sake of objectivity, say that he tormented me a tiny bit less this time), all the vulgar theatrical sudden reversals. The theater is not a church. Then again, even churches have their Iagos.

The rehearsals began with the "white" adagio. Except that at the time we didn't say "white," we used a number—the Act 2 adagio. The division into the "black" and "white" adagios came to the Bolshoi from the West. The foreign ballet troupes that began visiting at the end of the 1950s reinterpreted Odile, the daughter of the evil genius Rothbart, as the black swan. This division took root.

I learned the adagio quickly. I had danced as one of the six swans, then as one of three, and knew the entire ballerina's libretto. I simply improvised the finale of the act — Odette's exit. It turned out pretty well. And Elizaveta Pavlovna said, "Leave it that way. It really looks like you're floating away. The audience should like the exit." At the run-through I worked to add amplitude to the wavelike movements of my arm-wings. The result was an original twist. One of the dancers who attended said quietly, but audibly, "Plisetskaya will reap a harvest from this exit." It was a woman's voice.

Still, I wasn't counting on applause at that point in the premiere. But there was applause. And a quite a lot of it. And each of the eight hundred times, anywhere on the planet, the applause drowned out Tchaikovsky's quiet, ebbing, poetic music.

The third act, the "black" one, didn't go as smoothly. It was technically more difficult and complicated. The most treacherous part was the solo variation. By this point, you're already fairly tired, you come out onto the center of the stage on a musical pause. Bright, blinding light. It's so crowded on the stage — there's the corps de ballet, and the extras, and the brides who have danced their parts — all the characters. You're the center of attention. You have to show everything you're capable of. It's like an exam, a competition. The eyes of the troupe are on fire with the question — what shape is the ballerina in? The audience has grown quiet. It's time to begin . . .

Petipa (his version is usually danced along with his staging) pulled out all the stops: two turns from fifth position, the leg opens, a turn in attitude . . . and things really begin to take off. By the final pose you're feeling faint. And you've still got two codas to go. A fouetté and two rapid diagonals. Later I replaced my unstable fouetté — I didn't have enough training — with a rapid circle. But during the run-through and the premiere my fouetté turned out without a hitch, I landed right on the dime.

The fourth act didn't present any great problems. I felt relief — the major part was behind me, and there were few difficulties ahead. The most important thing here was the poetry and poignancy of the dramatic image. The tension of the ballet's finale music helps the acting. Tchaikovsky's famous swan theme, which everyone recognizes by now, resonates in its full glory.

My premiere, in spite of the matinee, brought together nearly all of Moscow's theater world. After the orchestral run-through, word spread that Plisetskaya's Swan was a success. That you had to see her in this ballet. There were many famous names in the audience. Sergei Eisenstein conveyed an elegant compliment through our dancer Susanna Zvyagina, "Tell Maya that she is a brilliant girl." The entire ballet world was there. They hashed and rehashed everything.

Lavrovsky liked my work. And he began to put me onstage on any occasion that was even the least bit serious: on holidays or during the visits of important guests.

I have danced my fill for guests. My *Swan Lake* was served up to everyone under the sun: Marshal Tito, Jawaharlal Nehru and Indira Gandhi, the Iranian shah Pehlevi, the American general George Marshall, the Egyptian president Gamal Nasser, the Afghani king Muhammad Daoud (who was later assassinated), the Ethiopian emperor Haile Selassie, the Syrian Shukri al-Kuwatli, Prince Sihanouk of Cambodia . . . I'll end the list here. It would take up an entire page. But I will talk about one VIP in detail.

Mao Zedong was coming to Moscow. The great helmsman of the Eastern peoples. What would we regale him with? There was no question: we could make

Chairman Mao happy with the revolutionary ballet *Red Poppy*. But we weren't informed of when the Party leader would arrive, so the management began staging *The Red Poppy* every other day. Ulanova would dance one day and Lepeshinskaya the next. But still no sight of Mao. Suddenly Lavrovsky called me (it was a Sunday), "Your day off tomorrow is canceled. You're dancing *Lake* for Mao Zedong (on Monday), so don't let me down." The calendar read February 13, 1950.

Security was increased tenfold that day. They thought that Stalin would attend the ballet with his bosom pal. Security went wild in their vigilance. A special pass which the zealous guardians managed to print overnight was checked at every door without exception. I had to keep it on my person in the brassiere of my tutu.

Please understand that you have to get fully warmed up before dancing in *Swan Lake*. So I had to keep showing my pass to the guards, pulling out a shiny piece of cardboard from my bodice and stuffing it back in. I had to get to the sixth floor, where the training studio was located. And there's a silent guard in a sagging jacket there, too. I'm warming up, and he isn't letting me out of his sight. His stare is stern, watchful, sexless. I limber up. And then I have to go through it all over again and show the same pass to the same guards.

But Stalin did not attend. The business of world revolution distracted the leader of the proletariat from the choreography. But big-cheeked Mao was right there in the Imperial Box.

And right in front of the entrance onto the stage, where the box of rosin is — the same faceless, sexless security agents, their eyes drilling through you, constantly comparing your pass with your suspicious person. And I dance the entire *Swan Lake* — both adagios, variations, the exit, and the fouetté — with the special pass in my bodice. The thought never leaves me: what if the pass suddenly slips out during a chaîné or jump, and the Voroshilov riflemen mistake it for the latest explosive device and open fire on me? It was nothing short of Kafkaesque . . .

At the end of the performance, a deeply moved Mao sent a giant basket of white carnations to the stage. It turned out that the Chairman himself had wanted to see *Swan Lake*. For an orthodox Chinaman, red poppies were a symbol for narcotics and vice. Not everything that blushes crimson is revolutionary.

I had many partners in *Swan Lake*. It would be a sin not to mention them with a kind word. I'll begin with the first one.

Vladimir Preobrazhensky did all the rough, preparatory work with me. When you learn a new ballet, the patience of your partner, who has already danced his part, is extremely valuable. Volodya was patient and decent. He responded in a calm, matter-of-fact way to all the nerve-wracking hassle of canceled rehearsals, reschedulings, new appointments. I fretted and rushed around; he would calm me down and take the trouble to intervene. He would even take on Shashkin: argue with and reproach him. He wasn't afraid of having words with Lavrovsky, either.

Preobrazhensky had a perfect athletic build; several successful Moscow sculptors had used him as a model. Half-dressed athletes in metro stations and parks of culture, good-looking pretty-boy workers, manly fighting men with open faces—all looked uncannily like my first partner in *Swan Lake*. He was a reliable and diligent partner.

Slava Golubin was my first love, and our *Swan Lake*s held for both of us something more than routine Ten-Day Celebration performances. He started out well, was the leading dancer in several ballets. But he began to drink, and it ruined his career and his life. He committed suicide at age thirty-four by hanging himself on a water pipe in the toilet of his apartment. Another bitter human fate . . .

Yuri Kondratov, who also died young, partnered wonderfully. He had a rare and innate sense of a ballerina's balance on pointe. I did ten to twelve pirouettes with him and could have done more, had Tchaikovsky's music allowed it.

I danced many *Swan Lake*s with Nikolai Fadeyechev. When I was allowed to travel abroad—when I became *vyezdnaya*—Kolya was calm and aristocratic. I loved to dance with him because our personalities complemented each other's. It was impossible to disturb his equilibrium. He would utter no more than ten words during rehearsals. His poise had a healing effect on me. Unfortunately, as time went on he put on weight and grew heavy. His passion for food and a round-the-clock appetite had their effect. He never could say no to food.

Alexander Godunov was powerful, proud, and tall. His sheaf of flaxen hair, which made him look Scandinavian, blazed in the wind of the incomparable Godunov pirouette. He danced better than he partnered. He was loyal, decent, and, in spite of his manly exterior, totally defenseless. His homeless, impoverished existence at the Bolshoi led to his sensational defection from the "Communist paradise." He was tortured, kept from dancing, and not permitted to go abroad for a long time, too. He languished penniless, which, considering his generous and proud nature, was a torment. It wasn't until just before he defected that he was given his own corner. I lost Siegfried, Vronsky, and José. Let fate be gracious to you now, Sasha! . . .

Another Sasha. Alexander Bogatyrev.

As handsome as a Greek god, perfectly built, romantic. An impeccable, attentive partner. I felt protected dancing with him. He cared less about his solos than about the ballerina's comfort. An impassioned warrior for truth. He didn't spare himself defending the downtrodden. The theater machine and its tyrant leaders rained a cascade of insinuations, lies, and slander on Bogatyrev. He defended himself to the last cartridge. The uneven battle undermined his strength and dried out his soul. He performed onstage only once every two to three months, and even then, in case of dire emergency. He left the stage unforgivably early.

Leonid Zhdanov, Yuri Gofman, Maris Liepa, Vladimir Tikhonov, Alexei Chichinadze at the Stanislavsky, John Markovsky in Leningrad, Nikolai Apukhtin and Valery Kovtun in Kiev, and Konstantin Sergeyev, with whom I had occasion to dance in China. Have I left out anyone?

I probably danced *Swan Lake* less than perfectly. There were successful performances and there were flawed ones. But my manner, principles, and some of my dance innovations stuck and took root. The "Plisetskaya style" went out into the world. Every so often I catch a glimpse of my splintered reflection on the stage or on T.V.: drooping wrists, swan elbows, head pulled up, body thrown back, poses fixed at their extreme.

I'm happy about it.

I mourn . . .

Chapter Seventeen

Youth Festivals

With *Swan Lake* my position in the theater improved significantly.

Among the new lists of of "talented individuals showing promise" after the war, the overly short ballet list began with me. This collection of names traveled from one newspaper to another and determined the selection of those would take part in the upcoming 1947 Summer Festival of Democratic Youth in Prague.

The ostentatious showcase celebrating friendship among the youth of "brotherly socialist nations" planned by the Kremlin leaders was supposed to become a grandiose Hollywood show, to impress the world with the luminous joy of those living in the Stalinist people's prison. Every two years one or another Eastern European capital city enslaved by Stalin was required to take up the baton of this diabolic charade.

And so I showed promise. Prague — that's already abroad. My first foreign tour lay ahead. I have to fill out the paperwork. What does this mean? The prophetic writer Mikhail Saltykov-Shchedrin had already summed it up in the nineteenth century: a Russian consists of a body, a soul, and some papers. Even more so by 1947.

First of all you have to fill out an application. The application consists of four pages. There are a good fifty questions about everybody and everything. Were you ever a prisoner of war, did you live in territories occupied by the Germans, for how long, your parents' background, your mother's maiden name, her employment record, and of course, everything about your father. Those of us who were selected were forced to fill out the application in a group, in a room of the Komsomol office crammed with faded red "day march" banners. It was torture. It was impossible to hide anything about my father, but writing the truth would mean that I wouldn't get to go anywhere. What was I to do? Their pens squeaking my neighbors were boldly scratching away. I kept vacillating. I wrote the truth, but messily and illegibly. It probably wouldn't do any good.

That, indeed, was what happened. Everybody left, and I remained in Moscow. Two days later, I was summoned to a talk at the Central Committee of the Komsomol. They asked me about everything under the sun. I squirmed like an eel in a hot frying pan. I hoped I wouldn't say too much! It seemed the danger had passed. The next morning I caught up and flew to Prague with a well-groomed Komsomol clerk. He said nothing all the while. Then he suddenly blurted out, "Have you been feuding with Lepeshinskaya long?" I gave him a guilty smile. What could that mean? Lepeshinskaya was also performing in the youth festivals and was already in Prague. I don't know the reason for the Komsomol question to this day. We'll rack our brains together, reader.

In Prague there wasn't the slightest mention of a ballet competition. In addition to the dancers from Moscow, there were dancers from Leningrad, Kiev, Tbilisi, and Tashkent — some "friendship of peoples"! There were no foreigners. With whom were we going to compete? Only the athletes and musicians competed. The judges didn't want to offend the musicians, so they divided first- and second-place honors among several Soviets. Everyone returned home as laureates, everyone met expectations. And yet Prague was where Mstislav Rostropovich's star flashed brilliantly for the first time.

The dancers simply performed for the audience as usual. I took a bad swing into a pirouette at the first rehearsal of the "white" adagio from *Swan Lake* and smashed Golubin with all my might right on the nose with my elbow. He was to be my partner at the festival. There was a horrible sound. I had broken Slava's nose. It was an open break, and Golubin returned to Moscow, his face covered with stitches. I danced everything with Kondratov.

Prague still looked prosperous that year. Private stores, small shops, and markets did not lack for goods. But we didn't have any money. We were fed Komsomol-style, in a herd. And so we only got to look and lick our lips. Still, the contrast was so palpable. Moscow's grip had not yet tightened around Prague's neck. That lay ahead.

We were not allowed to go "to town" alone. We could go in groups of no less than three people, so that at least one of us would inform on the others. We were transported in buses. The entire trip we sang Novikov's hymn to youth, "We are children of different peoples and we live inspired by the dream of peace," a hundred times, out of tune, but with dedication. There were many spies. If you didn't burst into song, you were considered incompatible, unreliable. So whether or not you had a good voice, you'd join in the singing . . .

There were many meetings at factories and plants. Interminable speeches. Sometimes in Russian, sometimes in Czech, sometimes in some other language. Then a concert. Folk ensembles, Cossack dances, accordions, peasant songs, with two or three ballet numbers squeezed in. My turn. Then a solo piece for voice, violin, or cello. It's a good life. We showed, too, that we hold the classics in high esteem, that the "progressive Soviet system" produces an abundance of stars. And for the closing, a general show of brotherliness. The participants would hold hands in friendship and sing the same Novikov hymn, ecstatically chanting, "Stalin, Stalin, peace, peace, friendship, friendship."

I was still dressed in my tutu and feathers, in my makeup, holding hands with a tall Greek man and pretty Greek girl, both wearing T-shirts emblazoned with the Greek flag, and I tried to sing along with everyone. I redoubled my efforts when I noticed the well-groomed Komsomol clerk's attentive eyes right up close. He'd undoubtedly write a report about how I behaved during my first trip abroad.

We were herded in buses to stadiums to root for our teams. To hear the newly composed "Hymn of the Soviet Union." Our countrymen kept winning. There really were many talented athletes. Light-haired, with ascetic peasant faces hardened by sweat and wind, fanatically involved only in competitive sports — they were nice, I liked them. But sometimes in the women's competitions, clandestine hermaphrodites took first place. There was no checking sex at festivals in those days. It was horrifying to look at these people. They looked like women, with mounds on their chests, but if you looked more closely — these were regular bruisers. If one of them would walk in the women's toilet and measure you up with a look, you wouldn't finish your business, you'd run out of there like mad . . . You just never know.

Two years later there was the Budapest Festival, then the Berlin one. But things essentially remained the same. The program which took shape in Prague became firmly entrenched.

In Budapest something resembling a competition took place, but again it was between our own teams. At the end they announced that five dancers shared the first prize. One gold medal for five people. I was one of them, awarded in alphabetical order. All of them were Soviet, all of them were from Moscow. A first-class couple from Tbilisi received the silver — so there, you should live in the capital! — and also shared it with their entire company.

This impoverished, loyal-patriot policy of giving all the prizes to the Soviet participants was in effect for many, many years. Only envoys from the land of the Soviets could dance, sing, play the piano, or walk the circus tightrope well. The birthplace of socialism. Everybody else, no matter how hard they tried or how brilliantly they sparkled, had to be inferior. Socialist brothers taking second prize, well, that was tolerable. But no one from the imperialist world — God help us! Education is poorly organized in capitalist countries. Over there, even talent is bought with money. They're beasts, they're corrupt.

The first glimmer of common sense was Van Cliburn's victory at the Tchaikovsky Piano Competition in Moscow. But what a lot of effort that took! I'm familiar with the behind-the-scenes battles Emil Gilels (chairman of the jury) had — the ultimatums, demands, and attacks — because we lived in the same cooperative building on Gorky Street for many years and would discuss the latest news in the courtyard. He was summoned to speak to the minister, accused of a lack of patriotism, shamed, and threatened. If you're not smart enough, then at least have him share first place with our Soviet pianist. Explanations that Cliburn's talent was head and shoulders above the rest were not taken into account.

The same was true in the world of choreography. I can testify to it as a two-time member of the Moscow Ballet Competition jury. Our score cards with numerical evaluations were carefully studied in the evening in the Ministry of Culture and reported "upstairs." The voting was secret but under their control. Express your will, and we'll see your patriotism and your love for your Homeland. The foreign members of the jury couldn't understand the ministry's machinations. The wool was expertly pulled over their eyes. To keep them from getting out of hand, the personal interpreters assigned to each of them force-fed them kilos of black caviar and washed it down their pickled throats with Stolichnaya vodka. At government expense, of course. And boy, do you sleep well after a government feast! Sometimes there were small rebellions by foreigners demanding fairness, but those occurred infrequently. The portions of black caviar were doubled, the guest was given a more comfortable personal car, one with better shocks. The rebels regained their composure. They behaved themselves. Late one night, Jerome Robbins, totally stupefied after an all-nighter, equably refused to vote, explaining that he, frankly, didn't understand what was going on. But he was an exception.

The "objectivity" of Soviet competitions grew legendary. Foreign competitors stopped coming over. Only the clumsy children of millionaires and over-excited amateurs ventured on the journey. And this was to the benefit of the Soviet brotherhood of athletes who were trained until they were blue in the face. You can't attract quality people with cheap bribes.

I saw my fill of idiocies during my first festival tours abroad. Everyone tried to show the full extent of his loyalty to the authorities and devotion to the "immortal ideas of communism." Someone might say something stupid, but it was a Soviet stupidity, ours, and they would break their silence, assenting — well put, true — and nod their heads in agreement. But if someone noticed anything foreign that was sensible or efficient, he'd be scolded immediately and criticized. I once cried out with delight when I saw a fluffy Saint Bernard out of the bus window, and the choreographer Rostislav Zakharov, director of our ballet guild, suddenly appeared and immediately chided me, "Plisetskaya, don't admire foreign dogs. Our dogs have better pedigrees." It sounds funny. But no one would smile. Rostislav Vladimirovich was right, it was serious business. And half the delegation, a third of the bus, were eavesdropping escorts. There were ears and eyes all around you. One small misstep and they'd send you home. You'd never get to go anywhere again. And they did send people home! People feared this most of all. They would smear you with stuff that you'd spend the rest of your life washing off.

There are details from the Berlin Festival that I recall: I had the opportunity to dance the *Dying Swan* in the open beds of four trucks that were pushed together. The bottoms of these vehicles, which had seen much in their day, served as the stage. I also danced the *Swan* on the grass of a freshly mowed lawn. My ballet slippers were very green afterward, like a wood sprite's shoes.

The Berlin of 1951 also plunged me into sadness. I had walked those still-undamaged streets with my father, not knowing what kinds of lives fate would deal us. And now . . .

I'm writing about the festivals because they were my first foreign tours, my first concert experience abroad.

Chapter Eighteen

My Injuries, My Healers

A performance of *Chopiniana* on April 16, 1948, at the Bolshoi. Semyonova was dancing the leading role; I was dancing the mazurka. I had no foreboding of the ill to come. During the final coda, when the soloists follow one another in sissonnes, Semyonova ran into me with all her might as she was doing a turn. The blow was unexpected, and I fell down. There was piercing, sharp pain. I couldn't get up. Everyone avoided me and kept on dancing. Unbearable pain in my right ankle. I seemed to have sprained my ankle badly. Everyone was dancing. I lay on the floor.

My right ankle swelled improbably right before my eyes, like in a Walt Disney film. I didn't move a muscle. Luckily, only a minute and a few seconds or so remained before the curtain fell. But time stretched for an eternity. That's how relative the sense of time is.

The curtain came down. I was carried backstage to the women's wing. The soloists took their bows. I could vaguely hear the applause in the house.

Slava Golubin and Rudenko crossed their four wrists to form a kind of chair and carried me to the dressing room. It was horrible to look at my ankle, all swollen and blue. Had I torn any ligaments? There was no physician in the theater. I had to get home, to Shchepkinsky; fortunately it was nearby. They brought me home. I was writhing in pain.

My bad knee had tortured me while I attended the school. My damned left knee. In medical terms, it was Hoff's disease, of the kneecap ligament. Now I think it was from the incorrect placement of my legs. When the foot leans into the big toe and not the little one, the entire leg turns in. The body bears down on the knee, which is used for support and pushing off.

At the age of fourteen I had beaten down the doors of all the leading Moscow orthopedists of the day. I begged them to heal me. Now their portraits hang on the walls of trauma clinics everywhere, and in the Central Scientific Institute of Traumatology and Orthopedics. The acclaimed Professor Boehm, whom I got to see through his daughter Tata, who was in her last year at the ballet school, carefully examined my knee. I felt pain wherever he pressed. He asked me to do a low plié. I couldn't. Boehm shook his head with regret and announced his verdict: "Young lady, you have to change your profession. You won't be a ballerina. It's impossible to straighten this knee."

These luminaries of healing now abide in another world. All that remains of them are rosy legends and stern-looking portraits lining the corridors that smell of carbolic acid. But I'm still dancing. I've been dancing for forty-seven years. Jumping, bending, spinning. My knee has endured without a whimper. How fortunate that I didn't heed the great prophet's advice and went to the "quacks."

The masseur Nikita Grigoryevich Shum saved me. He treated athletes, and someone recommended him to me as a last resort. He was a a giant of a man with hands like the widest country rake. In the 1920s he performed in the circus as a wrestler. He always wore a red mask, and that's how he got his nickname, "Red Mask." Once, while warming up, he laid the great Ivan Poddubny flat on his back. The undefeated champion became so enraged that he broke the rules, grabbed Nikita and threw him over a hurdle. His collarbone snapped like a matchstick from the blow and remained crooked and deformed for life. Shum treated people in his tiny, windowless room under a staircase not far from the Belorussian train terminal. He did it illegally of course; naturally gifted alternative healers weren't allowed to even come close to medicine—they were outlawed in Stalin's materialist heaven.

Nikita Grigoryevich felt my knee very slowly for about an hour and a half. He was in no hurry. In the tense silence I heard only the muffled, staccato steps of the apartment residents dashing up and down the stairs. Then he drawled, "You'll come to see me every day for two weeks. I'll need three or four hours of your time. You'll dance again, your knee will revive."

He performed his sorcery on my desperate, hopeless knee for two whole weeks. He limbered it up, straightened it, applied warmed paraffin and poultices, burned it with cold, stretched it, brewed herbal medicines. And he did all this slowly and methodically, without ever hurrying. Sometimes he asked me about dancing or about my family. But I rarely heard his voice. Shum was taciturn. I trusted him both medically and personally and told him about the ordeals of those close to me. On the fifteenth day the wizard gave me permission to begin dancing again. My knee felt weak, but completely healthy. I needed to pay him.

We hadn't made any previous arrangements about the price. My aunts and uncles pooled together a certain sum, which I brought to Nikita Grigoryevich in a small packet made from a theater bill, a few days after my last treatment. He very simply refused to take the money, without opening the packet and without a trace of posturing. "You'll need it yourself. The soccer players throw money my way. It's enough to live on and for tobacco."

Other dancers also came to see him. He helped everyone. He performed real miracles. After the war he was given work as a masseur at the Bolshoi. By that time he had started a family and expanded to a second room for space. It resembled the sanctuary of a sorcerer. The entire ceiling was hung with dried medicinal herbs, which reached nearly down to the floor. His wife, round-faced, plump, just as taciturn as the sanctuary's master, adroitly moved among the bristling, grassy tails, without ever disturbing them. Nikita's little daughter, Olga, followed her shadow around. The fragrance in the room was spicy and intoxicating.

The dancers idolized Shum. When his powerful body towered backstage, we danced more confidently, without giving it a second thought. Nikita was in the theater—in the event of trouble, he would mend it. His sudden death in 1954 sadly astonished all of us. People like him aren't supposed to die! It seemed as if nature had created such human power to last a whole century, But death . . .

There was a sea of flowers at the funeral service. Ulanova, whom he had miraculously helped on more than one occasion, placed an enormous wreath on his coffin. There are many bad, malicious people in the pages of my book. Our unendurable Soviet life spawned and multiplied worms and scum. But on this page I'm remembering the kindest person, who brought healing to many who suffered with an open, sacred heart.

I'll get back to my swollen blue foot. Shum was away. The all-powerful party patron of some soccer team had talked the management into allowing them to take the masseur with them on an important tour. The Soviet Cup or something of that nature. To whom could I appeal for help? I didn't trust anyone but Shum.

So there I was lying around and resting, pestering my visitors with inquiries about Nikita Grigoryevich's return.

Injuries accompanied me throughout my entire stage life. I tore a calf, pinched a spinal nerve, dislocated an ankle joint, broke toes, smashed my feet. Each of these injuries postponed premieres, canceled filming and tours. Each was a tragedy. I don't want my book to focus the reader's attention on my professional suffering. But I'll briefly describe one more incident.

I managed to dance in three mutually exclusive productions of Khachaturian's *Spartacus* by rival choreographers on the Bolshoi Theater stage. (Frankly, there have been a negligible number of premieres in the past few years. We keep repeating ourselves; we put on a new face, call it a new interpretation, and puff up with pride.) I began with the deceitful courtesan Aegina (Igor Moiseyev's choreography), then portrayed Frigia, the loyal wife of the leader of the slaves (this work by Leonid Yakobson is danced entirely on demi-pointe). And then I returned to the treacherous Aegina (I don't feel like mentioning the name of the choreographer).

This last production was praised to the skies by the increasingly decrepit members of Brezhnev's Politburo, who directly imposed their impoverished "revolutionary" taste. They said that the bushy-browed general secretary himself, heavily laden with the military decorations awarded to him a hundred times over, "wisely pointed out" the similarity between the rebel Spartacus and the false images of the Bolshevik leaders invented by clever little scribblers. They said that Communists hadn't descended from Mars to the peoples of the world but that they had ancestors predating the birth of Christ. Whoever doesn't recognize the Communist pathos in the history of ancient Rome and doesn't crow "Hurrah" with all his might is an enemy of the people. Sing "Alleluia" and cry "Hurrah" until you're hoarse . . .

During the rehearsals, my body rejected the choreography. There was something artificial, illogical. I forced myself. I didn't want to retreat. They would say that I was finished, that I couldn't dance any more. In the adagio with Crassus I had to grab my toe with my hand and pull away in attitude from my partner, who held me in counterbalance. The muscles of my spine were twisted like laundry being wrung out. I repeated the awkward position dozens of times. And I tore my muscles slightly. I had already danced five performances, but the sensation of a piece of wood stuck in my spine did not go away. No matter what I was doing as I danced, I kept worrying about how my spine would react.

An interesting tour in Argentina was coming up for me. It was 1978. The World Championship in soccer was just about to begin there. My fame was at its peak. I had already been to Argentina, and the audience there loved me. The organizers of the championship games had come up with the idea of Maya Plisetskaya opening the first match with a symbolic kick. I enthusiastically agreed.

Three days before leaving, as I packed, I pulled down a suitcase from a high shelf. Something shifted in my spine and I winced; it put me on guard. But the pain seemed to ease. That night unbearable pain suddenly hit me. The pain was so sharp that my teeth began to chatter involuntarily and I ran a high fever.

Shchedrin called an ambulance. The good-hearted, sympathetic woman physician gave me several injections. Going on a trip was out of the question. I fell into oblivion. Shchedrin manned the telephone constantly. We needed a brilliant specialist. Katya Maximova, who had just been seriously ill with the same spinal condition, gave him Vladimir Ivanovich Luchkov's telephone number. He had been a tremendous help to her. Shchedrin made arrangements with him by phone and drove him to our house. He made an excellent impression. "You'll fly in two days, now let's begin the treatment."

He did everything under the sun to me. But I really did feel better, and set off limping to the other end of the world.

I had to change planes in Paris. The pain had begun to return after the first four hours of flying. I spent the entire day in bed in Paris at the apartment of our most kind diplomat, N. N. Afanasyevsky (his wife, Larisa, played the violin in the Bolshoi Theater orchestra). I was already half-dead when they drove me to the airport late at night and put me on an Argentine plane. The twenty-hour flight to Buenos Aires was torment. My teeth began to chatter again. The people who met me at the airport were stunned by my appearance. The soccer match was impossible, dancing was out of the question. Impresario David Tsvilik tore his hair out, "Disaster, ruin!"

I was in bed at the Hotel Esmeralda, watching T.V. out of the corner of my eye — the championship game was opening without me. The pain drove me crazy. The local doctor, Dushatsky, gave me a barbaric injection in the hip which made me howl round the clock and let the entire hotel know. I talked with Shchedrin on the telephone. He was wearing Luchkov out with questions. The advice over the telephone didn't help. Maybe Luchkov's arrival would have helped, but it would have taken a Soviet physician a good half-year to do the paperwork for a trip to Argentina. Then Shchedrin called Melbourne. The legendary chiropractor Frank Foster lived there. He had magically put me back on my feet in 1970 during my Australian tour. He immediately agreed to fly over and bought an expensive ticket at his own expense. People like this still exist on planet Earth!

Frank's treatment did help, and I danced the last of the planned performances. I danced it with much trepidation, with half my usual output, at the theater in Colón, another city on the tour. Alas, it wasn't in Buenos Aires.

The impresario, trying to set his financial affairs right, announced in the press that Plisetskaya was well and would dance the program as planned at the Colón Theater. Above and beyond the call. People who had not yet returned their tickets to the box office were welcome. Journalists packed the rehearsal hall and informed the press of even the minutest details concerning the state of my health. There was a great big stir!

Frank Foster worked with me for the last time in the pool. He gave me his blessing and flew back home to Australia. He could no longer stay away from his clinic; his patients were protesting.

The day of the performance arrived.

Everyone was nervous. I didn't show it, but in the depth of my soul I knew that this was reckless, that I had agreed to a provocative offer for nothing. My spinal nerve had not healed completely, and I should have flown home instead of indulging in a risky venture.

I put my makeup on, warmed up fully. Everything seemed to be fine. I went to put on an Isadora Duncan-style tunic I would open with. And suddenly right near the door, I fell on the floor like a wounded bird, nearly losing consciousness from the sudden fierce pain. My right knee went numb and completely lost all feeling. God, what suffering!

A glum staff person from the theater management came out from behind the closed curtain and made the announcement in the graveyard silence: "The performance is canceled. Plisetskaya was taken to the hospital by ambulance." The audience gasped heavily. I myself didn't hear this. I'm going by what my partner on that tour, Valery Kovtun, told me.

Having suffered defeat, I returned to Moscow and went into the hospital for a whole month for treatment with Luchkov. Vladimir Ivanovich treated me seriously and thoroughly. He was expert with nerve blocks and gave me many of them. Then he sent me to a sanitarium in Piatigorsk for traction and radon baths.

I could go on and on with this long, joyless, and agonizing tale. It took a long time before I could get right after the severe injury. I'll end this part of the story by saying that it took three months before Luchkov allowed me to go on pointe, and four months before I could dance *The Swan* in a ballet concert. He himself sat in the first row of the orchestra; before my entrance onstage I looked at him through a metal-ringed hole in the curtain—he looked as if he were covered with flour, his face frozen and tense with anticipation. The talented physician was more worried than I was. How could you ever forget something like this?

Memories about injuries rush one after another. Every disruption and laborious healing is an entire small novel . . .

The premiere of *The Seagull* with a broken second toe on my left foot in Florence. Before every rehearsal and every performance I froze the toe with chlorethyl and spent a good hour painstakingly "stuffing" my foot into the ballet slipper, cutting out an impossibly strange pattern in the satin with scissors.

And the *Seagull* again. This time in Moscow. During the "flights" that open the ballet, where I am lifted up and lowered into a cube of black velvet by four partners in black suits, black masks, and black gloves who were invisible to the audience (the entire adagio takes place in impenetrable darkness, only the white top of my body and outspread arms are lit) one of the four, Lyova Trubchikov, tripped during the first turn, held onto my foot for a second longer than necessary and . . . A hellish sprain for me. Another freezing during the two-minute break backstage, the chlorethyl, the tight wrapping. I danced the entire ballet on cottony legs, drowning in cold sweat.

Another—the thousandth—reworking of *Swan Lake*. Distracted by chatting in a draft on the upper stage—there's a horrible draft along the floor—I began rehearsing with cooled down legs. What a dope! This time it's my calf. A tear. Misha Gabovich, Jr., carries me down below. The masseur Gotovitsky, always tipsy, burns my torn calf to the bone with chlorethyl. He didn't spare the state's poison, the dear. Shreds of skin, an open, oozing purple-red wound. There was no way to get near it. It was only when the wound started healing that they put a cast on it. Time slips by. I languish in agony at home in my bed. I hobble on crutches to the toilet. Golyakhovsky, the surgeon from the Central Scientific Research Institute of Traumatology and Orthopedics, travels clear across Moscow two or three times a day to my house to see me. Five months torn out of my life . . .

The legendary white-haired Polish professor Grutza, whom I especially fly to Warsaw several times to see, repairs my overworked knee. He uses the Bernard currents, a medical innovation at the time.

How many of my dancing days did I spend on the sidelines, out of the game! The number is horrifying. It's always so hard to find the strength within to rise from the ashes.

Chapter Nineteen

Who'll Get Whom!

I'll return to the theater, to my life in 1948.

In May, toward the end of the season — my fifth — a new director was appointed: Alexander Vasilyevich Solodovnikov. His "reign" was a dark period in my life in the theater. If everything up to that point had been attained through effort and mastery, then the malice initiating from the top turned my life into a day-in, day-out unfair fight. Today I can imagine that someone even higher in rank assigned him the task of "inhibiting" me. But at that time everything for me centered on Solodovnikov.

Unattractive, stoop-shouldered, with large eyeglasses, he always wore a white shirt and tie, but his suit was perpetually wrinkled, with protruding pockets. He could be preserved for posterity on any bulletin board of industry leaders. He also had a briefcase with which he never parted. In a word, the stereotypical Soviet manager with his briefcase.

Solodovnikov began his "anti-Plisetskaya" campaign with a newspaper article on young talent at the Bolshoi Theater. He gave all my sisters compliments and sent them on their way with useful advice. Me, he didn't mention at all. As if Maya Plisetskaya did not exist, either in the theater or in life. People read the few current newspapers in a particular way then — nothing was spelled out, yet it all meant something. Completely in the Chinese manner. The order the names were listed in, who followed whom, whose initials were used, whose names were written out, who was granted an adjective, and who received an entire sentence. Who was "talented," who was "gifted," who was just "young." And here I was — with photographs in *Ogonyok*, *Swan Lake*, a gold medal at the youth festival — well, I had disappeared, evaporated, I was missing without a trace. Solodovnikov's article did not go unnoticed by the theater world. Some people became anxious, others perplexed; some quietly sympathized, others began avoiding me. The pattern was repeated on more than one occasion. Only the stakes were raised.

I went to the director to have a talk. Bearing a grudge would have been worse. But just try and get through to the director's office past the Cerberuses. Dozens of times I tried to explain why, for what reason, in what connection. The long-awaited audience arrives. His eyeglasses flash, go dull.

"What article? Oh, yes. But it was about young dancers. You, you're a mature master. A leading dancer of the repertoire."

I hastened to note that the others named were ten to fifteen years older than me, with rank. I had been in the theater only five years. Solodovnikov got up from his desk. The conversation was over. He had government obligations, And there I was, bothering him.

Fedor Pimenovich Bondarenko, the previous director, whose years coincided with my first years there, did not bother with details — who danced which role, who sang, who danced solo. And he was gentle, accessible, forgiving. There was no room for such liberals in the imperial theater in 1948. The authorities had just taken care of Mikhail Zoshchenko and Anna Akhmatova, they had flogged the guilty formalist composers, various Shostakoviches, Prokofievs, Khachaturians. Order had to be restored in the theater as well, discipline had to be firmly established. And Solodovnikov rolled up his sleeves and worked himself into a frenzy. I don't know what things were like in the opera, but in the ballet he began controlling who danced in every troika and every group of six; and as for the ballerina parts, Lavrovsky didn't dare make decisions on his own, without the director. Here a sharp Party eye was needed. Otherwise someone with an unreliable family history might . . .

The choreographers tried to give me parts in their productions, as they had in the past, in order to get around Solodovnikov's "General Plan of Constructing the Ballet." Rostislav Zakharov gave me the likable part of the Maiden in *Ruslan*. That was the first breach of Solodovnikov's fortress. The vigilant Party knight hadn't paid adequate attention to dances in the operas. Dancers also got sick and sprained their legs. That's why I became necessary in *Swan Lake* once again, when I replaced the ailing Semyonova for a long time. To quote a Nikolai Tikhonov poem, popular at the time, you could "forge Bolshevik nails" from an iron woman like Golovkina, but even she caught a cold, came down with angina, and ceded *Raymonda*. I was still alive and kicking! Although from time to time on weekdays I would be bumped into some nonballerina part like a bride in *Swan Lake*. Or I'd see my name on the office bulletin board. But I had my own response to this. I took sick leave. I said I was ill. We'll see who gets whom!

And then there was the Komsomol. Thronged meetings: Plisetskaya raked over the coals there for not attending political lessons, shirking dialectical study. In the early morning, my eyes barely open, I performed the heroic deed of arriving twice by 9:00 A.M., all in a lather, on our day off from the theater (blessed Monday) at the House of Art Workers on Pushechnaya Street. That's where ignoramuses in the art world advanced their knowledge of the foundations of Marxism-Leninism. They gave unending, boring lectures: What hairy Marx had prophesied to the Russian proletariat a hundred years before, how Engels wrestled with the scoundrel Duhring, Lenin's April-May-June-July Theses from the armored car at the Finland Station, the divine revelations of the bewhiskered Stalin, and other mumbo-jumbo. I didn't understand a thing. I stared blankly, feigning genuine interest. I dozed. I wasn't able to attend a third time. Catching up on sleep was better; I had performances on Tuesdays.

And so I was punished: angry rebukes from Komsomol members, Party activists, and my colleagues, who raged most scathingly. I was a truant, an apolitical individual, an ill-intentioned element. I mumbled something in justification. (Noise of general condemnation.) Then for an entire month my name was displayed on the bulletin board of official notices near the office, singled out for general humiliation. So-and-so misses, doesn't attend . . . Oh, is that so? Now I really wouldn't attend. We'll see who gets whom!

It was Fayer's birthday on January 20, at the very beginning of 1949. I ran into him on our staircase landing, and he, deeply moved, suddenly invited me to a family celebration that evening. After all, he had conducted *Raymonda* for me the night before. It was supposedly a triumph.

And who were the guests?

The composer Nikolai Semyonovich Golovanov and his wife, singer Antonina Vasilyevna Nezhdanova, the airplane designer Alexander Yakovlev (Have you flown on any Yaks, reader?), the singer Sergei Lemeshev, and Ekaterina Vasilyevna Geltser. We were sitting and eating our crab salads, sipping our vodkas, nibbling hors d'oeuvres of pearly caviar—the shop counters were loaded with crab and caviar at that time. This may have been the period of terror, with the battle against cosmopolitanism at its heyday, but there was plenty to eat everywhere. The logic, of course, is idiotic. But that's how things were.

The doorbell rang in the foyer. It was Solodovnikov. He took off his fur coat and shook hands with everyone. His false smile slipped off his face when he turned toward me. A slight turn to Fayer. How do you explain this? Embarrassed, Fayer quickly said, "She's my neighbor, she's a neighbor, a neighbor . . ."

The scene was so painful that I left after ten minutes without making a sound or saying goodbye. I was proud. Why should I be treated this way? I won't be taken alive. Who'll get whom!

But that season I had more free time than usual. I joyfully agreed to an offer from Kasyan Yaroslavich Goleizovsky to do several concert numbers at the Tchaikovsky Concert Hall. We took the bull by the horns. The first rehearsal was in the ballet school in two days. We started with Chopin's Sixth Waltz.

Goleizovsky would have been a hundred years old in 1992.* A most striking figure in the history of the Russian ballet, who had nothing in common with anyone else, he was truly unique. An experimenter, an inventor, a visionary, an original, an eccentric.

Kasyan Goleizovsky's name had more resonance in the 1920s. He created the dazzling *Legend of Joseph* with music by Sergei Vasilenko on the Bolshoi stage. (Incidentally, Shchedrin's father, Konstantin Mikhailovich, graduated from the Moscow Conservatory under Vasilenko at that time. Just an aside.)

The Legend of Joseph was a real sensation. Back in 1916, even before the Bolshevik coup, Kasyan Yaroslavich had stunned Orthodox Russia with a mass spectacle featuring half-nude girls who formed miraculous wavelike images with their entwined arms. Twenty or so years later in Hollywood, they would call them showgirls. But showgirl revues had their origins in Russia with Goleizovsky.

And what was their creator doing in the 1930s and 1940s? Working as a night watchman in a grocery store next to his refuge. There was no unemployment in Stalin's empire; every citizen was required to be employed somewhere. And who was going to employ a pernicious modernist, a free-thinker, who hadn't the foggiest notion about socialist realism? They wouldn't hear of it. His wife, Vera Petrovna Vasilyeva, danced in the Bolshoi Ballet, and the family lived poorly on her wages and his watchman's salary and raised their son Nikita, an icon painter.

I came to Leningrad in 1959 to attend a Shchedrin concert and became seriously ill at the Grand Hotel Europa. I lay in bed. A young maid, who found out

*He died in Moscow in 1970.

that I was a ballerina, told me that the Moscow choreographer Goleizovsky had been living on the same floor a week ago (a wealthy amateur dance club had sponsored his trip for some production).

"What an interesting person! He's seen so much, he's traveled all around the world. He lived in Spain for several years. He knows every castle there."

But Goleizovsky had never traveled anywhere but Moscow, St. Petersburg, and the little village of Byokhovo on the Oka River, where he gathered mushrooms and odd plant roots. He was a classic nonexportable type! But his furious imagination took him everywhere, round the world, to Spain for several years, through the back alleys of Paris, to pray in the pagodas of Thailand, become intoxicated with the beauties of China, and hunt with the aborigines of Australia. He never lied, but he always fantasized freely.

Lamentable as it is to write about it, my creative romance with Goleizovsky never materialized. Naturally, I was to blame for this: my personality. A performer had to dissolve completely in Goleizovsky. The dancer is a blind person, and Goleizovsky is the guide. I wasn't able to do this; my native disobedience burst from every pore, challenging the choreographer.

We prepared that concert gradually for more than three months. It consisted of five ballet numbers with musical interludes: *Sleeping Beauty* in an eccentric interpretation with a half-mad Prince Désiré (Leonid Zhdanov). Chopin's Waltz with the pianist Yuri Bryushkov in the center of the stage. I was a cloud, which at times floated around the musician and at times caressed the piano. Scriabin, whom he idolized all his life (I still don't know whether they actually were friends, as he loved to say, or whether it was also just a phantasmagoria: Scriabin was forty-two when he died, and Goleizovsky was twenty-three at the time). Liadov's "Miniatures." And an incoherent (God forgive us our transgressions) whale of a number on a Soviet theme.

The concert could not have taken place without a patriotic tribute. My partner was the cumbersome, athletic Lapauri. He portrayed a disgusting fascist, and I a bold partisan. For ten minutes we rode around in white cloaks, crawled after each other on the floor, hid, and wrestled. But at the end, as befits the invincible Soviet warrior, I savagely strangled him. The German shuddered convulsively and froze. Finally, rising to my full height, I threw off my cloak, and the audience saw that the conquering hero was a woman. Who got whom? Even Lilya Yuyevna Brik, whom I'd met the year before, and who had her fill of Futurists, was completely baffled. (I had become acquainted with Brik the year before through the journalist Vladimir Orlov and his wife, Lusya—we met at the Matsesta baths, where I was finishing treatments for a sprain.) But how grateful I am to fate for those three miraculous months of work with Goleizovsky. How they propelled me forward!

In 1959 Kasyan Yaroslavich created a Spanish dance for me to Shchedrin's music. It also premiered at the Tchaikovsky Concert Hall, and Rodion himself played the piano (this piece is now part of the Bolshoi repertory; the composer called it "In the Manner of Albéniz"). But this was no masterpiece either.

But what a masterpiece Goleizovsky created for Vasilyev — *Narcissus* to Cherepnin's music. I was breathless with happiness every time I saw this incomparable number. And the series of Scriabin miniatures, Shaporin's *Incantation,* and finally the full-length feature *Layla and Majnun* (music by Balasanyan), staged by the master near the end of his days, when the artistic censorship of the Party relaxed its tentacles slightly. Nonetheless, this obsessed artist, full of creative imagination, could never fully realize himself in this terrible Soviet nation.

Swan Lake brought me out of this dark period again. The minister of culture, Vladimir Lebedev, attended one of the performances in which I was replacing someone. What else would Lebedev (whose name comes from the word for swan, *lebed*) attend but *Swan Lake?* His position was called chairman then, not minister. Chairman of the Arts Commission of the Soviet of National Commissars of the USSR. The God and tsar of performing artists and musicians.

I danced well that evening. The atmosphere was electric, as if for an opening night. The audience was thrilled and applauded for a long time. There were flowers and cries of "Bravo." The performance captivated Lebedev. He praised me right and left. I found out from a third party that our influential chairman insisted on including the "young ballerina M. Plisetskaya" in the list of artists recommended by the Commission of the Arts for the most important gala in the Kremlin to mark the occasion of Stalin's seventieth birthday. It was a long while before the performance, nearly a whole month — it was the end of December, and everything could change two hundred times. But something inside me repeated over and over that it would happen, that I would win.

Who'll get whom? . . .

Chapter Twenty

Stalin's Birthday

Historians could name the date without a second thought: December 21, 1949.

Gung-ho Communists on all the continents of the planet were rabid, despicably zealous to celebrate the bloody tyrant's birthday ever more grandly. Every hour, deceived laborers were instructed that this day was more significant than that of Christ's birth. Our socialist brother nations racked their brains looking for ways to surprise the benefactor of mankind on his bright holiday. They even created a museum of gifts presented to the crowned leader. The newspapers printed oceans of telegrams and letters addressed to "Dear Iosif Vissarionovich." People outdid themselves in servile flattery, trying to distinguish themselves and invent still more words and ways to more ecstatically lick the pock-marked, bewhiskered dictator's mug. Poets wrote odes, composers wrote songs, skilled weavers wove carpets. And artists dreamt of performing in the state's jubilee concert.

This is how I see it now. At that time, just participating in the jubilee performance eclipsed everything else.

The news reached us in waves. At times my name was seen on this most august list, at other times it disappeared from the list, and then later reappeared. Of course it meant the excerpt from *Swan Lake*. That's what Lebedev had decided. But it turned out otherwise.

The theater invited Vakhtang Chabukiani, a dancer as renowned as Ulanova and Semyonova, from Tbilisi to dance *Don Quixote*. Let all distinguished Georgians bring their art to their great compatriot on the threshold of this planetary holiday!

They selected the entire first cast, but there was no one to dance Mercedes, the street dancer, a secondary but vivid scene. Cherkasova, our leaping soloist, was ill. (How many times did I have to play the role of lifesaver?)

I mastered Mercedes in two rehearsals. And I performed the part with spirit, dressed in a black costume with flounces, lined with red ruffles, which I hastily made myself (Mercedes used to wear a white blouse with necklaces and a green skirt). It was a thundering success. Everyone praised me. My legs were light, and I jumped to the very heavens. The audience roared. Why not treat the generalissimo to a championship jump on his seventieth birthday?

Shashkin summoned me into his abominable little room near the main office.

"It falls to your lot to receive the highest honor. You'll take part in the Kremlin concert on December 22. Instructions from the Collegium."

(What sort of "Collegium" — the Creator?)

"You must dance the jumping variation from *Don Quixote*. The daily rehearsals are in the large hall of the Conservatory."

The many hours of waiting began. No class, no breakfast, just sit the entire day on the creaking Conservatory chairs. Wait till you're called. The orchestra seats were filled with focused, attentive gentlemen observers. The Commission, the Collegium, NKVD security — everyone was right there. They were comparing the performers' faces with their personnel files.

Every number was run through a hundred times. Bows, exits and entrances, curtsies to the god. I'm writing "god" in lower case because Stalin was short.

Kozlovsky and Mikhailov kept singing a duet over and over. A folk song. They were on the verge of losing their voices. They sang with all their might, no slacking off allowed. Vera Davydova, for whom the Caucasian heart of the People's Commander beat with secret passion (Moscow was filled with rumors), kept repeating and repeating her velvet aria. Quite a number of arias were changed, they wanted to choose one that was just right . . . Valeria Varsova, a famous coloratura of the time, a heavy, squat woman, became chilled and wrapped herself in her Orenburg shawl. The Conservatory Hall isn't the warmest in Moscow. Lepeshinskaya languished. State concerts did not take place without her. Stalin was fond of her and had nicknamed her "Dragonfly" (rumors again). Besides, concert organizers never forgot that the ballerina's husband was a comrade-in-arms of the cannibal Beria. NKVD generals were terribly feared.

Once again, things were not going well for me. The jumping variation is a little thing, some forty seconds. Hardly enough time for the birthday boy and his honored guests to examine the young talent, to admire the virtuosity of the jumps. I was supposed to repeat the solo twice the next day. I jumped a second time, but this time from the other foot. No good, either. The music was the same, it sounded like a street organ.

The following day, I simply sat around. I wasn't asked to dance. It looked as if I would be dropped from the concert.

Lavrovsky proposed an "artistic" solution to the commission. The pianist would play the jumping variation from *Laurencia,* and I would dance the *Don Quixote* choreography twice. The experts agreed to it. I tied things together with difficulty: I had to dance and choreograph. But the Conservatory stage is spacious, wide, and I leaped with all my might. I did my best. I couldn't be dropped from the concert—I'd be trampled, ridiculed: you didn't suit them. They'd consider it my fault.

The Collegium Commission was satisfied. They called me over, to ask if a red tutu wouldn't be better. It was a red-letter day, a great day for all of humanity. Naturally, I agreed. If they had suggested that I dance in a camouflage suit, I would have submitted. There was no going back. I'd be trampled, ridiculed.

And what color, Comrade Plisetskaya, will your headdress be, will it match? And your hairdo? They were interested in everything, the vermin. They were watching.

The jubilee was celebrated a day after his calendar birthdate.

Now everything in sequence: the details, trivia, fears.

The concert was to begin at 6 P.M. (maybe it was 7 P.M., I don't remember). But we had to be at the theater by noon. That I remember for sure. Makeup was to be applied in the theater. Nothing extraneous was to be brought. Better to put costumes on right then and there. We pleaded, "We'll cool down, we won't be able to get into character. It's December out there. Freezing cold. The opera performers are in tails and full-length gowns." You don't feel too cozy in a tutu with your thighs exposed six hours before going onstage. They gave us permission. There's a whole squadron of freeloaders and spongers escorting us. On their faces—profundity, devotion, and zeal.

We applied foundation, then our makeup. Lined our eyes. Arranged our hair. I pinned a red rose to one side. The guards looked the flower over carefully. It really was paper.

Then we sat in the director's box for a long time. We maintained a solemn silence. We vied with one another in conveying the most heartfelt trembling in our faces. Everyone was a super patriot, but who's the most?

In addition to the Bolshoi artists, the pianist Emil Gilels, and soloists from the Moiseyev Ensemble, there were several performers from the republics. The unshakable friendship between the brotherly peoples had to be shown in all its glory. I remember the Azeri Byul-Byul and Tamara Khanum from Uzbekistan.

A courier arrived noiselessly—the cars were ready. We slowly filed out to the first entrance. We got in. We were counted. Everyone accounted for.

We drove off.

There was a long security check at the Kremlin gate, the conversation in hushed tones. The contents of bags were checked carefully and unhurriedly. They went through our things vigilantly—tights, ballet shoes with ribbons, shoe horns. The accompanists' scores were leafed through from cover to cover. Everything in order. Nothing suspicious. Proceed.

At the entrance to the stage door, the procedure was repeated with redoubled effort. They checked passes against a list, cleared the list with a supervisor (each car had one), matched the supervisor with the passes and each pass with its mysterious numbers and stamp with a document from the theater. Of course, you had your pass with you. A lengthy comparison of your facial features in the pass photo with the real thing. Another glance at the stamp, "December 22, 1949, the Kremlin."

Proceed.

We did.

We were assigned to cramped dressing rooms. Our names were on the doors. Another long security check. You're probably bored reading about it. But the time before the call to go onstage lasted an eternity.

I whispered to Lepeshinskaya. Is there a toilet here? Yes, the next door over. I walked out. This startled the guards in the corridor. What's this? . . . I entered the bathroom, feeling guilty, like a shadow. At least there was no one there. Space and freedom. What if there was someone invisible? . . .

We took turns warming up, leaning on a table, in a cramped little room. Not enough room for two people to limber up. We seemed to be ready. We waited to be called.

General Vlasik, the head of Stalin's secret service, personally checked the bathrooms with a small flock of well-built, disciplined adjutants. He didn't greet anyone, just stared straight into your guts so hard it made your skin crawl.

The concert began.

The ceremony was held in St. George's Hall in the Kremlin. The performers took turns diving through a massive forged iron door opened by two light-haired grenadiers. There were probing eyes along the hallway—like searchlights, they burned right through you. Many eyes.

The little box of rosin was also guarded. A special guard stood by it. I waxed my shoes. I was trembling a bit. They had scared me to death. I was not up to dancing. Balaksheyev was emceeing the concert. I heard my name like an echo. Irina Mikhailovna Golovina, I can only guess at her rank and position, whispered in a panic, "Do your very best, Mayechka. . ." The door opened. I plunged.

Blinding light.

Everything was golden.

The emperor's bewhiskered face was in the first row at a long festive table, facing away from the stage and half-turned to me, blurred by my fear and the bright light. Mao was next to him. I took my preparation and the piano sounded. Lord, get me through this!

The first jump. Catastrophe. The floor was parquet, waxed and polished to a gleam. Just don't let me slip and fall; that's all I thought about.

I don't remember how well or how badly I danced. But I held out, I managed not to fall. I heard the muffled applause. Stalin bent over and said something to Mao Zedong. The face of the nameless translator floated up between them, as if on a paper tracing. What were the ones who control fates talking about? I bowed, smiled a forced smile, and, since I was told not to linger, dove into the gold and white half-opened door. I caught myself thinking that I had lowered my eyes to the floor during my curtsy. Years later, I can admit that it was too horrible for me to meet Stalin's glance. Intuitively.

No one responded. Everyone was busy with the next number. Drained, I wandered over to my little room. I sat immobile in front of the mirror for a long time. My face was drawn; it wasn't mine. I removed the red rose. I was dead tired. I would catch my breath and then change . . .

There was a short TASS communiqué in the morning papers about the holiday concert in the Kremlin. And my name was in it. This was a victory. Now I could fight for my future. Just wait and see, they would give me something new to dance.

Chapter Twenty-One

I Dance in Don Quixote, I Dance in Golovanov's Opera

The something new to dance was *Don Quixote*.

After the street dancer, I studied Kitri. This part, like the Swan, has been with me through my entire life. (Like the Persian in *Khovanshchina* when Nikolai Semyonovich Golovanov conducted.)

After the "Christmas" concert for Stalin's seventieth birthday, my ill-wishers tucked in their tails slightly. Shashkin began greeting me first and even cracking the slit of his thin mouth into the semblance of a smile: Plisetskaya hadn't let him down, she had acted bravely (word about the waxed stage of St. George's Hall in the Kremlin made its way to the ears of the company). Even Solodovnikov dropped by the director's box during one of my performances and waved his program from behind the edge, pretending to be friendly.

Summoning up my courage, I began a conversation with the head of the ballet about a pay raise, a conversation I felt demeaning to me. My pay had been frozen since 1945. I was dancing leading ballerina parts yet receiving the pay of a third-level soloist. Looking through my journal entries of those years, I came across a tearful sentence, "The brides . . . in the third act of my *Lake* . . . are getting paid almost a thousand more than I am. Whom should I ask?" And so I made up my mind. I asked. The material aspect of it was important but secondary. I still took every chance to participate in exhausting concert performances. That was the main source for my family's subsistence. But the prestige aspect, the issue of my position in the hierarchy of the ballet collective, was the primary one.

They now granted me more smiles, but my timid request was ignored. Yes, yes, they said, of course, we remember, we're not forgetting, we appreciate you, but it's difficult at the present moment, we'll work on it, don't worry. That's what the conversation was like. They didn't give me a damn thing.

But they gave me Kitri without any red tape. I threw myself into the work. Elena Ilyushchenko was the rehearsal coach. I've already mentioned her. Sharp-tongued, always cool-headed, and thorough. She usually wore something polka-dot or plaid. At rehearsals, Elena Mikhailovna called me "a force of nature." She carefully tracked how the choreographer's text was executed and punished improvisation with righteous anger. My partner was Yuri Kondratov.

Theater schedules came out three times a month and covered ten days. I was indescribably thrilled at seeing my name next to Kitri's part in *Don Quixote* on March 10, 1950. Would I really get to dance Kitri without the usual monkey wrench in the works?

The performance was a success. I was on a roll. It's easier to work and rehearse when intrigues are not being cooked up every day. The mention of my name in the press release by TASS about the jubilee concert kept me afloat for a good half-year.

There were amusing incidents during the premiere. In the first act, while finishing a variation of turns on the diagonal, I lost my balance and wound up on the floor at the end, perfectly in time with the music. As if that were the way it was supposed to be. You could rehearse for ages and never pull off anything like that. The audience appreciated my resourcefulness and applauded to their heart's content. In the dream scene I was eight bars late with my entrance onstage—the directors hadn't warned me that the dream would immediately follow the forest scene. I heard the music and ran toward the stage wing. This run took exactly eight bars. But it worked out all right—Amour turned to face me by the ninth bar. And I was right there, as if summoned. Everything went smoothly. In the final pas de deux I did eight fouettés perfectly, but during the last four I leaned off to the side. The final pose was not centered.

I took many bows. When the curtain fell, the entire troupe—everyone on stage—burst into applause. Ulanova came backstage, said cordial words, and gave me a copy of a book about Maria Taglioni, which she inscribed on the title page, "I wish Maya Plisetskaya a great life in art." She was animated and excited.

There was another spectator, whom I found out about many years later: thirteen-year-old Rudolf Nureyev, who happened to be passing through Moscow by chance that evening. When friends from St. Petersburg told me about it later, I inquired about his reaction.

"Nureyev cried after the first act," was their answer.

When we met, I ask Rudi whether this was true or just friendly exaggeration on their part.

"It's not true. I didn't cry, I sobbed. Sobbed from happiness. You set the stage on fire."

And there was *Khovanshchina*.

In those years the powerful musician Nikolai Semyonovich Golovanov was principal conductor at the Bolshoi Theater. He was married to the legendary Antonina Vasilyevna Nezhdanova (a cozy street in the center of Moscow bears her name; Shostakovich, Khachaturian, the entire Moscow Conservatory, Geltser, Meyerhold, Bersenev, Ermolayev, Obukhova, Maksakova lived on it; it's where the Composers' Union is located.)

Golovanov had his own scores to settle with the Soviet system. He was from a clergyman's family and always wore a bowtie, a shiny frockcoat, and a beat-up turn-of-the-century raccoon coat. He graduated from the Moscow Conservatory in Sergei Vasilenko's class as a composer, but became enamored of conducting; he had no equals when it came to performing Russian music. In the early 1930s Stalin smeared Golovanov in the press with a devastating, dramatic comment. He used the term *Golovanshchina* to castigate the conductor's naive, dictatorial tendencies. (And what conductor is not a dictator!) He was saying, in effect, "Rejoice, people, that you are lucky enough to be living in the most democratic and free nation. We won't let anyone trample on workers' and peasants' rights!"

It's a miracle that Golovanov was not imprisoned. Perhaps his wife's fame deflected the threat? Then again, did anything ever stop Stalin? These are my own speculations. The tyrant loved to play cat-and-mouse games. He loved it when individuals blessed with talent unintentionally flashed through his court retinue, occasionally even those with titles (like the writer Prince Alexei Tolstoy or Prince Ignatiev, author of the memoirs *Fifty Years in the Marching Column*), or were progeny of the clergy (Golovanov the conductor; Maxim Dormidontovich Mikhailov, the singer).

Golovanov may not have been imprisoned, but he was dismissed from the Bolshoi Theater. Why plant prerevolutionary nobility in the nation's main theater? Golovanov surfaced on the radio. And then he returned to the theater. I'm not aware of how things worked behind the scenes of his life, but Golovanov took up the conductor's baton a second time.

Nikolai Semyonovich had already noticed me in *Sadko*. I danced the sweet variation of the Needle Fish that Lavrovsky had created for the underwater scene in Rimsky-Korsakov's opera. I apparently danced it musically, because Golovanov, who still cursed everyone and everything as he used to (perhaps without obscenities now), was gracious and cordial to me. I once witnessed an entirely uncomplimentary flow of words from the conductor's stand across the silenced orchestra toward the stage to Vera Davydova, the leader's favorite:

"Come now, why are you howling like a wolf?"

The favorite, impossibly spoiled by sycophants, would run away from the rehearsal in tears.

He gave a whipping to Veronika Borisenko, a striking, lush contralto. She was the stout, full-breasted favorite of the Chief Musician Andrei Zhdanov, the ideologue of Stalin's court, who had no aversion to showing off in company in a general's military jacket:

"It's your boyfriend-generals who tell you that you sing purely. I'm telling you there's not a single live note . . ."

And the portly favorite minced off the stage in tears. It's difficult to believe, but Golovanov got away with it.

He was the one who chose me as one of the Persians in *Khovanshchina*.

To this day, Shchedrin is convinced that nature gave me the gift of perfect pitch, though I can (barely) read music. It's not for me to judge. But I do hear music, I distinguish the many half-tones an orchestra plays. Whether or not I have perfect pitch, I do genuinely have a good ear. It would be more accurate to say that I'm musical. This is why I think Golovanov was favorably inclined toward me.

Sergei Gavrilovich Koren choreographed the dances in *Khovanshchina*. He entered the annals of Russian ballet as an incomparable performer of Mercutio in Lavrovsky's Moscow production of *Romeo and Juliet*. Koren didn't create many works, and I think that the Persian is his most successful one.

Koren staged the whole role on me. After Prince Ivan Khovansky's words, "You there, in the women's quarters, send in the Persian girls," I was supposed to be the first, after the women's corps de ballet, to float into the boyar's rooms of the rebellious Moscow grandee. In the music there is languor, voluptuousness, and passion (at the time, Koren and I had never in our born days heard the word *sex*). Wrapped at first in a chiffon shawl, I then glide in circles, my navel naked in belly dancing style, clapping my hands like a tambourine, and arouse Khovansky's passion. I keep exciting him—there's a big crescendo in the music— while I'm like a lotus in the wind, and the Prince loses his self-control and lunges toward me . . . The chorus sings "White swan . . ." And that's when he is stabbed in the back. The rebellion is quelled.

I liked everything that Koren choreographed very much. And the music is exceptionally beautiful. But when orchestral rehearsals with Golovanov began, goose bumps began to creep over my entire body. At the culminating point of the music, which I secretly and greedily waited for every evening, a stream of goose bumps would turn my spine ice cold. I attributed this entirely to Mussorgsky. But when another conductor got behind the stand to take Golovanov's place, and the time for goose bumps came at the climax of the melody . . . they didn't appear. It was the same music, the same tempo, the same orchestra. And nothing—absolutely zero. No chills. This was when I realized what a conductor really is.

Lepeshinskaya also rehearsed the Persian, although she joined the work later than I did. Golovanov was a gentleman at the final orchestra rehearsals. The entire opera was rehearsed once, only the Persians were repeated twice: once for Lepeshinskaya, once for me. Then it was time for the dress rehearsals. And Golovanov openly expressed his preference. I was given three dress rehearsals and the two first premieres of the ballet. He really wasn't afraid of anyone. Someone grumbled indistinctly:

"We'll remind him of Golovanshchina yet."

That year Antonina Vasilyevna Nezhdanova died. She and Nikolai Semyonovich had spent their entire lives together, but she was a lot older than he was. Golovanov survived his wife's death with great difficulty. The theater decided to hold a concert in her memory on October 9. Golovanov met me in the hallway of the first floor of the theater and asked me to participate in the evening. I thought it appropriate to dance the *Dying Swan*.

An enormous portrait of Antonina Vasilyevna, covered in flowers, was raised at the back of the stage on a white background. And then, performing the *Swan*, near the finale of the number, with my back to the audience, I stretched my arms toward her in front of me, as if saying good-bye. The lights were slowly dimmed. Golovanov was deeply moved.

Within a short time, Nikolai Semyonovich was also gone. I cherish my memory of him.

Chapter Twenty-Two

Life on the Road and the End of the Stalinist Era

The next two seasons were quite ordinary for me. But I danced a great deal, both in the theater and, especially, at concerts. I traveled all over the country changing horses at every stop. I was earning money. North, west, south, east. There were no jet planes then. The flight from Moscow to Erevan, for instance, took fourteen hours. Today this sounds ridiculous.

The service was Soviet-style. The acrid odors of gasoline and passengers' sweat, the deafening roar of engines, the toilet door that doesn't lock. Filth. Cigarette butts. Sunflower-seed hulls. We brought our own food. The airline crockery shook mercilessly.

We arrived at our tour destinations at the very last moment, as was customary. The audience was already in the auditorium, and I was in a stupor from the jostling of the ride, attaching the swan headdress to my buzzing head on the way from the airport.

Imagine, as well, the Soviet hotels of that time.

Warm water would be available for two hours every twenty-four-hour period. It was always so rust-red that you couldn't wash it off when you got home. We brought our own soap. And stuck in a corner: boiling water in a rusty wooden tub, with a bashed-up cup fastened to it with a chain. This depressing setup was the hotel snack bar. There was a floor lady (sometimes even two) on every floor.

They drilled you with their huge, malevolent eyes: "Did the touring actress rip off a pillowcase or curtain? Did anyone go to her room to flout Communist morality?" When you checked out, they would count everything, check everything, and sign off on it—then the exit door could be opened. And every hotel, every one without exception, for sure, was under repair. Hammers would bang from sunrise on, pounding nails into your poor little head. This bad luck with renovations followed me all my life, all around the world. Am I the only one who's subjected to this kind of bedevilment, reader, or do you also get your share?

There were hundreds of trips. To the Kharkov Opera for the seventh anniversary of the liberation of Smolensk from the Germans, to the birthday jubilee of Stalin's gardener, Michurin, who made a bunch of promises to the Great Leader of Peoples that he would cross-breed varieties of rye with grapes that would bear fruit in the tundra on the shores of the Arctic Ocean. Minsk, Riga, Tallinn, and Ryazan; Bryansk, Kaluga, Leningrad, Kiev, Serpukhov, and Orel.

I'll stop the list. I traveled around the entire country. Siberia was the only place I avoided. Too far too fly there. Besides, the very sound of it was terrifying. It didn't attract me.

But what was I to do? I couldn't survive on my wretched theater salary. Plus, I had to pay for every trip in cash. And anyway, where could you earn better than in the theater? You'd wear yourself to the bone, but you'd have money in your pocket.

The biggest challenge of all was finding the time between dancing in the repertory and rehearsals. I always tried to plan trips around Mondays—our day off. There was bad flying weather. And in Russia weather for flying is bad all through the autumn, winter, and spring. Departures were delayed. You sat in the spit-covered airport waiting area, bedbugs eating you alive, freezing, nervous—you didn't want to be late for the morning rehearsal.

After the spring season they began renovations at the Bolshoi. And the dance troupe performed in the Green Theater in the Gorky Park of Culture. Later, in Hollywood, they made a popular film about spies of all nationalities and types infesting this park. They made the park famous. But this had nothing to do with us, the ballet. If the Hollywood screenwriters had known that Ulanova was dancing in *The Red Poppy* and I was dancing in *Swan Lake* at the Green Theater, no doubt they would have let a lot more film roll than necessary . . .

Moscow nights are cold, and it often drizzles. For warmth we had to put on something extra that was inconspicuous. Ulanova would wear a wool sweater under her Chinese silk pajamas, while I wore two pairs of tights several times. My admirers would get distressed—she's put on weight!

I did little that was new during those years. I danced Zarema in *Fountain of Bakhchisarai*, the *Walpurgisnacht* in *Faust*. I began rehearsing the ballet *Ruby Stars*, which Lavrovsky was staging. The composer was Andrei Melitonovich Balanchivadze, the brother of the great choreographer George Balanchine, who had lived in Georgia all his life (I had already managed to stroll along the small New York street near Broadway that bears the name of the American Balanchine). Stalin's Iron Curtain separated the brothers for decades on two continents. They didn't get to see each other until the years of Brezhnev's stagnation. The choreographer realized himself completely, but the composer ran aground with a simple ballet.

The plot of the ballet was not very impressive, but it wholly served the Soviet regime. The action took place in the Caucasus. The heroine's name was Dzheyran and, naturally, Lavrovsky's wife, Elena Chikvaidze, rehearsed the part. I was listed in the alternate cast, but Chikvaidze got all the work.

It's a love triangle: one of the rivals is a Russian, the other a Georgian. The front lines, a heroic deed and a heroic death, a young woman's loyalty, a victorious return. In short, "the invincible friendship of peoples," which the perspicacious Stalin proclaimed for all time. At present, this friendship has come apart at the seams, and it is saturated with blood. But at that time everyone obediently sat under the muzzles of machine guns, playing to the monarch in his Marxist anti-reality.

It was difficult to create action around an obviously false story line. Lavrovsky kept nervously shifting the core issue of the conflict: first the Russian would perish, then the Georgian would, then Dzheyran would decide to jump off a cliff, then both men would return from the front lines alive . . .

The dancers wound up utterly confused. Mikhail Gabovich tore his Achilles tendon and, because of the emergency, the main role was given to another dancer: Yuri Zhdanov.

We barely made it to the final orchestral run-through with an audience. A dress rehearsal, basically.

A large Central Committee commission arrived guardedly and without fanfare.

After the banning of Muradeli's opera *The Great Friendship*, the 1948 resolution against the Formalists in music, Zhdanov's foul speeches, the civil executions of Prokofiev, Shostakovich, and Khachaturian, the Myaskovsky Commission's own pants were full from sheer terror. Once again the action takes place in the Caucasus, once again the composer has a Georgian name, once again and again . . .

They shut it down, thinking it best not to let it get to opening night. But a lot of money was squandered.

Where was the management's vigilance? Where were they? Asleep at the wheel? Solodovnikov, the theater director, was dismissed (I rejoiced, my enemy was cast out) and so was Lebedev, the Chairman on the Arts Commission (that was a pity, he seemed well disposed toward me). There was nothing to be done, it ended in a tie, 1-1. The very experienced bureaucrats Alexander Ivanovich Anisimov and N. N. Bespalov assumed their positions.

The story of *The Great Friendship* is widely known. But the public thrashing of other shows on the Bolshoi stage remains in the shadows. In fact, after *The Great Friendship*, the newspaper *Pravda*, the official voice of the Party, lambasted the operas *Bogdan Khmelnitsky* and *From the Bottom of My Heart* and the ballet *Ruby Stars* (which concerned me peripherally), though they choked *Ruby Stars* quietly, through a pillow. Did I forget anything?

The 175th anniversary of the Bolshoi Theater was being celebrated in May 1951.

In Russia, anniversaries are always honored. Titles, little decorations, certificates are handed out left and right. As soon as a round-numbered date looms into view, people fall into confusion and frenzy—not to lose their chance, to grab what they can get. To get as much as possible. It'll be a long time before the next anniversary! You'll get old. Desperate plots, intrigues, petty scheming, and dirty underhanded tricks would begin, and many hands found the energy to write anonymous libel letters. Those who were sharp enough would force their way in to see important Party individuals tossing mud at anyone and everyone. And our theater anniversary celebration was preceded by a leapfrog of denunciations.

The ballet promoted me to the rank of Honored Artist. But the Komsomol organization stormily objected. I was politically immature, they said. Self-willed. But the union organization grunted, yes—I had visited hospitals and danced in managers' concerts.

The rivalry began.

The new management read my name in the TASS list of participants in the Stalin Jubilee. It noted my name. And that decided the outcome of one more small battle. On May 27, 1951, I climbed up a few more steps; I became an Honored Artist of the Russian Federation. The list of recipients of the award was announced publicly on the radio. From then on I was listed with this title in every theater bill and program.

Lenfilm began shooting *Masters of the Russian Ballet*, the first Soviet ballet film. You can still buy it on videocassette in America and Europe. Fate smiled at me: I was preserved for posterity in the role of Zarema and as Maria in a duet with Ulanova in that film.

But fate's smile was the opposite, a grimace, at the incomparable Leningrad ballerina Alla Shelest. She was another one of Vaganova's students and, of them, one of her most gifted. The film was shot on site at the Kirov Theater Ballet. I was the only one from Moscow.

This is how is happened: Shelest was preparing for the shoot, but a few days before starting to work on the film, Alla got into an automobile accident. Her legs and arms were not injured. But the windshield shattered and cut her face, and a powerful blow against the car's body broke her nose. There could be no talk of film shoots. I was hastily summoned from Moscow to fill in.

Many times while being interviewed all around the world, I've been asked the same question: Which ballerinas, to your taste, have attained Olympic heights in ballet? And all my life I have named three names: Semyonova, Ulanova, and Shelest. And I would still name them today. I haven't had occasion to see better ballerinas in my life. I didn't get to see Pavlova and Spessivtzeva while they were still alive. I can attest to the fact that they were great dancers from the amateur films and photographs which have been preserved. But I was being asked about my reactions as a viewer from the audience. And I answered, Semyonova, Ulanova, Shelest.

Ulanova and Semyonova left legends about themselves. Their names need no commentary. But people aren't familiar with Alla Shelest's name. I was always asked again. Who was the third one? Shelest? From the Kirov Theater? How's her name spelled? Sh? e? l? e? s? t? Is that correct?

Life is often unfair to talent. But a poet, a composer, an artist can break through the centuries. If he has a nuclear charge, that is. Schubert's Unfinished Symphony lay around in the attic of a Viennese house for fifty-two years. And it's all right, it didn't spoil. The masterpiece wasn't destroyed by decay. Van Gogh drew his sunflowers and landscapes. He was mocked; people laughed right in his face. That's all right. He outlived them, and only increased to millions in price. Marina Tsvetaeva hanged herself in Yelabuga. All by her lonesome, recognized by no one, not a single soul. But her time came, as it does to rare wines. Marina's sad face frowns from the windows of bookstores around the world. Reproaching us. And where were you, people, when I was looping the rope on the hook?

But it's more wretched for ballerinas. Once their time has passed, nothing remains of it. Emptiness. Those who applauded them, who sent them baskets of roses, already lie in their graves. They won't be sharing their delight with balletomanes.

In rare cases, when the ballerina is no less than brilliant, a photograph, even the most old-fashioned one, will reveal a great deal to a connoisseur. A bird, even when not in flight, is obviously a bird.

I can't forget many of Shelest's dancing roles: Giselle, Aegina, Zarema. *The Blind Woman* in Yakobson's production made me cry. And squeezing a tear out of a colleague is oh, so difficult.

But Shelest's life on the stage was unlucky. All her life something happened to her at the last moment. Things fell apart. She herself made fun of her rotten luck, recounting that at the age of nine, she got ready to go to the movies with a boy her age. She got dressed up in her pink Sunday best. She was clutching the money which her parents gave her for sweets and the movie ticket in her little fist. Suddenly the boy pushed Alla into a mud puddle, grabbed her money and ran away, whooping. Covered with sticky mud, she sat and wept bitterly, the unbearable injury wounding her in her very heart. That's literally how the rest of her life turned out.

The years of Shelest's prime were at a time when no one from Russia traveled anywhere. There were few premieres. Konstantin Sergeyev was the artistic director of the Kirov Ballet, and everything that was done was created for his wife, Natalya Dudinskaya. The traffic light was always red for Alla Shelest. She was quietly retired at the age of forty-plus years.

Shelest had the extraordinary ability to transform herself. She was unthinkably beautiful onstage. Divinely beautiful. After a performance died down, she would take off her makeup and get into the shower. And no one recognized her when she walked through a crowd of admirers who had been electrified by her, who blocked up the narrow artists' stage door. She walked home alone. She was that unremarkable.

I've gotten sidetracked again. Beyond the frosty windows of the Bolshoi and No. 8 Shchepkinsky Passage the Stalinist era still continued. Only the year on the calendar had changed—from 1952 to 1953. The bacchanalia of exposing the doctors, "the murderers in white coats," was going on. By the will of the NKVD conspiracy, they were all Jewish. Zionist agents. Horrible rumors circulated that Stalin intended to resettle the entire Jewish tribe to Birdobidzhan, in the Far East. He had already resettled entire peoples—the Volga Germans, the Crimean Tatars, the Chechens, and the Ingushetians. He drove them out in one night! The experience of the Soviet punitive service in this area was good. What lay ahead for me?

The otolaryngologist Valya Feldman was thrown out of the Bolshoi Theater

Polyclinic. The opera singers adored her; she treated them when their vocal cords went on the blink. But how could the daughter of the physician-therapist Professor Feldman, who had been blacklisted in the newspapers, work in an imperial institution?! Serves him right—he was already in jail. The theater Party organizer, a certain Yakovlev (party organizers were sent in from the outside, from the NKVD and the Central Committee), shook his clenched fists at the large rally of performers in the Bolshoi's Beethoven Hall.

"Vigilance, vigilance, and vigilance again. Our enemies are right under our noses, the daughter of the murderer Feldman built a nest in our Polyclinic . . ."

But the Lord was merciful. On March 2, 1953, in an icy voice Levitan read a news report indicating that the health of the real murderer, Stalin, showed little promise. It looked like we were about to become orphans.

On March 4 my name was on the theater bill in *Raymonda*. Would there be a performance? Or would it be canceled? Everyone asked each other under their breath. No one could answer. Shashkin, who had grown thin from effort, made the telephone dials spin. But no command "from on high" was forthcoming.

Nonetheless, I did dance *Raymonda*. A few of my friends, for whom I left requested tickets at the Box Office, did not come to the performance. They were scared. The tickets were wasted. How would things turn out? Would the miracle-working genius get well, or would the neighbors squeal that Family X was amusing itself, attending frivolous little ballets at that very critical, tragic moment of history . . .

Stalin died on the 5th. Endless crowds of people flowed to the Hall of Columns, where his frail, bewhiskered little body lay. As a participant in his seventieth birthday concert I was issued a "precious" pass. It seemed that the Party committee considered us acquaintances.

I managed to merge into the sea of people after I showed my pass to the double column of soldiers through the metro station Okhotny Ryad, which is opposite our theater (I did, after all live on Shchepkinsky Passage, which is right there).

The Hall of Columns, the former Hall of the Assembly of the Nobility, where, according to new Bolshevik tradition, Soviet leaders are mourned and have funeral services, was draped with black crepe. There was a symphony orchestra on the stage behind a black muslin curtain, and a vague silhouette of the conductor. The sounds of slow classical music. It sounded like Beethoven. I approached the coffin. Duped out of my wits by the propaganda, I wiped a tear. How would we ever live now? We would perish, we would die. Behind me, a man suddenly said in a half-whisper, "No one's afraid of you now . . ."

Horrified, I didn't even turn around. It was probably a provocation. They were testing me.

At home in the evening, I sat down to dinner with a suitably somber face appropriate to the occasion of the Great Loss. But my mother was cheerful among her kitchen dishes, exultant, and she didn't hide her joy: "The tyrant dropped dead, after all."

Why wasn't she afraid to say something like that out loud? I shuddered inwardly.

But a new era was beginning. An era without Stalin.

Chapter Twenty-Three

My Trip to India

This chapter is tragicomical.

In the slushy autumn of the same year, 1953, I was summoned to Neglinnaya Street, to see Comrade N. N. Bespalov. At the time, instead of the Arts Committee, we had the Ministry of Culture. The country was striding toward communism in seven-league boots. It was handier to use ministries to get there. We'd muddle our way over it more quickly.

After Stalin's death, the militant partisan Boris Ponomarenko was appointed minister. During the war, the partisan unit he led had bravely derailed German trains. The world of art was therefore right up his alley. But while Ponomarenko was up in the clouds, Bespalov sat grounded on Neglinnaya Street, across the road from the Bolshoi, and managed us mortals (I don't remember his exact position: he was either deputy or first deputy minister).

I was in his office. During the flowery conversation Bespalov wanted to determine whether I had "matured" enough for a real trip abroad. The festivals in Prague, Budapest, and Berlin were a test. A rehearsal, so to speak. They had been forging my socialist consciousness.

He asked in a roundabout way what kind of political regime India had, what its capital city was, whether the Indian working class was large . . . And then he came out with it: "We here have come to the conclusion that you should be part of the performing group leaving on a two-month trip across India. Can you handle it? I'm leading it."

I could have handled Australia, or mastered New Zealand. Even the islands of Fiji. But trips to those places were not envisioned yet. Their peoples had not yet begun the just struggle for social equality, whereas the Indian people, having just liberated themselves from English dominion, had stirred, had begun to gaze with interest at the dawn of a happy life rising over their Great Neighbor. The Soviet Union, that is.

The talk with N. N. Bespalov was just the beginning.

Two written recommendations from Party members were also required for the trip. Mikhail Gabovich and Olga Moiseyeva, a dancer in the corps de ballet, vouched for me. If I had tried anything, they would have been skinned alive. Again, the applications with hundreds of questions, the medical certificates, the decisions from various bureaus.

But I made it through the eye of the needle this time. I was included in the trip.

There were thirty-six such lucky ones selected. Maxim Dormidontovich Mikhailov and Leokadi Maslennikov, Bolshoi Theater singers. The pianist Yuri Bryushkov (do you remember the Goleizovsky concert?). The violinist Kaverznyeva. A group of dancers from the Piatnitsky choir (Russian folk dances: drumming heels in printed peasant women's caftans and shirts worn loose over pants). Beibutov, a singer from Azerbaijan (eastern folk melodies). The Uzbek dancer Turgunbayeva (her accompaniment was a tambourine). My partner on this trip was Yuri Gofman. The Fedorov sisters, popular folk singers of the time: Russian jazz (they all moved to the West together, marrying in turn). In sum, a hodgepodge, a mixed bag of high and low styles. The concert would last some four hours, a bit much for the delicate Indians. But they suffered through it.

And . . . our escorts.

Bespalov himself, the indispensable Shashkin (on top of everything), a pointynosed interpreter, and an agile administrator, who doled out the meager sums of money. Some one else . . . and two official representatives of the KGB: Shcherbakov and, I think, Stolyarov. They caused me serious troubles. I was unable to travel, was *nevyezdnaya* (unexportable) for six years after India. What can I say? It was a hell of a trip.

On a searingly cold December day, our entire seventy-two-footed delegation (I remind you, there were thirty-six of us) departed from Moscow by train to

Vienna. There we transferred to another train to Rome. From Rome we had to fly to Delhi (via Karachi). But fate granted us two days in Rome. Landing in the Eternal City, even on seventy-two feet — after Spitzbergen, Chimkent, and Sverdlovsk — is a joy.

What's the point of describing Rome? I breathed it in, marveled at and delighted in it . . . But we were not allowed to walk even slightly off our path, to linger near a fresco by Michelangelo. The escorts, like pesky flies, literally controlled our every step. Soviet Embassy staff diligently joined in as well. They all wore long gabardine raincoats. All the same color. They were showing Rome to prisoners, slaves. Just imagine my condition, reader.

We were in the air. We passed Karachi. We walked out on the gangway in Delhi in 35-degree heat (95 degrees Fahrenheit). Dark-eyed Indian beauties in saris encircled thirty-six Soviet necks with thirty-six garlands. The sound of unfamiliar speech. The grumbling of interpreters. The hosts bowed in "namaste" — the receiving side. Bespalov responded by giving a speech in which he mentioned the deceased Stalin at every other word. But without the previous trembling. And also merely for the sake of form. We were driven to the hotel. The road from Moscow took six days. The concert was the day after next.

The Indians had a fit of generosity and gave every performer with rank (and I was now an Honored Artist of the Soviet Union) a room to him- or herself. What freedom and space . . . It was not to be. The KGB were in the neighboring hotel room. Shcherbakov and again, I think, Stolyarov. I remember the latter vaguely — he had some other assignment, keeping track of someone else, too, whereas Shcherbakov — it was as clear as day — was my personal guard. As soon as my door squeaked, Shcherbakov would stick his head out of his room. He would look me over with a glance. Wherever I went, he went.

The surveillance was loathsome and exhausting. I'd step into a shop, Shcherbakov would pop up as if from the ground, bend over my shoulder, breathe loudly, and get a look at what I was interested in.

"You spend a lot of time in shops. You should chose things more quickly. This isn't Moscow," Shcherbakov would instruct me in good manners, bringing his sweaty face right up close to mine in the hotel lobby later. He had bad breath.

I was detained after a reception with the popular movie actors Raj Kapoor and Nargis. They wanted to take a photo with me as a memento. Shcherbakov nervously shifted his weight from foot to foot and fiercely glared at his watch.

"Don't separate yourself from the group. After all, you're part of a group. You gab too much," Shcherbakov scolded me in the passenger car on the way back.

I went off to the side in a museum to take off a shoe which had blistered my toes after a day. I sat down on a bench. Walking had tired me out.

No sooner had we walked out of the museum into the street and the sunny day than Shcherbakov hissed in my ear, "You've separated yourself from everyone again. And taking your shoes off isn't appropriate. Your shoes are dusty. You should clean them more carefully."

I lost my temper in response several times. I didn't have the patience to endure these moralistic teachings for two months. After every breakdown, my detective became more grim and spiteful. I understood that I was being foolish, that the payback would be painful, but I didn't anticipate the magnitude of the punishment.

There were concerts every day. We spent time in many cities. From the classical repertoire, the only piece the Indians took to was my *Dying Swan*. The *Swan* was a constant success. The audience greeted all the other numbers, including my own (I danced the pas de deux from *Don Quixote*, Khachaturian's waltz, and the adagio from *Cinderella*), only politely. What was important to them was what things meant and what they were about. And what is the pas de deux from *Don Quixote* about? I myself don't know.

Indians are an abstinent people. But Mikhailov sang only drinking songs: "Merry Shrovetide," "Pour Me Another Glass, Won't You?" "Let's Raise a Toast," "The Vodka and Liqueurs Are Sweet." His voice was shrill and powerful—it made your ears ring. It frightened the Indians. The singer portrayed the last stage of drunkenness, using pantomime to act out what was missing. The Indians were completely bewildered and sank deeper into their seats. The lengthy aria from the *The Bartered Bride*, which Maslennikova wailed through, elicited no sympathy. The audiences merely endured the violin and piano miniatures and yawned furtively, creaking in their chairs. Nonetheless we were received sincerely and amicably.

Jawaharlal Nehru came to the concerts, three times, a whole three times. Once Indira Gandhi was with him, along with a swarthy lad in a neat white Indian jacket. It was Rajiv, not yet torn to pieces by a terrorist's bomb. If people could see into their futures!

At a reception after one of the concerts in Delhi I was placed to the right of Nehru, which was how protocol seated us. The premier began a conversation with me in English, in French, looking at me with the most intelligent eyes. But I, illiterate one, like the entire population of my country (who in the Soviet prison could use foreign languages, and for what purpose — to court disaster?), made do with gestures and exclamations.

Nehru summoned an Indian interpreter and asked me several entertaining questions. Did I know that the swan is the most loyal of all living beings on Earth, that when the male of a pair dies, the female, soaring high in the sky, throws herself down to the earth like a stone, without opening her wings, and smashes herself to death? That the swan moans loudly, you might say sings, in its death agony? The sounds are deliberate and melodic. That the swan's sense of family must become a model for humanity?

They brought a steaming, peppery pilaf, and Nehru began to eat in a delectable way with his thin, aristocratic sandalwood fingers, after elegantly folding the tips of his two first fingers and thumb, and gesturing me to follow his example. Conveyed through the polyglot Indian translator, who sat frozen like a mummy behind our backs, this comment resounded:

"Eating this dish with a fork and knife is like making love through a translator."

I began to devour the delicious pilaf, using my fingers and enjoying it.

Shcherbakov was staring at me from the other end of the table like a statue. Throwing dirty looks. A piece of food stuck in my throat. The spy was on the lookout even here. He should have been stuffing his face with the free meal, the despicable soul, not getting distracted. They wouldn't treat you to a pilaf like this in Dzerzhinsky Square, now would they?

After the dinner Shcherbakov turned up beside me without making a sound, like a lynx.

"What did the prime minister talk to you about? Why didn't you call our Soviet interpreter?"

"Nehru asked me about you."

"Are you serious or . . ."

"Everybody's eating, but one man hasn't touched the food. Maybe he's pious and he's fasting?"

Shcherbakov realized that I was making fun of him. He turned white with fury.

But this was just a taste of what was to come — the worst awaited me in Bombay. After the first concert, Vorobyova, a former student of Vaganova's, passed the bewildered Indian security guards and came up onstage to look for me. Where in the world did she come from? How did she wind up here? Fate has scattered Russians all around the world; years later I met soldiers who were "missing in action," in Taiwan, Northern Ireland, and Peru. They hid themselves as far as possible from Stalin's bloodhounds in order to survive. They didn't want to place their heads on the executioner's block, or pan for gold in Kolyma,* or die in the Arctic circle.

I didn't know Vorobyova. A momentary meeting in Bombay brought us together for the first and last time in our lives. Hurriedly introducing herself and telling me that she'd been living in India since the war, she threw herself on my neck and, tears streaming, paid me compliments. This was an explosion of feelings from a meeting with the classical ballet, the native tongue, and forgotten compatriots. Dressed in a light cotton robe, with slippers on my bare feet, having just dried myself with a towel but still wet with droplets of water, I listened, embarrassed, to her confused speech.

In a rush of feelings Vorobyova proffered me her green-suede purse, woven in Indian brocade. There was candy in it.

"This is all that I have with me. Take it as a memento . . ."

Shcherbakov appeared in the doorway.

Vorobyova embraced me in parting and hurriedly left.

"What did that traitor thrust into your hands? Why did you take it? Why did you speak with her? The candy is most certainly poisoned. This is the most dangerous provocation." Shcherbakov flew into a rage. Ah, finally! Here they were, the émigré intrigues, bribery, poison. Now he would have something to report to the authorities in Moscow. He had neutralized a provocateur. The crowning moment of the trip. The government was not spending money on his per diem for nothing, he had earned it a hundredfold. Now they would promote him.

These sponging spies, who didn't know a single word in any language, looked for the slightest pretext to inflate an entire case (this tradition of torture ended only in 1990), to make a story, place themselves in a heroic light, and vilify the artist. They'd say he wanted to stay, to defect. If it weren't for us, for our vigilance . . .

If the trip went smoothly—and everyone was docile, meek, and taciturn, like good little children—then the Chekists would inflate results, and invent stories about how a spider's web of enemy conspiracy was woven around the Soviet individual, how he nearly succumbed, wavered, exhibited weakness, or was tempted by their offers. And he would have disappeared, the unlucky victim of misfortune, in the bottomless maelstrom of foreign intelligence services. But the Chekists sniffed out all the intrigues and machinations . . . The story's

---

*The forced-labor camps in the Kolyma goldfields were among the most deadly in the Soviet Union.

plausibility usually depended on an individual (or persons), who had difficulties going abroad. With blots and dark stains in their dossier. Although squeaky-clean people were also deemed suspect and written up in denunciatory telegrams for nothing.

To this day, I don't know whether Shcherbakov's surveillance was the zealous fulfillment of the orders of a superior or whether he was a sadist, the scum, operating on his own intuition. I'd give anything to just have a peek into the dossier the KGB agents concocted about me.

How much life energy these people without honor and conscience stole from me!

And I was a suitable individual. Someone to profit from. An unfortunate biography, an unyielding, impatient, and independent character, with an overpowering fervor. Shcherbakov and again, I think, Stolyarov, doubtless studied my personal dossier and smudged up its pages.

Shcherbakov brusquely grabbed the green purse. He fished out the candies and threw them out the window open to the night.

"I'm going to study the purse."

Downcast, I looked out. It was very dark in the street. I couldn't see the candy. A single one shone white near the street light. Should I pick it up when we went down? It wasn't poisoned. Vorobyova's eyes were clear, light, and shining. Had they had been washed by tears?

But the candy just lay there on the road. I was afraid to disobey.

The next day in Bombay the concert of Soviet-Indian friendship was performed again. Mikhailov frightened the Indians with drunken Russian feasting. Beibutov crooned sweet flourishes. The Piatnitsky girls seductively flashed the undersides of their peasant dresses, pounded their heels, drumming unbelievably. Bryushkov played Chopin for a long time . . . I danced my *Swan*. Life on tour continued.

And there were, of course, the shops and shopping.

I would be committing a grave sin against the truth if I ignored the most important, the main, the primary purpose of a trip abroad for any of my compatriots: to stock up on material goods, to deck oneself out (how to explain this in a foreign language?). India was my first nonsocialist, honest-to-goodness foreign country, and I got my education in shopping there.

No one has even written about this deplorable topic. Everyone lowers their eyes in shame. And truly, there is shame enough in this demeaning running from store to store. But whose fault was this?

Ours? The intimidated, harassed paupers with clumsy domestic products and department stores clogged with crowds? Or our government authorities—insolent, sanctimonious, inveterate liars wearing their quality Cheviot wool suits from special Central Committee ateliers? There was always so little money, it was a joke. But you had to be clever enough to compress all your innumerable desires into one farcical sum.

Do you need shoes? Of course. A lightweight coat? Desperately. A decent piece of luggage for your travels? A long-standing dream. A silk blouse for a severe suit? If you could only find it for a quarter of the price. What about gifts for your household? You can't return without them. Souvenirs for your friends? Absolutely. And so you rack your brains at night, in the bus, even while you're on the stage. And we were clever enough to manage. We made ends meet. Somehow. We did it. In other words, we applied Einstein's theory of relativity to the travel allowance of the first socialist nation.

But everyone is equal in shops, just as they are in death, including the respectable Bespalov, who got out of his black limousine a block before the hotel, and dove, hunched over, into the row of shops. Otherwise, his wife wouldn't have let him across the threshold of their home. And the ideological Shashkin, the impassioned unmasker of imperialist rapaciousness and the capitalist way of life, would leave the rehearsal, claiming a toothache, and go to the same place. I'm not talking about the performers—they were in plain view. What do you expect from them? Even the ascetic KGB guards, Stolyarov and Shcherbakov (who wouldn't taste Nehru's pilaf, just to remain true to his mission), would leave a performance, taking turns clandestinely, secretively, hurriedly (they had to be back at their battle positions), for the same shoes, lightweight coats, suitcases, blouses, stockings, souvenirs . . . Their wives had prepared the shopping lists in Moscow and wouldn't even open their doors without the desired little items.

Two Indian months came to an end. Everything that I bought with my per diem rupees fit into a sturdy new travel bag. In addition to the knickknacks and souvenirs, its contents consisted of patterned floral fabrics. I was going to have party dresses made.

Again the travel time was six days. Again Delhi, Karachi, Rome. The train, Vienna, the train.

Frozen, snowed-under Moscow. I returned to an overcast Russian winter. To a new year, 1954. What was in store for me?

This was how I took my first trip abroad.

Maya with her father, April 1926

Ra Messerer, Maya's mother

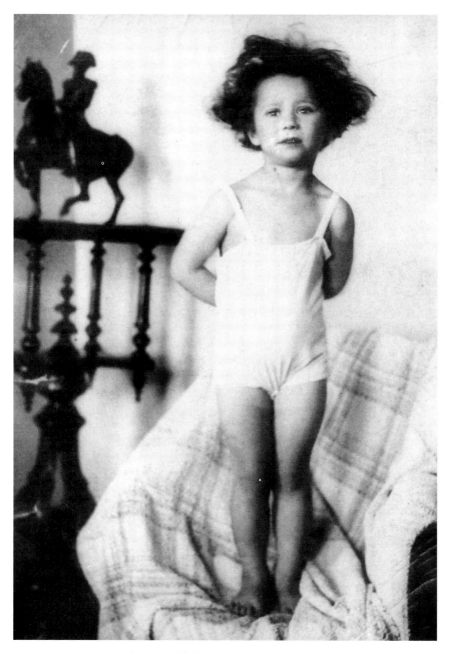

At age 3 in her grandfather's dentist office in Moscow, 1928

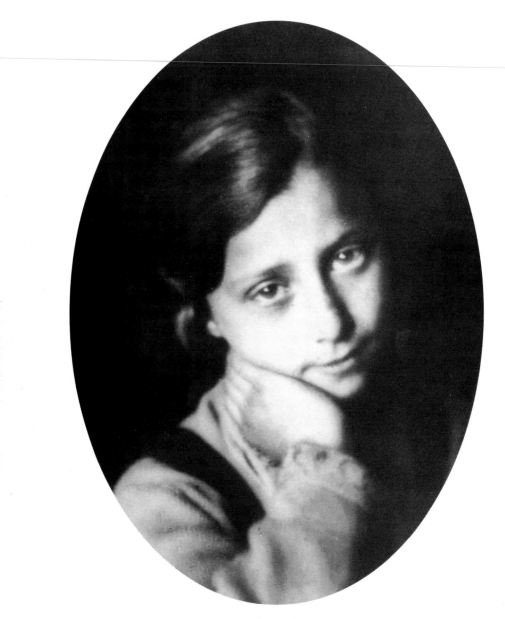

At age 8

With her mother and her brother Alexander, 1935

Rehearsal of Tchaikovsky's *Impromptu* at the Bolshoi Ballet School, 1941

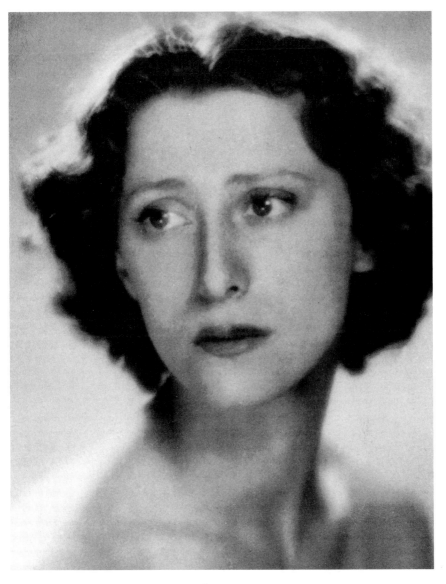

In 1949

In *Raymonda*, 1949

In *The Fountain of Bakhchisarai*, 1949

As Myrtha in *Giselle,* 1956

In *Swan Lake,* 1957

With Nikolai Fadeyechev in *Spartacus,* 1958

In 1961

In *Little Humpbacked Horse*, 1961

With Rodion Schedrin, Poland, 1961

With President John F. Kennedy, 1962

With the Bolshoi Ballet at the White House, 1962

With Yuri Gagarin, the first man in space, Moscow, 1962

With Roland Petit and Zizi Jeanmaire, Paris, 1964

At her dacha, 1966

As Kitri in *Don Quixote*, 1964

As Princess Betsy with Yuri Yakovlev in the film *Anna Karenina,* 1966

In 1966

At the shooting of the film of *Raymonda*, 1970

With Nikolai Fadeyechev in *Raymonda*, Paris, 1972

With Nikolai Fadeyechev in *Raymonda*, Paris, 1972

With Sergei Radchenko in *Carmen Suite*, 1970

With Dimitri Shostakovitch after a concert, 1972

With Boris Efimov in *La Rose Malade*, Paris, 1990

With Rudy Bryans in *La Rose Malade*, Paris, 1973

In *La Rose Malade*, Paris, 1973

With José Todero and Roland Petit after *La Rose Malade*, Paris, 1973

In 1973

Chapter Twenty-Four

Persecution

That was how I took my first trip abroad.

What was in store for me?

Time, which had been frozen to this point, took its first step. Nikita Khrushchev, backed by the guarantee of Marshal Zhukov's support, swept the head of the KGB punitive organs from the historical stage with a preemptive blow. Beria was arrested and executed. The coup d'état was perpetrated under the cover of a new premiere at the Bolshoi—Shaporin's opera *The Decembrists*. The entire troubled history of the nation "hovers near my theater," as the song says.

Foreign guests—heads of foreign governments—began calling in Moscow more and more often. It seemed as if a "thaw" had begun. They were all brought to the Bolshoi. To the ballet. And almost always to *Swan Lake*. The flags would be hung out. Anthems would be played. The house lights would be turned on. Everyone would rise to their feet. The chiefs would graciously wave their puffy, generous hands to the Muscovites from the central Tsar's Box: peace and friendship, good people. The gilded chandeliers would dim . . . and Pyotr Ilyich's swan music would flow.

Khrushchev would always be in the box with high-ranking guests. Nikita Sergeyevich got to see *Swan Lake* ad nauseam. He once complained to me, toward the end of his reign, at one of the receptions: "If I think about having to see *Swan*

Lake in the evening, I start to get sick to my stomach. The ballet is marvelous, but how much can a person take? Then at night I dream of white tutus and tanks all mixed up together . . ."

These were the kinds of jokes in vogue with our leaders.

And wherever there are guests, there are receptions. A new trend made its way around Moscow: going to receptions. If, in Stalin's time, foreign embassies sent crazy invitations to eminent artists on special occasions in care of the theater management's address, they inevitably wound up in the sieve of the theater's NKVD special sections. Besides, no judicious person would ever dream of heading off to an embassy lair. Only if he was tired of living. From there, there was only one route — directly to Siberia for torture.

But now they were calling on the house phone during rehearsals and apologizing five times: "Maya Mikhailovna, there's an invitation for you for Thursday. Please, would you be so kind, when you're finished, as to come by the director's box?"

You drop by and they give you advice.

"We recommend that you not go. But you decide on your own. But I wouldn't go. In any case, we've already let them know that you're not free. But decide for yourself."

An incident comes to mind, when tipsy members of the Politburo were overwhelming the popular tenor Sergei Lemeshev with requests: sing this, this, or that . . . And how the peace-loving democrat Stalin arbitrated, putting an end to the Party bazaar: "Don't force the artist. Let him sing what he likes. I presume that he'd like to perform 'The Heart of the Beauty' from *Rigoletto* for us."

But the opposite happened as well.

"They called from the Ministry of Foreign Affairs, Maya Mikhailovna. It's very important that you go to the reception at the French Embassy. The ambassador himself is a great fan of yours."

I vacillate, citing a dress rehearsal to excuse myself. These receptions mean only one thing — trouble.

"We'll request that the rehearsal be rescheduled. The ballet office will oblige us. Your presence is mandatory!"

I realized too late that two powerful organizations — the KGB and the Ministry of Foreign Affairs — had divergent interests.

The Foreign Ministry desperately needed vacuous, fashionable receptions for the diplomatic intrigues and ventures it calculated far in advance. Whereas the KGB did its own dirty work meticulously: surveillance, wire tapping, and informing. And I became the target of the activities of both institutions. If I danced

Swan Lake, foreigners would want to meet and admire me and talk about life; they were curious to find out if I had bones in my forearms.

And the KGB kept adding compromising materials to my bulging dossier: maintains friendships with foreigners; says too much, engages in free-thinking, is oppressed by the Party's policies, and besides, her décolletage is questionable. The wife of the esteemed comrade N. absolutely correctly expressed her dissatisfaction. And the wife of the esteemed comrade N. is the size of a sea cow. All six little swans would fit easily into her evening dress.

Alongside the *nomenklatura** wives, I truly stuck out like a sore thumb. No matter how I sit, how I smile, how I move, it's all totally the way humans naturally do. The Party wives were angry, envious, enraged. Everything they did was bovine and rhinolike. After every reception I sensed the number of my enemies — male and, most important, female — increase.

A refreshing breeze began to blow ever so slowly in the theater — new trends — a concert trip to Switzerland, then another to France were envisioned. And both times my name was included in the list of participants, but then things somehow fell apart at the last minute. Others went, while I was "desperately needed by the theater." That's how our authorities explained it to me. If that was the case, then I was really needed. I would go another time.

For the time being nothing put me on guard. I had taken a trip to India, had had two brocade dresses made, and my dress shoes weren't worn out yet. And there were people in Moscow for me to display my art to. Khrushchev would bring Chancellor Konrad Adenauer, the magnate William Randolph Hearst, or the Finnish president Urho Kekkonen. And new works absorbed me.

Lavrovsky produced *The Stone Flower,* Prokofiev's posthumous work. Sergei Sergeyevich had completed this score on the day he died, March 5, 1953. The great composer bid farewell to life on the same day as the great executioner Stalin. It was Prokofiev's final sarcasm, the orchestra wits quipped ironically.

I danced the Mistress of the Copper Mountain. Ulanova danced Katerina, Ermolayev the carousing merchant Severyan. Judging from everything, Lavrovsky had not put together a masterpiece. The dances were monotonous and impersonal. The main role of Master Danila (played by Preobrazhensky) turned out to be pompous, too, almost a pantomime. Danila kept hammering and hammering away on the flat theater hills depicting the malachite deposits of the Ural Mountains. He raised a lot of dust from the wings but never really offered much to dance. And the crowd scenes were lackluster, inert. But the original conception

*The *nomenklatura* was the Communist Party elite.

of the powerful, unique image of the magic Mistress of the Mountains, which was based on the resonant, beckoning melody of Prokofiev's trumpet voices, captivated me. It may not be appropriate to say so, but the part of the Mistress of the Copper Mountain turned out to be the most consistent, the most memorable, the most successfully drawn in the ballet.

Yakobson staged *Shurale* for me to music of the Tatar composer Yarullin. That was danced on the Second Stage. The composer himself had been dead for quite some time. He was killed at a very young age during the first years of the war, though his friends and colleagues had done their utmost to protect him. But he decided that there was no sense in sitting around in the rear scribbling musical notes. The Homeland needed defending. This slaughter was called the "people's militia." The recruiters gathered heaps of civilians of all ages—who didn't have a clue about rifles, bullets, or shooting, and were unarmed as well, without even a hunting rifle—and threw them in the path of tanks and the artillery. If not by skill, then by quantity. Directly contrary to Field Marshal Suvorov's strategy.

And hundreds of thousands of unlucky people perished in the snowed-over, frozen fields in bloody, senseless meat-grinders. The Germans had no idea that the people in the large chains on the offensive in the minefields who weren't firing on them were unarmed. And the soldiers of the Wehrmacht shot at the live targets without missing, just like at training sessions! How much talent did they kill needlessly in the hell of the first years of that war? How many geniuses did the Russian land which bore them lose? This was how Yarullin was killed, too. How much easier Salieri's goal of ruining Mozart would have been from the start if he had used all his high and influential connections to send him to the people's militia, to defend the Austrian homeland, the tidy city of Salzburg.

But I have strayed from the subject.

Shurale premiered on January 29, 1955. I danced the girl-bird Syuimbike, Levashov passionately danced the evil forest spirit Shurale, and my constant partner of those years, Yuri Kondratov, danced the heroic role of Ali-Batyr. Yakobson's ballet was a success; the audience received the performance very warmly. As in all of his works, Yakobson was original and inventive in *Shurale*. I won't enumerate all the choreographer's resourceful finds. I'll just recall how he presented me with the most interesting problem of transforming myself on-stage: first I am an ordinary village girl, then a sad, long-winged bird. All the changes were achieved solely through the art of rhythmic movement, the dance alone, without lighting tricks. There will be time to talk about Yakobson. For now, what went on offstage and in rehearsal studios.

Three more trips "whistled past" me. To the Netherlands, Greece, and China.

The theme repeated itself ad nauseam: "You are part of the concert group" and . . . and at the last minute others got to go. The arguments were the same as before: the entire repertoire depends on you, next month there are important high-ranking guests, the Muscovites want to see you, the theater, the theater, the theater . . . But new ballet supervisor Alla Tsabel's eyes were leaden, lying, as she gave me the same simplistic explanations, as identical as twins. Suspicions began to crowd my head.

Because of my foolishness at the time, I thought that these were theater intrigues caused by envy. That my ballerina friends opposed my worldwide recognition. Or that someone powerful in the theater was acting against me, or higher up, in the Ministry of Culture.

I finally succeed in getting a audience with the director (Anisimov served as director until September 1955). There was nervous, panicky casting about: "Why, Maya Mikhailovna, come now! Everyone loves you. Appreciates you. You are our pride. There's no malicious intent here. That's how it worked out. You'll go on the next trip without fail. I swear, I promise you."

"Everyone's looking askance at me, Alexander Ivanovich. It's not so much that I want to go, as it's embarrassing in front of others."

"You'll go, Maya Mikhailovna, you'll go for sure."

Time passed. The ministry offered me a trip to Sweden and Finland to perform with Kondratov. I spent a long time drearily filling out the paperwork. I brought all the references — after all, the director had made a promise. Two more days. It looked like I was going. My Indian travel bag was packed. My mother pestered me about not taking enough warm clothing with me. It was still winter in Scandinavia.

The day before departure, Tsabel came up to the rehearsal studio. She was our manager, replacing Shashkin who "left on promotion" (excuse me, this is Soviet jargon). Alla Tsabel had been a character soloist. She danced the "Spanish" dance in my *Swan Lake* but became more famous for her Party work. Now she was retired and managing.

"I must disappoint you. The passport wasn't prepared in time. Struchkova is going with Kondratov in your place. Raisa Stepanovna has just returned from a tour abroad and her documents are in order."

My heart stopped. Why had I bothered getting packed? Why had I lapped it all up in Anisimov's office? Why had I hoped?

Hurrying through the rehearsal, I rushed over to my place on Shchepkinsky. I was going to phone the minister. The mockery. The scum. The little liars.

We had a new minister. Partisan Ponomarenko was replaced by the philosopher Aleksandrov. The philosopher didn't last very long, but he did manage to do a lot of damage. He was dismissed when rumors surfaced that he spent dark Moscow nights in sexual orgies with young, appetizing Soviet movie actresses. Could you possibly refuse your favorite minister? Luckily, the short, balding philosopher liked women's bodies plump. His taste coincided with that of Rubens. Thin, bony ballerina figures did not arouse his lust. The Bolshoi Ballet maintained its primeval virginity.

I called on the phone for two days. An entire two days. From morning until evening. The ministry's secretaries were fed up with me, but I wasn't going to back down. I would call for a month, a year, until Himself picked up the receiver. I got my way. I heard Aleksandrov's weak voice through the crackling phone: "Don't worry. We'll clear it up. We'll help."

I asked Aleksandrov for a meeting. I also needed to tell him about my salary — I hadn't gotten a raise and was paid less than everyone else. And about my apartment. My contemporaries, Kondratov, Struchkova, the opera folks, had gotten spacious individual apartments in the high-rise Stalin apartment houses (on Kotelnicheskaya, near Krasnye Vorota). But I still lived cooped up in the Shchepkinsky building.

I prevailed upon him. The minister would receive me the day after tomorrow at four. I made some notes on a piece of paper, so I wouldn't forget anything.

I was in the reception room at ten minutes to four. Waiting nervously. At exactly four o'clock, the secretary opened the door. I walked in. An unattractive little man got up from his desk — the spitting image of Puss in Boots. He purred, "It's a misunderstanding. Why be so anxious? You are our hope. All the heads of foreign governments delight in your talent. We'll stick up for you. I saw you in *Don Quixote* and am proud that the human body is capable of manifesting such beauty and elegance." (The little philosopher had picked up Lenin's description of listening to Beethoven's Appassionata from the memoirs.)

The minister was a master of compliments. Fearing that he wouldn't hear me out, I blurted out about my salary and my apartment. He kept soothing me, promising me life in a land of milk and honey. I walked out reassured. I smiled at the secretary. Only the Politburo and God Himself were higher than the minister. My case was not all that hopeless.

But four days later Aleksandrov was dismissed. All my humiliating efforts were down the drain. What was his meowing now worth? Did I really have to start all over again?

After that, the minister was the former Komsomol leader Nikolai Alexandrovich Mikhailov. A cold and dry man with a curly forelock and a proletarian appearance. Fate brought us together several times at youth festivals. You couldn't get a yes or a no out of him. He'd beat around the bush. He was a zealot, a true Party soldier, dammit.

While I was pondering how and when and what to do, the French ambassador Dejean (with his nasal "r's") excitedly informed me about an invitation to Paris at a reception at the French Embassy.

I'm leaving out the details and how slowly the days passed as I waited to go on tour. But everything went like clockwork. Irina Tikhomirnova went instead of me. And I stayed home. Drank tea. Kicked myself.

The idiocy, the nightmare of the situation was that they continued to display me, as in the past, and feature me at all the honorary performances attended by eminent foreigners and our leaders. *Swan Lake, Fountain of Bakhchisarai, Stone Flower,* and *Shurale.* A mob of escorts would accompany each guest — journalists, businessmen, influential politicians — who would spread the news around the world in a second. Each of these visits flitted by in the *News of the Day* (our newsreel). Before every showing of a feature film, they rolled excerpts of my dances across the entire breadth of the Soviet nation. My fame grew.

On the days of high-ranking visits there were receptions and receptions. First the host would give one, then our people would compete in hospitality. I was invited to all the receptions, bar none. They talked, talked, talked at them and praised me — why haven't you visited our country, come on over, we have a good theater, the audience is waiting for you, why? And how was I supposed to answer?

And you, young readers, with whom I not acquainted yet, don't think that I'm letting my tongue run away with itself, that I'm exaggerating, that I've lost possession of my faculties. At that time our whole lives were muck, monstrous. I myself find it difficult to imagine, to believe today that all this actually happened, and happened to me. All the magical names that sounded like hymns and odes, like the names of ancient Greek military commanders, senators, and gods — Aleksandrov, Mikhailov, Khrapchenko, Bespalov, Kaftanov, Tverdokhlebov, Vartanyan, Solodovnikov, Shauro, Zimyanin, Kukharsky, Zakharov — belonged to ordinary mortals, inconsequential, uneducated men. A tragic misunderstanding. But they had power. The leashes led to the Kremlin, to Lubyanka, to Staraya Square. And we were conceived in fear, submission, silence, cowardice, obedience, and servility. We had chosen our lot, being born in prison.

I danced *Don Quixote* on October 5, 1955, for the Canadian premier Lester Pearson. Five, five, five — three fives! As usual, the next day there was a reception at the Canadian Embassy. Harassing phone calls — I had to be there without fail. I arrived. And I was immediately the center of attention. Pearson and his entire entourage lavished honeyed praise on me. And questions were asked right away: Why don't I perform in Canada? We shouldn't postpone it; incidentally, the Canadian impresario is here, dictate the repertoire you'd like to him. Really now, why not perform? You never know.

I sat down at the end of a table and painstakingly wrote out *Sleeping Beauty, Swan Lake* . . . It filled up a whole page. While the numerous agents pricked up their ears—they were perpetually hovering about (early the next morning they would squeal to their respective superiors): of course, she's giving away the blueprints of defense plants. But what was I to do? Say that I was illiterate, that I couldn't write?

A few days later, on October 10, there was a reception at the Foreign Ministry's private residence on Alexei Tolstoy Street. All the dates and mishaps are noted in my journals.

Vyacheslav Mikhailovich Molotov, our minister of foreign affairs, was standing near the entrance. Sadly, a historical figure, what's the point of describing him? His pince-nez flashed, he twitched his little whiskers. Shook my hand long and hard. He stuttered, "So glad to welcome you, Maya Mikhailovna. You danced well. Our guest just can't keep stop talking about you. The Canadians really liked you."

I smiled a sour smile in reply. My hand really hurt.

Pearson noticed me and walked directly toward me. He praised me again. Pearson was the center of the Foreign Ministry's universe that day. The wave of people attending rolled after him. It turned out that our leaders were standing right beside us. For the first time I saw Malenkov, Kaganovich, Shepilov, Pervukhin at close range. I scrutinized their well-fed, hemmorhoidal physiognomies, seen thousands of times in the newspapers. What repulsive faces.

And suddenly, something I never thought I'd live to see—Molotov suggested to Pearson that they raise their glasses to my health and art. To art in general, globally speaking.

Pearson clinked glasses with him. The leaders nodded their heads in agreement and drained their champagne glasses. Here was Pervukhin (who flashed like a meteor on the Soviet Party horizon and was such a loyal Leninist he flashed and sank into oblivion; he was thrown out soon after) who expressed his regret (from zeal, is it?) to the Canadian that the premier had not seen my *Swan Lake.* I seized the moment and, speaking a mile a minute, told Pervukhin that I was not allowed abroad. He was taken aback. His face abruptly changed its friendly expression. He was in a hurry to move away. And as he withdrew, he said, "I'll try to talk to the minister."

Days went by. All was quiet. There was no response.

My friends gave me the right idea: write a letter to Voroshilov to request an audience with him. They heard that he had helped someone. A few days later a call came from the reception room: "What is it that you actually want? You didn't state your request in your note. What is the matter?"

"That's exactly why I would like a meeting, in order to tell Kliment Efremovich everything in person."

"Fine. We'll report that to him."

Dial tone.

But again—graveyard silence. Again there was no response.

An official reception in the Kremlin. This time the Norwegian premier has appeared in Moscow. His Excellency, Mr. Gerhartsen. The Norwegian was treated to *Fountain of Bakhchisarai* with Ulanova and me.

I was so troubled and depressed by everything that was happening that I decided out of desperation to get dressed up in a costume that was almost theatrical. Let them look at me. I put on a long—floor-length—white brocade dress with a completely open ballet bodice, over which I casually threw a wide raspberry scarf. It was a spectacle. All eyes were on me.

Nikolai Bulganin was receiving guests at the top of an interminable staircase in front of the entrance to St. George's Hall. He had attended the performance of *Fountain* and, shaking my hand, paid me the compliment that the occasion required. As he did, he stared at me so intently that it began to seem to me that they were all in a conspiracy, that everyone knew something and was keeping it secret from me. Or was my suspicion?

Days later Bulganin himself came over to me in the Norwegian Embassy. He didn't even have a chance to open his mouth when I—surprising myself—suddenly said to him, "They're hurting me terribly, Nikolai Alexandrovich. Tremendously. They're not letting me go abroad. What did I do wrong?"

Bulganin raised his eyes and replied in a nearly Turgenevian sentence: "And I thought you were happy."

I didn't listen, I was saying my piece. There was so much pent up in me that required an outlet: "A ban has been placed on my leaving the country. All the soloists go, except me. In response to personal invitations made to me, they all go in my place."

"And why haven't you told me about this earlier?"

You go tell them. Just try. I was seeing him for the second time in my life. Up close.

I said that the ballet was a youthful art, that if I didn't go now, when everyone was inviting me, it would be too late in the future. Who would want me then? And it hurt me very much. Why? What had I done?

Bulganin frowned. But he heard me out to the end.

"I'll remember everything. I'll clear this matter up."

I'll interrupt my description of my efforts to get to the truth. The story had no ending. I have to exhale deeply.

There were changes in the theater again. We had a new director—the composer Chalk. And Gusev—my former neighbor on Shchepkinsky Passage—replaced Lavrovsky. Lavrovsky would return three years later, but the three-year period of Gusev's directorship enriched my repertoire. I began to rehearse Krein's ballet *Laurencia*, based on Lope de Vega's *Fuente Ovejuna*. It was Vakhtang Chabukiani's choreography.

I'm currently renting an apartment in Madrid at 47 Lope de Vega Street. Right across from the Prado. Life sure puts us through some funny numbers. The next street over is Cervantes Street. So did I dance *Don Quixote* for Pearson in vain? And could I have thought then—deceived, uncomprehending, confused, in a feverish delirium, imploring leaders, beating like a caged bird, driven to exhaustion—that the time would come when I'd click my heels walking around Madrid, not asking anything of anyone? I only regret that it's too late.

I'll use an ellipsis here . . .

And so what was next? On the eve of the new year, 1956, there was a New Year's ball in the Kremlin. Once again, I dressed up in a theatrical manner, loudly. Even provocatively. My evening dress for the ball was made of white lace. Foreigners surrounded me. They wore me out with questions. They were onto something, they had caught wind of something, these shrewd people. I fended them off with jokes.

This was when I had my first conversation with Khrushchev. He walked over to me with A. I. Mikoyan, pressed my hand, smiled; he reeked of vodka a meter away. "I've seen you so many times from far away. I wanted to see you up close. On the stage you're big, visible. Here, you're a skinny chicken."

Mikoyan giggled obsequiously: "I'm downright surprised."

Khrushchev, drunk: "Would you look at him, he's surprised."

Mikoyan followed his lead: "I wanted to say: captivated."

Khrushchev: "Now that's another matter."

(This is a quote from my journal. I haven't changed a single word, a single comma. I swear. Judge the manners and intellect of the Bolshevik leaders yourselves! This is how they subsisted on jokes.)

Maybe I should have confided to Khrushchev that I was not exportable, as they say. But something held me back, silenced me. It was somehow petty, humiliating. And Bulganin came over and invited me to dance a Russian dance with him. I took my place. We danced. All the bureaucratic dog muzzles showed emotion. Oh, how wonderful. Oh, how sweet. Well, what a great fellow the premier is. How adroitly he dances. No worse than the eminent ballerina from the Bolshoi. A scene from Gogol!

Nikolai Alexandrovich didn't bring up my request. Even though there was enough time. (It would have taken half a minute.) He just shook his gray beard, and exclaimed. I ground my teeth — should I ask, should I remain silent, remind him, give him a hint? My pride won't allow it. And so I just left the ball with nothing. Like Cinderella.

But my fleeting meetings with leaders continued. On the opening night of *Laurencia*, Khrushchev, Bulganin, Mikoyan, and Voroshilov turned up onstage after the performance with flowers (this was during the Twentieth [anti-Stalinist] Party Congress). They brought their pals to meet me; Maurice Thorez, Palmiro Togliatti, Dolores Ibárruri* extended their hands and smiled. I must have developed a complex at that time. I smiled in response but thought to myself: should I say that they're not letting me go abroad? But I merely thought it.

In May I danced for France's "big guns" Guy Mollet and Pineau. In June I was awarded a title. But still no progress. A blizzard of invitations was piling up in snowdrifts, everyone was traveling in response to them, but I was like the bogatyr Ilya Muromets, "sitting like a bump on a log." The fairy tale says that he sat that way for thirty-three years. I'd only had to wait for — it would soon be — three. I was tormented by a deplorable lack of information: What was the reason, who was behind this? Why try to evade it? Should I say nothing, lie? I came to the unhappy conclusion that it was the KGB. The denunciations by my Indian "educator," Shcherbakov.

Mita's second husband, the daring athlete Grisha Levitin, who raced a roaring motorcycle up a vertical wall wearing a helmet with goggles and who was friends with various people in the world of motor vehicles, shocked me one evening: "A man from the services whispered in my ear yesterday, 'Your famous relative,

*Three prominent members of the Communist International. Dolores Ibárruri was known as La Pasionaria.

the ballerina Maya, will never travel anywhere. That's certain. There's a ban on her.'"

And a new confirmation. The full cast of the Bolshoi Ballet was supposed go to England in the fall. With several ballets: *Romeo and Juliet, Swan Lake, Fountain of Bakhchisarai, Giselle.* Two of them were my very own.

In mid-June 1956 *Literaturnaya gazeta* published a detailed notice, informing readers of the Bolshoi's grand tour to Great Britain. It listed the ballets. It said Ulanova would star, and then gave the names of absolutely all the soloists.

My name was not on the list.

Chapter Twenty-Five

How I Didn't Go to London

"Foreigners will save us," Igor Moiseyev liked to say in those years. It was his motto, his mantra. He tried to console me with that aphorism, too.

They might save some people, but they only made trouble for me.

At a reception I was approached by a fair-haired, handsome young man. He introduced himself in fluent Russian. "I am John Morgan, second secretary of the British Embassy. I adore the ballet. I'm a big fan of yours."

We got to talking. Since I know no foreign languages, I could communicate only with Russian speakers.

Morgan was an amusing conversationalist. He was knowledgeable in the ballet, especially English ballet. Where what premiered, when, who was feuding with whom, who had changed partners. He had some gossip about our Violetta Prokhorova-Elvin. I was interested in it all.

"When are you dancing next?"

I told him the day after next, at Tchaikovsky Hall. A Strauss waltz in Goleizovsky's choreography.

Morgan was interested. "How can I get tickets? Will you help?"

I left two tickets for "Morgan" at the box office. Among the bouquets I received was one of white lilacs, with the card of the second secretary of the British Embassy in Moscow.

We met as old acquaintances at the next reception. I thanked him for the lilacs, Morgan praised the Goleizovsky. And suddenly, "Why are they saying that you're not going to London? How can that be?"

Because, I replied, the KGB put a red dot over my name, and that of my brother Alexander, in the theater's personnel list. (I had gotten the news as a top secret from Pyotr Andreyevich Gusev that very day; it was like a razor in my throat. And so I blurted it out.)

Morgan was unperturbed, in the British style. Not an eyebrow twitched. As if he hadn't heard.

"May I present you to our ambassador, Mr. Hayter?"

Was that going to be a help? Or a new burden? A trap?

Hayter was a tall, middle-aged gentleman. The compleat English lord. His Russian wasn't bad.

"Our side want you to come very much. The English public must see your *Swan Lake*. We shall insist."

Sensing that I had British support, I took a crazy step. I sent Chulaki, our managing director, an ultimatum. If my brother Alexander Plisetsky is struck from the trip to England (I did not mention myself), I ask to be freed from work in the Bolshoi Theater from such-and-such a date. And I left for vacation.

The letter was not smart, and harsh, of course, but it was to the point: would they really put my brother, six years my junior, through the same hell? Clearly, I was hysterical. What would I do without the ballet? Breed chickens, raise cabbages? But I was desperate.

In a thirty-second conversation, Alla Tsabel informed me over the telephone that my request had been granted. I was no longer in the theater. I should turn in my pass. Things were not good.

I spent August in Leningrad with my cousin Era. She always had a calming effect on me, like valerian drops. I traveled the length and breadth of the Hermitage several times. I stood for a long hour in the Pushkin house on the Moika Canal, where the poet slowly faded after his fatal duel. I went to Vaganova's grave. I wept and complained to her.

In the middle of August a telegram summoned me to Moscow. Minister of Culture Mikhailov wanted to talk to me. I hesitated, but went.

The conversation was conciliatory, not harsh. Why was I setting conditions? My brother was a separate issue. I should take back my impolite letter. The theater needed me.

Tsabel called my apartment on Shchepkinsky the minute I got back from the ministry, informing me that the rehearsals for London would start on August 20.

I had to be at the theater, I worked there. Whether I went on the tour or not was not her concern, but I did have to rehearse.

On the first day, instead of rehearsals, we had a crowded and noisy "meeting about the trip." I was literally led, although seemingly by accident, to the meeting. A whisper in my ear: I'd do well to speak. What about? To give an evaluation of my behavior. Oh, how the Bolsheviks liked to have people repent! To humiliate themselves, trample themselves.

The theater's Party organizer, French horn player Polekh who always wore a bowtie and makeup (after all he was a performer) gave the first speech, and he attacked me with the might of the Party. I was this and that and a so-and-so, pushy, conceited, shaming the name of the Soviet artist.

For three hours they spoke nonsense, exposing me. Let her speak, they demanded. I tightened my lips and said nothing. Toward the end I left, I got sick of it.

But I did go through two full stage rehearsals of *Swan Lake*. Before the third one, Tsabel again: "Karelskaya will rehearse. You are not going. It is decided."

I saw black. Sophisticated Chinese torture. I rushed to make calls from Shchepkinsky. Bulganin, Molotov, Mikoyan, Shepilov, Mikhailov (friends had given me their office numbers over the summer). I didn't call Khrushchev, saving his number for a rainy day. Would it ever be rainier than this? But no one came to the phone or called back after I spoke to their assistants and secretaries. Desperately, I called the British Embassy to talk to Morgan — his number was on the business card with the lilac bouquet.

It was a switchboard. I asked for Mr. John Morgan, second secretary. Just a moment. Click. Morgan picked up the phone. I spoke disjointedly, a flow of words.

"Where do you live? Shchepkinsky, 8? Right behind the theater? I have some brand-new books for you. About English ballet. May I drop them by this evening around six-thirty, after work?"

I had made the call.

But then I got cold feet. Scared. The phone at the embassy had to be tapped. God knows what they would think. And I couldn't receive a young man alone.

I called around. I reached Nikolai Simachov, at home with the flu. "Kolya, darling, come over this evening at six. I'm getting some new ballet books. About the English. We can look at them together."

He agreed.

Morgan visited me only twice. That evening and three days later. During both brief visits I was never alone. I have witnesses. Living ones, of sound mind and good memory. We barely spoke about the London tour. Morgan assured me that everything would be all right. I'd go. No more. We leafed through the books, made silly social chitchat. Had Georgian tea with cherry jam.

But the consequences of our meetings were out of a spy thriller. A KGB car dogged my every step, twenty-four hours a day. There were always three men in the car. Their silhouettes were clear against the setting autumn sun in Moscow. Wherever I went, so went the three heroes. Eliseyev's store, a studio, an exhibit — they would park not far away. Waiting. Coming out, I'd take a taxi or get a ride with a friend, and I could see them in the rearview mirror, keeping their distance but never letting me out of their sight. All the way to my house. And then they would wait, for hours. At a distance, but I could see them clearly from the window. On duty. Fine conspirators. Just like a movie.

At first I had thought they were new admirers. I was worried. What if they were robbers? But Grisha Levitin checked their license plate and said with certainty that it was a KGB car. "What's new now?"

Everything was tied in a very tight knot. Morgan vanished. He stopped calling, he did not attend receptions. Had he left, or was he coerced? I was really frightened. I wouldn't call the Brits myself. I had been burned. This was scary.

It was not until eight years later, when I was allowed to travel, that I met secretly with Morgan when I was in London. Don't get excited, reader. Secretly from the KGB, not from the rosy, neatly pressed Mrs. Morgan and three little Morgans in their polished, clipped, and tended house with green lawns outside London. It seems that when he came to visit me in Shchepkinsky, Morgan had parked his car near the Maly Theater. At a distance from my building. This caution must have worried the KGB — and ruined me completely. Their conclusion was clear: passionate love, Plisetskaya will remain in England, ask for political asylum. The other possibility was espionage: Plisetskaya was the new Mata Hari.

There were insubordinate people in the theater. Forty-five signed a letter in my defense to Minister Mikhailov: Plisetskaya is the mainstay of the repertoire, her presence is vital to the success of the tour. There were major names among the signatures: Ulanova, Lavrovsky, Fayer. Thank you, good people. If only you had known in your naïveté that the letter should have been sent to KGB Chairman Ivan Serov, at Dzerzhinsky Square. The letter didn't save me, but it did add kindling to the fire. Otherwise the flame of hope would have gone out completely.

Late one night Fayer called. He asked me to come immediately. I grabbed a taxi. The KGB car followed.

In a deep whisper, keeping away from his telephone, which might be bugged, Fayer told me that there had been a reply to the group letter. Not exactly a reply, but a reply . . . Not written, but oral . . . Fayer hemmed and hawed, avoiding any specifics. But it became clear to me that in order to save myself, I had to write a letter of *repentance*. To Mikhailov. The sooner the better.

I didn't sleep that night, trying to figure out what I could repent of without losing my dignity. I composed the letter as best I could. What would you have done in my place? I sincerely regret that I did not keep a draft and I cannot remember what sins besides my truly tactless ultimatum I could have blamed myself for.

And the very next day, breaking my own promise not to go to embassies ever again, I went to the Indonesian reception for President Sukarno. I was the only one from the Bolshoi who was invited. I was an attraction now, a subversive personage!

The first person I bumped into was Mikhailov. Fate. I pulled the letter out of my bag. Here, enjoy my repentance. Mikhailov's paw engulfed the letter, and he mumbled something.

A few days later he called me into his office. Gave me a long, unhurried speech. The solo aria: "It's a good letter. Courageous. Wise. Good for you. But is everything in there? Have you forgotten anything, hidden anything? Have you really understood all your actions, Maya Mikhailovna? You have a heightened interest in foreigners. That has to be taken into account . . ."

All in a smooth, steady voice, without periods or commas, but with small hitches on the letter "r," which sometimes stuck and bubbled in Nikolai Alexandrovich's throat. I could see that the minister was enjoying his own speech. It was flowing smoothly. He pushed a button to summon his secretary.

"Bring in Comrades Pakhomov and Stepanov."

I will explain who's who to the reader. Vasily Ivanovich Pakhomov was Mikhailov's deputy and had already been appointed head of the trip to England. Later he was director of the Bolshoi for several years. He will appear throughout the pages of my book. Vladimir Timofeyevich Stepanov, a soulful and not callous man, was in charge of foreign affairs at the Ministry of Culture.

The speech continued. "You have great talent, Maya Mikhailovna. A real talent, a major talent. And what did Comrade Lenin teach us? He taught us that talent must be protected. And that is why I dropped all my business to meet with you. I understand that you are suffering, perhaps not sleeping. But allow me to question which of us is suffering more. You or I, Minister of Culture Mikhailov?"

I am not angry at Mikhailov today. In essence, he was just another galley slave, like me. He was simply working two or three decks higher in the Soviet ship. It did not depend on him whether I would go to London or stay home. That was decided by a different institution. The KGB. But Mikhailov was the front man, who had to look good in a bad game. He was the visible part of the iceberg.

I ran into his wife, Raisa Timofeyevna, as I left Mikhailov's office. She was a crazy, uncontrollable woman but with a peasant's warmth and compassion. She took a most active and noisy part in her husband's work. She gave me a bear hug—the minister's wife was a large, full-bodied woman—and spoke right into my ear so that my head rang, "Nikolai Alexandrovich has nothing to with it. We both love you. But at the KGB, Serov has mountains of denunciations of you. You have to talk to him yourself. He decides everything."

Desultorily I made my way to the coatroom for my raincoat. It was pouring. The Moscow weather matched my mood—sleet, mud, puddles, slush. My head was pounding, filled with the words I had had to listen to all morning.

Someone hailed me cheerfully in the coatroom crowd. Victor Petrovich Gontar, Khrushchev's son-in-law. Director of the Kiev Opera. I had danced *Swan Lake* there at the end of the season. He asked how things were going. Helped me with my raincoat.

"We've heard even in the capital city of Kiev that Moscow is treating you badly. I defended you at the table at Tsar Nikita's (as he called his father-in-law). Shameless men, bothering a woman. Let her go—what's she going to do? It's all that Ivan Serov's fault. Trying too hard. Little shit."

There was that name again: Serov. It always came back to him.

"Victor Petrovich, could I talk to Serov? Raisa Timofeyevna told me today . . ."

"Why put it off? Let's go call him from the ministry on the spinner." (I have to explain to the Western reader that the direct government hotline was called the spinner. Creamy beige and tubby, the telephone had the Soviet emblem on the dial. The child of Edison perfected for Party needs, it was given to the highest Soviet *nomenklatura*. Only the most select. The "top," the most "reliable.") With our coats under our arms we walked up to the third floor. Gontar looked into offices, slamming the doors. He did not stand on ceremony. He was the Son-in-Law. He burst into Stepanov's office.

"He's got a spinner. He's a good fellow, not a coward, he won't refuse."

His well-trained secretary stood up respectfully and reported, "Viktor Petrovich, Vladimir Timofeyevich is with the minister. Shall I tell the minister's secretary that you are here?"

"Maya and I will wait in his office. We're not in a hurry."

No one dared contradict Gontar. The sophistication of Soviet subordination!

Gontar was merely a theater director. But . . . he was a relative. A close one. The husband of Khrushchev's daughter by his first marriage. And the denizens of the ministerial palaces knew who was a husband, a brother-in-law, a son-in-law better than the church calendar. Better than Stalin's *Short Course of the History of the Communist Party.* They never made mistakes.

Shutting the door, Gontar picked up the spinner. In the neat little directory, the size of an address book, he located the four-digit number (fortunately — or unfortunately — the all-powerful book was right next to the telephone). He dialed. And handed me the phone, gesturing that he was not there.

The line was picked up instantly. "Serov here."

The unexpectedness made me forget Serov's name and patronymic. Just a minute earlier, and quite inappropriately, I had been thinking that Gogol's character Khlestakov was also called Ivan Alexandrovich. I was losing my mind.

"Hello, this is Plisetskaya."

Serov did not respond to my greeting, nor did he say hello.

"Where are calling from? Who gave you my number?" His voice was hoarse and infuriated. The receiver resonated. Gontar could hear everything.

"I'm calling from the Ministry of Culture . . ."

Serov interrupted harshly. "What do you want from me?"

"I wanted to talk with you."

"What about?"

"I am not being allowed abroad. On the London tour."

"What do I have to do with it?"

My voice started trembling. I was losing my nerve. He was behaving like a real boor to me.

"Everyone says that you are not letting me go."

"Who's everyone?"

"Everyone."

"Specifically?"

I lost all self-control. My vocal cords did not respond to my brain. I heard my voice, no longer my own, a stranger's hollow tones say, "Raisa Timofeyevna Mikhailova . . ." He was screeching like a fishmonger, "That's just what she'd like! Mikhailov makes the decisions, I have nothing to do with it."

He hung up. The conversation was over. Gontar and I exchanged glum looks. Our act was a flop. Serov was a real bandit.

A half-hour later Stepanov's direct phone was removed. His innocent secretary was fired, tossed out onto the street from the ministry. The KGB knew instantly whose phone I had been using. Stepanov miraculously survived (my "diversion" took place in his absence), and to his great honor he never, not once, reproached me for my thoughtlessness.

Gontar, my dear, kindhearted Viktor Petrovich, the compassionate, noisy bull in the china shop — it doesn't matter, thank you anyway. You were a human being. Gontar, Khrushchev's son-in-law, damn it, had to pay, too. I don't know what Serov reported to Nikita Sergeyevich. But for more than two years Gontar was not allowed to cross the threshold of his powerful father-in-law's abode. His trips abroad were stopped. The disturber of the peace was punished.

I was still followed every day by the KGB car. Using up state gas, wearing down tires, making the agents' pants shiny in the seat. And people began avoiding me as if I had the plague. I was still invited to receptions, but I did not go. The one time I did go to the Kremlin — maybe some one in government would take pity and talk about my fate — I had to walk home across Moscow all alone. No one offered me a ride. I used to have to fight my way through the offers.

On October 1 and 2 *my* troupe flew off in two sections to London. There weren't a lot of ballet people left in Moscow. I was one of them.

Perhaps I have wearied you with the dates and numbers so thickly sprinkled throughout these chapters. When writing about my London epic, I kept looking into my diaries. I suppose I could have told this story more succinctly, in general outline. But I want you, my reader, to follow day by day, without haste, the path of my little Golgotha in the fall of 1956. This was the kind of "thaw" we had in Russia that year.

Chapter Twenty-Six

While the Company Was in London

The Bolshoi's "first team" successfully opened the London season. The hapless, the pre-pensioners, and the wounded stayed in Moscow. And I was among them. Suffering. My two "pleading" telegrams to Khrushchev, my letters to him, Bulganin, and Shepilov all went unanswered. None of the leaders would talk to me. I never heard a word.

But I was not alone. The "reserve bench" held a large armada of gloomy non-travelers. Like fallen warriors on the field of unequal combat. On the very last day, with great fuss and bother, they let out Lavrovsky himself. A fine Romeo they would have had without the choreographer. But they left the best Tybald, Alexei Ermolayev, back home. Someone must have ratted on him, saying that he planned to defect. Or something. The soloist Esfandyar Kashani, who, horror of horrors, was rumored to have a father born in Persia, was stopped at the last minute. Later, it turned out not to be true. Some had divorced a husband, broken up with a wife, fought with neighbors, or told a joke — they were all "unreliable." And each minor excuse was given a political coloration.

At first my telephone rang off the hook. Persistent British journalists thirsted for the sensation — why had I remained in Moscow? I did not answer the phone. Mother struggled with them, making up all kinds of stories, but then she got tired, too. Eventually the phone stopped ringing.

To keep myself busy and chase away glum thoughts, I decided to dance *Swan Lake* with the troupe remaining in Moscow. I had a hidden agenda: to show the world that I was healthy, in good form, and dancing *Swan Lake*. Then it would be up to them to figure out why I was dancing it here and not there.

The administration left in Moscow agreed. I don't know what they could have been thinking, but they agreed readily and complacently. They probably thought that people were more likely to buy the story that I was needed in Moscow than that I was sick.

The posters went up.

But the clerks had miscalculated.

The news flew around Moscow instantly. Crowds stormed the box offices; everyone wanted tickets for October 12. They had heard by circuitous routes that there would be a ballet instead of the opera. *Swan Lake*. With Plisetskaya, who was not allowed to go to London.

Our Soviet life has developed in us an incomparable and unparalleled form of speedy transmission of information. The speed of light! How did the city of millions learn in a flash what was a "must-see," where the hottest thing going culturally was that day, where the sensation was? Can cyberneticists explain it?

My morose companions cheered up. Shook themselves awake. Rehearsed at full steam. They learned new parts like lightning.

But our foes, the hostile forces, didn't sleep either. My telephone started ringing again. Call after call. Not only people wanting tickets but ministerial rats with warbling voices "sounding the alarm." "You must make sure there is no spiteful triumph, no demonstration." I'll name the people who called—Abolimov, Tselikovsky, Vartanyan, and Apostolov . . . Just for the information of future generations. Then there was a call from Furtseva. She was a member of the Politburo then.

"Maya Mikhailovna, Ekaterina Alexeyevna Furtseva wants to speak with you. I will connect you."

When I had called all those damned offices, the secretaries had been cold, their voices icy. At a meeting of the Council of Ministers. Gone for the day. Very busy. Tight schedule. Preparing a report. Receiving a delegation. Leaving tomorrow. Furtseva had not taken my calls, either. But now she was worried. She found the time. And her secretary was so pleasant.

"Maya, we need to talk. To consult, woman to woman, about your performance tomorrow. Come to see me at five today. The first entrance of the Central Committee, at Staraya Square. There's a pass for you. Don't forget to bring your passport. See you soon."

And there I was in the Central Committee's entryway. It was the first time I had crossed the threshold of the Party hive. All the founders of Marxism stared down at me from the silvery walls. Lenin, Marx himself, Khrushchev, Bulganin, Lenin again . . .

From behind a wide desk piled with papers a pretty, stately woman stood and approached me. Middle-aged, with a weary, crooked smile, neatly coifed, with a tight blonde knot at her nape, in a severe gray suit.

"So that's what you're like. Our famous ballerina . . ."

We talked for an hour and a half. About everything in the world. But the thread of our jagged conversation, like a sensible peasant horse, kept returning to its stable and its stall: I had to do something to keep tomorrow from being a success.

"There's only one thing I can do, Ekaterina Alexeyevna. Not dance at all."

And the pretty, charming woman would start her baloney again: "You must call all your fans. Explain that the foreign press will be there. A political provocation is possible. That would harm our socialist homeland, yours and mine . . ."

And on and on and on . . . I kept repeating, "I could not dance at all, Ekaterina Alexeyevna."

I do not want to digress, because I am recalling very painful days. But I will slow down. I cannot discuss Furtseva glancingly, in passing. She was a vivid figure in our soiled, miserable state. And her end was tragic: she poisoned herself with cyanide. Her boundless ambition put her on her deathbed.

After she had been in the Politburo she was "downgraded" to minister of culture. She replaced Mikhailov. And for a good fifteen years our lives crossed; we butted heads, I fought and made peace with Furtseva. She cannot be painted in just one color, black. Ekaterina Alexeyevna had a multitude of shades.

I will start with her last name. She looked very Slavic. But her surname was unusual and foreign-sounding. Many times, especially after drinking at artistic banquets, surrounded by gaping, servile Russians, she liked to boast charmingly and sweetly about how beloved she was by everyone. "But they especially love me in Germany. The Germans gather in huge crowds, I attract them like a magnet, they always smile when they kiss my hand, Madame Furtseva, Madame Furtseva . . ." Her ministerial henchmen lacked the sense to talk their minister into cutting back her trips to Germany, or to hint openly that her name was not the most aristocratic for Germans. To spare her being laughed at or protect her from humiliation and scorn. In the dictionary, *furzen* is translated as "passing wind," "farting." This is in Langenscheidt's Russian-German dictionary. Page 220. The most popular one. Yellow and blue. Sold on every street corner in Germany. Probably some serf ancestor of the minister's worked for a German landholder. The ancestor overdid certain sounds, and the German colonist called him Furtsev . . .

But seriously, she was a *live* creature, not an office puppet of papier-mâché. She could be touched, amused, persuaded, angered. She would pick up the phone while you were with her and take on some nasty bureaucrat. She would raise her voice at him. But . . . Even she could not challenge the KGB monster. Their sentence could not be appealed in the Soviet system.

Just before I left, she narrowed her gray-blue eyes and asked bluntly, "Did you say that people join the Party to further their careers and not out of conviction?"

"I don't remember. But if that's what it says in Serov's files . . ."

Furtseva shuddered. My mentioned of the omnipotent name was not pleasant. She quickly looked around her office. Could it be bugged, too?

And here was one more *Swan Lake.* In disgrace!

The theater was overflowing. I could see a boiling kettle of people through the peephole in the curtain before the house lights went down. The intoxicating hubbub of the audience, the buzz of a thousand bees. The side boxes seemed to be filled with clusters of grapes. A wall of people. In the aisles of the balconies, people were pressed together like coins in a purse. The orchestra seats were filled with hundreds of familiar faces. All Moscow was there. In solidarity with me. To support me. I had become a sort of dissident. One of the leading ones.

Someone tapped me on the back gently. The director's assistant, Sasha Sokolov. "Look, front center left, that's Serov and his wife."

I looked at the colorless, bedbug face of a eunuch, thinning pale hair neatly parted. A flash—a horrible association. He looked so much like Stalin's Commissar of Death Yezhov (his photograph appeared in the newspapers every day until 1937). Is it the executioners' profession or nature that makes them resemble one another?

I have never had a greater success in *Swan Lake* in my life. Perhaps later in distant Argentina there was something approaching it, but without the political coloration. The audiences there are royally generous with ovations.

From the very beginning, at my entrance—after a leap—when I freeze in the first swan pose in fourth position (freeze frame), the theater burst out in ecstatic welcoming applause. Through the waterfall of sound I heard syllables of their shouts: . . . ra-a-a-vo, . . . avi-i-i-issimo. And something else with As and Os.

It was time to do the glissade, my legs were going to stiffen. But I couldn't hear the music for the thunder. And I wanted to let the authorities have it. Let Serov and his wifie burst their gall bladders. Bastards!

I held the pose for a good minute, maybe two (a motionless minute in the theater is an eternity), I didn't move a finger. The applause and shouts increased (yes, yes!). At last, I came to life and rose up. The performance went on.

After the adagio I came out for bows six times. After the variations, four times. And the whole ballet went that way. (I have the figures in my diary.) I was not tired in the least, I didn't even work up a sweat, because I rested as much as I needed taking my bows, returning my breathing to normal. And at the end of each act and after the last curtain — I cannot describe what went on. A squall. A storm. An eruption of Vesuvius.

Just what the authorities had feared. A demonstration!

Later friends told me that there were muscular men in every box who grabbed people who clapped too hard by their hands and dragged them away from the barriers. The ones who shouted at the top of their lungs were taken out to the lobby. But they resisted, holding onto the legs of those who remained or onto other available hard objects, kicking and scratching. It was a mess. By the third act the "saboteurs" were left alone — it was too much trouble to get them out. The ushers in uniforms with the theater's gold initials tearfully begged the audience "not to interfere with the course of the performance," and to express their pleasure in a disciplined way, after the performance, when the curtain embroidered with the dates of all the great revolutions, the words "Workers of the world unite," and the notes for a line from Stalin's anthem "Indestructible Union of Free Republics" finally came down.

From the stage I could not see Serov and his reaction to what was happening. When the lights went up in the hall, crowds of frenzied Muscovites flooded the first few rows of the orchestra, including the short general. My friends also told me that he didn't watch the stage too much. The man had come to the theater to work. In civilian dress. He kept looking around at the boxes where his men were defending the Soviet regime. He reacted like a dog, ears and eyes perking up, to every muffled sound of scuffling in the dark of the dress circle and balconies. Every "battle of the boxes" elicited instant, lively interest. And he stared suspiciously at the distant sounds of struggle. I'm sure that the brave general came home with a crick in his neck.

The next morning Furtseva summoned me. She was furious. But she controlled it. "Why didn't you keep your word, Maya? You didn't talk to your admirers . . ."

"I didn't promise to do that, Ekaterina Alexeyevna. You imagined it."

This conversation lasted two hours and fifteen minutes.

And still, how can I forget that there were only two powers-that-be who had the courage to talk to me? Even if it was useless. But an open door, a human voice were like balm for me in those plague years. One was Furtseva, and the other bold official was Polikarpov.

Dmitri Alexeyevich Polikarpov was then chief of the cultural department of the Central Committee of the Communist Party. (After his death, Shauro held his post all through the years of "stagnation.") When squabbling writers denounced Polikarpov, Stalin wrote a playful resolution, "Get rid of the fool." The punitive organs decided that there was no rush to shoot a "fool"; let him get an education first. They sent Polikarpov to an appropriate academy. And so he survived. Dear Comrade Stalin, you should have written sentences without loopholes.

Polikarpov was elected to the Supreme Soviet from Latvia. Whenever he'd come to Riga, the local flunkies would send their whole motor pool of black government limousines to meet his train. Polikarpov hated it — perhaps sincerely — and took the trolley with his little suitcase. And the government motor pool followed in a file behind the city transport to the Central Committee hotel.

And Furtseva's last question: "When is your next performance?"

"The sixteenth."

"Well, could you get the applauders and shouters to keep from creating a demonstration this time?"

I did not answer and left her office.

The KGB worked over the balletomanes with their tried-and-true methods. My fans, male and female, were called into the precinct station at 38 Petrovka, one at a time, starting that same evening. The address to which they were called made it clear that this was not a political question, but a case of "hooliganism." They were allegedly disturbing the peace (so vigilantly guarded by the authorities) of Muscovites who came to the theater for a rest after a hard day's work. They were kept for many hours, threatened and warned. The interrogators looked for a conspiracy or secret plans. Did I buy the tickets for my followers? they demanded. What instructions did I give them?

From what they told me, my fans were firm and bold. They stuck to their guns. Plisetskaya's *Swan Lake* was an event. Why wasn't she allowed to go to London? When had they stopped letting people applaud in theaters? There was nothing to confess — they had bought the tickets and flowers with their own money, and there was no way you could force an entire theater to clap and bravo and toss flowers if the dancing was weak . . . I made friends with some of them, after their interrogations, for life. Shura Roitberg, Nelli Nosova, Valery Golovitser, Yura Pronin. Shura Roitberg was questioned for more than eight hours. And they interspersed the general questions with specific seditious questions: Who visits Plisetskaya, what do the guests discuss? . . .

But the second performance, on October 16, did take place. It was helped — don't laugh — by Soviet peace policy. Japanese Prime Minister Itsiro Hatoyama was in Moscow, and Khrushchev took him to the theater. The poor fellow hadn't seen *Swan Lake* in a long time. He must have missed it. (The ballet went on instead of the announced *Boris Godunov.*)

It was another thunderous success. Even Khrushchev felt it. Nikita Sergeyevich turned red and smiled; he wouldn't leave his box and kept sending his greeting to the stage. Recently a journalist who tried never to miss a single performance of mine mentioned in passing that those "disgraced *Swan Lakes*" were the crown of my career. They were so anxious, emotional, and nervous that I never managed to rise higher than their level.

The next *Lake* was for October 18. The guest this time was Muhammed Daoud, king of Afghanistan. And my beloved government officials were in the box with him. Once again Khrushchev (let us sympathize with him), Bulganin, Pervukhin. Applause, smiles, bravos.

But on those very same days, in that same October 1956, the same rulers who controlled our fates and lives, who gave me a standing ovation in their boxes after the performance, convened their villainous Politburo to hear General Serov's asinine report about the ballerina Plisetskaya, who worked for British intelligence. No one asked any questions about why it didn't make sense or observed that Serov's theories were nonsense. That the ballerina did not speak any foreign languages. That she was a deaf-mute who knew nothing about the defenses of the land of the Soviets, was aware only of theater intrigues . . . Instead, they resolved to confirm the report, continue surveillance, not remove her from her position, and not allow her abroad. (Khrushchev's memoirs have a chapter with pages that allude to my sad story and the similar one of Sviatoslav Richter, whom they tormented, too. Look into Khrushchev's book, reader, if you have the time.)

I learned about that creepy meeting from the girls in Moiseyev's dance troupe, who had all married the children of Party bigshots. (They were beauties, all of them; Moiseyev knew how to create an ensemble.) And the husbands whispered to their ballet wives about their miserable colleague from the Bolshoi. She's a dancer, too, but . . . Women in Russia never knew how to keep a secret. Agitated beyond bearing, they gave me all the details. The Big Theater of the Soviet Absurd!

✦

The tour in London was going well. *Romeo* with Ulanova was outstandingly successful. Timofeyeva and Karelskaya danced *Swan Lake* instead of me, and Velta Viltsin, called in from Riga "to save the situation," danced Zarema in *Bakhchisarai.*

My Party instructor — the idealist French-horn player Polekh — distinguished himself, too, but in a different way. He collected a sum of money from every troupe member for a wreath for Karl Marx, since the old man was buried in foggy London. The grave had to be accorded the respect of the artists from the land of the Soviets. Reluctantly everyone chipped in. How can you deny the dead founder? But the generous wreath from the Moscow artists did not warm the remains of the author of *Das Kapital.* The money vanished, bye-bye. Slipped through the fingers of the theater's ideological leader into his own pocket, for his personal needs. There was a scandal. They were willing to chip in for Marx. But for sly Polekh? No way. They elected a new secretary. And now, back from London, he sat as quiet as a mouse, still in his bowtie and makeup, in the orchestra pit, without making speeches exhorting the unconscious, and played his French horn solo.

And chief of the tour Pakhomov, whom you have already met, exerted all his Bolshevik energies on the most important issue: the order in which people enter and leave at receptions, press conferences, and meetings with the Soviet-British Friendship Society. The first to cross the threshold would be Vasily Ivanovich Pakhomov himself, naturally, the head of the delegation of sons and daughters of the great Soviet homeland. Next — Galina (as he referred with a worker's simplicity to Deputy Minister Ulanova), third, Raisa (Struchkova), fourth, Leonid (Lavrovsky), and then the rest. And the rest of the herd had its heads counted several times a day by special counters (from the secret police, of course) who were good at math and were brought in for this responsible task. The ballet tongues, razor-sharp, reported all this back to Moscow.

I want to say a good word about the people who expressed sympathy in those miserable "London weeks." Vakhtang Chabukiani, director of the Georgian ballet, persistently called on me to send all the torments of Moscow to hell and move to work in Tbilisi. But it would not have helped. The regime was Soviet, vile, everywhere. The artist Fonvizin, an old and respected master, whose eyes were bad by then, did several portraits of me. I posed gladly. Marina Semenova, who could read the suffering in my eyes, cheered me up: "Be brave, girl, it was worse for me. It's scarier being under house arrest. They didn't let me dance."

And I did have a meeting with Serov at last. Twenty years later, just like the Dumas novel. Shchedrin and I were on our way to visit the violinist Leonid

Kogan at his dacha in Arkhangelskoe. Leonid Borisovich had just bought the place and was having viewings for his friends. Amid the endless houses with high fences scattered outside Moscow, we lost our way. Were we supposed to turn right, or continue straight? Fortunately a small old man was making his way along the side of the road in a faded jogging suit. A covered tennis racket bounced in his hand. The man's hair was neatly shaved in the back, in a doughnut shape. We stopped. Shchedrin turned down the window. Greeting him politely, he asked, "Is Leonid Borisovich Kogan's dacha nearby? Are we going in the right direction? Should we make a right turn?"

The athlete turned and I felt a jolt of electricity. You remember faces like that to your dying day.

"What Kogan? We don't have people like that. These are government dachas. You've made a mistake."

Sensing hostility, Shchedrin drove on. Afraid to look back — I was scarred for life — I hissed, "That was Serov. Is he still alive?"

When we got to Kogan's, I asked him right from the doorway, Was it possible?

"You have a great memory for faces. Personal state pensioner Army General Serov lives nearby. He goes to play tennis with his pals every day. He'll outlive us all, the cutthroat."

Clairvoyant. Serov outlived Kogan.

Let me return to 1956. The KGB car diligently followed me, but I got used to it. It began to seem less scary and more funny. I began to recognize their silhouettes. I could tell which crew was working. One guard gave me a sheepish smile once through the window — it's just a job.

On October 29 I danced in Tula. In the homeland of Leskov's clever Lefty. I earned money. When I didn't have any, I put up with that, too. I began traveling not far from Moscow. Frequently. Ryazan, Kovrov, Bryansk, Tambov, Vladimir . . . I didn't have time to take longer trips.

I knew that on the 29th they were doing *Swan Lake* in London, while I was expressing myself in Tula.

My legs were aching from all the nervous tension, the overwork. The day before, I had a stabbing pain in my calf as I ran on the stairs to make a train. As if a dog had bitten me. I hoped it would hold! . . . On November 1, I would be dancing *Swan Lake* again in Moscow. For the Syrian premier Shukri Kuatli. Khrushchev would be there again.

I wanted to do something different in the second act. What could I come up with?

Chapter Twenty-Seven

How I Dressed

Whenever I notice a nun in a starched wimple or a manly, well-groomed lieutenant in a crowd on the street, I always wonder how they would be perceived if, let's say, the nun were wearing a Pierre Cardin dress with a plunging neckline or the lieutenant a dirty padded vest with oily stains over baggy quilted pants. How clothes do make the man!

Our exterior cover creates our image. It alone. We base our perceptions of character on image and use it to form our judgments of the individual. Clothes also dictate behavior. Manners won't save you (your palms can betray you only at close range). It even took an entire night to determine who the princess on the pea was.

So how did I dress? What did I wear? Where and from whom did I buy my wardrobe? After all, you can't find a good-looking dress in GUM. In my entire life, I didn't see a single one in GUM.

Once upon a time a sorceress named Klara lived in Moscow. She wasn't quite a sorceress, she was . . . an entrepreneur. Let's call her that. Klara made house calls to actors' homes, mostly to the *nevyeʒdnye*, nontraveling type. She always carried with her a bag of impressive size which could accommodate an entire wardrobe. Everyday dresses and evening wear, coats, capes, shoes, blouses, underwear, little purses.

All of Klara's treasures were imported and of good quality. The wives of Soviet diplomats regularly sold her their most popular items. The contraband trail was well-worn.

The items were always new, with the cheerful labels and brand names of foreign shops. The prices, however, were not cheerful — the luxury items were fabulously expensive. But you can't go around in rags. You have to dress as well as those who go abroad. People look at me; I'm in the public eye. But these un-worn clothes always gave off a slight trace of acrid sweat. Klara's young daughter would try on the entire wardrobe before her mother's next trips to the to the lairs of the actors.

Everything I wore I purchased from Klara. At three times the original price. She was no altruist.

If an attractive item was the wrong size or too tight, ballooned up or didn't suit you, Klara would neatly pack the dress back into the magical bag and solemnly pronounce, "I'll work with this some more."

She meant that the item would unquestionably find its buyer.

Klara had other clients at the Bolshoi Ballet, from the same tribe of *nevyezd-nye* as me. In a fit of blind rage, my theatrical pal Valya Peshcherkova's mother, who suffered excruciatingly for her nonexportable daughter, coined an immortal aphorism. For many years it, along with a bitter smirk, ameliorated the limita-tions of our ballerina wardrobes, the wardrobes of those of us who remained behind in Moscow: "We won't be seen in anything worse than them!"

And we weren't. But we had to do the rounds of thousands of tiny club stages with unheated, uneven dance floors, to traverse hundreds of torn-up, unpaved roads, blaze a multitude of onerous itineraries, chill and torture our feet, endure the ineradicable Russian boorishness to do so. Elegance attained by blood.

I've already written that my semi-theatrical, garish clothes were my rebellion, my revolt, my challenge to the system. Even our slow-witted leaders felt that there was something deliberate here, that I was dressed as if onstage, not "like us." It was in those years that Khrushchev said to me with a certain reproach, "You're dressed awfully beautifully. Are you rich?"

Things were more difficult when it came to furs. No matter how much I danced in clubs, I couldn't afford Klara's furs. And so I wore Mita's old astrakhan coat for seven years running during the frozen, snowy Russian winters. The gray lamb-skins were completely threadbare, worn out in spots, forming impressive bald patches. I had to resort to the theater furrier Mirkin's help; he picked over the decayed fur so he could sew wool of the same color into the sides. That's how an astrakhan hat was created!

People considered me a fashion plate. But my sense of fashion, of what was fashionable came to me much later.

When I returned from Paris in 1966 I put on another astrakhan coat, a black maxi-fur with leather appliqué, which Nadya Léger had given me as a gift. I dressed up in it and walked out of my place on Gorky Street to catch a taxi. The first Muscovite who saw me was perturbed by my appearance, crossed herself in the Orthodox manner and said, "Oh Lord, isn't she a sinner!"

In Moscow I was a Christopher Columbus when it came to maxi-length furs.

And then later, when Nadya Léger introduced me to Pierre Cardin, the great, incomparable, inexhaustibly inventive Pierre Cardin, and after I had spent time at his dazzling collections, I sensed intuitively that fashion was an art form. Full of mysteries, understatement, sorcery — art.

I firmly believe that it was because of Cardin's costumes that my ballets *Anna Karenina, The Seagull,* and *Lady with the Dog* received recognition. Without his refined imagination, which authentically conveyed the aromas of the times of Tolstoy and Chekhov to the viewer, I wouldn't have been able to realize my dream.

I wound up in Paris by the will of Fate during the heat of working on *Anna Karenina*. I was telling Cardin about my agony over the costumes for *Karenina* at breakfast at L'Espace. In Tolstoy's time, women wrapped themselves in tight, long, floor-length dresses, with an added heavy, protruding bustle in the back. You can't even walk properly in such an outfit, let alone dance, and here you were supposed to dance in it. I didn't want to turn the costume into an abstraction, but what kind of Anna Karenina would she be, dressed in rehearsal leotards?

Without any hope, more to think out loud, I said to Cardin, "Now, how marvelous it would be, Pierre, if you did the costumes for *Karenina* . . ." Cardin's eyes lit up like batteries. As if an electrical current passed through them.

"I know how to do it. You need . . ."

And then within a week I was in Cardin's boutique on avenue Matignon for a fitting. Cardin himself hypercritically controlled every pleat, every seam, every stitch. And asked me constantly, "Lift your leg in an arabesque, into attitude. Double over. Is it comfortable? Does the costume restrict your movements? Do you feel it? It has to be more you than your very own skin."

Pierre created ten costumes for *Karenina*. Each more beautiful than the others. Real masterpieces. They should be on display in museums.

"The last dress is a shroud. Like Christ's shroud. Gray on black. Gray like the puff of smoke from a steam engine." That's what Pierre said during the fitting for the dress in which Anna dies. (Please don't get the idea that I suddenly began to speak French so boldly. Our mutual friend Lili Denis, a kind, rare soul who was completely fluent in both languages, was always right there beside me, always assisting me as a friend.)

Before the premiere, Cardin sent me several boxes with company labels which contained the finished treasure-dresses. I can't forget the boxes either: they were made in the old-fashioned style — the kind great-grandfather's best Sunday to-phat was kept in — snow-white, with wide, patterned ribbons tied in bows. And two words — "Pierre Cardin."

The way Cardin solved the problem technically was simple. He lifted the side gathers of the Petersburg fashion plates toward the waist and liberated the legs, without changing the feminine silhouette of that time. Any movement became possible. And instead of bustles, Cardin made do with the widest possible bows, half-ethereal, with a wavy ribbon to the floor. He created my fur outfit with a velvet muff, crowned with a black satin rose, in the same way. I appear before Vronsky for the first time in this attire on a Moscow train-station platform in the gusts of a snowy blizzard.

The color range of the costumes is divinely radiant. Black velvet with a filmy scarf at the ball; decorative violet vignettes in Princess Betsy's salon; white wings, slightly covering the nude body in the scene of Anna's "fall"; ostrich feathers at the races; the chocolate-brown hues of the Wrede Garden; the heavenly azure of the happy Italian pas de deux . . . I won't enumerate all the costumes.

And also *Lady with the Dog.* Just one dress. But what a dress! You had to see it, my dear reader.

All the precious theater clothes (Cardin also created film costumes for me, such as the ones for Turgenev's *Spring Torrents*) were his regal gifts.

My dear unselfish Pierre! How can I convey my feelings to you in words?

But Cardin's name was not included in the Bolshoi Theater playbill. It wasn't mentioned. The costumes were all ours. Soviet ones.

It was the Ministry of Culture which panicked and forbade the management to mention a foreign name in the list of credits. And a name like Cardin at that. Pierre didn't bat an eye. Anonymous — then let it be anonymous. The time would come.

It was only years later, gradually, at first during a tour, in small print that the creator of the costumes for *Karenina* was mentioned. Then it was printed in the Bolshoi program, too. The Iron Curtain parted this way, at a turtle's pace, slowly but surely. And it parted until there was a Cardin fashion show in Moscow's Red

Square in the summer of 1991. I stood next to Cardin, my eyes not believing what they saw, asking him to pinch me harder, so I could be sure this was real and not a dream.

But in the meantime . . .

In the winter of 1957 I was being rocked in a frozen Russian train, monotonously counting railroad ties. Beyond the fogged-up window, a real live snowstorm raged. The crooked milestones flashed by. Women switch-workers with little yellow flags. I was wearing my gray Persian lamb fur with wool gussets along the sides. My astrakhan hat slipped down over my eyes from the jostling of the ride. I dozed.

The car was chilly, unheated, smoky with tobacco. A long road lay ahead. I was on my way to Kovrov, where I had two concerts in the evening. Five numbers each (excerpts from *Swan Lake,* Raymonda's variation, Gluck's "Melody," the third act from *Bakhchisarai,* and the truly immortal *Dying Swan.*) I wasn't feeling well. I had picked up the flu somewhere. At least I didn't have a fever.

But I would get paid *today.* I would have the cash to buy Klara's dresses.

Chapter Twenty-Eight

What a Person Needs

My little journal from the year 1957 records only grief and sorrow. They didn't let me leave the country until April 1959. I continued to write, sometimes angry, sometimes pitiful letters — petitions — but all of them remained unanswered. All of them. All.

Encounters with leaders became less frequent. I even avoided large gatherings of people where foreigners were present. If you're not careful, they'll make up new cock-and-bull stories for your dossier. I had quite enough nonsense in there already.

Obviously there was no going without conversations with the mighty of the world, but their response was lies. I was "passed" from the right side to the left, to center, to the umpire, like a ball in a soccer match. What's the point in listing the trips that I didn't take, the places I didn't go? It would be a bore.

Pyotr Alexandrovich Gusev was dismissed. Because of the red dots. The dots marked next to the names of those who were not allowed to travel. The fact that the artistic director could not keep a secret was leaked to KGB ears by an unknown route. Such people have no business in the silk-paneled offices of directors. Gusev left for Leningrad. Lavrovsky returned to the Bolshoi.

In the meantime, Igor Moiseyev began working on *Spartacus*. This was the Bolshoi's first crack at *Spartacus*. I was rehearsing Aegina. The subservient Moscow ballet folk, not unintentionally I think, pushed this work to the back burner. Needlessly! That was unfair. And all because the bacillus of servility deprived many of their conscience and memory: "Moiseyev's ballet is a bust, and that's all there is to it! To the garbage with it." But the present little dictator has created a great masterpiece. He's the one with the power. He's the one we're going to glorify. Naturally . . . while he's on the throne.

Time will put things in their rightful places. It's just that the waiting's too long.

The part of Aegina that Moiseyev created was uncommonly beautiful. My hand writes about it with pleasure. The production was luxurious, on a grand scale. No expense was spared. At that time the government threw money at the Imperial Theater by the fistful. It didn't keep track of it (anyway, it was the people's money, not the government's own). I appear in Crassus' palace from the lower trap on a hoist, in the colorful streams of an actual fountain. The entire male section of the troupe participated in the gladiators' duels. Everything shimmered with color; it gushed and blazed. Fayer disgorged Khachaturian's *tutti* on the audience so powerfully that their eardrums shuddered and warped. The costumes were lavish. They sparkled with mother-of-pearl, flashed with the colorful embroidery of theatrical stones. It was practically Hollywood on the Soviet square named after Sverdlov.

The choreographic movement was lush, earthly, and striking. My duets with Garmodius (Fadeyechev) were at the limit of the permissible, according to the tenor of those times, naturally. The viewer held his breath: would they really allow this? . . .

In the final scene I appeared in a gold helmet with long feathers in sparkling chain mail and an emerald chiffon tunic. I walked up a marble staircase to the castles of pirates (what were pirates doing there?). Pallas Athena from the bas-reliefs of the Acropolis . . .

The ballet's Achilles heel, and this really was the case, was Spartacus himself. Moiseyev set out to re-create Spartacus's physical image, one that was chronicled repeatedly by all the Roman writers: the leader of the slave rebellion was a mighty, powerful athlete. There was just such a handsome giant in the theater, Dmitri Begak. It's just that he had problems with . . . dancing. Moiseyev created Spartacus's part within the limitations of Begak's dancing capabilities. And he miscalculated. In the opera you have to sing. In the ballet you have to dance. There's no other way . . .

Moiseyev's inventive mind displayed itself most notably in the duets. At the rehearsals Igor Alexandrovich suggested an abundance of trick supports. Right then and there, when our muscles were warmed up enough, in the enthusiasm of initial discovery, we could manage them. But the next day it took a great deal of effort to effortlessly crown the culminating splashes of Khachaturian's melodies.

One lift didn't work, no matter what we tried. It worked once during the first production rehearsal, and elicited everyone's delight and the desire to perform it. After the high solo leaps, I was then supposed to jump up onto my partner's hip and wind up in the arabesque position, literally doubled over in half. A turn, a change of hand positions, a kiss across the spine. And then . . . No, describing ballet with a pen is a losing proposition. Just believe me that the weave of combinations was baffling but marvelously beautiful, striking, when we managed to do it.

All of Moiseyev's tricks worked for Aegina. In the story she is a courtesan. Moiseyev used all the bends, bodily languor, voluptuousness, and embraces he wanted. His taste did not betray him anywhere in the piece. But the show lasted an eternity. Khachaturian would not permit it to be shortened by a single bar. Battles commenced. Alas . . . Moiseyev retreated. The ballet lasted four and a half hours. No matter how tasty the dish, you feel nauseated if you eat too much of it.

I read all this and got to thinking, Aren't I writing about everything too maliciously?

But was I treated kindly? I was persecuted to such a degree that there wasn't a day that went by that I didn't contemplate suicide. There wasn't a single road to the other side that I didn't consider. Hanging myself, throwing myself out the window, lying down on a railroad track — all would be unaesthetic and painful. It would look disgusting.

The reader will shrug his shoulders: big deal, they didn't let her go abroad for six years. That was all. No big deal. She's a weak-nerved one, a sniveler. She wasn't sent to prison, wasn't forbidden to dance; they invited her to receptions, granted her titles; she had a salary, she dressed according to the latest fashions . . . What else did she need?

And so what does a person really need? I don't know about other people. I'll say what it is for myself.

I don't want to be a slave.

I don't want people whom I don't know to decide my fate.

I don't want a leash on my neck.

I don't want a cage, even if it's a platinum one.

When I'm invited somewhere as guest and I'm interested in going, I want to be able to travel, to fly there.

I wish to be equal with other people. If my theater is going on tour, I want to go with it.

I don't want to be rejected, shunned like a leper, branded.

I can't reconcile myself to it, when people run away, scatter from you, avoid you, are afraid to talk to you.

I don't want to hide what I'm thinking.

It's shameful to be wary of denunciations.

I don't want to bow my head and I won't do it. That's not what I was born for.

Every God-given day I was immersed in the thick of people. With the lasers of thousands of eyes boring into me. Rehearsal, class, performance, workshops, the cafeteria . . . I worked in the theater. I was supposed to smile in public, pretend lightheartedness, insouciance. Everything's fine, dear colleagues. Nothing to worry about. Things were all right. But my soul was being torn apart by tigers. You can master yourself for a week or a month, but six years? What if you have to live this way for six years? Two thousand one hundred and ninety days? It was very painful and shameful for me. Unbearably painful. Unbearably shameful.

Time heals all wounds, and heals them well. Today, even I look at my life of those years more calmly, with more detachment. But when you don't know what to expect the next day, what do you do with yourself, how do you save yourself and not let the art of ballet pass you by? — when there's no color except black for you in this whole wide colorful world?

I celebrated the new year 1958 in Tbilisi. In hospitable, beautiful Tbilisi, mercilessly destroyed now in the senseless, bloody slaughter. I was seriously thinking about whether to move there from Moscow. While Serov was the head of the KGB, there was no mercy for me. I began to negotiate with Vakhtang Chabukiani about a possible repertoire. We even sketched out a time line — after the first performances of Moiseyev's *Spartacus*.

But fate decided otherwise.

Chapter Twenty-Nine

Shchedrin

On March 11, 1956, the premiere of *Spartacus* took place on the stage of the Bolshoi Theater. The rehearsal period for the Moscow production dragged on so long that Leonid Yakobson, who had begun his work with the Khachaturian score in Leningrad after Moiseyev started his, nevertheless reached the finish line first. But he made cuts. While Khachaturian stayed Moiseyev's hand in Moscow, protecting his baby from any attempted cuts, Yakobson trimmed the plump score in Leningrad.

When Khachaturian saw Yakobson's *Spartacus*, they had an enormous, loud argument. Stubborn Yakobson and proud Khachaturian clashed on the field of curses at the Kirov Theater. The curses were real. For several years Khachaturian refused to greet Yakobson or shake his hand, spoke of him only in the third person in his presence, and addressed him through trusted envoys as Citizen Yakobson, as if he were a criminal in court.

Le tout Moscou attended the premiere. Theatrical Moscow. Musical Moscow. I invited a few friends, leaving tickets at the box office in their names. Two tickets were reserved for Rodion Shchedrin. We had seen each other a few days before the premiere at the house of Lili Yuryevna Brik, where I had spoken enthusiastically about the new work. He asked for tickets. I promised.

We met for the first time at the Brik house in 1955, when Gérard Philipe came to Moscow. Here is my diary entry for October 25: "Today I was at Lili Brik's. Their guests were Gérard Philipe with his wife and Georges Sadoul. They were all very nice and friendly. The couple expressed regret for never having seen me on the stage, but I 'consoled' them with autographed photos (very poor ones, but I didn't have any good ones). There were no other guests. (The composer Shchedrin was also there.)"

On that fall "French" evening, Shchedrin played a lot of his own music on the Briks' Bechstein, which delighted the company. A spark of mutual interest ran between us but went out immediately. Late that night the party broke up, and Rodion took the last guests home in his Pobeda. The route worked out so that I was the last one to get out, on Shchepkinsky. As we were saying good-night, I made a request—could he transcribe the musical theme of the Charlie Chaplin film *Limelight* just by listening to a record? I liked the melody very much, and I had talked with Goleizovsky about doing a number based on the plot of the Chaplin film. Goleizovsky liked my idea, but where would we get the music? Shchedrin agreed. A few days later he sent me the score. But something went wrong at the last minute, and that number never saw the light of day. In subsequent years we met fleetingly several times, sweetly exchanging a few witty remarks, but I had the feeling that he was angry about having done the Chaplin work for nothing.

And then came March 1958. The premiere of *Spartacus* was a success. All the participants received thunderous ovations, including me. The next morning Shchedrin called me with compliments. Then he went on to say, "I'm working with Radunsky on a new *Little Humpbacked Horse* for your theater. Radunsky is enlightening me as best he can about the ballet, but he insists that I come to class several times. Will that really help? When do you work? At eleven? Will you be in class tomorrow?"

The next day we saw each other in class. Shchedrin came with Radunsky. They sat down by the mirror. The class started. I worked in a black, clinging leotard . . .

I was one of the first to rehearse in a stretch one-piece. (In those days people usually wore tunics for class and rehearsal.) The black French leotard naturally came from the magic bag of the indefatigable Klara. The leotard looked great on my body, emphasizing its good points: I caught glimpses of myself with pleasure in the mirror. First there were seductive steps, then an hour's exercises in the garb that clung to my torso! Shchedrin was engulfed by a hurricane of Freudian thoughts. And then I added, "I have two more rehearsals after class. In Room 1. Would you like to watch?"

Shchedrin stuttered. "Thank you. But I have more than enough impressions for my first day."

But he called me that evening and invited me for a car ride. Old man Freud won. I agreed without a second thought. The upshot is that, as I write, we have not been separated for thirty-four years. Going on thirty-five.

We used to meet at the composers' apartment house on Ogaryov Street, where Shchedrin lived with his mother, and at my place on Shchepkinsky. It was a cold spring that year. And at night, lying still, we would listen to the shivering KGB men — the surveillance cars still followed me — turn on their noisy engine to warm up. From my second-story room we could hear them clearly. They were too lazy at the KGB garage to tune up the car.

This dizzying affair, which fell on my head out of nowhere, diverted me from thoughts of Tbilisi and my abortive trip to France and Belgium. The trip took place, without me, and the troupe did well. I stayed home. I couldn't get used to it. But this blow wasn't as painful. When you have a person to share your sorrows and joys, life smiles upon you, things seem lighter, and hope springs eternal. We'll find a way out of the catacombs together — we will!

A few days before the troupe left for Paris — their flight was on May 25 — Minister of Culture Mikhailov held a meeting at the theater to prepare the travelers. When someone asked why Plisetskaya was not going, he replied mysteriously, "Plisetskaya, comrades, may be going on another, no less responsible trip."

A wary hum went through the crowd. What could be more responsible than performing at the Paris Opera? Were they sending Plisetskaya to Mars? To perform swan dances for the Martians' delectation? About forty people who never used to recognize me suddenly started greeting Maya Mikhailovna Plisetskaya warmly in the halls. There's an example of our Russian baseness.

Mikhailov's argument was a joke. The performances of *Swan Lake* at the Paris Opera were on May 31 and June 2 and 7. I did not leave Russia on my "responsible trip" until June 14 — to Prague. Nevertheless, it was a small step, a shift from a hopeless situation. "A chicken's not a bird, Prague's not abroad," our old proverb goes. (Thank God, that no longer is true.) But the new passport for foreign travel was crisp in my hands. Customs, border guards, foreign speech, little shops, tempting Czech glassware . . . I could take a brief vacation from Klara.

The program in Prague and other Czech cities was called "An Evening with the Soloists of the Bolshoi Ballet." We called ourselves the "penalty battalion of the Bolshoi." An all-star team of dancers not allowed to travel abroad, performing in a fraternal people's democracy. None of us had been allowed to go to Paris, but we could go to Czechoslovakia. I guess they decided that they didn't want us completely embittered. And we couldn't run away from Czechoslovakia, anyway. There was a Soviet lock on the border there, too.

I danced only three numbers on that trip, Dvořák's "Melody," excerpts from *Swan Lake*, and — guessed yet? — *The Dying Swan*. I had always liked Dvořák's charming music, reminiscent of Tchaikovsky. So a few days before the trip I decided to do something from the "Czech repertoire." That ought to please the Czechs, no? Naturally, Dvořák. I took the music of his "Melody" and in just one rehearsal choreographed a duet. I chose Dima Begak, who had not gone to Paris and was a reliable escort, for my partner. The number was created all of a piece, on a single breath, and the audience liked it.

Shchedrin spent my "Czech month" in Sortavala. The Moscow composers had a vacation house there on the shores of Lake Ladoga.

After Czechoslovakia I packed up some goodies and headed for Karelia. The surveillance car followed me to the Leningrad Station and . . . vanished. Did they take a vacation, too? Or were they planning to follow me around the woods and lakes?

Shchedrin, tanned and more freckled than usual, met me at Sortavala. He and I came from the same stock — red-haired. Maybe it was nature's way of keeping us even closer together. A companion in the train pointed out the open window and said, "There's your brother with a bouquet." Shchedrin had an armful of field flowers. There really was a resemblance.

The summer in Sortavala was a high point. We lived in a tiny cottage in the woods, among granite boulders, completely isolated from people. The cottage consisted of one tiny room. Seven or eight square meters. The toilet was the great outdoors. The bath was Lake Ladoga. The mosquitoes were ruthless. Elk scratched themselves against our walls at night. On rainy days it was chilly in the house. The cottage had no heat. The roof leaked. But we radiated happiness. After all, what does a person really need, O wise philosophers of the universe, I ask once again?

In late August I had a new anxiety. There was every sign that I was pregnant. We had to go back to Moscow. Maybe I should have the baby and give up ballet? Oh, that would be a shame. After *Spartacus* and the Czech tour I was in good form. Thin. I'd put it off a bit. I had time. Dance or nurse babies . . .

I chose the former. Shchedrin was not delighted, but he agreed. A doctor in Moscow confirmed it. Pregnant. But there was no point in having an abortion before October. The fruit had not ripened.

Unexpectedly for ourselves, we set off on a long journey. To Sochi, just the two of us, in Shchedrin's car. I'd take the spa treatment at Matsesta, too. My knee was acting up. The troupe usually returned on August 26 to the theater. But this year, because of the French tour, we were not required to show up until a month later. In his youth, Rodion had done a lot of movie work, writing film scores. The pay was pretty good. And so he bought a car.

We set off.

Our route went through Tula, Mtsensk, Kharkov, Rostov, and Novorossiisk. Incidentally, I had danced in all those cities. They wouldn't let us into hotels. Our passports were not stamped to show we were married. So we were unmarried. Then go wherever you want, travelers, but not here. We had to sleep in the car.

On our first night in the car, on the side of the road in Mtsensk (the Mtsensk of Leskov and Shostakovich fame, where Katerina Izmailova bumped off her husband and brother-in-law), we left a bag of food outside in the cold, under a fender. It was crowded in the car, and the roast chicken would stifle in there. It was pitch black all around us. You could poke your eye out. Quiet, not a soul around. We slept soundly. In the morning, at daybreak, we opened the car door. We needed to eat before starting out. But the bag was gone without a trace. How could someone have taken it away in the night, without making any noise? Was it an animal? Or was is Leskov's clever left-handed craftsman who had invented a new way of stealing?

We were left without food. We drove to the railroad station, where they said the canteen was open round the clock. It was — but the food stank. The boiled potatoes were bluish, the stewed fruit had flies, the bread was stale, and the dishes dirty. I could tell that Shchedrin was watching me. Waiting for the ballerina to make a scene, stamp her foot, and complain. But I put the food away like a trencherman. I've always had a huge appetite.

We went on. We bought some watermelons from a farm stand. And we got some apples. We drove on.

This time we slept in the steppe beyond Rostov. We drove off the road to a small brook before dark. We washed our hands and filled up on fruit. What was left over, we piled up near the car and covered with branches. That was a reaction to the theft the night before, it was a little trauma, after all . . . We didn't really have to. Who would want our melons? The watermelon farms were all around. We didn't see any people.

We curtained the windows and slept soundly. At dawn, we decided to have a piece of melon. Early breakfast. We moved the branches — and found nothing. No melons, no apples. This was too much.

The third night we spent near Arkhipovka in Dzhugba. Right on the beach. A few meters away from the gentle splash of the Black Sea. This time we were risking roast partridges from the Novorossiisk market. We couldn't put them in the trunk — we had gasoline canisters in there, which would smell up the food. (There was only one place on the entire trip where we managed to fill up with gas, in Belgorod. There was no gas anywhere else.) Rodion spent an hour setting a trap for the robbers, should they try to take our partridges, too. As I remember it, the enamel pot in which the partridges lay was suspended by a thick cord above the ground. A line with a bell went from the pot into the car and tied to Shchedrin's foot for the night. We felt as inventive as Edison. If they dared — and there was no one on the beach — Rodion would wake up instantly and take a shot at the robbers with his starter's pistol. To scare them off.

We slept even better than usual knowing that our food supply was completely safe. In the morning, my first questions were, "Are they hanging there? Are they whole? Will we have breakfast?"

Shchedrin tested the line. The bell tinkled. He was happy. "The pot is safe. I can tell it's full. We'll have a feast."

We got up. First a swim. Then the partridge.

Unbelievable! Instead of the pot, there was a rock tied to the cord. And a penciled note: "Thanks."

Holy Mother Russia!

And that's how we got to Matsesta. I took ten spa treatments there. My knee got better. And then we went back. There was no one following me in Karelia or on the trip to Sochi. At least, we were not aware of it. No one drove right behind us, no one kept watch. I thought at the time that they were more worried about my meetings with foreigners in the capital. But then, what about all those thefts? . . . It was devilish. Could the KGB have been eating all our goodies? I still have no answer to that question.

Back near Moscow autumn was waiting for us. Trees in crimson dresses. Chilly mornings. Hoarfrost on the fields. Gorgeous.

This had been our honeymoon trip.

Back in Moscow, on October 2, 1958, we went to the registry office to join in wedlock. Today I can confess that it was on my initiative. Shchedrin did not want the official bonds of marriage. But my intuition told me that the authorities would ease up on me if I were married. They had hinted as much several times. And Furtseva told me so openly — get married. There will be more trust in you. They even promised me a new apartment.

Moscow's regional registry office. A dull building without windows, an office desk under felt. A harried, grim woman handed us the application blanks. "Go out in the hall and fill these out. Then come back to me."

We filled them out. Our hands are used to forms. And the questions are the ancient ones: father, mother, date of birth, place of work . . . No one's come up with any different ones. We did it. We came back. The lady did not even look at us. She was engrossed in reading our papers. She ran her pencil along the lines. And suddenly, she looked up.

"You are Maya Plisetskaya, the ballerina? I've never been to the Bolshoi, even though I was born in Moscow. Is there any way I could get tickets from you?"

I promised. I took her phone number. The lady became quite warm. She came out from behind her desk. She shook our hands. "May you grow old on one pillow. Congratulations!"

She stamped our passports with a rectangular violet seal. She wrote, "marriage registered . . . October 2, 1958, . . . Moscow."

Now we could spend the night together in a hotel. What progress. And we also got a marriage certificate, on parchment with water seals. And with the Soviet emblem in the middle.

We went outside. Sleet. Wind. A wet Moscow autumn. A fine drizzle. Sloshing through the slush, we headed for the nearest store. We needed vodka and champagne. Friends would be coming in the evening. That would be our wedding feast. A cranky old woman wrapped in a wool shawl — only nose and toothless mouth visible — gave me a nasty jab in the side. "Miss, don't jump the line!"

Shchedrin replied in an amiably edifying manner, "That's no miss. That's my wife."

Chapter Thirty

Life on Kutuzovsky Prospect

I'll begin with the prose. With apartment matters.

The entire summer while I was in Prague, Sortavala, and Matsesta, my mother was totally engaged. She was "breaking through" on the apartment scene. Her nature, as I wrote earlier, was quiet but caustic and obstinate to the extreme. She grew very concerned that I was beginning to suffer from insomnia because of the din of theater sets crashing under my windows in the middle of the night.

And she got her way! Her wedding gift to me was an authorization for new living quarters. Soon afterward, Shchedrin and I moved to our new apartment on Kutuzovsky Prospect. The apartment was tiny, not much larger than the cottage in Sortavala. Two tiny rooms and a kitchen. Twenty-eight and a half meters in all.

There was no foyer at all. And if you got a slight running start from the staircase landing, you could easily land on our conjugal bed in the bedroom. But the neighborhood was a good one. The Moscow River was right next to us. The Hotel Ukraina was across the boulevard. There were plenty of shops around. There was no noise from the theater beneath my windows. On Red holidays, from our little balcony, Shchedrin used to shout Armenian obscenities (taught him by musicians in Armenia) at Azaryan, a trumpet player and a neighbor on the same floor, driving him into indescribable embarrassment.

Three of us settled into our new little apartment: Shchedrin, myself, and Katya, the maid. Ekaterina Alexeyevna Zhamkova. She had worked for the Shchedrin family in the past, when Rodion's father, Konstantin Mikhailovich, was still alive. Later, after quarreling with Rodion's mother, she moved in with a Moscow army family.

On the second morning of our new life, Shchedrin managed to drop a fried egg on himself and, in a fit of temper, he got into his car and drove off to fetch Ekaterina. Barging in on the orderly household without any warning, he threw Katya's simple worldly goods into a suitcase, tossed her coat over her, and, accompanied by the wailing of the officer's wife loudly calling him to justice, dragged Katya off to our place on Kutuzovsky. Russians are inclined to submit to fate and pressure.

Katya slept in the kitchen near the gas burners, making her fold-away bed up for the night. In the morning Katya's bedchamber turned into a place for frying and steaming. When night fell, it reverted to a bedroom.

I have lived my entire life with Katya, and it would be a sin not to talk about her in more detail.

By birth she was a native of the village of Uspenskoye, near Arzamas, which means she was from the Nizhny Novgorod region. As soon as the war began, when she was seventeen, Katya was taken away to a defense plant to make cartridges. Bombing started. The warehouses at the plant were crammed with gunpowder. Who knows, a bomb could fall on it — everyone would be blown sky-high. The young collective farm girls who had been mobilized ran away in fright during the fiercest bombing. Each went her own way.

Having gotten past the barbed wire which encircled the defense site (the workers lived inside the barbed wire, like prisoners), Katya, together with a street-trader girl from the same settlement, rushed home to her native village. It was 40 kilometers to her house, but the escapees hid from people and made it to their native huts by the following night. On foot, naturally. Folks at home rejoiced but were frightened. Katya Zhamkova was a deserter!

And their fear was not without reason. An NKVD patrol began driving around the village along with the militia to hunt down deserters. They caught many of them, but a few still hid in gardens and woods for a long time. They were afraid to return to the plant.

This is a long story. I have to shorten my narrative.

Katya was on the lam from her persecutors for four years. It was a miracle they didn't catch her. She slept in logging areas, granaries, barns, and haystacks. She related how a search team stuck their pitchforks into a haystack in which she was hiding. She was also saved by the fact that the two deputized militiamen (Titov and Bodryashkin to be exact) had heart problems. Catching up with a resilient seventeen-year-old peasant girl was beyond their powers. They fired at her with their revolvers, but fate spared her. The former soldiers missed because of their shortness of breath.

But you get caught in the end.

Zhamkova was apprehended. She appeared before the tribunal. Lawbreaker, you must answer to the law. They gave her five years. One of them she spent in a Gorky prison (her story about it is terrifying), but the amnesty after the victory freed Katya before her term was up. Although freedom is always a relative concept in Russia.

The "freed" Katya was mobilized for peat-digging work, timber-cutting, and stump removal. Life painfully threw her here, there, and everywhere. After her father-in-law, who worked as an accountant in the collective farm office did some forging, Katya was released from the kolkhoz (collective) to go where she damn well pleased, and she headed off to the capital to get work as a maid. There was a rumor going around the kolkhoz that there wasn't a sweeter life in this whole wide world. Destiny brought her to the Shchedrin family.

We spent all our free evenings in the same place — on Kutuzovsky, with Lilya Yuryevna Brik and Vasily Abgarovich Katanyan, her last husband. They exchanged their walk-up apartment on the Arbat for the newly constructed Kutuzovsky building and moved in a few doors down in the same building. We had been very friendly even before — Shchedrin wrote music for Katanyan's play *They Knew Mayakovsky* and for a film of the same name, and Vasily Abgarovich wrote the libretto for Shchedrin's first opera, *Not Only Love*. Life as neighbors brought us even closer together.

It was always compellingly interesting at the Briks'. Theirs was an artistic salon; these were numerous in prerevolutionary Russia. But the Bolsheviks, who dealt brutally with all the "frivolities of the intelligentsia," sent Russian salon hosts to their forebears, to prisons, and to Siberia. By the end of the 1950s the Briks' was, I think, the only salon in Moscow.

Plenty of literature has come out about Lilya Brik in the past few years both here and in the West. I'm not going to be redundant and will direct those who are interested to the books in libraries. I'll just outline it telegraph style . . .

Lilya Brik, paramour and muse of Mayakovsky, a great poet of Russia: "If I wrote anything, if I said anything, it was the fault of the sky-eyes, the eyes of my beloved." Mayakovsky dedicated his entire collected works to Lilya. The French writer Elsa Triolet was Lilya's sister. Elsa was the wife of Louis Aragon, a great French poet. The sisters chose fiancés successfully!

Lilya was friends with Boris Pasternak, Pablo Neruda, Marc Chagall, Fernand Léger, Vsevelod Meyerhold, Sergei Eisenstein, Velimir Khlebnikov, Nazim Hikmet, and Isadora Duncan. With everyone from the "left front of art." She sculpted, acted in films. She was Agranov's lover, the Chekist who was Yagoda's deputy. It was Agranov's pistol that Mayakovsky used to shoot himself. Legally, she was the wife of Vitaly Primakov, the leader of the Cossacks whom Stalin executed in 1937. There is much talk and gossip surrounding her name. She was a complex, contradictory, unusual personality. I'm not going to judge her. I have no right to do so.

And the main thing, for me, is that Lilya loved the ballet very much. In her youth she had studied classical dance. She had even tried to dance herself, and flaunted faded yellowed photographs in which she was immortalized in a swan's tutu on pointe.

The first time I saw Lilya's photos I wounded her: "Your left sole is turned incorrectly."

"I wanted to astonish you, and you're going on about my left sole."

Lilya and Katanyan did not miss a single one of my performances, and each time they sent giant baskets of flowers to the stage. By Stalin's own decision Lilya received a third of Mayakovsky's estate, and she had a enormous amount of money. She squandered it. Didn't keep track of it. When she invited me over, she paid for the taxi. The same with all her friends.

The dinner table, cozily leaning into the wall that boasted original works by Chagall, Casimir Malevich, Léger, Pirosmani, and Mayakovsky's own paintings side by side, was always full of food. Caviar, salmon, cured sturgeon, pork loin, pickled mushrooms, and ice-cold vodka flavored with springtime black currant buds. And in honor of the French visit — fresh oysters, mussels, and pungent cheeses.

But one day Lilya became a pauper. Khrushchev, an unpredictable, eccentric leader, ordered the payments to the heirs of Mayakovsky, Gorky, and Alexei Tolstoy to be stopped without warning. Only grief and tears are stable in Russia. Lilya suddenly wound up on the rocks. She began selling her things. She summed things up good-naturedly: "The first half of our lives we buy, the second half we sell."

And even then Lilya made regal gifts. It was precisely then, in her penniless years, that she gave me diamond earrings as a gift, and I have them still.

And what about the ballet?

Film director Vera Stroyeva began filming *Khovanshchina*, based on Shostakovich's orchestration of Mussorgsky's opera at Mosfilm Studios, aligning it more closely with the original. I was asked to dance the Persian. Director Stroyeva — obese to the point of disease, a barely mobile woman with a kind, disarming smile — decided to take a decisive step in sexually educating the Soviet people.

"Maya, I would like to photograph you with your breasts bared. They say that you have the most beautiful breasts in the theater. I'd like to invite you to come by the studio by three o'clock tomorrow. You have to show your breasts to the cameraman. He has to set up some magical pink lighting. And I'll admire them myself at the same time."

I implored, "Vera Pavlovna, dear, I really would like you to film me. But in harem pants and a light embroidered bra — just like in the theater. My bare belly is enough to seduce Prince Khovansky and Soviet workers. The Art Council of Mosfilm won't let bare breasts pass censorship. They'll cut me out. I'll freeze for no reason. It's an icebox at the studio, and there are drafts."

Debates raged that evening on Kutuzovsky. Shchedrin was angry and suggested that I refuse to be filmed. He was jealous. Lilya Brik, to the contrary, reacted enthusiastically to Stroyeva's innovations. She begged me to take off the pants as well. Katanyan stayed neutral.

But my temperature rose at night. It was hard to swallow. Strep throat. The pink lighting rehearsal with the cameraman dropped by the wayside on its own. A week later, having gained extra weight from lying around in bed, I wrapped myself in warm scarves and came to Mosfilm for a night shoot. It was impossible to put it off any longer. The scenery in Khovansky's mansion had to be torn down in the pavilion. Stroyeva saw my pitiful appearance but still weakly insisted: "topless." I refused. The sexual revolution silently failed, and I was filmed in my usual theater costume.

At the theater, life took its usual course. I was very busy in the repertoire. From time to time I charmed distinguished visitors with *Swan Lake* and other ballets. I signed up for fewer concerts now. I began rehearsing the second version of Prokofiev's *The Stone Flower*. Everything at our theater was revised two and three times. I treated my knee again, getting Novocain at the Vishnevsky Institute.

Sol Hurok came to Moscow to plan the repertoire, choose the soloists, and assemble materials for advertising for an American tour. I know that he had asked about me insistently. Would they let me out? He tried to persuade the minister. Hurok thought that the minister, not the KGB, was the problem. Silly fool! He offered a guarantee. They replied, It's complicated. We could let you down. Prepare advertising about other dancers. . . At the theater people began to excitedly gossip about the three-month-long tour across the United States.

And suddenly, lightning on a clear day. Serov is dismissed with much noise. The daring fellow, he slipped up on the spy Oleg Penkovsky, who had disclosed all the super-secrets of Soviet jet fuel to the enemy. Instead of tracking the experienced spy colonel, he stubbornly made young KGB agents chase me on my good-for-nothing ballet trail. He changed the parasite-sentries three times a day! Those guys grew huge, fat faces from doing nothing! You pig, where was your Commie sense of smell?

Khrushchev placed Alexander Shelepin (the next Komsomol Führer after Mikhailov) on the throne as KGB leader. This same Shelepin would pay back his benefactor Nikita Sergeyevich a hundredfold in 1964: Shelepin removed Khrushchev from office and placed him under house arrest.

I traveled to one of the youth festivals in company with Shelepin, in the same train car. On the return trip, after championship beer and vodka libations, the Komsomol leader strolled about the railcar platforms in his underwear, with socks which had slipped down to his ankles and shuffled and squished like diver's flippers. He was inspecting the collective group entrusted to him. "The emissaries of Soviet youth," populating the festival train, gazed tenderly at their leader and snidely called him by his diminutive Shurik behind his back.

And here was "Iron Shurik" at the top of the Bolshevik hierarchic ladder, the head of the Organs, the Secret Services . . .

Should I start looking for the truth all over again? After all Iron Shurik and I had discussed my *Swan Lake*.

Beyond my Kutuzovsky windows—winter. The Moscow River was frozen over. Steam rose from people and cars. The New Year was upon us.

We were going to celebrate New Year's on Kutuzovsky at the Briks'. From 1959 on, New Year's Eve at Lilya Yuryevna's became a tradition for Shchedrin and me. We religiously followed this tradition for a good decade and a half. Louis Aragon and Elsa Triolet arrived in Moscow on New Year's Eve. They were going to be at Lilya's on Kutuzovsky.

December 31, 1958. Evening. In a few hours it would be 1959. We went up in the elevator, tracked with melted snow puddles and pine needles, and rang the bell to apartment 431 of our Kutuzovsky building. Katanyan, dressed in an attractive black frockcoat, opened the door. The Aragons are already there. We stamped our feet clean in the narrow foyer and walked over toward the table, crowded with an overabundance of delicacies. A pathetic fellow with a mug of beer in a Pirosmani painting squinted covetously at the food piled high on the plates. Lilya's maid, Nadezhda Vasilyevna, carried out a mountain of her rosy homemade pirozhki from the kitchen.

There was a gift near each place setting. A bottle of Robert Piguet's *Bandit* perfume near mine. Next to Shchedrin's — Dior cologne and Stravinsky's latest French recording. Elsa Yuryevna, Santa Claus, has brought it all from Paris. Ever since, I have preferred the scent of *Bandit* to all other French perfumes. The fragrance is marvelous, and the memory is dear.

During the dinner-table conversation we weren't silent about my six years "banned from the West." Aragon was indignant; he had a volatile and violent temper. They said that a meeting with Khrushchev was in the works. Vladimir Lebedev, the assistant to the general secretary on literary affairs, had maintained relations with him (all my life the Swan has been dependent on the Lebedevs).

"I'll tell Commodore Lebedev everything. I'll demand an answer. I'll complain to Khrushchev," Aragon raged, mangling Russian words. His Russian was staccato and amusing. At the beginning of a word he couldn't remember, he would hastily switch to French. Then Lilya would translate for us.

She, from her end, thought that we had to compose a most brilliant letter to Khrushchev which Aragosha (that's what she calls her brother-in-law) would pass on personally. "Serov was biased against you. Scoundrel! Fool! The new one will want to play a good guy in the beginning. For the sake of conversation around Moscow."

Twelve strikes. Veuve Cliquot champagne bubbled and foamed in our glasses. It came in Elsa's luggage, too. Aragon looked into Elsa's eyes without blinking through all twelve strikes. Lilya looked at Vasya. Imitating them, Rodion and I looked at each other.

We touched glasses.

We kissed.

Will the new year be good to us?

Chapter Thirty-One

I Go to America

Khrushchev did not see Aragon that trip. Leaders always have little time to spare for artists. They are men of government!

It turns out that we wrote the "smart letter" in vain. Aragon returned it to Lilya Yuryevna at the Belorussian Station when they were saying good-bye. It was a bust. But how we tried!

It had been the fruit of a collective effort. Something like the famous painting of the Zaporozhian Cossacks composing a letter to the Turkish sultan, but with flattery instead of cussing: the kindly tsar-batyushka is not aware of his ministers' intrigues. Three writers had a hand in it—Aragon, Triolet, and Katanyan. And Shchedrin and Lilya. The first line I wrote was the only line they left—the greeting, "Dear Nikita Sergeyevich."

Now I'm tearing my hair out. This letter got lost when we moved to another apartment. It should be included in Aragon and Elsa Triolet's complete works; it might be useful to researchers.

I was rehearsing *The Stone Flower.* I tried to immerse myself totally in work in order think about the April American tour less. But how can you cut yourself off? The theater was buzzing like a beehive: he's going, she's staying, and that one's on the reserve list . . . suffering, tears, complaints. And the closer April approached, the more intense the electrical outbursts of passions. The theater is only Bolshoi ("big") in name; the people in it are small and vulnerable, defenseless against insults.

Lilya Yuryevna didn't let me lounge around and suffer. "Aragosha's campaign fell through. We'll find another way!" Lilya, Katanyan, and Shchedrin worked out a plan for a "spring offensive" that they kept secret from me. Rodion was supposed to importune until he got an audience with Shelepin to brilliantly explain all the confusion and suffering that was going on. Katanyan added a little fall-back plan: "And it also wouldn't be a bad thing, Lilik, to see his deputy too."

Mayakovsky, in his memoirs, admitted that Lilya was always right about everything. If she said that we walk around on our heads, well, then, that's how it was. With regard to people who live in Bolivia—that is how it is.

"No Deputies. Only Number One. With the Soviets the distance between Number One and Number Two is the same as the distance between Number One and Number Forty in the British Isles."

She unearthed the phone number of Shelepin's reception room on Dzerzhinsky Square. It was a city number, not the "hotline" used by top officials. Even then Lilya Yuryevna had powerful contacts everywhere. Shchedrin didn't delay; he dialed the mysterious digits from the Briks' apartment. Lilya was listening in on an extension. Vasily Abgarovich also put his ear to the receiver.

Shchedrin introduced himself, briefly explained who he was and the reason he was calling, and requested an audience. They asked him on the other end of the line to leave his number just in case. They asked when it was convenient to call. They politely said good-bye. Lilya was dissatisfied. Angry.

"You spoke timidly. Without passion. That's not the way to request an appointment. You won't be received. I wasted time getting hold of the phone number." But for the first time in her life, Lilya was wrong.

A few days later the telephone rang in the morning. A man's low voice asked for Rodion Konstantinovich Shchedrin. I handed the receiver to Rodion. Many people called us, and I didn't attach any importance to the early-morning bass voice. Except that I thought: it's not very nice to telephone a theatrical home so early in the morning. The "spring offensive" plan had been created in strict secrecy, behind my back and, I wasn't aware that my fate was being decided. And my sixth sense was dozing—there wasn't a clue.

I overheard Shchedrin repeating a request for names and patronymics unfamiliar to me, and some other nonsense. I headed to the kitchen to have tea and chat with Katya.

Shchedrin, without waiting for my departure for the theater, suddenly dashed off to the Briks' place. This was not his habit. We got together as friends more often in the evenings.

Now I'll tell you what Rodion told me. This early morning phone call was from the Lubyanka. From the KGB. From Shelepin's reception room. The chairman, as they explained, pardon us, was very busy, he couldn't receive him, but his deputy — Yevgeny Petrovich Pitovranov — would see him. Got that? The pass would be at such-and-such a place, such-and-such an entrance, you must call the following number there. You will be met. After rehearsing the long-awaited speech for the last time at the Briks', Rodion headed off to Dzerzhinsky Square.

Pitovranov listened to all his husbandly lamentations attentively, without interrupting once. He asked some questions. Rodion later told me that Pitovranov, like Tolstoy's Khadji-Murat, knew how to listen. That after the end of someone else's sentence he would pause a bit — would the speaker add anything else? There's no point in describing what Rodion said. Read all the preceding chapters, reader. My entire *nevyezdnaya,* nonexportable, odyssey.

The "conspirators" informed me of what was going on. Shchedrin explained, "It seemed to me that the deputy believed me. You aren't planning to defect. I swore on my life. He stared into me so intently, to the core of my being."

There was an outcome to the conversation: I had to write another letter to Khrushchev. A very personal one. A sincere one. A critical one, as Pitovranov put it (critical toward myself, of course). A convincing one (go try and convince them, I'd been trying for six years!). A brief one (that brevity is akin to talent, as Chekhov had philosophized, I had learned at Moscow telegraph office windows. I sent my telegram petitions to the government — which never got to their destinations — from there). And so on. What was new and significantly humane was Pitovranov's promise that he would personally hand my letter to Khrushchev.

Yevgeny Petrovich Pitovranov kept his word. His comrade from the institute, Vladimir Lebedev, Khrushchev's assistant (I've already mentioned his influential name in the previous chapter), personally handed the letter to "Tsar Nikita." But I learned about all this much later.

The letter was immediately written and brought to Pitovranov's secretary. All that remained was to wait.

Now, alas, it's a time of utter ingratitude out there, in the country where I was born. People have completely forgotten all the good that others have done for them. Simply mentioning that someone occasionally helped you is seen as bad form. And people have even forgotten their teachers: they say, I'm like Bach —

self-taught, never studied with anyone. I got into fifth position and began dancing right away (the virus of forgetfulness has especially infected Vaganova's
students. Poor Agrippina Yakovlevna).

I, for one, have not forgotten, nor will I ever forget, that Yevgeny Petrovich
Pitovranov was part of my tangled fate. Then, in 1959, and later . . . Yes, he
worked for the KGB. Held the rank of general. For us today the KGB is a terrible, faceless tarantula, which stung millions of people to death. This monster
killed my relatives, too. But there were different kinds of people there. I swear
I'm convinced of this. Scoundrels, bloodsuckers, executioners, soldiers who un-
questioningly fulfilled whatever orders they were given, and sadists. But there
were also exceptions. My life has brought me in contact with them.

For a short time Pitovranov was the head of counterespionage in the Soviet
Union. Our Soviet Admiral Canaris,* if you like. A professional counterespionage agent. In 1952, after a malicious denunciation, he was arrested and sentenced
to death. He was tortured in the basements of the Lubyanka. His wife, Elizaveta Vasilyevna, survived with their three small children by selling books from
their family library. The courage which he exhibited at his interrogations — and
Stalin's death — saved his life. I don't know all the twists and turns of his biography. But I know and feel that the misfortune of his own fate was reflected in his
participation in my mishaps. And what if Shelepin had had a different deputy?
An out-and-out unfeeling, callous scoundrel? Some indifferent bastard? The vile
surveillance would have gone on for years, leading me one bleak day to leap out
of a window or swallow a handful of sleeping pills. People have the same livers,
intestines, and bladders. But their characters and virtues are different. Don't try
to convince me otherwise.

The American edition of the book *KGB* that I happened to see about fifteen
years ago begins with the description of a summer evening in Nice. A tall, charming Russian in a well-tailored dinner jacket has just beaten all his rivals on the
tennis court. He plays the piano, quotes poetry, and drives all the Frenchwomen
who are in love with him crazy. The author of the book maliciously warns his
female readers: Ladies, don't be in a hurry to fall under the spell of this Russian's
charms. He is General Pitovranov, a major Soviet spy. I don't know what he's
like when it comes to intelligence work, but this man really possesses quite a lot
of charm. An agent 007, but with red hair and glasses!

*Head of German military intelligence during World War II who was executed following
the failed assassination attempt against Hitler.

A few days later Pitovranov called us at home. "Maya Mikhailovna, this is General Pitovranov. Our chairman, Alexander Nikolayevich Shelepin, will receive you tomorrow at 10 o'clock in the morning. You do know him, don't you? Your pass will be at . . ."

Here it is, the happy ending, just as in Perrault fairy tales.

Or not?

A half an hour before the appointment, I walked out of the metro at Dzerzhinsky Square. The menacing building loomed across the square. Felix,* made of stone but known as Iron Felix, dressed in a mile-long military overcoat, frowned as he suspiciously scrutinized the Moscow crowds. Who's that over there, emerging from the metro? The stone handshake of this *Don Giovanni* Commendatore would drive anyone to an early grave. I'm not indulging in fantasy. This thought became etched into my memory—the analogy between Dzerzhinsky and the Commendatore. How could I get away from associations with the theater? But the statue's no longer there. It was torn down. Serves him right.

I walked into the gloomy, dirty-red entrance. Clicking his heels, a disciplined aide handed me a pass by the crudely fashioned, heavy marble staircase. Two young guards in new caps with blue bands concentrated as they checked my passport against the pass. Today these caps are being sold for German marks to curious tourists at the Brandenburg Gate.

The aide did not rush the sentries. It was the Secret Service. A serious institution.

We moved on.

My arms and legs were chilled. I was numb with terror. How many here were . . .

Through which entrances?

Along which hallways?

Up this staircase?

Which way down to the terrible basements of hell's underworld?

Where did the executions take place?

Or is this entrance just for the characters from Perrault's fairy tales?

The aide opened an impressive door. A spacious reception room: assistants and secretaries at desks with thousands of telephones. So many, it dazzled the eyes. No doubt all lines from every part of the country lead here. Two hundred and twenty million living "under a bell jar."

*Dzerzhinsky, head of the Cheka at its founding in 1917.

At exactly 10:00 A.M. a tall, well-built man walked out with attentive gray eyes behind glasses. "Hello, Maya Mikhailovna. I am General Pitovranov. I called you yesterday. You're punctual. Alexander Nikolayevich is expecting you." I went in. An iron . . . no, it's not Felix, it's Shurik Shelepin. He appeared from under Khrushchev's portrait. He smiled. Pulled up a government chair.

Shelepin was wearing a black suit, white shirt, and maroon tie. This was the punishment for being a leader—Politburo members and the most other important Party birds always have to wear dark colors and a white shirt. Should a photojournalist by chance capture him, the beloved leader would be seen in all his official glory by the people.

Black shoes on his feet. I realized with loathing that I was being inappropriately mischievous: I had expected the slipped-down socks that squish like flippers in the festival train.

Shelepin twisted his mouth, which was edged by thin, unkind lips. "Have a seat, Maya Mikhailovna. I haven't seen you for a long time, since the festivals." I sat down.

"I know all our literature and music from those festivals. And I remember your husband from the Warsaw festival. He received a prize for his *Little Humpbacked Horse*."

It's customary for Soviet bosses to begin far afield and postpone business to the very end. But we were getting to the point, I think. I became tense. The flight to America was three days away. Would they tweak my nose again?

"Nikita Sergeyevich read your letter. He asked us to sort it out here. We consulted and think that you should join your colleagues who are going abroad."

My heart leaped. Would they really let me out?

"Nikita Sergeyevich believed you. We don't have any reason for not trusting you. Much of what was said about you is nonsense. The ill-will of colleagues. Professional jealousy, if you like. But you, too, made many mistakes. You should control your speech and behavior."

I still couldn't believe my absolution. I expected some kind of dirty trick. And then suddenly: "Your uncle, Mr. Plesent, died on April 7, 1955, in New York. There are two sons with their own families. You can see them. We won't create any obstacles against it. It's your business." In general, he said what I've already related in Chapter 3.

In the doorway, Shelepin asked me to convey his regards to Shchedrin. He stretched his thin lips into the semblance of a smile. "Let him go on playing piano concertos in peace. We're not going to chop off his hands as collateral. Now if you don't return"—the chairman wagged his finger menacingly. Black humor.

I feverishly packed at home. This time I hadn't even prepared a toothbrush. I was afraid of jinxing the trip.

John Martin's review in the *New York Times* about my first performance at the Metropolitan Opera House ended with the words
"Spasibo Nikita Sergeevitch!" *

* "Thank you, Nikita Sergeyevich!"

Chapter Thirty-Two

Seventy-three Days

April 1959. I'm thirty-three and a half. For the first time in my life, I'm going on a real tour with my theater. The entire tour will last seventy-three days and take us to the major cities of America.

I was on board the plane with my ballet family. I stretched my neck toward the windows and surveyed the melting fields on the outskirts of Moscow. The pilots warmed up the engines and steered toward the runway. But it still was not too late to order me off the plane, if they should want to. There have been instances of that.

The plane soared up into the April sky. In Russia, the sky seems higher in April than at any other time of the year. Damn, we were flying!

On this tour I danced in *Swan Lake*, *The Stone Flower*, and *Walpurgisnacht*. Ulanova danced in *Romeo and Juliet*, *Giselle*, and several concert numbers. Both of us were centers of attention. Political interest toward me also escalated. The ballet world and journalists knew that I hadn't been allowed abroad, that the Soviet authorities were afraid that if they weren't careful, I would defect.

The most improbable thing about it—almost like a fairy tale by Hans Christian Andersen—is that neither I nor Rodion had any thoughts whatsoever about defecting to the West at that time. Today, in hindsight, I could change my story, fib a bit, talk nonsense, and make up some excuse about fearing the totalitarian monster. But if you want the truth, the truth alone, in those years I never thought about defecting. Was I a fool?

I was. I'm crying over spilt milk now. Again, if the truth be told.

We were born in the bottomless, swampy labyrinths of the Stalinist system. Surrounded round the clock every day by bellicose lies. They penetrated our ears, eyes, nostrils, pores, brain. We were stuffed to stupefaction, to dullness with them. One of the Bolshoi's quiet artists, torn apart by Communist propaganda, suddenly wound up abroad with the troupe, where the abundance of goods in the shops and shop windows crashed down on him (though he had memorized the doctrine that all America went around with their hands outstretched, begging for alms), and he went crazy, out of his mind. Really. This is a true story. Our Soviet life.

The quiet man's insanity was violent. Hysterically, he begged the theater management and the staff of the Soviet Embassy, which had arrived on the scene of the "scandalous flashpoint" to return him to his homeland immediately. Everything there was clear to him. Everything was logical. But here? And he was sent back immediately . . .

The summer flight path passed through Scandinavia, with stops to change planes. The mood in the cabins was festive. Euphoria. Jokes. Laughter. "Let the unlucky one weep."

There was a crowded, noisy welcome in New York Airport — it wasn't called Kennedy Airport yet. Correspondents. Questions. The popping of flashbulbs. Long-stemmed roses. The smell of cigars. Casual customs agents. This was the first time the Bolshoi Ballet was in America!

Sol Hurok, in a black velour hat, floated over to me. He extended his arms and kissed me on the cheeks. "You've arrived? They let you out? They listened to me?"

The indomitable naïveté of foreigners!

The opening night performance was *Romeo and Juliet*, with Ulanova. The second night was mine: *Swan Lake*. We prepared diligently.

The troupe was put up at the Governor Clinton Hotel. (Who's he?) On Seventh Avenue, near the old Metropolitan Opera House. We walked over. But in groups. We were not allowed to go alone. No ex-cep-tions! New Yorkers were all FBI agents. Every single one of them. They had all changed into civilian clothes and put on carefree faces, but they were looking to instigate a provocation, to weaken communism. They were choosing the right moment, targeting their victims. Whoever walked out on Seventh Avenue alone would immediately pay for her political carelessness.

It wasn't until we reached the hotel that the euphoria began to die down. I began to notice that I was surrounded on all sides. They had put me up at the Governor Clinton Hotel with what they thought was subtle craftiness. The ballerina Plisetskaya must not betray Khrushchev's trust. But even a small child would have noticed: the neighbor to one side of me was an escort from the KGB. Those on the other side were from the Bolshoi, but they were, as chance would have it, more curious than cats.

They would knock on my door in the morning: "I forgot my toothpaste in Moscow." Or in the evening thrust themselves on me to brew up some tea in my hotel room because they had eaten too much salt at dinner, or make a phone call from my room because the phone in their room suddenly wasn't working . . . I'm not even mentioning the street, the theater, the receptions. I was always, again as if by chance, surrounded by people — do you need translation from English, Maya Mikhailovna? Can we help you buy anything? Can we help pack your things and carry them downstairs?

That's how it went the entire trip. All seventy-three days.

But it's time to talk about ballet.

The opening night of *Swan Lake* had arrived.

I was more nervous than usual. It was as if I were taking an exam. People gossiped, expounded, sympathized: what if I didn't dance well or if I wasn't liked?

The remarkable stage of the old Met helped. Spacious and springy, it had an ideal incline toward the footlights. Only the stage at the Bolshoi Theater is more perfect than the one at the old Metropolitan Opera House. The proportions and construction at the Bolshoi Theater are ideal for classical dance. Maybe that's why I didn't think about defecting?

I'll mention here how important the incline of the stage area is! It is two meters at the Bolshoi. The viewer's eye doesn't notice this, but the body does (by virtue of the law of gravity). And how! Without a doubt, the old choreographers took the incline into account when they staged their productions. Wise classical masters knew quite a number of clever tricks. Ekaterina Geltser told me (she heard it from Petipa) that it is best to dance diagonals in a precise line from the top corner of the stage to the bottom corner. If you go the other way, the dancer's height diminishes. It's an optical illusion.

Milan's La Scala stage was built for opera. And its incline is too high, though the singing voice projects more resonantly into the auditorium. Dancing *Swan*

Lake at La Scala, it was hard for me to go "uphill" during the manège (circle) of turns in the "black" act. And going "downhill" was so easy that I had to summon all my will not speed up and rush the tempo! Of course, I'm speaking about micro-movements, but every ballerina must make corrections on an unfamiliar stage.

The Fathers of the Russian Sovereign State designated the stage of the Bolshoi for ballet. It was fortunate that they had love affairs with ballerinas. The weaknesses of our monarchs came in handy.

My first American *Swan Lake.*

The performance went smoothly, without major mistakes. Both Kolya Fadeyechev and I did our best. The soloists and corps de ballet did their utmost. Fayer conducted comfortably, passionately, with the American orchestra. I was personally satisfied.

What else do I remember about the American debut? The audience. It was very knowledgeable and very kind. At the end of each act, we took innumerable curtain calls on the Met stage. My swan "exit" at the end of the "white" act was crowned with such an ovation that I lost the thread of the musical accompaniment. I had to strain my hearing, grow still; but I couldn't hear a thing except for the cannonade of applause and squall of heartrending cries. Not a single orchestral note! I wound up finishing the act by intuition.

At the end of the performance a crowd of fans gathered at the backstage entrance. Autographs, smiles: everything as it was supposed to be. Several of those fans accompanied me through the entire tour, across the entire continent. And then through my entire life as well.

Alisa Vrbska, a saintly soul — she just died, may she rest in peace — raised the KGB alarm: no one would follow you around like a shadow just out of love for ballet. They began frightening me with talk of FBI nets. I didn't heed them. Then one of the escorts (I remember his name — Chernyshev) switched weapons: "We have evidence, Maya Mikhailovna, that your new fan Alisa is a lesbian . . . Be careful. Distance yourself from her."

"But I'm not a lesbian."

They let up.

Reviews came out. They praised me. Walter Terry, I think he was writing for the *Herald Tribune* at that time, compared me with Maria Callas. "Plisetskaya is the Callas of ballet." And who was this Callas? I asked Elena Ilyushchenko. She was informed about everything.

"Don't bring shame on yourself, ignoramus. She's a singer. Don't ask any more questions; don't parade your lack of education."

Reader, you're waiting for my impressions of America and my travel notes? You've gotten impatient for them, I dare say? Be disappointed, because there won't be any. Alas, during my first trip, I didn't get a good look at the country. The nerve-racking hassle of the departure, being followed, opening-night performance jitters, and waiting for meetings (this was the only time in my life that I didn't keep a journal during a trip and now have to rely on memory alone). Of course, I craned my neck at skyscrapers, marveled at the scope of life, the space and freedom, gasped at cars, wore out my feet walking, forgetting everything in the world, like a child in fairy-tale Disneyland.

America is a great, blessed nation, and I don't want to be off-hand about it. But one thing was clear to me — immediately! — that America was a working land. Not a land of parasites, as we had been persistently taught since childhood.

There were a great many receptions. Wealthy ones, elite, ceremonial ones. Evening dresses, limousines, dinner jackets, ice-cold champagne, eminent notables. I was introduced to the artistic elite of the States. Oh, if only I could speak English! Either someone standing nearby (and it was clear who stood there) would translate, or I would lavish smiles instead of words.

I made friends with Leonard Bernstein. We had a good relationship until the end of his life. He played Shchedrin's music. Bernstein and I both received the Via Condotti Prize in Rome in 1989. And Lenny teased me about my "polyglotism": "What, Maya, didn't you ever learn any English?"

It was easier to socialize with Artur Rubinstein. He spoke Russian. When Rubinstein came to Moscow, I dropped by the darkened dressing room of the big hall of the Conservatory after his concert. "I thought I'd see you completely fatigued after such a massive concert, and here you are fresh as a daisy."

"I have enough energy to dance a pas de deux with you," and — not deliberating too long — Rubinstein lifted me in the air and made a few turns.

Gene Kelly, whom I saw several months ago in Los Angeles at the home of Gregory and Veronica Peck, reminded me that in 1959 we were taken by the half-crazy idea of performing together in an amusing musical. But how could I, when I was sentenced to hard labor?

I danced something devilish to a bewildering improvisation that Ella Fitzgerald created in my honor. A mixture of boogie-woogie with "the Kamarinsky muzhik."

Later, during the days of his Moscow pilgrimage, Rodion and I treated John

Steinbeck to an aspic of veal knuckles with pickled horseradish at our house on Gorky Street. The famous writer really took a liking to this dish. And truly, nothing better was ever invented as an hors d'oeuvre with Stolichnaya vodka. But then, in 1959 in America, Steinbeck drummed into me through an interpreter that the seamy side of the backstage ballet world could become the most interesting novel, full of conflict . . .

These are a few of my New York acquaintances from that memorable year.

In Hollywood I met Mary Pickford, Humphrey Bogart, Frank Sinatra, Clark Gable, Audrey Hepburn, Henry Fonda, Yma Sumac. In San Francisco a well-known American painter whom everyone enthusiastically recommended (I won't name him, because he really is a good painter) had the idea of painting a large portrait of me in oils. A full-length one. I made three attempts to convince our director, Orvid, to grant me permission to spend time on my day off at his studio with my interpreter and a special escort. I barely succeeded. Permission was granted. I made time, washed my hair for the occasion, put on my face, my tutu, and my pointes. I neatly tied the pink ribbons on my shoes ("If you're Maya Plisetskaya, why aren't you wearing a tutu?" a little girl once asked me in Vilnius).

I posed for about three hours. At the end of the session, limbering up my numb back, I took a look at the easel: a ragged blue-white stain the entire length of the canvas. Where was my freshly shampooed hair?

And what about my American relatives?

On the second day of rehearsals at the Met, Edward Perper, Hurok's stepson, called me aside. He worked in his stepfather's office and spoke fluent Russian. Edward's face barely concealed an expression of confusion. It was obvious that Perper was keeping some secret. "Maya, do the names Michael, Lester, and Stanley mean anything to you?

"They do. Michael is my father's name. Lester is his older brother. Stanley is Lester's son."

"Did you know that you have relatives in New York?"

"I did."

"Do you want to meet them? Will this cause you any harm?"

"It already has. But I want to meet them. Why not today? They're kin . . ."

Tears came to Edward's eyes.

The next day my cousin Stanley Plesent came backstage with Perper. He speaks no Russian. And I don't speak English. The epochs and family chronicle had carried something vague and obscure about each other across the ocean.

We were the same age. Born the same year. Both in November. I was born in Moscow, he in New York. Stanley was a successful lawyer. The head of a large, harmonious household. He was now part of Senator John Kennedy's team in Washington. He came especially to see me. I was a ballerina of the Bolshoi. I danced for the heads of foreign governments. On the square named after the famous Bolshevik Sverdlov. I chatted with the Kremlin leaders. Life certainly does throw us unexpected curves!

The first thing that my cousin told me was, "My father went to see the film *Masters of the Russian Ballet* eight times. He liked your *Fountain of Bakhchisarai*. This film played here. You probably don't know that my father died."

"I do know. On April 7, 1955."

Stanley stopped in his tracks. "How do you?! Who told you?"

After the rehearsal, which pleased Stanley enormously, we headed off to lunch. Edward Perper had business to attend to. One interpreter from the platoon that never took their eyes off us stepped in to help. What else could we do?

In a week and a half, after my *Swan Lake* and *Stone Flower,* after the excellent press, the New York colony of my American relatives arranged a noisy, interminable, ten-hour reception at the home of Uncle Philip (he's my thrice-removed cousin and is ninety-two years old). My relatives gesticulated. Argued. My relatives were talking loudly, incessantly. They interrupted and did not listen to one another. Only one of them was full of melancholy and shyness. He smiled a shy, friendly smile. The bedlam of the relatives seemed oppressive to him. This was my second cousin Emmanuel, a first-class professional athlete.

The large house in Greenwich Village was bursting with people. Were they really all my relatives? I tried to count those present. I lost count. My uncle thrice-removed nodded in a contented way: all of them there. My mother would have been thrilled by the sight of this intimate idyll of relations.

I couldn't understand how they were related to me — there's no way. My brain couldn't take in their spirited explanations. I was finally alone at this familial apotheosis. Without escorts. But even without this reception the Moscow scribblers would have enough to inform to the authorities.

Everything was fine. And yet I was counting the days. There remained 47, 46, . . . 31, 29, . . . 20, 19, 18, 17 . . .

Rodion was also counting the days in Moscow. Katya told me: there's a table of seventy-three numbers next to the telephone on Kutuzovsky. Every day he crosses out a number. That's how each day ends — with this ritual. It's our Mendeleyev table! It is more precious to us than all the minerals of the world.

We talk for a long time, almost every other day, and even twice a day when the angry, highly strung Moscow telephone operators connect us. The KGB agents, who were eavesdropping on our conversations, probably had to work very hard—so much work! Katya was desperate; with ritual lamentations, she would head off to the savings bank near the Hotel Ukraina to pay for the astronomical bills. They made a laughingstock of her every time. Of course Plisetskaya had bewitched her husband.

And now there remained 3, 2, an entire long day . . .

We returned to Moscow.

No one defected. Everyone's intact. Safe and sound down to the last person. In the fall I will be graciously welcomed into the ranks of People's Artist of the USSR. This was the highest rank an artist could have in the land of Soviets. It seems that they were thanking me for not slipping away.

But then in sultry June, in the sweltering, dank Vnukovo Airport, in the excited, flushed crowd of people meeting me, I hungrily searched for Shchedrin's dear face. We hadn't seen each other for exactly seventy-three days. A whole eternity.

There he was, standing over there, with a gigantic bouquet of pale pink peonies. Peonies grown in the outskirts of Moscow are insanely fragrant. My head spun.

Ever since that day, the astringent, intoxicating fragrance of peonies returns me to 1959.

To the long, happy, seventy-three days under surveillance, when I discovered America.

Chapter Thirty-Three

How We Were Paid

In America in 1959 I received $40 per performance. And on the days when I did not dance, nothing. Zero. The corps de ballet were given $5 a day. Per diem. Or per dummies, as they joked. Later, when I danced *Lady with the Dog* in the States, the American dog I appeared with on the Yalta pier got $700 a performance. But that's just an aside.

Financial arrangements with performers in the Soviet state were always deep, dark secrets. It was forbidden, not recommended, strongly advised against, to talk to anyone about that delicate subject. Especially, as you can guess, with foreigners. It was clearly hinted that the sums we earned went to the treasury for the urgent needs of the socialist state.

To support Castro? Buy wheat? Recruit spies?

Later it came to light where the hard currency went. For instance, the son of Andrei Kirilenko — twice awarded Hero of Socialist Labor, former Central Committee secretary and member of the Politburo — and his gang of layabout pals regularly went off on African safari. To hunt elephants, rhinoceroses, oxen, and other African game. For the amusement of the scions of Party fat cats, performers were deprived of their hard-earned wages, while sables, ancient Scythian wares, and paintings were sold for next to nothing. They took away the winnings of athletes.

How are you supposed to survive on $5? Satisfy the needs of your family? Buy presents for friends? A puzzle.

Fainting from hunger became a daily occurrence. Even onstage, during a performance. ("We are a shadow theater," the dancers used to joke.)

The very clever Sol Hurok figured it out quickly—the Moscow dancers wouldn't make it to the end of their tour this way. He began giving the troupe free lunches. Things improved instantly. Cheeks grew rosy, cheekbones filled in, everyone was dancing fine. Success!

When travel abroad became common, and there were no more calculating impresarios like Hurok, the members of the Bolshoi Ballet troupe began packing their bags with long-lasting food. Just in case. Canned goods, smoked sausages, processed cheeses, grains. An ordinary mortal couldn't budge a piece of luggage like that. His ligaments would snap. But a dancer trained to do lifts easily managed the extreme weights. Customs officials sometimes stood in the way of the hoarders. It depended on whom you got. Sometimes they confiscated, sometimes you got away with it.

We all remember this so well, I wonder whether I should even write about it. But I'm writing for future generations. Let them know about our humiliations.

Hotel rooms in America and England were turned into kitchens. There were cooking and steaming going on. Cooking odors wafted down the corridors of fashionable hotels. The aroma of canned pea soup overtook the local ladies and gentlemen in their clouds of Chanel and Dior. The Soviet performers were in town!

Toward the end of a trip, when the Moscow supplies were used up, the dancers would switch to local fare. Cat and dog food were particularly popular. Cheap and vitamin-rich. You felt very strong after animal food. We fried canine beefsteaks between two hotel irons, boiled hotdogs in the bathroom. Steam billowed out from beneath doors on every floor. Windows steamed up. Hotel administrators grew panicky and confused. All the immersion heaters turned on at the same time blew fuses and stopped elevators. Pleading didn't help—we don't *andestan po-angliskii, mademoiselle. Verstehen Sie?*

Somewhere Nikolai Leskov wrote that the Russians display miracles of adaptability in very difficult times (I'm not quoting accurately, just the sense). And this was the perfect example. Every per diem dollar was strictly budgeted. When I asked one of my partners to join me in a café for a snack, he replied with disarming frankness, "I can't, the food sticks in my throat. When I eat a salad, it feels as if I'm chewing on my son's shoe."

A bacchanalia of locusts descended on hotels that had buffets. In a few minutes, everything was consumed, plates wiped cleaned, bottles emptied. Bottoms up. The lazybones who arrived too late threatened the staff, grabbing their shirt fronts and demanding more, pleading . . .

It was shameful. Hideous.

I'm describing only what I saw for myself. My own Bolshoi Theater. But the same thing happened with other touring groups. Though there may have been differences in minor details. For instance, the Folk Dance Ensemble of Georgia had a per diem of $3.

Who's to blame for this shamefulness?

The impoverished, dependent performers or those who invented and wrote the immoral laws? While the dancers fried canine steaks on hotel irons, our leaders — members and candidate members of the Politburo of the Central Committee of the Communist Party — never left home without their own food. The special rations were kept in zinc-lined boxes under seal (to prevent poisoning of the loyal Leninists, who might get an upset tummy). Special guards in special cars accompanied the big shots everywhere — in case they got hungry!

Solo tours were "arranged" through Gosconcert. Gosconcert had a state monopoly on every performer from one-sixth of the world. That organization was truly from hell. I don't want to blacken every single person who worked for Gosconcert, but it truly was the kingdom of complete cover-up. Next to the Gosconcert mafia, the most vicious Sicilian mafia looks like an institute for young ladies of the nobility. So many artistic fates mangled there. So many artistic hopes dashed.

A long road begins with the first step. At Gosconcert that step is an invitation arriving from a foreign impresario. For ballerina A, pianist B, or singer C. Should the performer be informed that the invitation has arrived safely and has been languishing unanswered on an official's desk at 14 Neglinnaya Street, at Gosconcert USSR? Is the artist worthy of being invited? Is he politically mature? Had he smiled pleasantly enough at the desk chief at the last meeting for, say, Germany and Austria? Will he understand that out of the pittance mercifully left him after state taxes, he should use a hefty portion for gifts for his patroness desk chief? Will he have the sense to ask in a polite whisper what his patroness particularly needs today? Will he figure out that he must inquire about the sizes for winter boots, summer slingbacks, a warm coat, a raincoat? Will he know which French perfume she prefers?

The contacts between the shy curators and the far-flung impresarios are confidential and businesslike. A true collective of Communist labor. If you want X, all right, we'll give you X, but you have to invite Z, as well. This young talent has not shown his full strength on the concert stage. But he will, we have no doubt; in fact, we place great hopes on him, predict a great future . . . And he's so considerate, so full of smiles! As for Y, he's busy, too bad, he just can't make it, or—What do you need with him, he's had bad press, he's hard to get along with, he's cranky . . .

A few cynical impresarios, chuckling smugly, admitted out loud, "That desk chief at Gosconcert gets a monthly salary from me. Not in rubles, naturally. And I bought a coop apartment for that one."

I can think of a thousand examples.

Each director of Gosconcert—and there were dozens of them in my time, ruined by greed—had a deputy director from the KGB officially attached to him. Now those were real connoisseurs of the fine arts, let me tell you.

I'll mention one—Golovin. Deputy Director of Gosconcert USSR Comrade Golovin, once he started work at this cultural establishment, turned out to be a collector of new suits. Where did a peasant's son develop such a baronial hobby? This proletarian liked to stroke the fabric, select different shades, be measured. And on Fifth Avenue or the Strand, of course. Hurok told me that after every trip Golovin made to America, Hurok's office received a big bill for seven to ten expensive suits. Hurok paid without a murmur. Business was business. The devilish aspect was that Comrade Golovin always showed up in his office at 14 Neglinnaya Street in the same gray shiny suit. Modestly. In the best Leninist traditions. Did he try his new suits on at night, like Gogol's lieutenant with his boots? The man accepted bribes, he did. But the Borzoi puppies were updated: to new suits.

Before a trip each artist was thoroughly briefed. Not only how to behave, where to go and with whom, or what to say at a press conference, should there be one. But how to subtly introduce the latest Party policy, the decisions of the latest historical congress of the Communist Party, and the brilliant wisdom of the current leader and his angelic love of peace. And also how much of his fee to turn over, to whom, and in what manner. It was a university for us. But even that was not all.

David Oistrakh, a man of great distinction, politeness, and restraint, told me of one assignment—among others—he was given by Gosconcert administrators. They had developed a suspicion that a certain impresario was cheating

Gosconcert by underreporting the sizes of the halls where Oistrakh was performing. So they gave the great violinist a simple task: to count the seats in the philharmonic halls where he was going to be playing.

He resisted in embarrassment: "How can I do that? There isn't enough time! Rehearsals."

"During the concert, while the orchestra is playing without you. It's very important for us to know whether Gosconcert can continue working with this impresario in the future."

It sounds like a joke. But it's no joke. It's the vile truth.

In ninety-nine cases out of a hundred, Gosconcert sent an escort with the performer. From Moscow. (Oistrakh, Gilels, and Kogan were exceptions.) Allegedly to help during the travel, at the hotel, to count the money, to protect you from fans. In fact, what were they for?

In fact, this is what it was like. Just two examples from my own experiences.

I was flying to Argentina to dance. They gave me a young woman who could barely speak English. Not a word of Spanish.

We flew from Moscow on separate flights. The impresario sent me a ticket on Air France, via Paris, the shortest way. The girl was flying on official funds. On Aeroflot. Via Cuba, Mexico, and Peru. Every Soviet citizen was required to fly on the Soviet airline Aeroflot.

Gosconcert always tried to get the impresarios to cough up for the tickets and hotels of the escorts. They negotiated. If the producer refused outright — it was too far, too expensive, as in this case — Gosconcert sent someone at their own expense.

The girl arrived in Buenos Aires on the third day. Jet-lagged, with no sense of day or night. The impresario was paying for my hotel, a comfortable one next to the Colon Theater, in the center of town. The girl, thanks to the patronage of the Soviet Embassy, was settled in a fleabag for prostitutes and their pimps on the outskirts of town. Gosconcert hadn't given her money for a hotel. And why should they? Every day the entire country repeated Brezhnev's high-flown nonsense, "The economy must be economical!" Therefore, young lady, you must sleep with the whores in a sleazy hotel on the outskirts of Buenos Aires. The economy must be economical.

The girl was shy and got lost easily. She couldn't get into the theater or the hotel. On the fifth day she tugged at my sleeve at the exit after the show. "Maya Mikhailovna! I am your escort . . . I was sent by Gosconcert. How can I be of help?"

After that we talked on the phone—how much did the impresario pay, how many more performances would I be doing, what paperwork must be done, and where I should turn over the money. We turned in a different amount every time—it was never a set percentage, you could never find the rhyme or reason. They clearly tried to muddy the waters so that the performers would not ask importunate questions: Why, How come, What for? . . . Instead, the performers were always tense and burdened with calculations. Whatever you did not pay in hard currency, you had to pay in rubles tenfold. No slack for anyone.

The example with the simple girl is a curious one. I truly felt sorry for her.

The other example is scarier and more typical.

My partner and I were flying to Florence in May to dance *La Rose Malade* in a gala program. We had an escort, as required. Comrade Victor Berezny from Gosconcert. A hail fellow, well-met: sharp, affable, smiling, blue-eyed. Comrade Victor Berezny was a bolt out of the blue as far as the festival administration was concerned.

"We have rooms reserved for Signora Plisetskaya and her partner. For Signor . . . Gosconcert, alas, no."

Berezny made himself at home in Efimov's room. (Boris Efimov was my partner on that trip.) The room was a single, with only one bed.

"Not to worry, Boris. We'll manage with one bed. We're friends, aren't we?"

Signor Gosconcert's snores could be heard throughout the hotel floor. The walls shook, and Efimov couldn't sleep. He showed up at rehearsals worn out, wan, and yawning. He blew the lifts. At least, the brave escort from Gosconcert had no homosexual tendencies. There was no need for the hotel maid to give funny looks to the two men sharing one bed.

The first thing Comrade Berezny did was empty the mini-bar of its contents. He filled the refrigerator with jars of black caviar. "So it doesn't spoil in the Italian sun."

"How did you get all that through customs, Victor?" Efimov asked.

"I had a pass from the ministry for Sheremetyevo customs. I go through a special door. They don't look there."

Berezny would disappear for long periods, and the caviar jars vanished one after the other. He was not interested in our rehearsals or performances. By the premiere, my partner had regained his strength, and the lifts went smoothly. Efimov got used to the snoring in his bed. He shaped up.

After the final show there was a buffet reception. No sign of Berezny. Signor Gosconcert was up to his neck in something else. The theater director—tactful, aristocratic Alberti — invited me to come back in three months. "But please, come solo, alone. Without a partner. What is there in your repertoire that you can dance alone? Isadora?" We agreed on *Isadora*.

"Gosconcert demanded a huge sum from us: $7,200 for each *Rose*. Without a partner, your visit will cost less, I hope. The festival, the audiences love you, but you must agree to that."

"What do you mean $7,200? I have a copy of the Gosconcert contract for $4,000."

"If only it were so. It is $7,200 for each performance."

"That must be a mistake. Here's the paper." I took out the typed contract from my purse, with a translation of the contract into Russian, which was given me in Moscow.

Alberti did not know Russian, but he could read the figures: $4,000. He called his bookkeeper. "Bring the Plisetskaya contract" (our astonishing conversation was translated by Zhenya Polyakov, who had been working as head of a local ballet company in Florence for several years by then). The bookkeeper brought the papers.

"Why are there two contracts for Plisetskaya? For $4,000 and for $3,200?" The bookkeeper gesticulated in agitation. He explained. I turned to Zhenya. What was he saying? What's going on?

"For some reason Gosconcert asked them to divide the sum in half. And this is more convenient for the local impresario Giancarlo Carena."

I was confused. What a mess!

The next morning Alberti called a meeting. He demanded that Signor B., the accompanying person from Gosconcert, be present.

Berezny sat there, red, his face flushed. Frowning. Wiping his forehead with sweaty palm. Babbling pathetic nonsense: "I'm a minor person, I'm just a minor person. No one explained anything to me. I'm just a minor person."

When we got back to Moscow, Efimov and I were grilled by the customs people — how much money we were bringing, how much we had taken for ourselves? (Let me note in passing that I had the right, according to my typed contract, to keep $300 for each concert — this was 1981 by then. Efimov got a per diem — this really was a per dummy — of $12 a day. That wasn't enough for dinner with a meat course. Try dancing on coffee and a sandwich. Berezny also got $12 — without dancing or rehearsing, for the caviar and snoring in someone else's bed.)

We watched with narrowed eyes as our minor person Signor Berezny brought eleven bulky cases, almost his height (eleven, Efimov and I counted), through the diplomatic exit, giving instructions to the sweating porter, bustling, and looking around stealthily: had we passed through customs yet or not?

I demanded explanations. From Gosconcert, from the Ministry of Culture. But neither the then-director of Gosconcert Kondrashov nor Deputy Minister of Culture Barabash could explain a thing. They evaded the issue, promised to look into it, and switched topics.

I haven't heard an explanation to this day. Not a word.

I once told Katya Maximova about this comic opera. She exclaimed at my naïveté. "This was the first time you discovered it? Gosconcert has been working with two contracts for quite a while. One for the treasury, the other for their own pockets. They share the profit among themselves in the top offices of the ministry and Gosconcert."

"And what was in the crates?"

"The crates were full of video equipment."

The ministry officials preferred to get news about the flowering of mature socialism from the screens of Japanese television sets.

So, judge for yourselves how well the state monopoly on performers in the first country of socialism did its work.

And then you had to drag your earnings around with you, hauling them from country to country, from hotel to hotel. Tucking the money into locked luggage, counting and recounting it, wetting your fingers and the bills. Gosconcert didn't trust checks too much. Cash was more reliable. The easiest way was to turn in your fee at a Soviet embassy and get a receipt with a seal: "Received from so-and-so, such-and-such amount." That was allowed, but they always added, It would be better to turn this in to the cashier at Gosconcert.

The embassies — with the rare exceptions when there were no funds for paying salaries — did not like accepting piles of money. Several hours went into counting the piles. If you make a mistake, you pay for it. So any excuse possible — We're having a Party meeting, women's committee meeting, the consul has the seal — was used to get rid of the uninvited visitor with money. And always with a grim and hostile attitude.

"Come Monday after three."

"I'm afraid to keep money in the hotel. You never know."

"Too bad. Be careful. Or take it to Moscow."

And so one time I was carrying $40,000, plus French francs and Finnish marks. There had been performances with Roland Petit's troupe and television shows in Marseilles. From there, Finland for *Carmen Suite*. Three Bolshoi soloists were waiting for me in Helsinki. The French paid me on the last day before I left. They added all kinds of documentation, including a note from the bank on the exchange rate between the dollar and the franc the day I was paid my fee. Without that paper, the artist had to pay a penalty, that is, a large fine.

It was a Saturday. The Soviet consulate was closed. Out fishing. Willy-nilly, I had to put the money in my suitcase, which I checked at the Marseilles Airport to Helsinki. According to French law no more than 5,000 francs (or something like that) could be brought out of the country. Carrying all the money I had earned on the tour was risky. Sometimes the customs agents looked into your hand luggage. But sending the money in baggage was scary, too. What if my suitcase got lost in transit?

Everything went well. I had the money, and I kept it in a locked suitcase in the hotel room. From time to time I would re-count it. After *Carmen Suite*, I added Finnish marks to the dollars and francs. All the things I had to turn in to Gosconcert.

I was returning to Moscow by plane. Alone. My three partners, by the will of Gosconcert, were making the trip by train. I had accumulated a lot of things over the month. I asked Sergei Radchenko (the stalwart Torero) to take my roomy ballet bag with him on the train. It had my costumes, makeup, headdresses, shoes, and rehearsal leotards.

I got back to Moscow. No end to my stories. So many impressions. We were in the kitchen, having tea. Shchedrin recounted the Moscow news. Katya tsked over the market prices. I was in a wonderful mood. Before going to bed, I decided to unpack. In the morning, first thing, I would go to Gosconcert, report on my tour and turn in the money. It made life easier that way.

The big suitcase, where I had kept the money throughout the trip, had no money. My heart sank. I felt a chill. Rodion and I went through the contents. Piece by piece. No money.

Nervously, I opened the second, soft cloth suitcase. It couldn't be in there. But, just maybe?

We knelt tensely over the second suitcase. Going through it with icy hands. To the bottom. No money.

I turned the purse that I had on the plane inside out. I couldn't have put the money in there. It wouldn't have fit. But what if? By some miracle? . . . No money.

We went through the big suitcase again. Feeling around, like blind people. In slow motion . . . No money.

Once again. Back to the second case. No money.

The money was gone!

Where could it have been stolen? In that quiet Helsinki hotel? By that sweet, light-eyed maid who smiled gently in the doorway of my room and slowly, diligently, put bouquets of flowers from the theater into vases? Or by the grumpy albino Finn who repaired my shower the day before yesterday?

Or had it happened at the airport? Someone opened the suitcase, took out the money, and relocked it. Everything was in it . . . But no money.

Which airport? In Helsinki? Or here in Sheremetyevo? Probably here in Moscow. "In Russia, they steal," said Nikolai Karamzin centuries ago.

And what was I supposed to do now? Tell Gosconcert the truth? That the money was stolen? They wouldn't believe me. Never. They would tell the whole world. Adventuress, thief.

But it was my money. Hadn't I earned it? Hadn't it been paid to me for my dancing? The truth would sound like a lie. Your good name is worth more than money. There was only one way out: I would have to borrow it. But the total I had to give to Gosconcert seemed astronomical to us. We were Soviet citizens in Moscow, after all. It came to around $65,000. A fortune. It would take me to the end of my days to repay it. But there was no other way.

Whom could I ask?

We decided on Nadya Léger. She was wealthy and at the same time kind. She would believe what had happened and help me.

A sleepless night. Hundreds of times I tried to remember how it had happened, when I had seen the money last, when this calamity could have befallen me.

I went through the days in every way possible. We talked and talked. The most likely thing was Sheremetyevo Airport.

In the morning my brother Alexander brought over the bag with my ballet stuff. He had met Radchenko, Fadeyechev, and Lavrenyuk at the Leningrad Station. The Helsinki train arrives very early in Moscow. He told me that Radchenko had fought a major battle with our customs agents at the border. He had carelessly let slip that he was bringing Maya Plisetskaya's bag with her ballet costumes. The agents made a fuss, stating that carrying things intended for others was against Soviet customs regulations.

"So what that it's Maya Plisetskaya, so who cares about ballet? It's against the law. We have to confiscate other people's property." Radchenko barely managed to persuade the fierce guardians of the law. The bag was merely zipped, there was no lock, and the agents went through its contents for a long time. Convinced that there was nothing illegal in the bag, only ballet accessories, they reluctantly handed over the bag to Radchenko. They made him promise that he would never bring other people's things across the border ever again.

I began taking out my ballet things for class. I decided not to go to Gosconcert that day. I would put off the terrible conversation for a few days. I had to talk to Nadya Léger first. I would go to class instead. The work would distract me from my grim thoughts.

But what was in the rectangular knit pack with threads, scissors, and ballet ribbons and laces?

Oh, a bottle of vintage Framboise, a gift from Gaston Defferre in Marseilles, from his own wine cellars. I had forgotten all about it. To keep it from breaking before I got it to Moscow, I had wrapped the bottle in threads and ribbons. I had to show it to Rodion. We would open it in the evening and try to drown our sorrows with ancient French liqueur.

But what was that under the bottle?

Oh, ye gods! My dear sweet gods!

The damned Gosconcert money. There it was, damn it. Several packs, held by round, colored rubber bands. There were the dollars. There were the francs. There were the Finnish marks. All the receipts and notes. With an electric shock my memory restored the images of my actions. After the Finnish Opera gave me the final accounting, a few days before my departure, I took out all the previous honoraria from my big locked suitcase. I put all the money together. But just then, the albino Finn knocked at the door to fix my shower, and I hastily shoved the Gosconcert capital under the bottle. And, naturally, forgot about it. The momentum of memory still had the money in the locked suitcase — safe. Oh, thank you, my kind gods, and the vigilant but useless guardians of the Soviet customs at the border, infinite thanks to you!

When I told Radchenko about my fortunate discovery, he almost collapsed. He turned pale and swayed. That would have been some scandal, a hard-currency affair, contraband, with a trial and prison, had a custom agent's hand found $65,000 beneath the bottle of Framboise, wrapped in threads and ribbons.

This chapter is getting long.

But I want to tell you more about our shameful experiences. I can't stop myself. Endless suffering and humiliation fills my memory. I should mention this, and that . . .

Every day or every trip was in the shadow of the scorn in which your human dignity was held. The spitting at your pride and honor. Most terrifying is the fact that while we considered many things vile and disgusting, we accepted them as a matter of course. It was to make slaves consider their slavery normal that Stalin killed sixty million people. It's no exaggeration to say that there wasn't a single family in the country that had not been touched directly or obliquely by the ax of the Stalin terror. The cement binding the system was fear. And it entered the genetic code of the next generation as the main component.

And what about the foreigners, those sweet, well-kept, washed and perfumed, perfectly dressed foreigners? The free people from the free world? What did they do? Protest? All the impresarios from every continent who yearned to work with the Soviets—and I would swear this on a stack of Bibles—knew better than us what Gosconcert and the Ministry of Culture were doing to Soviet artists. How they treated us.

But the impresarios diligently participated in the hellish, dishonest game. They supported and facilitated the prison guards. They stuffed their pockets on the vile behavior of communism. They bought islands, castles, yachts, and hotels. And in the meantime, Gosconcert was listed as a deficit-running organization in the state budget—it was in the loss column and received millions in subsidies!

Soviet artists were a very profitable business. Enough to tailor a new suit for a collector, buy wives all kinds of little nothings at Woolworth's, feed Soviet officials a meal of caviar, vodka, and lobster at expensive restaurants during contract signings—all small costs that would be written off as business expenses. And the impresarios could pretend to be as hospitable as tsars.

Then the semiliterate and unsophisticated Party clerk, barely sobered up, returns to Moscow and reports that the gentleman who had wined and dined him was a true friend of the Soviet Union, prepared to propagandize Soviet art selflessly. He should be given preferential treatment. A primitive game.

Now that communism has died, thank God, the monster is mourned less by former members of the CPSU than by its ideological supporters—our kindly, altruistic impresarios. How could they not grieve? They have lost their golden goose. The ability to catch the golden fish in murky socialist waters. Some will put a good face on their loss. They'll give interviews and spin out memoirs claiming that they fought for freedom, for human rights, defending and supporting the artist persecuted by the Communists. They invited him to come on tour . . .

And how about your bank accounts, dear ones? How many zeros were added? They won't answer that one, even though they love to hear themselves talk. Why dwell on the prosaic aspects of life?

When the evil deeds of communism are finally brought to trial, when at long last the Nuremberg Trials for the CPSU are held—I fear I won't live to see them to speak out—don't forget the collaborators, the co-conspirators in the crimes. Without their help, communism would have left the stage of history much sooner.

Chapter Thirty-Four

Paris Meetings

I was a seven-month baby, a preemie. When Mother was having me in a small maternity hospital in Bolshoi Chernyshevsky Lane, in the middle of Moscow—right across from the Conservatory—the midwife tried to cheer her up by saying, "Your girlie is a strong one. She'll travel to Paris yet. Mark my words." This family legend was the first commentary I ever heard about my appearance in this world.

The midwife must have had a crystal ball. I did go to Paris. It was in 1961, October. The Paris Opera invited me with a partner (Nikolai Fadeyechev) to dance three *Swan Lake*s in Vladimir Burmeister's choreography. Burmeister had first done this production in Moscow on the stage of the Stanislavsky and Nemirovich-Danchenko Musical Theater in April 1953. And in 1960 he moved it to Paris. I had the chance to dance it, and I remembered the new text of the ballerina's part. But Fadeyechev didn't know that version, and he didn't have time to learn the entire ballet, so we replaced Burmeister's pas de deux in the third act with the more familiar Bolshoi variation. The rest followed the Burmeister. It's a good thing that our choreographer wasn't in Paris just then. He was a proud man, and he would never have accepted such free-thinking. The French, after vacillating a bit, did not resist, even though the orchestra had to play the music of our pas de deux. We had cleverly brought along the score and orchestral parts.

Georges Auric, the famous French composer—who soon took over as director of the Opera—even supported our innovation, noting that the music of that pas de deux was more closely tied to the whole.

I did not stay in a hotel. Or rather, I spent the first two days at the Hôtel Scribe on the boulevard des Capucines, where Fadeyechev and I were brought from the airport. But Elsa Triolet practically carried me by force to her two-story apartment on the rue de Varenne. The staff of our embassy made faces, as if they had been sucking lemons, about my living at the Aragons' place. But Aragon was a Communist, editor-in-chief of the Communist newspaper *Lettres françaises,* and a friend of Picasso and Maurice Thorez, so the embassy, to my great relief, accepted it. I lived an insouciant, almost French life. And there were no reprisals upon my return. So there!

Elsa took a very active part in my "French life," including the rehearsals at the Opera. She helped with the French, interpreting at interviews and telephone calls. You can't get lost with a guide like that in Paris!

Le tout Paris attended the first performance. So Elsa said. I was nervous, of course, but in moderation. The day before the *Lake,* fate arranged for me to watch a rehearsal of the same part by the French ballerina Josette Amiel. Either she was marking the rehearsal, or the part didn't suit her too well, but suddenly I felt completely calm, and I even thought, "Well, I'll show you . . ." Smugness usually ends up with embarrassment. I've been the victim of overconfidence and conceit more than once. But that Parisian "push" did me a good turn, fortunately. I didn't lose a milligram of strength or a drop of emotion through stage fright.

Don't laugh at me, reader. Yes, once again I'll be writing down that I had a great success and that they applauded incessantly. But what else can I write when I did and they did? And this was in Paris, not Tula. Mark Zakharovich Chagall* once said to me, "Paris made my name. In general, Paris makes you or breaks you." It seems that it was the former for me. The press noted the number of curtain calls we had—twenty-seven. For Paris that's not too bad.

Why did the French like me? Did I strike the right note? I asked that question of a dozen super-French friends—Louis Aragon, Roland Petit, Jean Vilar, Yvette Chauviré, Jean Babilée . . . They all agreed on one thing: I had forced the audience to switch its interest from abstract technique to soul and plasticity. When I danced the finale of the second act, people's eyes were glued to the line of the swan's arms, the angle of the neck; no one noticed that my bourrées were not so perfect. There were quite a few ballerinas with the Opera who could do a

---

*The painter Marc Chagall, who was born in Russia.

more refined bourrée, with a better extension. But could they sing Tchaikovsky's theme with their arms and neck?

I'm switching to today. Technical problems no longer exist for twenty-year-olds. A properly trained ballerina (she must be properly trained, that's essential) can dance anything now. Without a slip, a trip, or a hiccup. A double fouetté is nothing. Five pirouettes on pointe — no problem.

At the dawn of the Silver Age of Russian poetry, Alexander Blok noted wryly, Gentlemen, who writes bad poetry in our time? Everyone's learned to write well . . .

Naturally, sport has supported the technical breakthrough in classical ballet. And videos. I myself have progressed tremendously ever since I got the opportunity to review my dancing in class and onstage. But to this day I am convinced that you can't conquer the world with technique alone. Today and 150, 200 years from now, dancers will have to first and foremost touch the heart, force the audience to share emotions, shed tears, and get goose bumps.

It was amusing living with Aragon and Elsa. Both writers got up at dawn, had a cup of black coffee, and wrote, sitting up in bed, until noon. During those hours, I did not exist as far as they were concerned. They did not answer questions, much less the doorbell or the phone. When I went off to class, the first few days I politely tried to let them know — I'm off, don't worry, I'll lock the door, good-bye . . .

Silence. Only the scratch of pens on paper and heavy breathing.

Aragon was working on a history of the Soviet Union in those days, and he was immersed in his research and conclusions. Once, when I came back from the theater, I had to ring and bang on the door for a long time. No one answered. At last, the door opened. Gray-haired Aragon opened the door in his birthday suit. He was muttering in French, not even deigning a glance at me. Still muttering, Aragon hurried back to his study, with a flash of his skinny, lean buttocks (he had good legs for ballet) . . . There was one word in his mutterings that I understood: Bukharin, Bukharin.

That evening at dinner, when the maid Maria, a hulking, stooped southerner, was serving salads through the hatch in the kitchen wall, Elsa grumbled, "Aragon is besotted by those stupid Bolsheviks" (she never had time for them). "This is the third day he's worrying about why Bukharin got into a confrontation with Kamenev or whomever."

We went to the Aragons' country house a few times. "The Mill," as they called their cozy, spacious dacha. The yard was filled with nettles, and Aragosha whacked the vicious weeds with his knotty stick. I suspected that he was still angry with Bukharin and took out his fury on the nettles. At the Mill (the house had once been a mill and was situated on a stream that lazily turned its mossy oak wheels) there was a huge fireplace, in which knotty dried trees smoldered and crackled for hours. The heavy peasant table was always covered with fruit and Elsa's obligatory salads in coarse, wooden bowls. The ancient candelabras held massive twinkling candles. Two white doves murmured under the high eaves. They were accompanied by the measured sound of the water. In their will, the Aragons specified that they be buried at their beloved Mill.

Now there are two graves there. The nettles have spread, there's no one to be angry at them anymore . . .

I've been in Paris many times. I showed the audiences — in addition to *Swan Lake* — Maurice Béjart's *Isadora, Leda,* and *Bolero,* Serge Lifar's *Phèdre,* Roland Petit's ballets, and my own *Anna Karenina, Lady with the Dog,* and *Carmen Suite,* as well as concert pieces. On my very first visit to Paris with *Lake,* I was visited by a special audience member. Unusual. Ingrid Bergman had come especially to see my *Swan Lake.*

This is how it happened.

My official interpreter in those days was Mme Lotar. The same Lotar (this is for the Russian reader) who in the 1920s in Paris tried to put a halt to Mayakovsky's advances and told the poet in self-defense, "Vladimir Vladimirovich, leave me alone. I won't give myself to you. I'm a virgin. I am going to marry Vova Pozner." Mayakovsky quipped, "Better Pozner than never." (*Pozner* sounds like *pozdno,* which means "late.")

A lot of time had passed since the 1920s, and now in the 1960s, Mme Lotar was hard of hearing, forgetful, and occasionally she got things confused. I found it a bit annoying, so I tried to get help from Elsa whenever I could and often overlooked Lotar's messages. One such garbled message was that some movie star (whose name I didn't catch) wanted to see me. And for this she was making a special trip to Paris, to see the show and speak with me.

After the final bows, while I wearily removed my makeup and took a shower, Lotar kept nagging me impatiently to hurry, that we were late. Over the running water in the shower, I missed the movie star's name again. Lost in thought, I entered the darkened side room of Maxim's with Lotar, thinking that there was no one there. Ingrid Bergman rose from a distant table and quickly came toward me. She embraced me and spoke in French. Lotar translated a tenth of what she said. Bergman and Lotar's biorhythms did not correspond. There were tears in Ingrid's eyes: "You told about love without a single word. You have divine arms. I lost all sense of time. I read that you are persecuted by the Russian government. Our photographs were in the American *Vogue*, on the same page, you in a blood-red tunic on one side, my face on the reverse. And quite accidentally, in candlelight, I saw us next to each other, together. We were meant to meet. It's fate. Flee communism. I will help you . . ." I am giving the sense of her words. I repeat that this is what they sounded like, more or less, in Russian in the mouth of Mme Lotar.

I told her that I was amazed by the meeting, it was unexpected for me, I had seen her films, and she was beautiful and majestic.

"Which films have you seen?"

Out of nervousness and the unexpectedness of the question — we were still in the middle of the darkened room — I could only name one film: *Gaslight*. I had seen it twice in a closed screening at Dom Kino (the Cinematographer's Union club) in Moscow. I had seen other things of course — I recognized Bergman's face in an instant — several other films. But my memory shamefully failed me. I mumbled, unable to think of anything else.

"Only *Gaslight?* That was so long ago. Have you seen *Aimez-vous Brahms?*" I'd never seen any *Brahms;* foreign films were rarely shown in Russia in those years. Only once in a while were there closed screenings at Dom Kino. But, averting my eyes, I nodded: I've seen it, of course, I have.

"Have you seen *Anastasia?* It's about Russia." This time I told the truth: No, I haven't.

Bergman looked saddened. She led me to the table. There was an intense gentleman seated there. But I never found out who he was. Husband? Friend? Throughout the dinner, the intense man said almost nothing. Ingrid did all the talking. Lotar tried to keep up. Bergman talked about Anastasia, her mystical fate, Bergman's own belief in the lovely legend, the miraculous rescue, about Russia, which kept calling to Ingrid, and her dream to play Anna Karenina — in her own way, a different way.

"Would you like to play her? Can it be danced? Could you tell her drama without words?"

In 1962, when John Kennedy received the Bolshoi troupe at the White House, Jacqueline greeted me with the words, "You're just like Anna Karenina."

That was the second heavenly sign of my future. Perhaps the furs I was wearing made the two women think of Tolstoy's tantalizing image? At the meeting with Bergman I was wearing a white fur stole from Elsa Triolet's wardrobe. Elsa liked lending me her clothes. And I stood before Jacqueline Kennedy in a black coat trimmed with black mink and a small, black fur hat.

While I didn't take Ingrid Bergman's advice to flee to the West (even though it was quite timely, on the night of October 6, 1961, outside the doors of Maxim's), our conversation about Anna took serious root. So when in the 1970s I watched one of Bergman's last films, *Autumn Sonata*, looking at her lovely, regal face, touched, alas, by age and illness but still enchanting, and the premiere of my *Anna* was behind me — the anxiety and the dancing done — waves of emotions brought a lump to my throat. My clairvoyant, great Ingrid!

In that same room at Maxim's I was introduced to an eccentric artist with whom we spoke playfully in Russian. The Alphand family (its head was a minister of France) had invited me to lunch at Maxim's. The maître d'hôtel seated us at the same table where I had dined with Bergman. Or was it just my imagination? ... It was daylight. A well-bred, mustachioed gentleman no longer young sat at the next table with his back to me, his companion younger than young — a tall, blonde beauty, her flaxen hair tumbling down her bare back. Our minister was a bit late for lunch, and as he headed toward us, he greeted the man at the next table. "Bonjour, Salvador."

We were introduced. Our neighbor turned out to be Salvador Dalí. His companion was called Michelle, and I thought how nice when a name can belong to a man or a woman that easily. Oh, those French ... Upon learning that I was from Russia, Dalí switched to Russian: "Bojiia korovka uleti na nebo dam tebe khleba" (a nursery rhyme).

Everyone laughed.

"Ballerina. Maya. Rossia."

"You speak Russian? I never expected that."

"Galia. Zhenshina. Lenin. Rossia. Ballet."

After every word he managed to produce with difficulty with his Spanish vowels and consonants, Dalí put a period. His famous mustache vibrated and swayed. The blonde beauty waited patiently, tapping her foot on the floor and playing with her massive bracelets, so big on her thin and well-tended wrists. And this was our fine Russian conversation.

When Dalí left, having clicked his heels and kissed all the ladies' hands, majestically and dramatically (just like the exit of the King in the prologue to *Sleeping Beauty*) — his straight back was in sharp contrast to the bent spines of the maître d'hôtel and waiters seeing the artist to the door — Alphand said to me, bending close and lowering his voice, "Did you realize that Michelle was a man?"

"A man? Impossible."

"No . . . It's just for the shock value, there's nothing between them, it's merely *épatage.*

And then there was the ballet world of Paris. Motley, noisy, relaxed. Serge Lifar burst into my dressing room after the "white" act of *Lake*. "You reminded me of Olenka Spessivtzeva. She was the best ballerina of the ages. Like you, she danced with her soul, not her body. Well, with her body, too. A wonderful body."

At first, I didn't realize that it was Lifar. Rudely, defensively, I recoiled from the obnoxious, loud visitor. But I quickly figured out who he was.

"Each time I danced with Olenka, I realized each time that she had no equals." And here Lifar kicked around every famous ballet star, past and present. Tact keeps me from mentioning the names of his unlucky victims.

"Olenka, Lord, forgive me, was passionately in love with me. But that's not why I found her so delightful, believe me. She was a real angel." (Toward the end of my meeting with Olga Spessivtzeva at the home for the aged at the Tolstoy Foundation near New York, I asked Olga Alexandrovna—-out of sheer curiosity—whether Lifar had been a good partner. She smiled gently and without any ado, quietly said but one word: "Bad.")

After the "black" act Lifar burst in once again without knocking. I wasn't dressed, and holding up a towel and squirming, I had to listen for a good quarter-hour to the continuation of the panegyric for Spessivtzeva. Suddenly, without any connection, Lifar switched to politics. "I avoid Soviets. They're all agents of the NKVD. Every single one. Bastards. I trust only you. No informer could have such arms, such wings." My eyes swiveled to my pale and bare shoulders, smeared with insect repellent.

"I read, naturally, that they wouldn't let you travel abroad. They tormented you. I came to London in 1956 especially just to see you . . . I did, what can I say? Why the hell are you sticking around in Moscow? Stay here. Shall we go to the police tomorrow morning?"

I wailed, "Sergei Mikhailovich, I won't have time to get into my white tutu. Please, take pity . . ."

Lotar moved on him, impressive bosom leading the charge. He went on talking. "The Bolsheviks will never forgive me for my telegram to Hitler the day the Wehrmacht took my native Kiev. But I couldn't know the Germans would be such animals! . . . I have many of Pushkin's letters and other memorabilia."

In total, over my many trips to France, I must have spent a hundred hours of my life with Lifar. He coached me in his *Phèdre*. He told me fascinating stories about Diaghilev, Kuznetsovo porcelain, and iconography; he took me all over Paris on foot—he knew the nitty-gritty of all the secrets of every tiny street in the city—and he was my Virgil in the long, long catacombs of the metro underpasses.

I've never seen Lifar dance, and I can't judge what kind of partner he made for a ballerina. But I have danced his choreography. I can firmly say that if not for his *Phèdre, Icare, Suite en blanc,* and *Daphnis et Chloé* (he created more than two hundred ballets), there would be no Béjart or Roland Petit. Actually, there would be, but they would be different . . .

The next day, after class Lifar was waiting for me at the backstage door of the Opera. "Coco Chanel is expecting us. I told her about you. Let's go."

I was stunned. Lifar's appearance was so unexpected. But meeting Chanel? "I have an appointment. I shouldn't let people down."

"I'm a poor man, I can't afford a present worthy of you. Everything I earn goes for my Pushkin archives. So my present to you is a meeting with Coco. Come on, let's go, damn it. They're waiting for us."

Obediently I walked faster. We went down into the metro.

Lifar had told the truth. We were expected at the Chanel boutique. Straight-backed, anorexically thin and severe, surrounded by leggy models, Channel held out her wrinkled, knobby hands in welcome to me. The skin on her hands gave her age away treacherously. She was in her eighties. And so for an audience of two, Lifar and me, there was a show of the fall and winter collections of the House of Chanel. This was the first French collection I ever saw in my life. And up close like this.

The models worked hard. The tried to hit the beat of the vague melody Chanel was humming off-key. The mistress was displeased. Annoyed. An angry tirade in lilting French. The action came to a halt. Coco got up from her armchair. "Roll your shoulders forward more gracefully. Shoulders forward. Pelvis forward. Shorten your stride."

Coco showed them how to wear her clothes. A miracle. Magic. The mistress of the boutique looked a little over twenty. She moved so elegantly, so sedately.

"Pick what you like, Maya. It's all yours."

I mumbled hesitantly.

"Well, then I'll pick. There, the white suit on Jeanette. It's yours."

Chanel's present is still in my closet. I wear it on special occasions. Amazingly, the cut and shape are still in style. Wonders! Heavy stitched white silk. Navy-blue narrow trim on the jacket. Gold semi-military buttons, which ornament the whiteness of the garment like war medals or regimental insignia. Under the jacket, a simple sheath hugging the body.

"Jeanette, take off the suit, let Maya put it on. And let's have her walk for us. We'll see how a ballerina from Russia wears an outfit from the House of Chanel."

Brown-eyed Jeanette helped me into the white suit, and I came out. Coco hummed. I tried to copy her walk. I made a diagonal and two turns. Chanel burst into applause. "Now I believe Serge that you are a great ballerina. I'll hire you to work in my boutique. Agreed?"

I noticed that Lifar was pleased that I had passed the tricky test. The degree of our relationship rose sharply.

"Serge, Maya, come upstairs to my place."

Chanel's apartment was exquisite and luxurious. Ninth-century painted Chinese screens (an entire room), Bourbon furniture (another room), an encrusted trunk that had belonged to Marie Antoinette, Italian Renaissance tapestries. All kinds of stuff that I don't remember precisely.

"Would you like to see my collection of bracelets? Did I ever tell you about it, Serge?"

A cupid-pretty youth and a lovely shepherdess of a girl brought in an ancient chest. It contained treasure, a whole island of treasure. The cupid opened the mother-of-pearl lid. The shepherdess, like a magician, pulled out bracelet after bracelet, trying them on Chanel's wrists. Two or three on mine. She gently babbled pleasantries. On thin platinum and white-gold chains nestled diamonds, emeralds, sapphires, garnets, and rubies. Large ones, the size of a woman's fingernail.

I began to have doubts — could this be costume jewelry? It really was too much to be real. Coco saw my suspicions. "The bracelet with emeralds is a Russian gift. From Grand Duke Dmitri Pavlovich, a cousin of your sovereign Nicholas II. I had a long affair with him," Chanel told me conspiratorially. "This ruby bracelet came from the wrist of Marie Antoinette. And my favorite ruby necklace was hers, too. Bring the ruby necklace!"

The cupid noiselessly, with feline stealth, vanished through a low camouflaged door. The ruby necklace, which Coco put on immediately, was incredibly, unimaginably beautiful.

And now, a small mystery-story epilogue to this Paris story . . . A few years after the death of Coco Chanel, when I was back in Paris, the telephone rang in my hotel room. A woman speaking broken Russian introduced herself as Mrs. Conan Doyle. Ho, ho! I thought. Not bad.

"Yes. I am the wife of the son of Conan Doyle. I'm calling from London. I wonder, do you remember ruby beads on the neck of Mme Chanel when you visited her with Lifar?"

Yes, I remembered. How could anyone forget?

"You see," the ingratiating voice continued, "the night Mme Chanel died all her jewelry disappeared. It was stolen. The ruby necklace vanished, too."

"What does it have to do with you?"

"Mme Chanel willed the Marie Antoinette necklace to my sister. We are looking for it."

Was she pulling my leg? If she was, it was based on fact. Or could it be?

"Since you really are Mme Conan Doyle, keep up the investigation. Good luck."

The lady never called back.

On the last evening of my life in Paris, Elsa and I went to the Folies-Bergères. Aragon had planned to go with us, but he was apparently still having problems with the relationship between Bukharin and Kamenev, which kept him at his desk on rue de Varenne.

O sneaky and mysterious Muse of Parisian fame! The topless chorus girls recognized me. They introduced me to the audience. Brought me a bouquet of red gladiolas. Made a speech. The chorus girls applauded. Their bare breasts jiggled with the ovations. The most talkative, most seductive, and most beautiful one came down the stage steps into the audience to kiss me. Elsa grumpily translated the greetings in the most short-hand way.

"Our Lilya likes to bare her breasts. She should have gone to the Folies-Bergères with you. Not me. I'm a serious French writer, the wife of Aragon. Tomorrow the newspapers will carry ridiculous photos with vulgar captions."

When I got back to Moscow, Lilya Yuryevna Brik greeted me with a question, "Well, did Elsa tell you a lot of nasty things about me?"

It was the Soviet embassy staff that said nasty things about me after the first time I met Paris and Paris met me. On April 14, 1992, the Moscow newspaper *Komsomolskaya Pravda* published several denunciations from the secret archives of the Central Committee of the Communist Party. It was almost as if the newspaper staff had prepared this amusing information for me specially just when I was working on the Paris chapter. The heading for the "secret file" was this: "On Improper Behavior During Business Trips Aboard."

6.7.77. Embassy of the USSR in France. Secret.
To the Minister of Culture, Comrade P. N. Demichev.

Dear Pyotr Nilovich:

I would like to raise several issues with you, relating to the publication by bourgeois periodicals of interviews with M. M. Plisetskaya, which she gave to French journalists during her stay in France in June of this year as part of the ballet troupe of the Bolshoi Theater. First of all, M. M. Plisetskaya expressed a thought about stagnation in our ballet art, its alleged ossification and conservatism. Secondly, M. M. Plisetskaya criticized the Bolshoi Theater. . . . Third, M. M. Plisetskaya heaped praise (undeserved, in our opinion) on contemporary Western choreographers, most of all on M. Béjart. . . . As Comrade Butrova reported to us, she tried several times to talk to M. M. Plisetskaya about her interviews. The ballerina's reaction was, unfortunately, not self-critical. Apparently, it would be useful in Moscow to have a talk with M. M. Plisetskaya on the level of responsible persons, whom she considers authoritative, without giving this whole story much publicity for the time being.

—Ambassador of the USSR to France S. Chervonenko.

This was scribbled in 1977! When I was in Paris for the twentieth or twenty-fifth time . . . When I had the highest regalia of the land of the Soviets bestowed upon me . . . When I had received awards from France (later, President Mitterand would pin the Legion of Honor to my black Cardin dress and I would receive an honorary degree from the Sorbonne) . . . When I had been recognized by the ballet world . . . When I . . .

Damn it, then what had the embassy hounds written about my first Paris tour in October 1961?

I hailed a taxi on the corner of place de l'Opéra and rue de la Paix. I handed the elderly driver, ramrod straight like a military man, a slip of paper with an address on the other side of the Seine. We said nothing during the entire long trip—we were stuck in traffic. We approached my goal. I took money from my purse, crumpled bills, like every woman's money on this planet. And suddenly . . . in pure Russian, with prerevolutionary pronunciation (I could almost hear the old orthography), "I won't take your money, Miss Plisetskaya. This ride is in lieu of a bouquet."

Paris had acknowledged me.

Chapter Thirty-Five

Work with Yakobson

The Parisian dream was over . . .

Awakening.

I was in Moscow. Hordes of foreign visitors. State performances. *Swan Lake* after *Lake*. Khrushchev, that martyr to art, must have memorized the ballet! What would the Soviet government have done if Tchaikovsky hadn't written *Swan Lake?* And with Nikolai Fadeyechev and *Swan Lake* yet again, I opened the Kremlin Palace of Congresses on December 23, 1961. The clumsy, bureaucratic building, appended to the ancient Orthodox churches of the Kremlin, was intended for Party congresses, anniversary sessions of the Supreme Soviet, and international congresses. But there couldn't be government ceremonies every day. So they gave the palace to the Bolshoi. Six thousand theatergoers could watch us there.

After yet another *Swan Lake,* this time for the king of Laos, there was a reception. Shchedrin was in the capital city of Kiev with his concerts. I went alone. Now our leaders were once again condescending and kind to me. The ballerina had not run off, she had come back — she was ours. In an insouciant mood, Brezhnev, all dimples and wriggling eyebrows, offered me a lift home. The leader was flirting. I had to go, otherwise he might bear a grudge. My place really was on Brezhnev's way — along Kutuzovsky.

Brezhnev was the Number 2 man in the Soviet state then—chairman of the Presidium of the Supreme Soviet of the USSR. He had an armored car. Black and roomy, like a catafalque. Another one hastened after us. With the bodyguards.

Leonid Ilyich had had quite a bit to drink in the name of "eternal" Soviet-Laotian friendship, In a deep voice, he recited poetry by Sergei Esenin to me:

Everything will pass, like the apple tree's white smoke . . .
I will no longer be young . . .

He sobbed. Our leader was very sentimental. Yet another bodyguard, up front with the chauffeur, turned and nodded sympathetically to me, as if to say, Look how educated our leaders are now . . . And then gave a quick look at my purse, checking for dynamite or grenades. It would be terrible for the country to lose an educated leader . . . You can expect the worst from those bitch ballerinas.

After the poetry, Brezhnev started singing—the leader was also an amateur musician. With a wheeze he warbled, "The Broad Dnieper Roils and Moans" while, like a bear, he pawed at my knee. I moved over into the corner and—appropriately—cried out, "Leonid Ilyich, oh! There's no left turn here! Driver!"

"I can turn here, Maya Mikhailovna," the poetry lover insisted smugly.

Traffic was stopped. The traffic cop saluted. And the two black limousines went across the intersection on a red light. The tires squealed as we turned left. The leader started some social chitchat. "What new work will you bring to your fans this season?"

"I've started rehearsing *Spartacus*."

"But I've seen *Spartacus*."

"You've seen Moiseyev's version, and this is Yakobson's."

"Yukhanson? The hockey player?"

"Yakobson. Leonid Veniaminovich. A brilliant choreographer."

We had reached my house. I rushed out to my entrance. On the run, I turned back to say good-bye. "Thank you. Good-bye. Come see the new *Spartacus*."

We were rehearsing *Spartacus* day and night at the theater. Sol Hurok, who had seen Yakobson's ballet in Leningrad, wanted us to bring it on our fall tour of America. If the Bolshoi did the premiere by April, then the sets would make it by ship in time.

Hurok's second condition was my participation in the ballet. Two messengers from the theater—Preobrazhensky and Nikitian—came back from Leningrad and informed the administration that Plisetskaya's role was Phrygia. So I started learning Phrygia.

My coach was Maria Nikolayevna Shamsheva. She was from Leningrad, from the Maryinsky, and she had a phenomenal choreographic memory. And the right schooling—Vaganova.

In Yakobson's style, there was a movement for every note. And Khachaturian had a lot of notes, many more than necessary. And that meant that there were thousands of movements. I would have to memorize them all. And none were familiar—none of those pirouettes, développés, or jetés en tournant for him. It was all freshly minted, never existed before, pure Yakobson.

In my entire life I've met only a few creative choreographers who had a God-given talent for creating dance. God is very stingy with choreographic talent at birth. You see a brilliant dancer, smart, educated, well-read, with a good ear, who is a mediocre, useless choreographer. And that pseudo-creator will start refinishing, borrowing, and redoing successful ballets of the past. Filling musical space with primitive class combinations without rhyme or reason and then add something fashionable—a strained attempt at modern dance, borrowed from videotapes or spied on the stages of the contemporary pillars of modern dance. The result is a Joseph's coat, a patchwork of borrowings.

Would you like me to give you an example? I've staged *Raymonda* in Rome and *La Fille mal gardée* in Madrid, and I would begin with the best intentions to be innovative and come to the finish line in humbleness—Why try to outperform the best? I did the Spanish dance in the second act of *Raymonda* on pointe, tricking it up with all sorts of things. But then I returned to the Gorsky,* retaining only my idea for a characteristic dance on pointe. And hand on heart, I can say that I couldn't come close to Gorsky. At least I understand that. But what about the others?

Yakobson the choreographer was anointed by God. But as a dancer, he was just the opposite—quite average. I saw him when I was a teenager on the Bolshoi stage in a few episodic roles. My memory retains only one small part as a fellow with a balalaika, where the dancer was distinguished not by his leaps but by his humor.

My exhausting work with Shamsheva would be interrupted by the refreshing appearances of Yakobson. During warm-ups he proposed innumerable variants.

---

*Alexander Gorsky restaged Petipa's *Raymonda* for the Bolshoi.

His imagination was infinite. And everything was right there, on the spot, without doing homework, improvised. Really, it was Mozartean.

That does not mean that he did not insist on unqualified obedience to his text. He insisted, and how! He was — and this is the other side of the coin — stubborn and pedantic. But also an extravagant improviser and fount of imagination. How did that coexist in one man?

I was mastering Phrygia's final cry. In the text, a good half of it is walking, crawling, and jumping . . . on my knees. I refused loudly. My bad knee was sensitive to extravagance. Straining it was easy. And then? My reasoning persuaded Yakobson. He began proposing one variation after another. A good hundred variations. Each one better than the next. Just that day's instantaneous perceptions were enough for a whole new ballet. A marvelous one. Now the hold-up was in deciding which suggestions to settle on.

Yakobson's version of *Spartacus*, like each of his ballets, is flawless in its sense of style. He had no equals in terms of style. Yakobson, I always thought, seemed to get under the skin, get right into the kidneys, the fate, the era of his heroes. How else could the Roman woman Phrygia weep — in movement, without a single word — over her beloved's dead body? Tear out her hair, rend her clothes, beat her chest, howl, wring her hands, kiss his armor, wash her hands in the blood of her dead husband?

April 4, 1962, was the premiere of Yakobson's *Spartacus* at the Bolshoi. The audience and all of theatrical Moscow divided into two groups. Pro Yakobson. And contra. That was par for the course. He was used to it. At one pole were his admirers, at the other those who rejected him and could not accept his work. And that extended throughout his entire professional life — the ones who were outraged were the bosses, the commission-givers, the commanders of art. They tormented and berated Yakobson mightily.

Leonid Veniaminovich's reputation in official circles was clouded. He was considered leftist, a formalist. His talent was obvious; his innovations, endless; but his intentions?

Yakobson's talent did not easily fit the usual bureaucratic paradigm. Yes, he did show an interest in revolutionary themes: *The Twelve*, based on Blok's poem, *The Flea*, based on Mayakovsky. That was laudable. But why drag shtetl motifs onto the stage: the wedding procession, and those Chagallian plots? And why was there so much eroticism? *Rodin Triptych* was a corrupting influence on Soviet youth: the dancers in the pas de deux start making love in public.

A groundbreaker has a hard time in any social system. But it is hell for him in a totalitarian system. Yakobson had to beg, plead, scratch, and implore for permission from the authorities for each new ballet. And then he had to fight them off, disobeying, disregarding orders. A Yakobson premiere was always, without exception, a battle, a scandal, and a nerve-wracking experience.

Leonid Veniaminovich kept an autograph notebook with evaluations and opinions about himself. He collected autographs, either jokingly or seriously. Perhaps the kind words in that book were a balm to compensate for all the slings and arrows in his life? For the dim-witted ignorance of his contemporaries?

When we finally performed *Spartacus* in America, with Yakobson there — the first time he had ever been allowed out of the Soviet Union — it was the most bitter experience for me to hear how cruelly and devastatingly the American press attacked him. And not for essential things but over trifles. Smug people, who had created cozy nests for themselves in the arts sections of famous newspapers, did not see or sense the choreographer's genius or his martyred and tortured fate as a creator.

How many times is that clichéd and shameful story repeated: in his lifetime, the artist is trampled into the dirt, scorned, and rejected, but once he dies, he is remembered lovingly: what he said to whom, which pub was his favorite for drinking beer, what streets he strolled . . . Now there are all sorts of societies, foundations, memorials dedicated to Leonid Yakobson all over the world, the United States included. And what about back then, in 1962?

I worried, seeing how Yakobson suffered and agonized, and how the ministry hacks who accompanied us gloated — so, Mr. Yakobson, your Western innovations got what they deserved. Yakobson tried to not show how dispirited and burdened he felt. His animated, mobile face was hidden behind a mask of indifference. Only after the last performance of *Spartacus* in New York (the ballet was quickly replaced for the rest of the cities on the tour), did Yakobson sit down on the metal stool in my dressing room at the Met and break out into silent weeping. Large, heavy tears dropped from his blue eyes.

"Maika, you were brilliant today. Your weeping scene was so powerful, that I . . ."

"Leonid Veniaminovich, don't pay attention to the critics. You saw how the audience applauded, how they didn't want to leave."

"I'm afraid my tormentors in Moscow and Leningrad have been given a big trump card."

The seamstress Nyura Zaitseva came in to pick up my tunic costume, but seeing me still dressed in it, she quietly shut the door.

"The critics wrote that there weren't enough dances. It's all dances, there isn't a single nondance movement, not a single pantomime."

"They were expecting fouettés and manèges of pirouettes . . ."

"This is the most danceable of all my ballets! They're sending me home the day after tomorrow, since *Spartacus* won't be performed any more. Let me take a picture of you in your dressing room wearing the tunic. I filmed your dancing today from backstage. There wasn't enough light. I'm not sure how it will come out."

He took all the per diems allotted to him in America and bought a small eight-millimeter camera and a few rolls of Kodak film. For his stock. "The camera will be a great help in my work. I don't have the money for a luxury like this in the Soviet Union."

Yakobson spent his entire life in need. What profit could a fighter have made? Because of his permanent battles and fisticuffs with the Ministry of Culture, the Leningrad Party gave him a small salary as choreographer. The Soviet regime knew it could stifle a rebellious artist with rubles as well. His wife, Irina, drew a salary as a dancer at the Maryinsky. But the magic wand to save them when things got very tight was folk dance: Yakobson would set off for Moldavia, to Kishinev. To work with Zhok, the famous folk ensemble. The audiences loved the flavor and authenticity of the Moldavian folk dances, and no one ever suspected that they were all choreographed by Leonid Yakobson. He was a virtuoso stylist.

The Moldavians paid generously, with only one condition — anonymity. Yakobson agreed without a murmur. Even a genius needs to feed his family.

When I was ready to implement my ideas of a dancing Anna Karenina, I was a bit worried about doing it all alone and talked to Yakobson.

"Go ahead, Maika, you'll do it. If you stumble, I'll help."

I began with my solo dances — the mazurka at the ball, "The Blizzard," the final scenes. I wanted to test myself. I called Yakobson and then went to see him in Leningrad.

Despite everyone and everything, L. V. used the thermonuclear energy of his zeal to create a ballet theater toward the end of his life. It was a chamber theater — the very name explained it — Choreographic Miniatures. But it was his own, understand, his own ballet theater. Just imagine what that meant to him. It took blood and guts, but he got the city authorities to give him a cramped space on Mayakovsky Street with two rehearsal halls. It was cramped but his own.

For microscopic pay, enthusiastic, decent dancers who believed in him joined the theater. Even premier dancers of the Kirov, Alla Osipenko and John Markovsky, shunned high pay and prestige to join Yakobson's troupe.

Shchedrin taped excerpts of the music for *Anna* and I took the tape with me. Before looking at my sketches, L. V. wanted to hear the music. The assistant turned it on. Yakobson couldn't sit still. On the ninth or tenth measure he got up and started dancing, covering his eyes with the back of his hand, slowly dancing to the sound. It had nothing in common with what I had done. Nothing at all. My own creation started to pale for me.

He improvised throughout the entire tape. The few people present were mesmerized by the unchecked flow of Yakobson's imagination. A miracle was being created. Freezing on the last note, Yakobson turned to me. "Maika, did you remember it all?

"Of course not."

"If you had, you'd have the key to the entire ballet. But you're too lazy!"

I had to unkink my legs and start showing him my baby. But how could I miss Yakobson's inspiration?

"L. V., improvise one more time. And we'll film it. Where's your American camera? Is it still working?"

The camera worked, and film was found. No Kodak, of course, but some black and white of Soviet manufacture. My Leningrad sister, Era, who had come with me, could handle a camera. She got ready to film.

The assistant turned on the tape. Yakobson started improvising, but it was all different. Something had scared off his inspiration. Maybe it was the annoying clacking of the camera, maybe it was the long search for film, maybe . . .

Something was lost. The miracle was not repeated. Yakobson sensed it himself. Angrily he said to Era, "Expose the film. Throw it away. We'll do it again tomorrow fresh."

"Tomorrow I have to be back in Moscow."

"You're always like that! Well, then, next time."

There was reproach in his voice, which pricks to this day.

I started showing him my steps. Yakobson made a few inconsequential remarks. He was a moody man, and he was bored and depressed because his vision of Anna had slipped away.

Naturally, Era did not throw away the film. She had it processed and sent it to me in Moscow via a conductor on the Red Arrow overnight express, along with a tiny editing table so that the "beautiful" moments could be stopped, and every movement could be rerun, back and forth, back and forth. My sweet Era! (The film eventually dried up and grew wavy, but it's still in the desk of our Moscow apartment.)

I did use a lot of Yakobson from our rushed meeting on Mayakovsky Street in Leningrad. I mixed it with my own. I developed and extended some dance combinations. And I blame myself over and over for not staying longer in Leningrad and calling in sick for the rehearsal at the Bolshoi. For not using all my energy to try to summon once again the vision of Yakobson's Anna.

Our next meeting was much later. At the filming of *The Bluebird*. I was supposed to dance Yakobson's choreography with Alexander Godunov — the roles of Water and Fire. I was struck by how much weight Yakobson had lost, how tired he looked. He was irritable.

"Are you well, Leonid Veniaminovich?"

"My ensemble is exhausting me. The Leningrad authorities have lost their minds. Every ballet they automatically ban. Then you have to bargain for every lift, sewing on color strips on flesh-colored leotards. They fear the naked body and sex like fire. Do Party members make babies while wearing fur coats?"

I looked anxiously at Yakobson's sunken eyes, which had lost their former heavenly blueness. His skin was yellow and dead-looking. "Are you well, Leonid Veniaminovich?"

"I'm not feeling very good. I've seen doctors. Did tests, didn't find anything. They say I'm healthy. It must just be age. I've worn out my nervous system. But only physically. My new works I think are the best I've ever done!"

Work on the film, unfortunately, was never completed. Even though what L. V. proposed for Sasha Godunov and me was brilliant. Our duet showed the mutual dependence of fire and water. I foamed, streamed, fell like a waterfall, splashed at the fire. The fire hissed, moved back, rushed around in blazes. And all that only choreographically.

Yakobson was hospitalized. In a ward for ten. The equipment for tests belonged in the Stone Age. There was no medicine. The syringes were boiled on a hotplate. They were used and reused. Filth, stink, the moans of the suffering. The hallways were filled with cots and patients. Indifference and harshness of the personnel. God keep an ordinary person from ending up in an ordinary Soviet hospital. Even a healthy person would die on the spot.

Ira Yakobson — who always managed to "ameliorate" L. V.'s problems — rushed to Moscow. To the ministry. She got all the way to Minister of Culture Demichev (who replaced Furtseva, when she called it quits with cyanide). Pyotr

Nilovich Demichev responded to Ira's plea. He was a gentle and kindly man. He did a lot for the people who asked. But it was very hard to get to him. Two Gennadys—the numerous bodyguards didn't count—Gennady Gennadievich and Gennady Alexeyevich, ever-vigilantly guarded every precious moment of their minister's time. They apparently considered Demichev's compassion a fatal flaw better hidden from people's eyes. And they performed unimaginable feats to keep their boss from excessive contact with his countrymen. Every citizen of the USSR, as far as they were concerned, was a potential sponger.

Demichev immediately arranged for Yakobson to be transferred to Kuntsevo Hospital in Moscow. The minister was a candidate member of the Politburo, and this was within his power. The strict subordination of the Soviet system— who was allowed what—was circumvented this time. And Yakobson went in for further testing.

I have to mention that Demichev arranged for Shchedrin to go to the Kunt- sevo Hospital twice, when Rodion was having heart trouble, thereby violating the rules of Party etiquette (Shchedrin had never been a member of the Party). I have no intention of forgetting the good deeds Demichev did for our family.

The first serious test showed that Yakobson had advanced stomach cancer. All his anxiety, suffering, and stress had taken their toll. And now, when he had finally gotten a touring ballet company of his own, Yakobson, weakened, squashed, and fully rational, was fading in great pain. Fading away in the Kremlin Kuntsevo hospital.

How do you like that irony?

But his creative imagination was at full speed even in a hospital bed. He listed hundreds of new ideas, choreographic projects, and dreams for Irina, who was constantly at his side. But it was too late. His martyred life ended in more suf- fering in the Kremlin hospital.

Yakobson died on October 17, 1975. His remains were taken to Leningrad and buried at the Serafimovsky Cemetery.

Why did I isolate my work and meetings with Yakobson into a separate chapter?

I worked with him more often and for a longer time than with any other of my contemporary choreographers. My first participation in a production, my first role made for me, my first public appearance in something new, was *Disarma- ment Conference* (I was a Chinaman, a war-monger) in 1934. Choreography by Yakobson.

Several ballets for an entire evening, concert numbers, production work on all these, alas unrealized, projects. Choreography by Yakobson.

My delight at the premieres of Choreographic Miniatures. Choreography by Yakobson.

Shchedrin's *Daring Ditties* at the Kirov Theater. Choreography by Yakobson.

Making movies. Choreography by Yakobson.

Choreography by Yakobson.

But not only that, not only . . .

The fate of Yakobson, like that of another great choreographer of my country, Kaslan Goleizovsky, is a tragedy for me. No less tragic than the fate of millions who spent time in Soviet prisons and rotted away in the Gulags. A man burning with creativity who could not express himself fully. Who could not tell people what his fiery imagination saw, heard, and sensed. With a gagged mouth and tied hands, banging his head every day, like torture, against the bans of Soviet ideology and the stupidity and zealousness of its proponents and executors. Forced, in order to survive, in order to preserve his talent, in order to protect the creative future of his son, Kolya, to make compromises. Not capitulation, do you hear that, Western analysts, inexorable judges with weak, politicized brains? Compromises. Don't you make them every single day?

The system is ruthless, deadly; and open rebellion is perilously dangerous. Now we know how they jabbed a poisoned hypodermic into Solzhenitsyn in a crowded store in Rostov, how they put poisoned cigarettes into the hotel room of Vladimir Voinovich. And to make it worse, to be forced to stew in your own juices, to be isolated from the rest of humanity, the latest discoveries and achievements of world culture, the work of your Western colleagues.

And to worry about feeding your family, finding shoes and fruit and schnitzel.

And with all that, with all that, to create astounding masterpieces that will outlive the ignoramus Brezhnev as well as their creator, who was hounded to death.

I have to turn to the words of Andrei Voznesensky once again: Warriors, sculptors, glory to you!

Chapter Thirty-Six

Why I Did Not Stay in the West

I began this book in February 1991 in Spain. I went through my diaries, reread my letters to Shchedrin, and decided to pick up my pen. I would be another George Sand (my husband was a composer, too).

Time rushed by like a meteor. In a few days, epochs can crumble. The world is completely different today. What will tomorrow be like?

Nowadays I can't give a single interview that doesn't begin with the question, Why didn't you stay in the West? I'll try to explain to everyone, including myself, why I didn't run away after all.

My generation was brought up as if we were at the front, as if there were a war on—us and them, we were at war. He who runs to the enemy's side is a traitor. The punishment for a turncoat is revenge. All the films, plays, radio shows, and newspapers shouted that constantly. When I asked my mother why we didn't stay with Father in the West in 1934—the whole family was in Norway—she said, "If I had even breathed a word about it, he would have abandoned me with the children instantly. Misha would never have been a traitor."

It was the code of honor of the times for our deceived fathers. Abroad seemed farther away than Mars, and foreigners were aliens from other worlds.

When I discovered America for myself in 1959, even though I was surrounded by surveillance and nannies, rehearsals and performances, I had enough sense to see that Americans were free and we weren't. That they lived in abundance, and we in poverty. That they had comforts, we had problems. And so—should I have rushed over to the police to ask for political asylum? In Moscow I had family. They would feel the aftershock. In Moscow was Shchedrin. He was like a hostage. I was counting the days until I saw him. And I should just run after comfort, after a filigree doorknob?

Today I write like that, but back then all my thoughts were on other things, and I didn't think about running away. Of course, like everyone else I suppose, I had the brief naive thought, a second's desire to try out a different lifestyle—ah, it's so free and lovely here, wouldn't it be nice to earn a lot of money and buy that house on the hill beyond the chestnut lane and live happily ever after with Rodion? Would they ever let us live happily ever after? They'd arrange a car crash, squash my legs, and then what—beg in the subway if I survived?

Every similar dream was erased by fear. That is the first explanation that I can give. Yes, yes, simple *fear*. I was afraid they would kill me. There were so many incidents like that with refugees . . . More than one could count.

In 1961 word flew around the world that Rudolf Nureyev had stayed in the West. He had asked for political asylum in a Paris airport when he was separated from the Kirov Ballet troupe leaving for London, and an attempt was made to force him to fly back to the Soviet Union. That meant that his ballet life was over. He would never go anywhere again. In a similar situation I would have done the same thing. I would have screamed even louder, I think.

But my life wasn't over. It was only beginning. After six years of torture I was allowed abroad. And with Ulanova's retirement from the stage, I was the prima ballerina of the Bolshoi. An enviable position. That also held me. If our famous fugitives had had this, maybe they wouldn't have fled after all?

But they beckoned and tempted me every time.

During my second American tour in 1962 I received a fairy-tale bouquet of salmon roses. I had never seen a rose that color. There was a miniature envelope with the flowers. A note inside. It was from Nureyev. He wrote that he congratulated me on my success and hoped that someday we would dance together . . . Rudi did not supply a telephone number or an address, and there was nowhere to send my thanks. And would I have dared to call? I don't know.

Our propaganda depicted the fugitive as the devil's spawn, and Soviet people were afraid even to say the name Nureyev. Any form of communication with the incomparable dancer carried the threat of the grimmest repercussions. It's hard to imagine it decades later. But try living then, not now, brave people.

I asked the maid for a large vase, trimmed each stem, and set the flowers a bit apart from the theater offerings. I didn't tell anyone about the bouquet. I kept it to myself.

The next day I had a surprise visit from one of the keepers who accompanied us from Moscow. A meaningless chat about this and that. Looking around. Surveillance. Ah, what lovely flowers. These orange ones are the best. Who sent them? I blushed. I came up with some lame story, I don't remember, but I naturally didn't mention the name Nureyev.

The keeper had perfect smell, the way some people have perfect pitch. "Have you heard? They say Nureyev is in New York."

I replied that I hadn't heard.

"It's too bad about him, what a dancer he was. He's being wasted here in the West."

And all the time, he was sniffing Rudi's bouquet. "What if he sends you flowers, too? What would you do with them?"

I got scared. Was he trying to provoke me, or did he know something? That's how we lived. That's how fear ate away at us.

Now there have been reports in the press that the KGB, on orders from on high, was planning an "accident" to break Nureyev's legs. It's a rumor, but it sounds real.

In 1963 I made a trip to England. That's when I finally got there — seven years after the first time my Bolshoi toured there! A call from Svetlana Beriosova, prima ballerina at Covent Garden, with an invitation for a late supper. At her house. Tactfully, she warned me, "Maya, Margot Fonteyn will be there, you know her, and . . . Nureyev. Will that be a problem? If it is, I'll understand."

I accepted instantly. The year had softened the blow of my first reaction (and later I even carried parcels and copies of Rudi's films for his mother and sister). But how could I get out of the hotel unnoticed in the evening? The eternal problem. I invited Nikolai Fadeyechev to join me. He was an honest person, he wouldn't turn me in, and we would be safer from prying eyes if we were together.

I had met Margot in 1960 in Finland, when she was dancing *Giselle* and I *Swan Lake* at a ballet festival. We hit it off right away, simply and naturally, as if we had known each other all our lives.

Svetlana picked us up near the hotel, and we went off. Margot and Rudi weren't there yet. They were performing that night. Svetlana's husband, a Pakistani Grenadier, was cooking dinner. All the spices in London were being used in those dishes, and Fadeyechev was looking forward to the meal. A pealing ring of the doorbell. In comes Nureyev and with him Margot Fonteyn, whom I didn't even notice.

Rudi and I rushed into each other's arms. An eternity went by. This is how the most ordinary things suddenly become—damned politicians!—emotional explosions.

"Did you get my flowers in New York?" We used the formal form of address in Russian. We had not known each other well before.

"I did. Thank you."

"And the letter reached you? Will we dance together?"

Only then did I notice Margot Fonteyn, patiently awaiting her turn to embrace.

Rudi smiled and said, "I provoke such fear in my former countrymen. You are the most daring of the lot."

"Kolya is no coward either. We'll hang together."

Margot was wearing a black suit, probably French. I'm not going to describe Margot Fonteyn's wardrobe and face. She was so famous, every step so well known, that I dare add only a few words.

We had gone to each other's performances more than a few times, and we participated in the same concerts in Japan and Australia. I was always impressed, no matter what we were doing, by her impeccable manners and the perfection of her breeding. I had never met a better brought-up person, and not only in our rather vulgar ballet world—in my entire life. How I envied her ability to get on with people. Even the press. How they persisted, like sticky June bugs, those uninventive reporters with the same question, over and over, in Australia and in Japan: When will you retire? Now I get it all the time too. My answer is simple: when I'm 107, not before.

Margot always replied with the most charming smile, which was intended to say that she was hearing the question for the first time in her life. "I haven't decided yet." She once told me, however, that she would come out onstage as long as she was asked. "I'll come out in a wheelchair. I need money for my husband's medical bills."* She had personal experience with wheelchairs, alas.

We spent an unforgettable evening. Rudi gave me a huge volume of Goya reproductions. How had he borne that weight to Svetlana's house? I treasure the luxurious book to this day. Not wanting to burden Svetlana Beriosova with chauffeuring duties again, Fadeyechev and I took a taxi back to the hotel. Kolya carried my two-ton book.

---

*Fonteyn's husband, Panamanian diplomat Roberto Arias, spent his life in a wheelchair following an assassination attempt.

In the lobby, despite the late hour, familiar characters were waiting for us. "Where have you been so late, friends? Actually, we know. At Beriosova's. Right? Did we guess?"

Kolya almost dropped Rudi's present.

"We almost went to Mrs. Beriosova's house. But an uninvited guest is worse than a Tatar," he said, quoting an old proverb.

"But not worse than a Bashkir," said the other, with a grin. Had they prepared that clumsy joke, or was it an improvised quip?

We said nothing. We pretended not to get the reference to Rudi's nationality.

"What's this fat tome? A present, no doubt?" Goya quickly moved from Fadeyechev's hands to the vigilant eye. The eye leafed through it. "Gorgeous. Would someone have dared to sully this volume with an inscription?"

Wise Rudi had not inscribed the book for safety's sake. Bravo!

"Goya does war, and we're at war. I won't write anything. You'll remember anyway."

Bravo, Rudi. Thanks.

Later we comforted each other. They were just trying it out. If they had known for sure, Fadeyechev and I would still be in Moscow. We would never have traveled again.

The reason I'm writing about this is to explain clearly to people of the future why I was afraid to stay in the West, why I feared for my life. I don't doubt that Nureyev and Baryshnikov spent more than one night in nightmares. None of them, in all their fugitive years in the West, ever said an unkind word about the criminal Soviet regime. They limited themselves to stating that they wanted to dance a new, modern repertoire. Good for them. They would have been wiped out in a flash. They were hunted, seriously.

Besides their Soviet spies, the KGB had a wide network of amateur informers in the West, who worked out of ideological belief. And worked as hard as they could. One bookstore in Europe that sold Russian émigré books had a bespectacled clerk who served the Soviets. Not for money, but for an idiotic idea, he supplied the appropriate departments of the Soviet Embassy with photographs he took surreptitiously behind the counter of everyone interested in the latest from the foreign publishers Possev and YMCA Press. They paid dearly for their curiosity about émigré anti-Soviet literature.

At that same time in London I received a serious proposition. Fonteyn introduced me to a gentleman called Mr. Summer. He spoke Russian freely, albeit with a heavy accent. "Wouldn't you like to sign a contract in England for, say, five years? You would get annually . . ." Mr. Summer named a sum that sounded incredible to my Moscow ears.

"For five years? What about Shchedrin? I can't leave him."

"We'll find something for him, too. Well? Will you stay?"

Oh, those secret services. Maybe he was from Lubyanka? They confused a poor ballerina.

There were many more such Mr. Summers in my future. Many. The approaches changed, the accents, and . . . the amounts. (Interested? You guessed, big sums.) In that same London period, as if it were planned, I got jabbed by the frisky British press. Used to adoration from Moscow audiences, spoiled by the instant acceptance from America and France, I was not prepared to passages like, "We are visited by Madame PLI" or "Apparently, a tavern keeper's daughter suits her" or "Isn't it time to bury the poor bird?" Today I know that reacting to jibes from the press is stupid. But make allowances for my complete lack of that sort of experience in 1963. The audiences went wild, but the press was giving me nasty little flicks on my nose. I was furious with the entire British Empire, and the royal family to boot. And then, Wouldn't you like to stay here?

A coincidence? Fate? Character?

Maybe I should have omitted my British bruises. But I want to tell the truth. To hell with the rose-colored lights.

And *Shchedrin* was another reason I did not stay in the West. We rarely traveled together. I would go and come back, then he would . . . I traveled much more, naturally. The rare occasions when we both found ourselves abroad together were always made out to be exceptional by our authorities and permitted only by the very top of the Central Committee hierarchy. And always came at the last moment, like an unexpected Christmas present. And what we usually asked for was permission to stay an extra few days so that we could hook up in, say, Paris, where we were going on different professional (and not overlapping) programs. Sometimes with a gap of only two or three days.

Of course, we would have needed only an instant to decide to cross the fatal border. But we didn't! So blaming it on our rare stays in the West together is pure self-delusion.

It went deeper than that.

While I adjusted easily to changes in location, to hotel life, and moves, Shchedrin, on the contrary, was a homebody. Any trip, no matter how enticing, was hard on him. He was permanently tied to Russia, to Russian culture, history, and mores by, invisible iron threads. Taking Russia away from him was not easy. Every nasty crack about his people went to his heart. He was not a bystanding observer. When he had to leave, he would sit down, make everyone else sit down in silence for a few seconds, then say "Godspeed," and only then set off. Even if he was going somewhere close by.

Then there were his thousands of superstitions. A woman with a bucket crossing his path was a bad omen, a teapot pointing its spout at you meant illness, going back for something you forgot meant a bad trip, and you had to watch out for black cats, or shaking hands over a doorsill—all bad luck, bad, bad luck. I found that kind of "Russianness" in trifles annoying.

Of course, there is an explanation for it. Shchedrin's grandfather was a village priest in the Russian town of Alexin, on the Oka River, in Tula Province. It was in his genetic code, to use a scientific explanation. He couldn't escape it. But why am I telling you this? You can hear it all in Shchedrin's music. Just listen closely. Please!

I couldn't imagine life without Shchedrin. Even in a crystal palace on some island in the Canaries. We spent so much money on telephone calls every single day. Our family budget suffered from them. But the dear voice gave me strength to keep on and shortened our separation. I couldn't break off our connection. Nor did I want to. Taking Shchedrin out of Russia would have been cruel, and I wasn't up to it.

And *conscience* was another reason why I did not stay in the West.

Not the conscience that tormented Tsar Boris in Pushkin's play. There were no bloody boys in my eyes.

Staying in the West meant deceiving people who believed in your decency and sincerity. Without deceit, you can't run away. They would use you to poke someone else in the eye: you sluggard, idealist, trusting fool. You see, we were right not to trust that dishonest con artist. How happy and cocky it would have made some Serov, who would lecture others: "Never, ever trust anyone, no sentimentality, no faith. Listen to me, you fools," he would brag. I really didn't want to make my enemies happy. I know it was naive, it was childish. But I was self-conscious, abashed, somehow embarrassed, even before Khrushchev. Before Yevgeny Petrovich Pitovranov.

In October 1959, after the first American tour with its happy ending, Khrushchev came up to me in Beijing at a reception, leaving the entire group of Chinese Party bigwigs. His narrow eyes sparkled. Satisfaction, total satisfaction beamed from his pancake face. "Good girl, coming back. Not making me look like a fool. You didn't let me down. I wasn't mistaken about you."

Some reason, sophisticated people might say. Embarrassed before Khrushchev. Have you forgotten that he gave the order to shoot at the workers in Novocherkassk, that he sent missiles to Cuba?

No, I haven't forgotten any of that. But a person has — maybe not every person — a hard-to-verbalize sense of conscience; I don't know what to call it. Is it shame? Does that sense help or hinder people in life? Today I see that there's little use in it. Brazen people flourish and prosper. Conscientious ones have a harder life.

In Pushkin's day a nobleman's word of honor was more reliable than a Swiss bank account. I've read a lot about the honesty of the Decembrists, how faithful they were to their word. How they did not lie to Tsar Nicholas, did not try to twist the truth in order to lighten their prison sentences. I keep thinking about a story, I don't know whether it's appropriate or not, of how in the early years after the October revolt in 1917, Felix Dzerzhinsky, chief of the Cheka, allowed a group of Russian aristocrat anarchists out of a Bolshevik prison on their word of honor. They had asked permission to attend the funeral of a fellow nobleman for just one day, promising to return to prison after the obsequies. And they all came back. Even though they had promised the chief of fiends and knew full well that what awaited them in prison was execution. Would you say that they too were fools?

I don't know the answer myself. I'm just thinking aloud.

And perhaps I should be upset when today I see a practicing Catholic or Protestant shamelessly deceiving his client, then hurrying off to church to pray, and then go back out to deceive and trick some more. Doubling his capital . . .

And there was also the *Bolshoi stage*. The divinely wonderful stage of the Bolshoi was another reason I did not stay in the West. I have danced in all the prestigious theaters of the world. But there was no stage so comfortable, the most comfortable in the entire solar system, in the entire universe, as the Bolshoi!

Before my entrance, standing in the wings, I awaited my music, my cue with a shiver of joy, a feeling of incomparable happiness spreading throughout my body. Three more bars. Two more. One more. There. My music. I step out onto my stage. It was a familiar creature, a relative, an animate partner. I spoke to it, thanked it. Every board, every crack I had mastered and danced on. The stage of the Bolshoi made me feel protected; it was a domestic hearth.

Like a soccer player, I played better, and preferred playing, with the home advantage.

Did that answer the question in the title of this chapter for you?

It didn't for me.

Maybe future generations will live freely and simply, like cranes and swans, without visas, applications, travel commissions, seals, idiotic limits on days, ridiculous forms. Maybe the clever Japanese will invent miracle pills that will make learning languages easy. Maybe people will stop fleeing — from whom and to whom? (I hope you realize that I meant the Eastern and Western worlds.) Maybe people will not be hampered and oppressed, hobbled like horses, deprived of freedom of movement only because they were born to their sorrow in Eastern Europe.

And then, maybe those who left won't play the national hero, proudly sashaying from state-supplied limousines to television cameras and murmur to the bootlicking — the shamelessly, horribly bootlicking — reporters about their exploit: leaving in time, running off, being sensible, and now returning with foreign passports and bursting with the greatness of their own heroism.

Maybe the ballerinas of the future won't be asked the daily, persistent question, Why didn't you stay in the West?

Chapter Thirty-Seven

Marc Chagall Draws Me

"Is that first position?"

"No, second."

"What's first position?"

I show Chagall the first position in ballet.

"I can stand like that, too." Mark Zakharovich turns out his feet, but he can't hold his balance in that unnatural position. He stumbles. "*Quelque chose!* What else does a dancer need?"

"A high arch."

"Is mine high?"

Chagall takes off his shoe and rolls up his trouser leg to demonstrate his arch.

"Well, it's smaller than Anna Pavlova's, but it'll do."

Vava Chagall, the artist's wife, whose full name was Valentina Grigoryevna, announces, "It's too late for you to go into ballet, Markusha. You're better at drawing. Let Maya do the dancing."

Chagall is greedily interested in everything. The artist likes to interrogate his visitors. He discusses with the same thoroughness flutes, key signatures, and conductors with Shchedrin.

Our conversation is taking place in St.-Paul-de-Vence in the south of France. We are in the garden, bursting with color, in the shade of an orange tree. The fruits are deliciously bright and large. But they need to ripen. It's only the peak of summer. July.

Vava invites us inside for tea. The calendar on the wall shows 1965.

Nadia Léger drove us to the Chagall place in her roaring Pontiac, screeching in the sharp turns on the seaside road. Nadia was born in a Belorussian village called Zembino. She went to the parish school and herded cows. Back then she wasn't Nadia Léger but a tanned farm girl with springy pigtails called Nadezhda Khodasevich. Feeling a desire to draw, the farm girl set off on foot for Warsaw. She made the walk in 1927, when you could still wander from country to country along village paths. From there she headed for Paris. Knowledgeable Poles explained to Nadia that you had to study art from the French, in Paris.

With the handsome young artist Georges Baucquier, whom she married without a second's thought, she visited the studio of Fernand Léger. As behooves a French master of the brush, Léger immediately set his practiced Don Juan eye on the well-built, small-waisted young Slavic girl with strong, developed calves. Nadia has a slight Mongol cast to her face, hair pulled tight into a bun, and a piquant snub nose. Léger depicted her like that in many of his canvases.

Before Paris, Nadia had managed to study Suprematism with Kazimir Malevich and "finish a course at a ballet studio," as she informed me. The latter I leave to her conscience, because the generosity of her Slavic soul encouraged her to add fantastic touches to her life story, telling a ballerina that she had also been a ballerina, a surgeon that she had removed an inflamed appendix, and a pilot that she was a pretty good navigator.

Nadezhda Khodasevich became Nadia Léger. What was the power that drew French and Spanish artists to Russian women? Picasso and Khokhlova, Salvador Dalí and his Galya?

I met Nadia at the Aragon house, on my first trip to the French capital. Whenever the Aragons expected Nadia for dinner, Elsa always included a boiled chicken on the menu. Maria, the servant, obediently headed for the butcher shop. A Belorussian stomach was hungry without boiled chicken. If Nadia missed a visit, Elsa would say, "We haven't seen Nadia one chicken." The chicken was a unit of measure for their meetings.

That spring Nadia—who like Fernand Léger was a fervent Communist (the fact that her brother had been shot in 1937 because of his sister's travels around Poland and France did not cure Nadia of the Communist virus)—sent an invitation to Rodion and me. She addressed it to Minister of Culture Furtseva, who sought advice and permission and then blessed us on our thirty-day private trip.

"On the responsibility of Nadia Léger." Our authorities trusted the Légers' Communist ménage; Nadia had been in the French Resistance and was a bosom buddy of the Soviet ambassador's. We were allowed out. And until the mid-eighties, this was our freest voyage abroad.

In addition to the friendship between the two artists, Léger and Chagall, Nadia's Belorussian roots endeared her to the latter. Vitebsk, Chagall's hometown, was very close to Zembino. And the fact that my father was from Belorussia delighted Chagall.

In October 1961 the Chagalls missed my performances — they rarely stayed in their Paris apartment — but they had heard good things about me. They had seen the friendly French reviews.

At the table Vava mentions that Chagall is working less than usual, being lazy. "It's not like him. Usually Markusha does not stop work for more than an hour, no matter who our guests are."

"But you're wrong. I've been working all day. I'm creeping up on ballet."

I knew that Chagall had done the scenery for ballets by Balanchine, Lifar, and George Skibine. I saw the set model for *Daphnis et Chloé* in illustrated ballet dictionaries.

"What do you mean creeping up? I don't understand."

Chagall explains that he is working on a mural for the new Metropolitan Opera House in New York. It is a continuation of his ceiling for the Paris Opera, which he created in 1963 on a commission from André Malraux. "I'll have the various arts there, and animals, and Muses . . . And the ballet. What if you were to show me a few movements?"

"Pose? For Chagall? My pleasure."

We climb up to the second floor. Later they had an elevator installed, when his hernia acted up. Shchedrin and Nadia stay downstairs with Vava. "We'll call you."

A spacious, airy studio. No different from any other studio I have ever visited. Stacks of stretched canvases. Splashes of paint. Books on the floor. Scraps of colored materials. Dirty brushes.

"What pose interests you, Mark Zakharovich? An arabesque? An attitude?"

"I would like to see movement. The most simple kind. And please, loosen your hair."

I start a simple improvisation. A few port de bras. Then I kick off my shoes and do a barefoot bourrée on high demi-point. I spin. I hold poses.

Chagall is sketching with charcoal on drawing paper. His eye is narrowed like a hunter's. Mouth open. I have no idea what he is drawing. You can't see through an easel. Out of the corner of my eye I follow the routes of his artistic, light hand. It is gently performing its own dance. The hand pauses to think. I stop.

"It's hard without music. I feel constrained. Would that be a radio, Mark Zakharovich?"

Chagall does not reply. He's not there.

"If that is a radio, Mark Zakharovich, let's find some melody for me."

"Sorry. What did you say?"

"Let's turn on the radio. It will be easier for me."

Chagall starts looking for suitable music. He turns the black ridged dial of the transistor radio. Nothing but spoken French. Just to spite us. Or snatches of commercial jazz, parts of ads. Then more talk. The latest news. And then suddenly a elegiac, tender melody. Violin and orchestra. I think of Pushkin's line, "Radiant is my sorrow." Now my improvisation has meaning and poetry. Music helps me so much!

I dance. Chagall sketches without a single word. We are both caught up. I don't know how long it went on. But Chagall interrupts the silence. "What marvelous music. Who is it?"

I stop my dance and say that I'm not familiar with the music either.

"Call Shchedrin, maybe he knows." I call Rodion.

"That's a Mendelssohn concerto. Excellent recording. Who's playing? They'll announce it at the end." The announcer tells us it's Yehudi Menuhin. When I went to London in the spring of 1991 at Menuhin's invitation for his anniversary concert — where he conducted Shchedrin's new composition, among other works — I told him about my dance to his recording in Chagall's studio. The mysteries of meetings and crossed paths never cease to amaze me.

Chagall asks me to take a few more poses. The most classical ones, he says. I obey.

"Do you know, your dance to the Mendelssohn concerto was charming. If only the brush could convey what the eye sees. Or perhaps it's better that it can't?"

It is interesting, listening to Chagall. He speaks with biblical measure. Chagall talks about his youth in his hometown of Vitebsk. How he was a commissar, going around in jodhpurs and a leather jacket, painting sidewalks and buildings. He tells us how he believed in the ideas of world revolution.

"And was I alone? Fernand," he says, turning to Nadia, "wrote a letter to the first Soviet government with an offer to design work clothes for the entire Soviet country. If work was a holiday then the clothes should be festive, he felt. He didn't ask for a single centime, either. And then Schoenberg decided to teach music to everyone for free. Corbusier wanted to build sun cities in Russia. I heard that they never even got a reply. I went to see the Party secretary in Vitebsk and said that we needed a museum. 'We don't need a museum, Comrade Chagall, we need a bridge,' he replied. And so I left. And here I am in Vence."

I hate lying memoirists to whom great people they barely know start unburdening themselves. In long monologues, which seem to be recorded by hidden microphones. In my diary I wrote down only the contours of the conversation on that hot July day with Chagall. Later I had quite a few other meetings with Mark Zakharovich and Vava—in New York and Moscow, in Paris and St.-Paul-de-Vence. They saw me dance on a real stage. But Chagall was so disarmingly frank only on that first meeting. Remember, it was 1965; the Iron Curtain had only shifted a bit, and Shchedrin and I were among the first messengers that the world was starting to change for the better. Chagall must have enjoyed conversing in his native tongue with a ballerina and a musician who had Soviet passports, not French ones. And who would be going back home to Russia in just a few days.

It was only when the thick southern night fell outside that we got ready to leave. The Chagalls suggested we spend the night. But we had promised to return—before dark—to Nadia's cozy house in Calian, where we were awaited by the artist Georges Baucquier, who had remarried Nadia after Fernand Léger's death; the helpful Communist servants; Vatan, a grim German shepherd; and Cocquelicot, a bandit of a cat.

We look around once more at the light walls covered with blazing treasures—Chagall's paintings, from the earliest to the latest. Fish swim above the city, cows fly in the skies, village fiddlers poignantly play Vitebsk passages, huts list drunkenly, and eternal lovers melt in wild kisses. Enchanted, we stop in front of a picture of a pink pregnant mare with the colt in its belly, hitched to a wagon. A peasant wearing a peaked cap holds a whip.

"I used to wear a cap like that," Mark Zakharovich chuckles.

Chagall gives us signed lithographs. A massive academic monograph, which is autographed up and down generously with colored markers: "To Maya and Rodion . . . in memory . . . with love . . . Vence . . . Marc Chagall." And some early ceramics.

I respond with a memorial medal depicting me, created by Elena Alexandrovna Yanson-Manizer.

Chagall looks the medal over at length and very seriously. "Realistic. But . . . beautiful."

A year passes quickly. To be exact, ten months.

In May 1966 Chagall and I are having lunch in New York. We are Sol Hurok's guests in a luxurious restaurant. Mark Zakharovich is finishing his mural for the new Met. And I will be closing the old Met tomorrow. So the table conversation is about the theater and artists.

Chagall is grumpy today. He attacks Hurok unexpectedly for a clumsy opinion. "Hurok, you are an ignoramus. You don't understand a thing about art. Why are you involved in it?'

"I brought Anna Pavlova and Chaliapin . . ."

"Better you hadn't done it at all."

Hurok takes offense. "I'm bringing the Bolshoi Ballet to America for the third time. The third time I'm bringing Maya Plisetskaya here."

"*Quelque chose* . . . I'm going to see Maya tomorrow. And I'm going to put impresario Hurok in my mural dressed as a usurer. I'll follow Michelangelo," Chagall says, returning to his customary irony.

The next day comes. A Sunday. May 8. The last performance on the stage of the old Metropolitan Opera House. At nine in the morning on Monday, the theater will be blown up.

I appear twice in the gala concert. I dance the *Swan* and the first act of *Don Quixote*. My *Swan* ends the first part of the show, the part with the speeches.

The famous John Martin is speaking. He is listing everyone and everything that took place over an entire century within the walls of this glorious theater. A huge screen fills the stage and familiar and unfamiliar faces flicker on it — slides of the stars who had appeared here. Old photographs, blown up to gigantic size, break up into their component parts, large dots. They remind me of Impressionist paintings, done in a black and white palette. A whiff of marvelous eras. Where are these smiling, handsome men and beautiful women, proudly puffing out their chests, their bodies encased in corsets, wearing straw boaters and flower-trimmed hats? In retirement homes, in wheelchairs, in cemeteries?

I watch Martin's slides from an angle, squinting. And at the same time, I do my pliés — I can't cool down.

At last, Martin introduces me. Saint-Saëns, *The Swan*. Isaac Stern's violin solo. Stern plays from the orchestra pit. The audience goes wild, and we must do an encore. Isaac, whom I bring out for the bows, remains onstage. The orchestra is in the pit. Fayer conducting. Stern is in the spotlight by the footlights. Once again I float out in bourrée . . . After the intermission we blasted out the *Don Quixote*. With scenery and in costume. I am Kitri. My partner is Vladimir Tikhonov.

I can't come up with a better verb than *blasting*. We really did! I warmed up very well on the two *Swan*s and I didn't get too cold during the intermission. The electric, extraordinary atmosphere whips my body to do more than it had ever been able to do before.

The evening is crowned by a grand polonaise. Everyone who performed tonight, the old guard of the Met, steps out in solemn couples for the last time onto the legendary stage. Martha Graham, Alicia Markova, Alexandra Danilova, Pierre Vladimirov, Anna Pavlova's partner Anton Dolin, Jerome Robbins, Agnes De Mille, Tamara Toumanova, Igor Youskevitch . . . The audience rises for a standing ovation. I see Chagall's gray head next to Vava. They are applauding with the rest.

When I return to New York once again — the 1968 tour — the new Met is open. We are going to perform there, too. I hurry to rehearsal. But I stop in my tracks in the plaza by the fountain. I look up. Chagall's tall murals. I look at the left one, reddish orange. A flying sunny angel with a trumpet, a marvelous Ivan Tsarevich playing a green cello, birds of paradise, a two-headed creature with a mandolin at its equine chin, a glazed violin and bow on a blue-sparkling tree.

And right in the middle a slender, bosomy dancer with loose red hair, holding her feet diligently in first position. She's tense and contorted by the effort, about to fall if she's not careful . . .

In the top left corner, a colorful flock of ballerinas. With tight calves, wasp waists, in various poses: some leaping, some frozen, some on pointe, some with arms folded in a sweet wreath, others ready to spin with a thin partner.

And one is certainly me, pelvis forward, tight as a bow string, arms behind her back, feet in second position. I did something like that for Chagall to the Mendelssohn Concerto. And Mark Zakharovich had captured that moment.

The disgraced Hurok is not there.

There is little resemblance between me and the dancers on the mural. But when you look for a long time, attentively, you can see that the great artist's hand had caught something of me. There is something there.

At our next meeting, Chagall questions me closely — have I seen the mural, did I recognize myself? "*Quelque chose.* Will you pose for me again?"

"Of course I will, Mark Zakharovich. I love you very much."

Chapter Thirty-Eight

November 20

Madrid television was doing a program about Valentina Koshuba, a Russian ballerina from the legendary days. She had joined Diaghilev's troupe in 1914. She was incredibly beautiful; they'd call her "Miss Diaghilev Ballet" today.

I took part in the show. I made the proper complimentary noises. The reporters attacked Koshuba with pointed questions about her alleged affair with the Spanish king Alfonso XIII. Koshuba refused to respond. Yes, he had been slightly in love me, he used to send flowers and made royal gifts. But as for intimacy? . . . There had been nothing like that at all . . . Finally a pushy female journalist said angrily, "At your age, esteemed señora [Koshuba had hit ninety!], you'd be better off lying to us. The king is long gone, and it would be much more interesting for our viewers."

"But why should I lie?" Koshuba replied hotly.

I met the Kennedy family in 1962. During my second American tour. On November 12 the Bolshoi Ballet had reached the capital. Before Washington, there had been New York, Philadelphia, Los Angeles, San Francisco, Chicago, Detroit, Cleveland. And the Cuban crisis.

Once in my clean hotel room, I turned on the bath taps, in anticipation of a luxurious bath. But the loud and persistent telephone rings signaled our leader Pokarzhevsky, who called me back downstairs.

"Did you get a rest from the trip?" And without waiting for my reply, he grabbed my elbow and dragged me toward the exit. "We're going to a press conference. The reporters want to see you. It's important after Cuba. But please, be restrained and responsible in your answers. Our interpreters will help you with that."

After the press conference we all headed over to the Soviet Embassy. A reception. That was the way it was done, apparently. Our ambassador, Anatoly Dobrynin, led me over to a tall, slim American, whose face seemed familiar. "Attorney General Robert Kennedy. He asked me to introduce you. Maya Plisetskaya."

So this was Robert Kennedy. I hadn't recognized him right away. The rest of our conversation was interpreted by Dobrynin.

Robert Kennedy told me that he had seen me in Moscow in 1955. He remembered my *Swan Lake*. And he had learned from the papers that I would be dancing in Washington. "I can't come tomorrow, but the president and his wife will be there."

In response, I blurted, "I know you, too." Kennedy smiled shyly. "I read in the magazine *America* that you were born in November 1925. So was I. When is your birthday?"

Kennedy was surprised by the sudden turn in our conversation. "The 20th..."

"The 20th? Then we're twins. That's my birthday, too."

In my entire life I had met only one person with whom I shared an exact birthday, day, month, and year. My twin. Robert Kennedy.

The attorney general became emotional and kissed my cheek awkwardly. The coincidence made an impression on Dobrynin as well. He rubbed the bridge of his nose.

"Where will you be that day?" Robert Kennedy asked.

"Boston, I think."

"Yes, in Boston," said Pokarzhevsky, nodding his red head, as he appeared next to me out of nowhere.

The continuing coincidences amused my conversational partner. "Boston is my hometown. What will you be doing the night of the 20th?"

"I think I'll be dancing *Swan Lake* again."

"Yes, yes, *Swan Lake*. Maya will be dancing *Swan Lake* in Boston," Pokarzhevsky preened. A convenient opportunity to show Ambassador Dobrynin how he knew and remembered everything. Pokarzhevsky had been brought in on the tour from somewhere else — and we knew where — he was not part of the theater. But how quickly he had learned everything. Dobrynin would report in, and the Wunderkind would be promoted.

"I'll send you a present," Robert Kennedy said.

"So will I," I promised, swept up in the momentum.

The next morning, the day of my first Washington *Swan Lake,* I came to rehearsal. To warm up. I try never to break my rule of warming up very well on the day of a performance.

There was an audience. Jacqueline Kennedy and little Caroline. The First Lady was accompanied by a retinue: translators, bodyguards, and the administration of the Bolshoi Ballet, deferentially bowing and scraping in unnatural politeness. I wasn't at my best that day. I had a cold, and the day of our Washington premiere coincided with the first day of my period. However, seeing the large-eyed beauty Jacqueline, whose attentive, Velázquez-like face was multiplied by the room's mirrors, I pulled myself together and lasted through the whole class. Even the jump combinations. After class we were introduced, and I gave little Caroline the black and white contact sheet of my ballet slides, which I had in my purse.

Evening came. Before the start of the ballet, they played our anthems. The president was there. His attendance of a performance by Moscow dancers after the Cuban crisis was a blatantly political step to better relations with the Soviets. That is why our embassy people were so electrified and the reporters for Soviet newspapers and the theater bigwigs were all so excited.

After the second act, almost before the curtain went down, President Kennedy came onstage. A marvelous gesture. He and Jacqueline headed straight for me. She and I kissed like friends. I smeared her tanned cheek with my stage makeup.

Praise. Raptures. The president said that little Caroline was delighted by my slides. "She told Jackie and me that she will be a ballerina like you. The first ballerina in the Kennedy clan." The president mentioned that he knew of my meeting yesterday with his brother and the amazing coincidence of our birthdays.

But Pokarzhevsky stuck his red head into our group. Stepping on my toes with his broad peasant feet, shouldering me away gradually from Kennedy, our leader placed a book in my hands, trying to be unnoticed in the maneuver. *The Bolshoi Ballet* had been published in Moscow a good decade earlier. Heavy, clunky, with blurry photographs of artists who had retired and no longer danced. The ink left marks on your hands, and the book reeked of a gluey and stinky substance. All through the third act I could smell the vile Soviet glue coming from my black swan wings. I thought my partner would worry that Odile, the daughter of the Evil Genius, had been eating strong cheese. What about the poor president! He had held the book in his hands a longer time.

In the morning, John Kennedy received the Bolshoi troupe at the White House. He paid me lots more compliments. I began with naive explanations: that I hadn't danced my best, too bad he and Jacqueline had come that night. The theater in Washington in those days was cramped and unsuitable, with a slippery and uncomfortable stage.

"You were incomparable. I was knocked off my feet." (That was the translation the cultural attaché from our embassy gave. A clairvoyant.) I hadn't been able to sleep after the performance the first night, and I had taken a sleeping pill toward morning. Now, after a glass of the presidential Dubonnet on an empty stomach, I was seriously tipsy.

"When will you be dancing again?" the president inquired politely.

"Tomorrow."

"What?"

"*Bayadère* and *Swan Lake*. Come with Jacqueline. I'll dance better . . ." Actually, we were doing *Giselle* the next day. I had gotten it all mixed up. I was intoxicated and gesticulating with doubled heat, my fur hat off to one side and my hair loosened. And it was there at the White House that Jacqueline Kennedy predicted my future. "You're just like Anna Karenina."

November 20, *our* birthday, was approaching. The Bolshoi's administration was showing "paternal" interest in me. "Now what can you give Robert Kennedy on the 20th?"

And what could I? And how?

And with syrupy voices they said, "Well, by the way, we just happen to have a hand-painted Russian samovar for a friend, his anniversary, but it would be better, probably, to give it to you. For Robert Kennedy. We'll find something else for our comrade with the help of the embassy staff. Write a friendly note to your co-celebrant—in Russian, of course—and we'll translate it and hand it to the attorney general exactly on the 20th along with the samovar. He'll be so pleased. It's exhibition quality."

"Is it very big?"

"It's not small, Maya Mikhailovna, not small, or cheap."

"Where could I have gotten it? What will he think? Let me see your hand-painted marvel."

The samovar was enormous, as I had feared. The size of a toddler. Now where could I have picked one up like that in America? And no one brings something that size along just in case they might meet someone to give it to. I refused, no matter how they tried to persuade me.

I wrote a letter, actually, just a few words. And added a half-dozen wooden spoons. No value to them, but they were mine. My spoons.

They regretted that the samovar did not suit me, but our "activists" agreed to give Robert Kennedy my best wishes.

On November 20 I was awakened by loud, persistent knocking at my door in the hotel in Boston (I had unplugged the phone for the night, as usual). Struggling to open my eyes and cursing, I opened the door. There was a gigantic bouquet of sweet-smelling white lilies swaying at my door. The messenger holding them was blocked from view. Another messenger handed me a delicate box tied with a broad golden ribbon. And a letter in an envelope from Robert Kennedy. He was the first to congratulate me that day.

I untied the bow and opened the box. On a raspberry-velvet pillow lay a lovely gold bracelet with two encrusted charms. One was a Scorpion, our astrological sign. The other, the Archangel Michael killing a dragon with a spear.

A little later Robert called me. With great difficulty I sought the few words I knew in English through my sleep-fogged brain. Thank you . . . Also . . . Best wishes . . . It's awful being illiterate! I'm illiterate thanks to the Soviet system, my own laziness, and my constant certainty that someone will translate, explain, help me. But I was alone. And so I bleated like a two-year-old . . . Thank you. Also . . . Best wishes.

I ran to class. But at the door I bumped into yet another messenger, bearing a case of wine from Kennedy. But I wasn't about to break my lifelong habit and not warm up on the day of a performance.

I was met by a party in class. Cakes. Flowers. A card signed by all the leaders of our trip. Congratulations from Ambassador Dobrynin. Pokarzhevsky made a lofty speech, "Our dear Maya Mikhailovna, you . . ." he was literally singing my praises. The good tooth in the mouth of our leader smiled at me. Lots of applause. Look what being born on the same day as the attorney general of the United States does for you!

That evening, the third Kennedy, Edward, came to the performance. He come up onstage afterward, said, "Fantastic," and kissed me on both cheeks. That was from Bob, he explained.

And then Sol Hurok gave a reception in my honor. He handed me a telegram from Rodion. We partied until late. Poems, dancing, everyone loves me, everyone likes me . . .

The maitre d' walked softly to the table. "Telephone, Miss Maya." Pokarzhev-sky stopped in mid-sentence—the tension was unbearable.

I took the phone in a cramped booth near the bar. It was Robert Kennedy again. He explained something at length and with heat. I did not understand a thing. It was impossible for any normal Westerner to believe that I did not comprehend English. Not a word. I just turned on my record: Thank you. Also. Best wishes. The attorney general would think me a fool for the rest of his life. You can't even flirt with a vocabulary like that.

A few days before my next birthday, which I was celebrating at home in Moscow, Robert Kennedy made another appearance.

Anastas Ivanovich Mikoyan, who had just returned from America, sent his assistant to my house with a birthday wish. From Robert Kennedy. Five pale lilac porcelain carnations of royal beauty. With veins, petals, and leaves. They seemed alive and real. I leaned over to smell them automatically. And caught myself. This was art, not nature. Those carnations are always in a vase on my bedside table in our Moscow apartment.

Two days after my birthday, November 22, we had more guests. We were finishing up Katya's delicious food—I would be fat at the next performance, I wouldn't be able to get into my tutu. The telephone rang: turn on the T.V., someone shot John Kennedy! We watched, listened to every word. The president was killed. Poor Jacqueline. I can still feel the shock, the emptiness of that sleet-filled, horrible Moscow night—Who? Why? The bastards!

The next time the Bolshoi went to America was in the spring of 1966. By tradition, Robert Kennedy and I tried to find a way of congratulating each other on our birthday. Our congratulations were no secret, certainly not from the KGB. A week before our departure to New York, Mikhail Nikolayevich Anastasyev asked me to his office. He was the first deputy director of the theater then and appointed to head the American tour of 1966.

I remember Anastasyev with kindness. A failed musician, brother of a famous theater critic, he was a friendly and sensitive man who, I think, chafed at his official duties. He ended up badly, throwing himself out of a window after a public Party scolding for his passionate affair with a woman half his age. Other people may shake their heads and complain that Anastasyev did not help them and that he was a so-and-so. I won't argue. But he was kind to me.

"Maya Mikhailovna, please meet Mikhail Vladimirovich. He will be one of my deputies on the trip." Of course, Mikhail Vladimirovich had a surname, but in keeping with his high position, Mikhail Vladimirovich kept it out of the picture. And so we all called the people's leader Mikhail Vladimirovich, with respect and a show of love. I get all those leaders without surnames mixed up: the Mikhail Vladimiroviches, Sergei Ivanoviches, Ivan Daniloviches — but there were so many of them in my life.

"Maya Mikhailovna," our new leader said at last, revealing his infrequent teeth. "I saw *Sleeping Beauty* last night, you know. You are such a marvelous dancer. I came away with so many impressions!"

Once he ran out of clichés, he got to the point. The expression on his gray face gave away his obvious idea. "You know, I was leafing through the encyclopedia, seeing who was born when, and you know, I came across an amazing coincidence. You and Senator Kennedy were born the same day! Two important people, you know . . ."

What a brainless game: why bother with an encyclopedia when the whole theater, half of America knew all about it!

Lubyanka, KGB headquarters, had sent us all kinds of people over the years. Businesslike ones, smart ones, like Kalinkin and Felix Perepelov, the troupe accepted and treated with sincere respect and friendship. Horses can distinguish a good groom from a tormentor a mile away. But . . . in their case, evil prevailed over good. Some of our brother artists (I burn with shame) denounced them for being too soft and kindly as overseers. Perepelov, to make things worse, fell in love with a ballerina and planned to marry her. There was no place in the Bolshevik sun on Dzerzhinsky Square for people like them. They were replaced.

"It would be so good, Maya Mikhailovna," the surnameless Mikhail Vladimirovich continued, "if you and Robert Kennedy became friends."

This was as silly and hopeless as the dreams of Manilov for undying friendship with Chichikov in Gogol's novel *Dead Souls,* love which would make the tsar so touched that he would "make us generals." Everyone was uncomfortable: Me, Anastasyev, even the author of the great project for indestructible friendship across the ocean.

So when the new tour of the Bolshoi Ballet in America began a few days later, I tried to avoid Mikhail Vladimirovich. And avoid everything that could be avoided. Nothing happened, but I still felt uncomfortable. A terrible mood . . .

Nikolai Fedorenko, the USSR representative to the United Nations, gave a reception for us on May 20. Who was there? I'll write the names from my diary: Leonard Bernstein, Jerome Robbins, Mike Nichols, ambassadors and their wives, Sol Hurok, Mikhail Anastasyev, Jacqueline Kennedy, Robert Kennedy . . . and I. These are the ones who got into my notes. And naturally, Mikhail Vladimirovich. He did not speak any languages except his native Russian (rather, Soviet).

Not even Best wishes and Also. Totally ignorant. More ignorant than I. But he manifested great activity at the reception. His face got all blotchy. Sweat poured from his forehead right into his champagne glass. His hands trembled. The cocktail frank fell from its toothpick onto the floor. And to top it off, he spilled his champagne and sweat onto my party dress. And he never got more than a few feet away from me. He had an important job.

Bobby picked me out as soon as he came in. He rushed toward me. We kissed and embraced. With Fedorenko's help, we chatted sweetly. Blotchy M. V. stood like a statue near us. Listening. Wheezing. Worrying. Spilling champagne. Kennedy kept looking over at him and trying to figure out who this stiff was. If you really did want to become friends, the tenacious M. V. would scare off not only the senator from New York but a hotel doorman.

Bobby said he would drop by the Governor Clinton after rehearsals to show me New York. At one o'clock. Then Bob gave a speech. Or a toast? To art. To friendship of peoples. To the emissaries of Russia. To Maya Plisetskaya, who is better than diplomats . . . We touched glasses. This is when my Lubyanka matchmaker spilled his drink on my dress.

As often happens with me, I was late. About twenty-five or even thirty minutes. But Robert Kennedy was waiting. He had come with a driver, who parked right by the entrance to the hotel. Seeing me hurrying toward the car, Bob got out with a bouquet of white tulips.

Through the glass doors of the Clinton I saw the focused face of M. V. He seemed to be pleased with the way things were going and expressed satisfaction through his narrowed eyes.

Of Kennedy's greeting, I understood only the word "lunch." He was probably asking if I had eaten. Just in time! I hadn't gotten to the free lunch arranged by Hurok at the hotel today. And I was always starving after class and rehearsals.

"Lunch, lunch," I said in agreement. We got in the car. M. V. was hanging out of the hotel doors. We were off.

We went to a restaurant. After a delicious and filling meal, we walked around New York. Just the two of us. Passersby recognized their senator. We stopped at Tiffany's. Bob took me by the hand and led me into the store. We looked around the impressive room. We slowed down in the watch department. After some conversation with the saleswoman, he bought me an alarm clock in a leather case. An old-fashioned clock, without batteries. I understood that this was a silent rebuke for my lateness. We couldn't talk without a translator, about anything.

We returned to the car and finished the city tour.

The tulips faded . . .

To make things worse, we got stuck in traffic. A jam. I started worrying—
I didn't want to be late for the evening performance. And I think that Bob was
getting sick of my company. Boredom filled the back seat.

And yet we met a few more times.

Jacqueline Kennedy later threw a soirée in my honor. In a severe black dress,
a funereal frame for her dramatic face, Jacqueline greeted her guests. I looked
deeply at her faded but marvelous Velázquez face. And I thought, it's a moot
point which of us is more the Anna Karenina.

At the party, I had an interesting chance to talk with Balanchine. He came
with Lucia Davidova, his close friend and awed fan. In the aristocratic tones of
the first wave of émigrés from revolutionary Russia, Lucia called Balanchine *bozhenka,* the diminutive form of "God." He responded to her unearthly nickname
without a murmur.

"Maya, who is your teacher?" Balanchine asked unexpectedly.

"On this trip?"

"No, always. Who keeps an eye on you?"

I hesitated. The KGB kept an eye on me. Mikhail Vladimirovich had brought
me from the theater to the door of Jacqueline's apartment. He didn't have the
nerve to go in himself, without an invitation: she was the president's widow,
after all. Even though he was dying to do it. He might have still been out there,
stamping his feet. Who knew? . . .

"I can't name just one teacher. I studied with Gerdt. I go to Asaf Messerer's
class. I rehearse with Ilyuchshenko and Semyonova. But to tell the truth, I'm my
own boss."

"Being your own boss isn't bad. But, don't be angry, Maya, you need a good
teacher."

Then Lucia Davidova asked her own question: Had I seen bozhenka's *Don
Quixote?* I replied that I had not had the time. But some of our troupe had gone.

"Well, what did they say?"

"They said they didn't like it," I burst out like a simpleton.

Lucia Davidova frowned. Pressed her lips. Got in a huff. "Oh, I forgot. Soviet
taste. But you, you of all people, Maya, you absolutely must see it. It is a masterpiece for all time."

Among the last to come were Bob Kennedy and Ethel. That evening my English tongue was Lucia Davidova. She translated for me. My diary says that we
spoke about Vietnam. That was a most painful subject then. Bob asked what I

thought about it in faraway Russia. I replied that I felt very sorry for the American boys dying in rice paddies and swamps.

"I feel sorry for the Vietnamese boys too. If I run for president and win, the first thing I'll do is end that hellish slaughter. Should I be a candidate in '68?"

I replied — and I quote from the diary — "Why not?"

A sudden flight of English.

After the party, Bob and Ethel gave me a lift to the Clinton Hotel. We spent a few minutes in the lighted doorway saying good-night. I noticed Mikhail Vladimirovich pacing, head down, in the shadows. I even managed to see that he was not happy. He was angry with insensitive Ethel, the third wheel.

The next day I was invited to the Kennedy house.

It was filled with children. Noise. Laughter. One of the Kennedy heirs had a cold and coughed with a terrible rattle. Bob picked him up. A girl demanded Ethel — urgently. Two older children went off to ride ponies. Normal American life.

I looked around the Kennedys' New York place. A photograph of two brothers — the president and Robert. They are facing each other, in profile to the camera. Arms crossed on their laps. Faces sad. The light emphasized the mood — diffused and low.

"It's a good photo," I said. "But very sad. As if John foretold what fate had in store for him. But you, Bob?"

"Who can predict my fate?"

Semyon Semyonov was helping me with English that day. Everyone called him Semyonchik. Cheerful, quick, with rolling "r"s, a former dancer of the Russian Monte Carlo Ballet. He worked with the Hurok organization in the ballet department.

"I'd like to give you this photo. Will you take it?" Bob removed the prophetic photo in its dark wooden frame from the wall.

Bob Kennedy came to the theater a few more times, dashing in for my performances. Tight-fisted Hurok grumbled. "Senators should buy tickets at the box office. Why does he sneak in without paying through the stage door? That door is for *my* artists. Why is he hanging around, like a boy, backstage? Distracting a ballerina from her work?"

And that's how my few days in New York passed . . .

What was it then?

I think back on it now. It wasn't a flirtation. It wasn't a game. It wasn't a passion. But there was an attraction. There was interest. There was curiosity. There was a newness. There was an unfamiliarity . . . The marvelous coincidence of our appearance in this world. And our amazement about it.

I've heard gossip about Bob Kennedy's relationship with Marilyn Monroe, that he had been a Don Juan. How much of it is true? And how much was made up? And how much is ordinary envy toward extraordinary, talented, vibrant people? What part is desire to dirty, to hurt? . . . I don't know. But I do know what happened with me. With me Robert Kennedy was romantic, elevated, noble, and completely pure. No seductions, no passes.

And I gave him no cause. I have to disappoint the audience, like Valentina Koshuba on Madrid television. "It didn't happen."

Another factor was the shadow of Mikhail Vladimirovich, who dogged my every step. I felt bitter and anxious. I felt pulled into a dirty conspiracy. Like a decoy. That would be enough to turn you as cold as the Ice Maiden.

Robert Kennedy and I were not fated to meet in 1968. The Bolshoi's tour that year began in late May. We started in New York. This time we were not at the Governor Clinton but the Empire Hotel at Lincoln Square. Right near the new Metropolitan. Now I could look out my hotel window and enjoy the Chagall murals, seeking undeniable resemblances with the red-haired ballerinas (I even changed rooms for this purpose).

That first evening Robert Kennedy called me at the hotel, and I gathered that he had decided to run for the presidency and had to travel to many states. Of course, the newspapers were full of this news, including the Moscow papers. Bob would be in New York in early June, and we would have dinner on the 11th. Keep the evening free, he said.

Word that Robert Kennedy was a presidential candidate excited the intrigue-filled offices of Mikhail Vladimirovich. They started up the present business again in Moscow: Maya Plisetskaya should bring the candidate presents worthy of the great moment. Stun the future president with Russian generosity. To continue and deepen contacts and friendship. Another samovar (Soviet spies are low on imagination). And caviar. Lots and lots of caviar. This samovar was gigantic — the size of a well-muscled teenager. But heavier. Ancient, tubby, pale copper with a filigree spout. They showed it to me surreptitiously in the Bolshoi studios, where I was trying on ballet slippers, and warned me gently that it would be shipped to me.

I was furious. "The hell with your samovars! Send it under the director's name. Don't get me involved."

So now it was people from the Soviet mission to the U.N. who were in charge of the samovar. They were of a higher order than my unforgettable thug M. V. There's a big difference between a senator and a presidential candidate.

But the samovar was never given. It had been dragged across the ocean for nothing. Where is it now? The caviar, naturally, was eaten by the mission staff . . . There was a lot of caviar.

On June 5 Robert Kennedy was shot in Los Angeles. He died on the 6th.

On the evening of June 6 I had a performance at the new Met. I was supposed to dance *Sleeping Beauty*. The pas de deux. But my heart was breaking. I had to do something. Scream! . . . let my pain come out somehow. Before the ballet, someone from the Metropolitan came out on stage. He said, "As a tribute to Robert Kennedy's memory, Maya Plisetskaya will dance *The Dying Swan* by Saint-Saëns. Choreography by Mikhail Fokine."

The curtain rose slowly. The audience stood up. Quietly. But I could hear them rise from where I was on the stage. They all got up.

Icy stillness. The harp's four introductory arpeggios. The solo cello began singing the melody. I lost myself in the dance. The spotlight pulled my hands, arms, and neck out of the darkness.

People were frozen still. No one moved. Stifled sobs joined the music. From all sides. Like streams of tears.

The dance was over. The spotlight held my final, fatal pose for a long time. And then faded . . .

There was no applause. Just a sorrowful silence. The people stood there wordlessly. The curtain covered the darkness of the stage ever so slowly.

"Silence, you are the best of what I have heard," Boris Pasternak said. And the most horrible, I thought that evening.

It was June once again. This time, June 1992. Twenty-four years had passed.

I was in Washington. As a spouse. As Mrs. Rodion Shchedrin. It was the day before the premiere at the Kennedy Center of Rodion's new piano concerto, which—do you remember?—he was writing in Nerja, in southern Spain. The pianist is Nikolai Petrov. Conductor, Slava Rostropovich. Now there is a marvelous theater, a marvelous concert hall, in the American capital. The Kennedy Center!

Everyone was at rehearsals. I took a taxi and told the driver, "Arlington Cemetery, please." I was carrying a huge bouquet of white lilies. I walked slowly down the swept path past countless identical white obelisks. It was a hot, sunny day. Groups of Japanese tourists with cameras.

In *Swan Lake,* 1977

With Nikolai Fadeyechev in *Swan Lake*, Paris, 1972

With Alexander Bogatyrev in *Swan Lake*, 1977

With Anatoli Berdychev in *Fantasia*, 1975

With Alexander Godunov in *Carmen Suite*, 1979

Rehearsing *Bolero* with Maurice Béjart in the Cour Carrée of the Louvre,
Paris, 1976

In *Bolero* at the Théâtre de la Monnaie, Brussels, 1977

In *Bolero*, 1980

With Maurice Béjart, Fête de l'humanité, 1976

Costuming *Anna Karenina* with Pierre Cardin, Paris, 1972

In rehearsal for *Anna Karenina*, 1972

With Alexander Godunov in *Anna Karenina*, 1975

With Maris Liepa in *Anna Karenina*, 1973

With Alexander Godunov in *Anna Karenina*, 1979

With Maris Liepa in *Anna Karenina*, 1973

As Anna Karenina, Paris, 1979

With Jorge Donne in *Leda*, Paris, 1979

With Alexandra Tolstaya, New York, 1976

With Olga Spessivtzeva at Tolstoy Farm, New York, 1976

With Rudolf Nureyev and Michael Edgley, Australia, 1977

With Pierre Cardin, 1980

In *Isadora*, 1985

In *Isadora*, 1978

In *The Dying Swan*, Tokyo, 1993

In *The Dying Swan*, Tokyo, 1986

In *Swan Lake,* 1985

With Boris Efimov in *Lady with the Dog*, Paris, 1986

In *Phèdre*, Paris, 1985

In *The Queen of the Underworld*, Paris, 1986

Taking class with Mikhail Baryshnikov in New York, 1987

With Mikhail Baryshnikov and Martha Graham at a rehearsal at Graham's
studio, New York 1987

With Gregory Peck, 1990

With Frank Sinatra, 1990

Receiving the Légion d'Honneur from President François Mitterand, 1986

Receiving Russia's highest civil honor, the medal for service to the Russian state, second degree, from President Vladimir Putin, 2000

The path rose gently along the slope of a broad hill. I stopped. The grave of John Kennedy. The eternal flame was almost invisible in the blinding sunshine. All I could see was the rhythmic trembling of the hot air. On the black slab I saw the name of the dead president and a small carved black cross. I dropped a single lily from my arms. It fell onto the flagstones, covered with grass, by the chains framing the grave.

Rest in peace, John!

Not far away was Robert's grave. I had never seen it before. Engraved in gold on the small white marble plaque was "Robert Francis Kennedy" and below that, "1925–1968." I had not known his middle name. Two meters from the marble slab stood a severe white cross. Its harsh shadow fell on the marble, like a sharp pencil line right in the middle of the name Robert. On the name Francis lay a solitary white carnation. Did it come from a human heart, or was that the way it was supposed to be by etiquette? The lawn was neatly mowed, but the tractor tracks were like scars on a face.

I threw the flowers hard. They covered the grave and the earth around it like white snow.

Rest in peace, Bob!

Chapter Thirty-Nine

How Carmen Suite Was Born

I was still dancing the old repertoire. *Swan Lake* again, *Don Quixote* again, *Sleeping Beauty* again . . . Then *Swan Lake*, then *Don Quixote*, then *Beauty* . . . One more *Swan Lake*, one more . . . Would it really be like this to the end of my ballet days? Just *Swan Lake?* . . . Anxiety tormented me. Frustration. I needed something new, something my own. Definitely new. Definitely my own.

What to do, with whom? And where?

I had always wanted to dance Carmen. Well, not since early childhood, of course, but so long that I can't even remember what first prompted it. Maybe I could make something up . . . The thought of my Carmen lived in me constantly, glowing deep inside, occasionally rushing to the surface demandingly. Whenever I talked to anyone about my dreams, the image of Carmen was at the top of the list.

I began with the libretto. Using the Mérimée and Bizet opera, I naively sketched the contours of the action: Carmen, José, the flower, love, toreador, jealousy, cards, knife, death . . . Very naively.

I decided to involve — go for broke! — Shostakovich. I wrote out a neat copy of my libretto and handed the manuscript to Dmitri Dmitrievich. I thought he seemed sincerely interested. "You know, Maya Mikhailovna, it's a very good theme, so to speak, for a ballet. And you've done it all, so to speak, grammatically.

I'll think about it." Outwardly, Shostakovich was a gentle, shy man, who was too embarrassed to refuse. But internally he had a powerful backbone, harder than diamond. What he decided to do, he would do, and what he didn't, couldn't be forced.

A few days later, D. D. telephoned and haltingly, with many "so to speaks," he invited Rodion and me to his dacha in Zhukovka. "I want to talk about your libretto for *Carmen.*"

We set off. We spent the summer of 1964 with the Shostakoviches, with Dmitri Dmitrievich and his wife, Irina Antonovna, in the mountains of Armenia, not far from Lake Sevan. It's gorgeous there. Majestic, biblical.

We had had a good relationship before that. Rodion adored the great composer, and Rodion's father, Konstantin Mikhailovich, had even worked briefly in Kuibyshev as Shostakovich's secretary. Shostakovich had faithfully given their family a lot of help. He got Rodion's mother back from the Stalinist labor front, got her reinstated at work after being fired, and even managed to help Rodion's uncle, Victor Mikhailovich, get an apartment in Tula. The summer we spent together brought us even closer. That was why I had dared to approach Shostakovich with my idée fixe.

The Shostakovich dacha in Zhukovka was almost directly across from Andrei Sakharov's. Certain plain-looking men liked to stroll through the bushes and ravines. They kept watch on who visited, who left. And when the forlorn Solzhenitsyn later moved into Slava Rostropovich's dacha nearby, the entire neighborhood was filled with "lovers of fresh air" tromping around.

Shostakovich gently but firmly refused to write the music for *Carmen.* His main argument (according to my diary) was, "I'm afraid of Bizet," though he said it half-jokingly. "Everyone is so used to the opera that whatever you write, you'll disappoint them. The opera is unsurpassed. Perhaps Rodion Konstantinovich can come up with something special, so to speak?" (D. D. preferred using our names and patronymics.)

I remember 1964 for another event as well. I received the Lenin Prize. That was the highest award for an artist in the Soviet land. The decision was taken by secret vote of the members of the prize committee (which included writers, architects, musicians . . .). The recipient had to get more than two-thirds of the secret ballots. Then the results of the voting were approved by the head of state. The laureates were solemnly announced to the entire country on Lenin's birthday in April. This was started by Khrushchev in the years of the post-Stalinist "thaw." While for Khrushchev himself, 1964 was the year that he was forced out of office.

Only three candidates got two-thirds of the votes—Slava Rostropovich, the actor Nikolai Cherkasov (*Ivan the Terrible, Alexander Nevsky*), and me. Solzhenitsyn was nominated that year for *Ivan Denisovich*. Sensing that the artistic sympathies of the majority of the committee were silently on the side of the rebel writer, the official Party newspaper *Pravda* published a tooth-shattering article on voting day, accusing Solzhenitsyn of every mortal sin, especially political ones. The writer's candidacy was recalled.

Everything went haywire. Khrushchev refused to approve the secret decision of the committee, complaining that all three winners were performers and not creators. A second round of voting was set up. The poet Alexander Tvardovsky, editor of *Novy mir,* noisily refused to vote again. Wouldn't it be shameful, he said, to wear a little medal wheedled out of the authorities unjustly? Some of the more daring supported him. Nonetheless, another three "creators"—a writer, an artist, and a journalist—found themselves among the nominees.

Looking back now, I can laugh: Maya Plisetskaya, a laureate of the Lenin Prize. How could that be possible? . . . But back then, receiving that highest accolade of Soviet recognition, I was proud and happy. I won't be a hypocrite about it. I was given preference secretly, paying no attention to the swirl of nasty letters from my "well-wishers" addressed to the presidium of the committee. Only two people had gotten the Lenin Prize in ballet before me: Ulanova and Vakhtang Chabukiani. I became the third one in that series. The musicians with the title that I can recall are Prokofiev, Shostakovich, Khachaturian, Oistrakh, Richter, and Gilels. And the same year as me—Mstislav Rostropovich.

Now the minutia of former Soviet regalia lies on the dust heap of the shift of the times. But people always live in the present. Only the present.

(I was never deemed worthy of the Stalin Prize. I was once on the list of contenders for *Khovanshchina,* at Golovanov's insistence. But my family's ideological impropriety brought that notion to naught.)

Returning to *Carmen.* After Shostakovich's refusal, I tried to approach Khachaturian. Our dachas were close by, in the settlement of Snegiri near Moscow. Dacha residents, as befits Russians in the country, took constitutionals, and on our walks I told Avram Ilyich about my idea. But things never went beyond talking.

And then a new character appeared. In late 1966 the Cuban National Ballet came to Moscow. My mother, a tireless theatergoer, attended their performances and enthusiastically bade me to come see the Cubans. It was winter. The performances were in Luzhniki. Snow, dark, ice. I was lazy. But still I went. They were doing a ballet by Alberto Alonso. From the dancers' first movement, I felt as if a snake had bitten me. I sat on a hot seat until intermission. This was Carmen's language. Her movements. Her world.

I rushed backstage at intermission. "Alberto, would you like to do *Carmen?* For me?"

"That is my dream." The dialogue took place without "how-de-do's" or introduction. Instantly. To the point. Like thunder on a clear day.

Alberto had to go back to Cuba in a few days, but if the official invitation from the Soviet ministry arrived in time, he would come back to Moscow . . .

"With the completed libretto," he promised.

At nine the next morning, I was in Furtseva's waiting room. Her secretary Lubov Panteleimonovna (Lubov Po-telephonovna, as callers dubbed her) frowned. "How could you just drop in without calling, Maya Mikhailovna? Ekaterina Alexeyevna is . . ."

But luck was with me. The minister appeared in her doorway and asked welcomingly, "Are you here to see me so early? Instead of ballet class?"

"Ekaterina Alexeyevna, I simply must see you. It's so important." Haltingly, not very clearly, I began to ask Furtseva to invite Alberto Alonso to choreograph *Carmen* at the Bolshoi.

They did not invite foreign choreographers to the Imperial Theater. In fact, they wouldn't let them get within a hundred meters of the place. They might infect the virginal Bolshoi with various degenerate Western influences. Pervert it. Destroy it. But this was a Cuban, from a people's democracy, whose troupe successfully strengthened friendship among the peoples of the socialist camp.

"You say it would be a one-act ballet? Forty minutes? Like a little *Don Quixote,* right? In that style? A festival of dance? Spanish motifs? I'll confer with my comrades. I can't imagine it meeting serious opposition. It would be good to strengthen Soviet-Cuban relations."

Furtseva agreed so easily to *Carmen* — after my Lenin Prize. The prize supported my position. I could collect on it for two or three years. It would have looked bad to deny a prize-winning prima ballerina a small ballet outside the theater plan. Ministers knew which way the wind was blowing! My reputation as a classical dancer was impeccable — they couldn't possibly expect me to let them down with any of that modern dance stuff. At last, the brotherhood with bearded Fidel could reach euphoria.

It came to pass. Alberto flew in to Moscow on a freezing day with a month-long visa. As a youth he had danced with the Russian Ballet of Monte Carlo and he remembered a few Russian words: "One month. Visa. Little for ballet."

Alberto had a tropical insouciance toward the Russian winter and arrived without a fur hat, assuming that his luxuriant Spanish head of hair would protect him from the frost. Not so. That first day hot Alberto got such a chill in his head that he not only needed a fur hat with ear flaps but also a doctor, who was jolted into diagnosing the chilled choreographer from the Cuban Republic with no less than an inflammation of the brain.

And so, the new ballet . . . *Carmen* . . . We begin tomorrow. But to what music?

Shchedrin has promised to write the music for me, not really believing that it would be so easy to "transport" Alberto Alonso to Moscow. He made the promise to keep me quiet, so that I would leave him alone. Yet the next day at noon is the first rehearsal. What's the pianist supposed to play? I know that Shchedrin is up to his ears in composing. Piles of scores lie on his desk. He's involved in his *Poetorio,* a concerto for poet and orchestra (the poet is Andrei Voznesensky). And he's got his film work. And they're always in a hurry in the film world — they need everything "yesterday."

He calms me down. Use the Bizet. Remember what Shostakovich said? "But which parts of the opera should we use?" I ask. Deep into the night the three of us sat up working at our place on Gorky Street — Alberto, Rodion, and I. Alberto in a Russian-English-Spanish mix tries to explain his concept. He wants us to read the story of Carmen as a fatal confrontation of a willful person — born free — and a totalitarian system of universal slavery and submission, a system dictating the mores of lying relations, perverted brutish morals, and destructive cowardice . . . Carmen's life is a corrida watched by an indifferent public. Carmen is a challenge, a rebellion. Blinding against a gray background! Alberto doesn't have the words. He starts showing us. Dancing. He moves plates and glasses on the table. He gets up on chairs.

"Why chairs?" we ask in almost Gogolian unison.

"Do you know what is power? Power, no liberty, prison? Do you know? Power is always death to freedom . . . Do you know that?"

Alberto is turning red. Agitated. His eyes blaze madly. The entire ballet is in his head, his heart. The text of the libretto is just a tiny, crumpled piece of paper, scribbled over in Spanish, which he leaves at our house, covering it with the herring plate in his excitement.

Rodion tries to soothe him. "Maya will be there tomorrow with the music.

Don't worry, Alberto. After Bizet. I'll do a montage of the music tonight following your plan. Maya will come with the music! Don't worry!"

The clock said two A.M.

"What will you start with?" We began with the duet. Carmen and El Torero. Sergei Radchenko and me. Alberto worked in a frenzy. Enchanted, we plunged into the world of his choreographic fantasy. Every movement was a word, a phrase. Everything was concrete. It was all "about" something. Seriously. And uniquely. It was like nothing I had ever danced before.

A glitch. Bizet's music has an acceleration, a bursting forth — this was the part from "Arlesienne." But Alberto needed something hidden and mysterious. He showed us subdued, cautious movements, whispered conversation of the legs, eyes, and forearms. But it didn't match the music. It didn't coincide. At all. After the theater at dinner I complained to Shchedrin. Alberto would be over in the evening. We were stuck. Rodion promised. I'll drop by class tomorrow. We'll see. What time?

When we showed him what we had, I could see in the mirror that our excerpt impressed Shchedrin. We danced the part that comes after Bizet's acceleration. It is set for silence, for pauses. Rodion picked up the music and sketched out a musical text, making variations in the Bizet to match our choreographic state.

That is how the Bizet-Shchedrin *Carmen Suite* came into being that is produced, played, and performed in every corner of the globe to this day. At competitions for figure skating, gymnastics, and synchronized swimming . . . It has been read in surprisingly different ways by many choreographers (the last was a brilliant production in 1992 by Mats Ek). It started in the second rehearsal hall of the Bolshoi, on the fifth floor. At the barre of the class mirror.

That year — 1967 — the genre of musical transcription was totally forgotten. The "avant-garde" was self-indulgently "feasting on Bald Mountain." It was fate itself that urged Shchedrin to revive the neglected genre.

Rehearsals moved on. Borya Messerer was completing his filigree red, black, and yellow set. Fadeyechev was rehearsing José, Lavrenok, the Corregidor, and Kasatkina was learning the part of Fate. The three solo tobacco girls were Kokhanovskaya, Ryzhenko, and Domashevskaya. Ten men for the accompaniment. A total of eighteen people. A dozen and half. There was no second cast. The theater never saw other dancers. If someone got seriously ill, the work was down the drain.

But Heaven was on our side. We overcame great obstacles to extend Alberto's visa — Oh, how hard that was! We paid for his hotel ourselves, but private Soviet citizens were not permitted to pay for a foreigner. Not allowed, that's all. But we managed to do that, too. Alberto kept being evicted, but they never got him out. Hurrah!

The backstage shops couldn't keep up. They gave us the tiniest time possible for rehearsals. The costumes were completed the morning of the premiere. The dancers didn't get a chance to accustom themselves to them. We were able to reserve the main stage only once: that was the lighting, the staging, and the dress rehearsal. One — one for everything, for everyone. The ballet was made in a frenzied rush. A day before the dress rehearsal Shchedrin asked the participants to go up to the top stage to hear the orchestra sound. A surprise awaits you! Gennady Rozhdestvensky was conducting the Bolshoi orchestra, and he was doing it brilliantly.

Rodion had told me that he was writing his score for strings and percussion (the composition took only twenty days — miraculous — of which four Shchedrin spent in Hungary for the funeral of Zoltán Kodály). I danced for him in our cramped kitchen — right in the middle of dinner, with a piece of chicken in my mouth — doing every new episode staged by Alberto, doing my part and my partners' parts. Shchedrin watched my staccato movements closely, seeking some mysterious accents. What was that all about?

It was only when the orchestra played that I found out. The music was so unusual, vivid, dashing, three-dimensional, contemporary, juicy, agitating, colorful, doomed, and lofty that we were stunned. Now that was something!

"Genius," Natasha Kasatkina whispered in my ear.

The orchestra played with unfeigned delight. The musicians' faces — and on the upper stage you're almost above the orchestra, right up next to it and above — showed that they liked the piece. The bows flew up and down, up and down diligently, the percussionists banged away on the drums, rang the bells and caressed exotic instruments I had never seen before, crackling, creaking, and whistling. Now that was something! Music kissing music, as the most august Bellochka Akhmadulina later said about *Carmen Suite.*

"We have to do our best, too," Radchenko lectured Fadeyechev in paternal tones.

Did we ever do our best at the premiere! We turned ourselves inside out. But the hall was colder than usual at the Bolshoi. Not only Minister Furtseva and her entourage but the Moscow audience, always so kind to me, had expected a second *Don Quixote,* sweet variations on a familiar theme. Mindless entertainment. But this was serious, new, strange. They applauded out of politeness and respect, love for the past. Where were the pirouettes? Where were the chaînés? Where were the fouettés? Where were the tours en manège? Where was the cute tutu of the naughty Kitri? I felt the audience sinking, like a drowning signalman, into confusion.

(Among those who wholeheartedly accepted the ballet at its premiere I will name the great Shostakovich, the originally berating Yakobson, Lili Brik, and V. A. Katanyan, and the music critic Irina Strazhenkova. That's all. No one else. The rest were either silent or brought up other topics like the early spring and the ridiculous prices at the markets.)

Before the start I caught a glimmer of Furtseva's insouciant and happy face in the director's box—long live the new celebration of friendship between the Soviet and Cuban peoples, born through her efforts by the Ministry of Culture she oversaw. There had been almost no officials at the sole rehearsal because of the rushed deadline. And if any of the minor vigilantes of ideological order had reported his concerns to the powers-that-be, he was not heard because of that rush. Or maybe they did, but they didn't get around to it. After all, I had the Lenin Prize in my buttonhole. Who would dare lift a hand against the medal with the bald profile?

When I came out for my bows, a quick glance at the director's box revealed an empty red-and-gold armchair instead of Furtseva. Ekaterina Alexeyevna's happy, insouciant face was not there.

The second performance was listed on the poster for a day later—April 22. We planned a banquet on the 22nd for everyone in the production, reserving the restaurant at the House of Composers. The advance payment was made. However, things became complicated. On the morning of April 21, I heard the baritone voice of the director Chulaki on the telephone: "Maya Mikhailovna, Rodion Konstantinovich, I'm not supposed to be calling you. But tomorrow's production of *Carmen* has been canceled. Instead of the triple (that was the evening of one-act ballets, the last of which was *Carmen Suite*), they'll do *The Nutcracker*."

"What? On whose orders?" I asked in confusion.

"The order came from Vartanyan. I can't disobey. Don't mention my name. But try to talk to Furtseva. Maybe you'll be able to break her. Good luck."

Vartanyan was a small, stooped Armenian who was in charge of all the musical institution of the land of the Soviets. Above him at the Ministry of Culture were only the deputy ministers and Furtseva herself.

Arms missing the sleeve holes, lacing up our boots in the elevator, we rushed to the Ministry of Culture. Lubov Po-telephonovna inadvertently gave away a state secret—she hadn't heard about the reaction to *Carmen* yet—the minister was at the Kremlin Palace of Congresses attending the run-through of the Lenin Concert (every year Lenin's birthday was marked by the most stultifying, endless speech and—after an intermission—a "concert by masters of the arts").

Blinded after the sunlight outdoors, we made our way by touch into the dim auditorium. The minister and her retinue were busy with important state business—spending an hour on deciding whether the choir of Old Bolsheviks and their revolutionary songs should go at the beginning or the end of the concert. We sat down quietly behind the backs bent toward the wise minister. The dispute ended. The Old Bolsheviks would sing at the end, before the exultant apotheosis. The lights went on. Seizing the moment, we started talking to Furtseva. All our arguments were brought to bear. But the minister was implacable.

"It's a great failure, comrades. The production is raw. Nothing but eroticism. The opera's music has been mutilated. The concept has to be rethought. I have grave doubts whether the ballet can be redone. It's an alien path . . ." I'll leave out the depressing dialogue. We were speaking different languages.

Furtseva headed for the door. Her minions awaited. Walking beside her, Shchedrin brought out his last argument. "Ekaterina Alexeyevna, we've paid for a banquet at the House of Composers. All the participants are invited, the entire orchestra. And now the Voice of America will mock the Soviet regime all over the world."

"I'll cut out the love adagio. We'll leave out all the lifts that shocked you. We'll just do a blackout while the music plays," I begged at the door.

"Can't you cancel the banquet?" Furtseva asks, coming to a halt.

"Everyone's been invited, Ekaterina Alexeyevna. Whether the show goes on or not, the people will come. If it's not a christening, it'll be a wake. Word will get out. Is that what you want?" You never know what will work on the minds of the higher bureaucrats. Go figure . . .

"The banquet—that really is bad. But you'll get rid of the lifts? You promise? Vartanyan will come to the rehearsal in the morning, and he'll report to me. Change your costume. Put on a skirt, Maya, you have to cover up your bare thighs. It's the stage of the Bolshoi Theater, comrades."

I can't describe the entire scale of emotions we went through in those two miserable days. It's too hard on my nerves. This was just a brief outline.

Shostakovich helped, too. He called the ministry and expressed his delight over *Carmen Suite*. So there!

Nutcracker was canceled, *Carmen* was put back. The second performance did take place! But the thousands of "what ifs"—what if Chulaki had been too scared to call, what if Lubov Po-telephonovna hadn't spilled the information, what if we hadn't caught Furtseva in the darkened hall of the Kremlin Palace, what if Shostakovich hadn't made the effort, what if? . . . Our ballet would have been lost for eternity. Amen.

But we did have to cut the love adagio. What else could we do? At the rise of the strings, at the highest lift, when I freeze in à la second, the curtain with the head of Messerer's threatening bull suddenly fell in front of Carmen and José, keeping the audience from seeing the erotic arabesque, when my leg embraces Jose's hips, the split, the kiss. No need to see that! Only the music carried our adagio to the end. Vartanyan, who had come to his political career from playing third clarinet in a band and was therefore considered a great connoisseur of the musical theater, had followed his minister's instructions thoroughly. There would be no sex on the Soviet stage.

Moscow audiences gradually got used to our baby. The success grew with each performance. Nikolai Fedorovich Kudryavtsev, an impresario from Canada, aristocratic child of the first wave of emigration, who was organizing a summer tour of Canada for the ballet as part of Expo 67, had been to a performance and wanted to include *Carmen Suite* in the repertoire of the tour. It was just what Expo 67 needed.

As is typical in Russia, the right leg didn't know what the left was doing. So the sets for *Carmen* set sail across the ocean to Canadian shores. But Vartanyan's department was not asleep and set off the alarm: Everyone topside!

A meeting was convened in Furtseva's office. Around fifteen or twenty people. The minister's plan was simple: Plisetskaya publicly recognizes the faultiness of the new ballet, denounces it and herself in it, and asks that it not be included in the foreign tour as an immature work to be replaced by something classical. How about my crowning *Swan Lake?* That was the real face of the Bolshoi! According to Furtseva's concept, my self-denunciation would take a quarter-hour, twenty minutes tops . . . Kudryavtsev was ordered to await the decision in the waiting room, under the wing and eye of Lubov Po-telephonovna. As I passed through the doors of the ministerial office, I greeted my bleak-looking and pale impresario, nervously tugging at his lush, polka-dotted bowtie.

The meeting began with a harsh attack: We allowed you to show a highly controversial ballet, but that does not mean that an experimental performance should be shown to foreign audiences. And more about the face of the Bolshoi . . .

"Do you understand, Maya Mikhailovna, that you should be the one to refuse its performance and explain the reasoning to Mr. Kudryavtsev?" insisted V. I. Popov, Furtseva's deputy on foreign contacts, pushing me up against the wall.

"I'm not going to Canada without *Carmen*. They've seen my *Swan Lake* three times there already. I want to do something new," I replied.

"I haven't seen it myself," Popov went on, "But everyone says that it doesn't work and that you've lowered yourself."

"Why don't you come see it, Vladimir Ivanovich, instead of depending on hearsay?"

Furtseva exploded. "The show will not live in any case. Your *Carmen Suite* will die."

"*Carmen* will die when I die," I replied harshly.

Silence. Everyone held their breath.

"Where will our ballet end up, I ask, if the Bolshoi starts putting on such formalist production?" Furtseva demanded angrily.

I was angry, too. I couldn't keep from saying, "It won't go anywhere. It'll keep on getting moldier and moldier."

Furtseva's face broke out in red blotches. She turned in a fury to Chulaki, who sat as still as a wax figure. "How can you keep silent, Comrade Chulaki, when you hear that? Respond! While you're still the director . . ."

That was a threat. Chulaki was a massive man, with the large, balding head of a bull, who had gone through fire, ice, and copper pipes in Stalin's day. He was a tough nut. Hysterical women didn't faze him. He gave his minister a near-sighted, grim look through his thick horn-rimmed glasses. "I took two pills so that I could keep silent." Chulaki's plump fingers played with the pill bottle.

"Why weren't you watching, Comrade Chulaki? Why didn't you want us there? What, do you like this outrageous ballet?" Furtseva kept pushing Mikhail Ivanovich.

"Not everything in it is bad, Ekaterina Alexeyevna. The fortune-telling scene is quite interesting . . ."

"Aha! You're a co-conspirator."

And here our cultural minister spoke her historic line: "You" — casting lightning bolts at three faces, mine, Rodion's, and Chulaki's — "You have turned a heroine of the Spanish people into a whore."

That was too much. That was one for my side. Furtseva's ball landed in her own court. All present lowered their eyes. I saw that some of them had actually read Mérimée. But they said nothing.

"*Carmen* is not going to Canada. Tell that to the entrepreneur Kudryavtsev," Furtseva commanded.

Popov rose.

"Vladimir Ivanovich, tell Kudryavtsev that I'm not going to Canada either," I hasten to say.

"Is that an ultimatum?"

"Yes."

"You will go to Canada without *Carmen!*"

"And how am I supposed to explain why I'm not dancing the announced new ballet?"

"You will say that *Carmen* is not ready yet."

"No, I will not say that. I will tell the truth. That you have banned it. You'd be better off not sending me."

"Maya Mikhailovna is right," Shchedrin said, spacing out each syllable.

Furtseva looked as if she had been struck by lightning. She started screaming. "Maya is an unconscious element, but you . . . you . . . you're a Party member!"

Dead silence. A long silence.

"I'm not a member of the Party," Rodion said even more clearly.

Furtseva fell back into her chair.

"If *Carmen* is banned," I said, adding fuel to the fire, "I'll leave the theater. What do I have to lose? I've been dancing for twenty-five years. Maybe it's enough. But I will tell people the reason why."

"You are a traitor of the classical ballet," Furtseva screeched.

I said nothing. What could I say?

"All the musicians are upset. Yesterday the respected composer Vlasov tore his hair. Our Vartanyan is in despair."

Vartanyan had tormented me with his puritanical advice. I got my revenge: "The mediocre Vartanyan doesn't like it, but the genius Shostakovich is delighted by it. What can you do about that, Ekaterina Alexeyevna?"

Furtseva grimaced, but she didn't dare throw stones at the legendary name.

Carmen Suite didn't make it to Canada. The sets traveled there and back, though. They breathed that tangy ocean air. For six years I had been not allowed to travel, and then I created a production that wasn't allowed to travel.

I didn't go to Canada, either, no matter how much they threatened me. I lost the whole summer. I fell seriously sick for a long time. Nervous stress. Lost my voice. Good thing I wasn't a singer. Shchedrin and I spent the summer as recluses at the dacha in Snegiri until the season started. I didn't want to see people.

Poor Nikolai Fedorovich Kudryavtsev, who had waited in the minister's reception room a good three hours instead of twenty minutes (Lubov Po-telephonovna plied him with tea), paid a major no-show fine, which was hard on his finances.

The production didn't play in Moscow for a long time because the sets were gone. And it was also an anniversary year, damn it, 1917–1967. Fifty years of the Great October Revolution. The theaters were expected to offer the Soviet audience nothing but the immortal ideological masterpieces of socialist realism.

When the cannonade of universal joy died down, *Carmen Suite* began finding its place slowly in the Moscow repertory of the Bolshoi. It's a mobile show. Not many participants. The sets don't change. The orchestra is only strings and five percussion players. The audience, which was kinder to *Carmen* with time, started coming in droves. Everyone was happy. Me most of all.

I loved that ballet so much it made me dizzy!

And now for the happy ending.

Alexei Kosygin came to one of the performances in 1968. After it was over he applauded politely from the government box and . . . left. No one knew what he thought of *Carmen*.

The next day Rodion bumped into Furtseva at a reception.

"I heard that Alexei Nikolayevich Kosygin attended *Carmen*. Is that true? How did he react?" Furtseva asked apprehensively.

Shchedrin bluffed spontaneously. "Marvelously. Alexei Nikolayevich called us at home after the ballet and praised it highly. He liked it."

Furtseva broke into a blissful smile. "You see, you see. We were right to insist on additional work. I've had reports that much has changed for the better. We must keep working."

The following year I toured in London. The English impresario asked Popov if they could have *Carmen Suite* for England. And suddenly Popov, without blinking an eye, replied pleasantly, "Of course. If you like the ballet. We won't argue. The production has matured. Plisetskaya has grown. This will be a colorful addition to the repertoire."

In faraway England, at a distance from Vartanyan's black eyes, we felt so bold that we reinstated the finale of the love adagio. And three years after that we performed it in Moscow. And it went all right, can you imagine? The passage of time must have helped.

I want to defend Furtseva. Don't be surprised. She said what every Soviet boss inside the walls of the office of the Minister of Culture of the USSR had to say.

If he or she were to say anything different, they'd be gone in a flash. Ideology! A system of mutual interdependence.

But Furtseva also helped me. She gave orders in the theater, she invited Alonso, got him a visa, removed the ban from the second performance, did not behave too stubbornly, and thereby determined the fate of the production, did not keep a grudge after our clash at the ministry—so unusual for those Soviet times—and gladly accepted the simplistic lie . . .

I danced *Carmen Suite* about 350 times, 132 times at the Bolshoi alone. I've danced it all over the world. The last *Carmen* was in Taiwan with a Spanish troupe in 1990. And it may have been the best *Carmen* of my life. Believe me!

I've been praised by the press and I've been criticized. But the audiences have taken to the production with delight, enthusiasm, and joy. Isn't that the highest reward for my stubbornness, faith, fanaticism, and conviction?

On September 3, 1967, the Bolshoi troupe gathered. A bit later than usual because of Expo 67 in Canada. I was beginning my twenty-fifth season. My twenty-fifth!

When I entered the class the dancers gave me an ovation. At first I thought it was because of the anniversary. But no, it was something else. It was too long, too warm, too marked. Could it be for my refusal to go to Canada without *Carmen Suite?*

Sergei Radchenko leaned over to my ear: "They're applauding your civil courage. Understand?"

There was a lump in my throat.

Chapter Forty

Work with Roland Petit and Maurice Béjart

After Soviet television showed François Mitterand, the president of France, giving me the order of the Legion of Honor and making a gracious, truly French speech in my honor, a tall, loud, Soviet official I didn't know came up to me at a Kremlin New Year's party and said, "I thought, Maya Mikhailovna, that the Legion of Honor was given only to members of the Resistance. And suddenly, they gave it to you . . ."

"I've been resisting all my life," I replied, laughing sincerely.

Resist or not, I never dared to dream of working with Western choreographers. I saw films of productions by Serge Lifar, Roland Petit, Jerome Robbins, and Maurice Béjart and grew intoxicated by the freshness of ideas, vocabulary, and form, but dream . . . huh-uh, I didn't dare. Our hobbled, servile existence was so far from the unfettered inventors, iconoclasts, and challengers.

On a visit to Paris, I ran into Roland Petit at the Repetto store (which Roland's mother owned) and heard the unexpected words, "We must work together. I have a great idea for you, Maya — to make your role on port de bras alone." Bumping into the counter and knocking the leotards I had selected onto the floor, Roland began his strange dance: his arms wove designs, loops, knots, his hands talked to each other, had conflicts.

"What do the legs do?" I asked.

"I don't know yet. Are you in Paris for long this time?"

"Just a few days."

"I'll invite you to Marseilles."

I had met Roland Petit during my second Paris season. Roland and Zizi Jeanmaire were friendly with the Aragons, and it was Aragon who gave Petit the idea to dance to the poems of William Blake. Critics said Aragon had done a brilliant job translating Blake into French. And it was Aragon who was responsible for my *Rose Malade.*

But the theater didn't let me go to Marseilles — there were too many performances at home. So Roland, intending his dancer Rudy Bryans as my partner, flew to Moscow with him for a "look-see." Would he suit me, would he be too short?

At first Rudy seemed like a shrimp. His jacket was right in fashion then, and it hid his height. But when he changed into ballet clothes, Bryans was transformed. He stretched out and grew more slender. We tried a few lifts. The Frenchman had strong and smart hands. I like that expression for the hands of my partners: smart hands. You can't dance with dumb hands. They're bound to drop you, hold you too long, or rush you. Well, then, we'd try.

The rehearsal was set for noon the next day. Roland, for the historic moment, dressed himself in white from head to toe. He was fragrant with perfume. He had appeared in Moscow — it was cool autumn — decked out in a full-length raccoon coat. Muscovites hadn't seen a French gentleman like that in their lives. Not since the War of 1812! To top it off, Roland had shaved his head in preparation for his role as Mayakovsky — Elsa and Aragon had gotten him involved in that idea, too, and gave him the famous photograph by Rodchenko of the Russian poet with a shaved head. Roland immersed himself in the image.

A rumor flew through the theater, that Petit had come to rehearse with me, but he looked so bizarre that everyone kept sticking their nose in the door of the rehearsal hall. When else would you get a chance to see something like that? . . .

Roland had staged our duet in a single breath. In just a few days. He had roughed it out with Bryans in Marseilles, with a double for me. The choreography was done well, and we changed only a few lifts that did not suit my body. The music for *La Rose Malade* was from Mahler, excerpts from the Fifth Symphony. The famous Adagietto.

Raising a ruckus among the customs and border guards at Sheremetyevo, filling the Moscow airport with the strong scent of French perfume for days, Roland in his raccoon coat and Bryans majestically quit Moscow.

It was so easy. Maya Plisetskaya wanted to be in Roland Petit's new ballet —

well, then, here it was on a tray, tied in a blue ribbon, here's the partner, brought to Moscow, no problem . . . If not for Aragon, my naive reader, who had appealed to "dear Comrade Brezhnev" with a complicated letter (not very comprehensible for ordinary mortals), there wouldn't have been any *Roses*, Petits, or Bryanses.

I flew to Marseilles on January 1, 1973, the first day of the new year. I wore a mink mini-coat and white fur beret. I was Snegurochka, the Snow Maiden. That was my response to Roland's long raccoon. My fur coat was becoming and youthful. The fuzz-faced youth at passport control at Sheremetyevo took a long time comparing my year of birth in the passport with my Snegurochka look.

In Marseilles there was no hint of winter. It was pouring rain ruthlessly. The mink was in danger. I had been a bad geography student in choreography school.

I had a few days to polish the Adagietto with Rudy Bryans and learn the third, leaping act of the ballet with six men. The first part, which is called Garden of Love, does not involve me. The premiere was going to be in Paris at the Palais du Sport. They were waiting for me to try on costumes, created by Yves St-Laurent.

Roland himself rehearsed with me, not trusting the coach. He showed me the movements thoroughly, at full power. He dangled in Bryans's arms. He tore open his legs. I wasn't used to working in such a frenzy. Roland was angry.

"Are you this lazy just with me — or always?"

"The important thing for me is to memorize the text, then I'll add on."

"Strange Russian school," Roland summed it up.

"What's so strange? I want to dance until I'm a hundred."

"And if you weren't lazy?"

"I wouldn't get past forty."

I seemed to have infected Roland with my laziness. When we later did a ballet based on Proust, he told me on several occasions, "Improvise, simply improvise."

"But at least in what manner?"

"Whatever your Russian school tells you."

Gaston Deffere, mayor of Marseilles, came to our last rehearsal. Roland Petit had founded his troupe under the mayor's patronage. Roland came to my dressing room before the start. "Don't be lazy today, Maya. Gaston doesn't know anything about the customs of the Russian school."

This was the first time I went through the *Rose* full-leggedly. I think I caught the mood. Roland was satisfied.

After the rehearsal, our whole noisy group headed off to a popular restaurant to eat seafood — oysters, clams, sea urchins, hot bouillabaisse. Roland sat next to me wearing snow-white kid gloves. The restaurant's regulars recognized him and gazed delightedly at the kid gloves.

The premiere in Paris. First came *Mayakovsky*. The stage was covered in red banners. Woytek Lowski soared in leaps as the stormy petrel of revolution. Denys Ganio was the poet's youth, the love of Lilya Brik, Barbara Malinowska. Roland, with shaved head, was Mayakovsky in the last years of his life, the suicide leitmotif. Two fingers made a pistol.

The audience was not thrilled by the revolutionary subject, despite the marvelous, refined choreography. But Roland was not depressed. He shouted "Bravo!" loudly to his troupe from the wings, blew kisses to the detractors whistling in the audience. How wonderful that he believed so strongly in his work and infallibility.

Then came our turn. *La Rose Malade*. The first act—Garden of Love—has three couples in love: a young man and a maiden, two voluptuous women, two sensual boys. The garden of love.

The second act was us, Rudy and me. A brilliant twelve-minute pas de deux, closely following the plot of Blake's poem. The young man, fatally in love with a rose, dries it up with his passion, the rose fades in his embrace, dropping its petals.

I love this tiny masterpiece of Petit's. After that Paris premiere I've danced it a good two hundred times. On every continent. At the Bolshoi, in Argentina, Australia, Japan, America. After Bryans, I danced the duet with Godunov, Kovtun, Berdyshev, and Edema.

The third act. I was surrounded by six men. Their powerful leaping variations. Then me. Then all together. Leaping in unison. Yves St-Laurent had created amusing costumes. Costumes drawing the naked body. Muscles, ribs, loins. I was alone among them in a black tunic with a flame on my head.

Roland Petit judged my choreographic opuses as well.

"How did you like my *Anna*, Roland?"

"Everything in it is good except for the choreography."

I talked about my dream to dance Princess Tarakanova with him. The one I was so afraid of as a child in Sretenka. I got him books, which were in Russian, unfortunately, and lithographs. Roland was curious and asked me about the Fortress of Peter and Paul and the floods in St. Petersburg. I sent him to read Pushkin's *Bronze Horseman*. He didn't have a translation handy. So we went to the statistics instead—how high does the Neva River rise in a century? But we never got further than statistics. There was no ballet.

My communications with Béjart began with a letter.

Having spent a day in Dubrovnik in the summer of 1974—there was a big festival there—I ended up at an evening of ballet. Dushka Sifnis was dancing Béjart's *Bolero*. It was unbelievably good. I went crazy. I was delirious. *Bolero* had to be mine. It didn't matter that I wasn't the first. I would become the first. It was my ballet. Mine!

When I got back to Moscow I started the letter: "Dear Maurice, I'm delighted, delirious, I want to dance it, could you try it with me, *Bolero* is my ballet," and so on, and so forth. Our polyglot friend translated my agitated letter into French, got an approximate address for Béjart (all Belgium must know where the creator of *Bolero* lives), and the mailbox swallowed my wails. Would the Soviet censors hold it up?

There was no answer. Obviously, my letter had never reached Brussels. They intercepted it, those postal bastards.

Moscow life gradually cooled my ardor. I dreamed less often of the red table, the assembly of men around it, and me, dancing in bright lights on that table.

A year passed. Suddenly—unexpected luck. André Thomazo, a representative of a Parisian literary and artistic agency, invited me to make a film dancing Béjart's *Bolero* in Brussels. A Franco-Belgian production for television.

"But I've never danced *Bolero*. Only dreamed of it."

"But you've seen it? You like it?"

"I'm mad about it."

"Béjart himself will teach it to you. Will a week be enough? There will be four performances before the filming," Thomazo tries to persuade me.

"I accept, I accept, I accept, I accept."

"Television pays well. Gosconcert, if you accept, has already given its approval."

At the Brussels airport I was met by the Dobrieviches, a Yugoslav couple. Both had formerly danced with Béjart, both were coaches now, and both spoke good Russian. Luba Dobrievich had danced *Bolero* herself, and Béjart had selected her to coach me. She would show me the ballet.

"Is it a difficult part?" I asked after the first hellos.

"Difficult for breathing and memorizing. We'll start tomorrow. Béjart wants to see you a half-hour before we start."

Maurice and I met like old acquaintances, even though I was seeing him up close for the first time. His pale blue eyes outlined in black pierced me. His gaze is questioning and cold. It has to be held. I refused to blink. We stared at each other. If Mephistopheles existed, he would look like Béjart, I thought. Or does Béjart resemble Mephistopheles?

Luba translated, "Here is your letter, Maya. In good French. I was told you don't speak it."

"So, you did get my letter, Maurice? I thought it hadn't reached you."

Béjart tucked the letter back into the book he grasped tightly. "We have only one week. Focus. Your predecessors had trouble with their memory. Luba, tell Maya the names for the episodes that you gave to the music as an aid. Start with that."

The legend has it that Ravel ran out of time when he was writing *Bolero* at the commission of the dancer Ida Rubinstein. And so the composer, in a rush, kept repeating his Spanish-like melody, merely changing its orchestral dress. So they say. I don't believe it. But Ravel did set a task for dancers!

Béjart's episodes were called

Crab

Sun

Fish

B.B.

Hungarian Woman

Cat

Stomach

Samba.

All sixteen versions of the melody (that was the name for my part in the program, Melody) were given names.

The name Sun came from the widespread arms, like rays of the sun, fingers spread, as if raising a prayer to the heavenly light. The name Crab also came from hands, which turned — suddenly — into pincers that pinched crosswise into one's own ribs.

"B.B." meant Brigitte Bardot. She was then the most famous woman on the planet, and Béjart turned the manner of her walk and gestures into a choreographic image.

"Stomach" — well, you must be tired of this by now.

But which followed which? Before each appearance of the melody Ravel has two measures of rhythmic break. For those two measures Béjart tamed the fireworks of his imagination and repeated a hundred times a simple formula of springy squats in plié. That moment is the time the dancer tries to remember which episode comes next: Cat or Hungarian Woman? You lower yourself and in a panic try to recall what now, what next?

Bolero came hard. All the movements were new for my body. Béjart had studied Eastern dance seriously — Indian, Thai, Persian — and something of that vocabulary entered his own. Plus there was the diabolical inventiveness. Asymmetry. Absence of squareness. Polyrhythms. Ravel used a triple beat, Béjart used four. Even dancers trained on Béjart lost count. And for me, after all those *Lakes* and *Beauties* — think what it was like.

Finally, I stopped sleeping. Deep in the night, in the illumination of the nightlight, I danced the entire text I had learned thus far.

I remembered it.

Now, let's go over it all in order. From the very beginning. Here's the beat, here's the squat, and now? I had forgotten again. Maybe the Crab . . . or is it the Sun?

Angela Albrecht, my Brussels predecessor in *Bolero*, gave me her crib sheet. A secret piece of paper. Tiny drawings and scribbles. It really helped. But at the last rehearsal with the men — there are thirty of them, accompanying me — the wind carried off kind Angela's crib sheet. Gone forever. My brain was muddled. I kept getting confused. A shadow crossed Béjart's features.

No, I wouldn't be able to do it. I had to give up. You can't learn a thousand movements in dizzying alternation in just a week's time. I had to give up. Albrecht came over to console me, told me that it took her three months to learn *Bolero*. Oh, if I had another three days! But the first performance was the next day.

I went over to Béjart. "Maurice, I'm leaving. I can't memorize it. It's beyond me."

"You'll go back to Russia without dancing *Bolero?*"

"I don't know what to do about it," I muttered my favorite preamble.

Luba translated.

"I'll stand in the aisle at the back of the hall," Béjart said. "In a white sweater. I'll be illuminated by a flashlight. I'll prompt you. Cat. Now Stomach. And now B.B. This way. Do you understand me?"

"With a prompter like you I could dance it tonight."

People sometimes ask me which was the most unusual performance in my life. This was. *Bolero* in Brussels with a prompter hidden from the audience in the far aisle, lit by a beam of light from below. With a prompter dressed in a white sweater. With a prompter who was Béjart. At every breather Ravel created, as I bounced in my plié, I stared at the spot illuminated at the back of the hall, giving me signs, like a traffic cop, where to move next. Hand scratching ear in a feline way — do the Cat. Hands flickering in a czardas, now Hungarian Woman. Hands weaving the ornament of a belly dance — Samba.

I didn't get confused, I didn't mix it up. The prompter knew the ballet. Knew it well. My frozen gaze awaiting prompting gave my movements a ritualistic, prayerful aspect. People liked that.

I did the second performance myself. The stress of the first firmly fixed the plethora of information in my brain. I no longer needed prompting. But I retained the manner. Rather, the absence of manner. Just the frenzied player. The alienation.

Then we did the filming. Béjart corrected my *Bolero* for the film. He had become kinder to me. He believed in me. Therefore, when we were saying goodbye, and I told Maurice that I would like to do something else with him, something my own, something new, he replied kindly, "Well then, propose a theme. I accept."

Every city has its own smell. I always sense it at the airport. Munich smells of automobile paints. Prague of chimney smoke. Tokyo of soy sauce. Madrid of almonds. Moscow of garbage in the streets ("I almost hate my homeland," said Pushkin), and Brussels of wet, mossy conifers.

I danced and recorded *Bolero* in November. The third performance was on my birthday. I turned fifty. Dancing the sixteen-minute ballet alone, on a table, barefoot, without a moment's breather (the men accompany the soloist on the floor, around the table), increasing the energy level—you have to correspond to Ravel's mighty crescendo—is an achievement of which I'm very proud. And pleasing the difficult prompter, too.

When I sent Maurice a whole list of suggestions with the first person traveling there, I picked *Isadora*. *Isadora* was Shchedrin's idea. We were taking turns reading Duncan's fiery book *My Life*, which was handed back and forth around Moscow in a Rotaprint copy from a Riga edition from 1937.

I had rehearsed *Bolero* along familiar paths. The choreographic notes were written down, and I merely had to execute them. *Isadora* was created for me.

I came back to coniferous Brussels, with an invitation from the director of the Théâtre de la Monnaie. Every morning I went to class at Mudra, Béjart's school, getting a receipt from the cab driver per Gosconcert's instructions. Always in a hurry, I would toss a knit robe over my damp leotards and order a snack of steak with fries from the hefty Regina at the Mudra cafeteria.

Béjart's pianist Babette Cooper made the selection of music for *Isadora*. Maurice intended to do the whole ballet to the music of a solo piano, making the pianist part of the performance. After a brief prologue—Isadora's death—the pianist slowly comes out in black concert dress to the center of the stage, musingly looks at the prostrate body and walks to the piano. Isadora, reviving, rises from the floor and says to the audience, "I did not invent my dance. But it was asleep until me. And I woke it up." Turning to the pianist, "Exercise."

Chopin sounds. Then come excerpts from Schubert, Brahms, Beethoven, Scriabin, Liszt . . . How was the music selected? Béjart would explain his concept to Babette, read the text that introduced each dance number. The text was from Isadora Duncan herself — quotes from her book. In response, Babette would flip through the piles of notes on her piano, play a few measures, and then ask, "Will that work?"

Béjart would agree or reject. It was very simple. It took a half-hour, no more, to select the music. How did Béjart create? He improvised. But he also prepared ahead. The music had just been chosen, but he adjusted his prepared steps to it. When the steps did not fit the musical phrase, Béjart invented an excellent variation, not going too far from his original idea.

We made *Isadora* in three rehearsals. The fourth went for tiny details and polish. One number — the *Marseillaise* — intentionally fell out of the chamber-music accompaniment. The *Marseillaise* was done to an orchestral tape. It was like a quotation too, a documentary insert, an appliqué. Isadora liked to start her concerts with épatage — the *Internationale* or the *Marseillaise*. Béjart showed me that piece in five minutes. It had been composed — without a doubt — earlier.

How could we manage without Sergei Esenin? Béjart asked me, "Maya, recite something from Esenin. Whatever you remember." I read the first thing that came to mind:

Unsaid,
Blue,
Tender . . .
My place is quiet after storms and thunder,
And my soul — an endless field. . . .
Breathes with the fragrance of honey and roses.

Béjart did not understand a single word, but he nodded his Mephistophelean head. "That's fine. We'll keep it." I liked that Béjart devoted only the barest minimum of rehearsal time to pondering. If he had wasted time the way our Moscow semiprofessionals do, Béjart would not have created so many varied ballets.

The premiere of *Isadora* took place in Monaco. It was there, in Monaco, that

Isadora died, strangled by her own scarf. Fifty years earlier. When she was fifty. We were marking two dates: I was also fifty, just a little bit over by then . . .

At the end of the ballet, children run out onto the stage. Béjart gave them action, not dancing. But the children were important. They expressed the idea of Isadora's school. I say to the public, "I spoke of my school . . . but I was not understood." Did they understand me? It's all a mystery. A girl with blond curls curtsies and hands me a bouquet of wildflowers. Béjart had picked them himself at a flower stall that day. Was it the right bouquet? That was important, too. From the very edge of the stage I tossed flowers into the audience. Isadora used to do that. The flowers were her soul.

Screeching brakes, a 26-meter scarf, a scarf across the entire stage, entangling the dancer like a silk cocoon. Darkness . . .

My work with Béjart upset ballet Moscow. I did not miss an opportunity — in every interview and television program — to talk about the great choreographer from Brussels, the discoverer of new worlds. It drove the bureaucrats crazy and the administration of my theater, too, but I stubbornly continued the "enlightenment the people."

Recently I was told that the prisoners in Alcatraz penitentiary near San Francisco always had warm showers. So that their bodies would not get habituated to cold — the water in the bay there is icy. None of the fugitives who tried to swim to shore made it. Their bodies, used to warmth, became chilled and perished. Our audiences were also washed in warm water. The meager ballets of whatever chief were presented as undying masterpieces. There were no other horizons, and that was that. My propaganda, when combined with the lure of forbidden fruit, had its effect. Béjart's name acquired a mysterious aura.

After *Isadora* there was *Leda*. A twenty-minute ballet with Jorge Donn. It was 1979. But first, a prequel.

A year earlier, on my thirty-fifth anniversary of dancing on the stage of the Bolshoi, with enormous difficulty I had gotten permission to include Béjart's *Bolero* in the program. I had to scramble to get it. The conflict reached the government, and the final permission came the day before the performance. I'll describe that in more detail in another chapter. What happened to Béjart's creation has to be of interest.

My struggle with the authorities over *Bolero* came back to haunt me the following year when I received Béjart's invitation to make a new ballet with Donn, and I — nothing had changed in Soviet life — starting doing the paperwork for travel abroad. This must have been my hundredth trip abroad. But like everyone else, and as before, I had to get character references. With three ill-starred signatures: Administration, Party Committee, Party Local. Without the references from the theater, Gosconcert was powerless to do the paperwork.

The secretary of the Party committee was the cellist Shchenkov. And he did someone's evil bidding to block a new meeting between Béjart and me. It was done quite simply, simpler than anything: "Shchenkov is gone. Won't be back today. Oh, he didn't have time to sign it. He was called to the Central Committee on urgent business. He can't do it on his own, he must confer with other members of the Party bureau. The Party bureau meeting is next Wednesday . . ." When they used to sing this song to me at the start of my career, it was disgusting but somehow logical in an idiotic way. Now this mockery was intolerable.

Like an angered lion, I attacked the doors of higher-ups. But everyone — of the few I found in August, when all are on vacation — sent me back to the elusive Shchenkov. We can't tell the Party committee secretary what to do. We have a democracy now (when was there ever or will there ever be a democracy in Russia!). Shchenkov will sign. It's just all these things . . . Béjart's name did not help. Official ears apparently could not hear it.

Shchenkov never did sign a reference for me. All was lost. There would be no *Leda*. Desperate — I was alone, Rodion was out of Moscow — I rushed to my former savior Pitovranov. Many years out of the KGB, he put me in touch with Filipp Denisovich Bobkov, gave me his number. Bobkov was the deputy chairman of the KGB. The spawn of hell, according to the logic of Soviet life, but . . . I got him on my first try. He picked up the phone himself. He did not rush me, he patiently listened to my rambling moan: all is lost, there will be no *Leda*, the first session with Béjart is set for the day after tomorrow . . . And right off the bat, without any hemming or uncertainty, he said calmly, "You will go. That's for certain. This is the fault of your director Ivanov."

(I'll get to Ivanov later. I promise, dear reader.)

I know for a fact that Filipp Denisovich Bobkov helped many people, pulled many out of trouble. Later I had to seek help from him again, to cut through a new knot that our servile Soviet life tied on my fate. To cut through a new web of intrigue and vileness into which I had carelessly fallen. My genetic code calls on me to remember kindness. And I can't deny that call.

(When I read this chapter to Vladimir Voinovich, he harshly noted, "It wasn't hard for Bobkov to help a famous ballerina. And at the same time he did vicious things. Think it over."

I mumbled, "Bobkov helped other people, too. I can name a lot of people —

Bella Akhmadulina, Yakobson, Bogatyrev, Myagkov . . . What if someone else were in his place?"

"I believe you when you say he helped. But at the same time, Bobkov was doing hideous things."

"But he did good for me! If not for his interference, Béjart's *Leda* would not exist. I am recalling how it all happened. I want to write the truth."

"But you can't write only about your own personal truth. There was also the truth of the nation."

Our conversation ended in a stalemate.)

And so I did go. I flew! To Brussels! Without the references. Without the insignificant signature of the cellist Shchenkov. Nonsense . . . Abroad without references? It must have been the first time since 1917. Gosconcert handed me my passport and ticket an hour before take-off. I made it to the plane.

The embassy borzoi hounds meeting someone at the airport were stunned to see me: "What? You're here? We weren't expecting you! The ambassador had objected. Plisetskaya is a ballerina with the Bolshoi, not Béjart's troupe."

Who had told the ambassador to object? He didn't have enough things to worry about without the repertoire of a Moscow ballerina? That's what my life was like. All my life someone was keeping me from going somewhere. And I fought, struggled, and strove to be let out. That's what my life was like.

No one met me at the Brussels airport. They had given up expecting me. I took a taxi to Mudra. I remembered the address, rue Bara 103.

Béjart was happy to see me. And then, as if it were an ordinary occurrence, "Change, warm up, and we'll start."

Late at night, Sonya, Béjart's secretary, took me with my suitcase to the hotel. And I repeated what Maurice had just created for me and only calmed down toward morning.

We rehearsed in two sessions a day. Like madmen. At 12:30 and at 5:00. The work involved me totally.

The music was Japanese, from the Noh dramas. A solitary flute soared plaintively, sobbing, and drums jingled. I had never danced to such sounds before. But the ballet began with Saint-Saëns's *Swan*. And so Maurice warned me, "Don't dance *Leda* and the *Swan* on the same night."

Béjart united two ancient legends in the plot — the well-known Greek myth about Leda and the Swan and the Japanese tale about a young fisherman who fell in love with a talking bird. The fisherman wants to strip the bird and takes off her feathers. From Japan came the music and my costume. I started the ballet in a swan tutu, which my partner later tore off me, dressing his own arms in my swan feathers (then the fisherman was the Swan). I remained dressed in a short tunic. But then its turn came — the Swan tore it off, too, leaving me in a flesh-colored leotard and tights. That is to say, naked. Then came such lifts that if Comrade Ivanov and the Soviet ambassador were to peek into the rehearsal hall, Comrade Ivanov and the ambassador would have had the hiccups till they died.

My partner, my unforgettable, kind Jorge Donn, was brilliant. He was handsome. Sculptured. Regal. During rehearsals Donn was patient and extremely focused. Every word Béjart spoke he took seriously and attentively. Donn tried to execute every detail, every tiny part of the choreographer's textual movements. He obeyed Béjart. But Béjart had a brilliant, exhaustive knowledge of the dancer's nature and abilities. Jorge's cap of flaxen hair tickled my wrists and neck, large drops of sweat dampened my rehearsal togs, falling down his long spine and chilling mine. We worked without a single break.

One interesting observation. I would come to rehearsal, as is customary in ballet life, with an aching foot, or crick in my back, or something else. Before we started I would wonder in trepidation, Maybe I should ask Maurice to spare me and give me time off. But seeing Jorge's severe, concentrated face, I would drop my capitulating intentions. I would start at half-steam and then get cracking. And miraculously, by the end of rehearsal the pain would be gone, each time. Vanished. I would be healthy once again. *Leda*'s choreography healed me. Like yoga.

The premiere was held in Paris. I danced *Leda* — always with Jorge Donn, I never had another partner in *Leda* — in Brussels, Buenos Aires, São Paulo, Rio de Janeiro, Tokyo . . . But I could never show it in Moscow. Muscovites never have seen *Leda*. Béjart had created a ballet that was too free, too unfettered. And now Donn is dead.

Béjart and I had had other plans. We almost started on Gogol's *Nevsky Prospect*. Even set a date.

Of course, it wasn't hard to get Béjart excited. The more unexpected and paradoxical the task proposed, the easier it was to get a response from him. Sitting one day after a performance late at night in Maurice's house, I mentioned Tolstoy's *Death of Ivan Ilyich*. Béjart stopped in mid-word and hurried to his library. A few minutes later he returned with an open book — he was reading Tolstoy's novella.

"*The Death of Ivan Ilyich* is a man's ballet. If it were a woman's.," I joked. But Béjart did not hear me, he was deep in his reading.

Béjart's troupe was coming to Moscow. At last! Beethoven's Ninth Symphony, *Petrushka*, *Sacre du printemps* . . . I was not in the program. And why shouldn't I dance Isadora in Moscow? Why not recall her on the stage where she performed so many times, why not read to an audience that can understand Esenin's poem, "Unsaid, blue, tender. . . . Quiet is my place . . ." Why not?

They hammered it into my head: the program was approved by Gosconcert a long time ago, nothing can be changed, adding something would be too much, the audience would get tired, wouldn't put up with it.

I spoke with Maurice. He said nothing. He did not want a conflict. My admirers — not at my prompting, get that straight — showered the Bolshoi Theater and Béjart with letters. The Poles in Béjart's troupe, knowing the value of nostalgia, explained to Béjart that he should give Maya the chance to dance with us at least once in Moscow, they love her here.

At the third performance at the Bolshoi, Béjart added my *Isadora*. Babette Cooper had remained in Brussels, and Natasha Gavrilova would play for me. We picked out a dress for her. I hastily taught the children for the final scene. A bouquet of wildflowers was already in an enameled pail in my dressing room. We were ready.

I really did drag out the show. I came out after *Isadora* for curtain calls for thirty-two minutes (according to the stage director's stopwatch). Alone, with the children, with the pianist, I brought out the agitated Béjart, then alone again . . . Multicolored rose petals rained down from the galleries. That was a happy night for me. Muscovites expressed all their love and admiration for me, enjoying with me the justice of the evening.

I received two presents for the *Isadora* in Moscow. Béjart, who was a bit abashed by his early fears regarding Gosconcert, gave me brooch with a lilac enameled pansy, ornamented in the center with a tiny diamond. An ancient Russian Fabergé piece. I've got in my hand right now, Maurice . . .

Jorge Donn — my unforgettable, kind Jorge Donn — at our next meeting doing *Leda* gave me a miniature leather box. Inside, a gold ring with a sapphire. "This is for you, Maya, for *Isadora* in Moscow. Do you remember?" I am writing these lines with Donn's ring on my finger. I treasure it.

Do you hear me, Jorge Donn?

Chapter Forty-One

A Lyrical Digression

A lyrical digression.

I am galloping through my life. Through my entire bustling life. It keeps getting clearer that it is impossible to tell completely about what you have lived through. Only excerpts. Blurred contours. Shadows. Did that really happen? Yes, it did. My diary of those years confirms it. But my memory has already mixed it up, put it in different years . . . Premieres, flowers, struggle, hassles, frustrations, impulses, meetings, packing, suitcases, the daily grind . . . What else would you like to learn about me?

That I am a lefty and do everything with my left hand? But I write with my right hand; with my left I can write only in the opposite direction, mirror writing.

That I have suffered from insomnia all my life? That I've swallowed kilograms of sleeping pills: Nembutal, Luminal, Tazepam, Roginal, Valium?

That I always got into conflicts? Got into trouble for nothing? That I could hurt someone just like that, without thinking, unfairly. And then repent.

That I was a creature of extremes—I could be extravagant and greedy, bold and cowardly, queenly and modest?

That I believed in nourishing creams for the face and liked to put them on thickly and then play solitaire in the kitchen?

That I collected curious surnames, cutting them out of printed publications?

That I was a fanatic soccer fan (of the TsSKA team)?

That I loved herring?

That I never smoked and had no pity for smokers, and that a glass of wine would give me a headache?

That I was stupidly trusting and just as impatient? I could never wait for anything . . . Was harsh and impetuous . . .

That for my whole, entire life I adored and idolized Shchedrin? And that I wrote thousands of pages of letters to him — from every country, every city, every hotel on all my tours? Those letters stand me in good stead now — colorful, crumpled pieces of hotel stationary with the crests of my havens: Holiday Inn, Palace, Intercontinental, Meridien, Osaka Grand, Savoy, Windsor. Day after day they record all my unkempt, unpolished information — from the most serious to complete nonsense. The chronicle of my life!

Or should I tell you, my reader, about my ballet, my professional habits? That before every class, every performance I poured warm water into the heels of my ballet slippers (to make the foot sit more firmly).

That I twisted Soviet one-kopeck coins into my leotards at the hips to tightly pull the ends of the ribbon at the waist: that made the leotards fit better?

That more than anything else I worried that I might forget to look at myself in the mirror before going onstage — to make sure my mouth was juicily painted, that my eyes were well-outlined, so that I wouldn't look like a colorless moth in public?

What about all this — is it just nonsense and trifles? Or do the trifles complete your picture of me?

What have I learned from my life, what philosophy?

The simplest. As simple as a mug of water or a gulp of air. People are not divided up into classes, races, and state systems. People are divided into bad and good. Into very good and very bad. That's all. Bloodthirsty revolutionaries, who swore in a frenzy that the bad people would at last be replaced by only good ones were lying. There were always more bad people throughout the centuries, many more. The good ones are always an exception, a gift from above. So much wisdom, so much that is obvious was spoken through the centuries — by Christ, Buddha, Confucius, Avvakum* . . . Did people listen and understand? And so blood flows, lives are lost, fates and hopes twisted. And this will continue, there

---

*Seventeenth-century leader of the Old Believers, who separated from the Russian Orthodox Church.

is no doubt about that, alas. Human biology is such. Envy, greed, infidelity, lies, treachery, cruelty, ingratitude . . . How can responsiveness, sensitivity, compassion, kindness, and self-sacrifice withstand them? They can't. It's an unequal combat. But in every generation, in every corner of the world, in god-forsaken areas, good people are born and bear their cross. Our world depends on them. There's a Russian saying that covers it very well: there isn't a village without a righteous person.

Reducing my problems and struggles just to that damned Soviet system would be frivolous. It all happened; it did. It was vile and disgusting. But so many of my problems were caused by common envy, ambition, puffed-up conceit, slander, and ridiculous rumors. One of our musicians who now lives in the West once cried out angrily, "That prima donna X has a bank director husband. That's worse than a secretary of the Party committee."

Hardest of all for me was retaining my independence. Now that's a luxury. Busybodies kept trying to push me into their groups, hustle me under their mediocre banners, tuck me into their ranks. I was guilty of many things, but that's not one of them. Let me reiterate: I was *independent*. I worked very hard at that.

We *never* had any privileges from the powers-that-be, no special meals, no state-owned apartments or dachas. We earned everything by our sweat and labor. The delirium of a Western journalist who scribbled a fat book about the grim life in the Soviet Union (without ever having come anywhere close to either Shchedrin or myself) parrots the vicious lie heard from some envious slanderer that we got special food parcels from the Kremlin: slander. Plisetskaya and Shchedrin didn't even know the address of that heavenly institution. We bought all our food at Moscow markets. And we got some goodies from the buffets of the Bolshoi.

For an envious, jealous person, a little Salieri, to say that Plisetskaya can't dance or that Shchedrin writes bad music would be unreliable: a journalist could watch and listen and realize that it was just envy talking. But if he hears about the food parcels, about the establishment, the journalist's politicized ears will perk up, and he'll quickly divide things into black and white, good and evil—after a leg of veal and boiled asparagus, followed by a bottle of good burgundy: I am a famous Sovietologist, ladies and gentlemen, and I know all kinds of secrets about Russia. (When in fact he's spent only a few months in Russia, doesn't speak the language, and whatever lies he was told at the slanderer's house between the borscht and the chicken Kiev, he sticks in his book.)

I despise both—the slanderers and the pseudo-scholars.

Oh, if only I could be born today in some prosperous place like Iceland or Connecticut. And start from scratch. With a free passport, which doesn't require you to beg for a visa, to hang about consulates and embassies, encountering nothing but dryness and hostility at the very sight of a Russian passport. Worrying that there are only a few pages left in my passport, two or three more countries and the passport is over, and I'll have to go plead for a new one. All that humiliation, suffering, stress.

And it wouldn't be bad to be born in Canada or Luxembourg. But I was born in Moscow. In Stalin's kingdom. Then I lived under Khrushchev, under Brezhnev, under Andropov, Chernenko, Gorbachev, and Yeltsin . . . And I'll never be born a second time, no matter how I try. Live the life you have!

So I did. I tell myself it was lived honestly. I did no harm to children, old people, or our younger brothers the animals. I did not betray friends. I paid my debts. I never envied anyone. I lived for and by my work. I lived for ballet. I did not know how to do anything else well.

I didn't do enough. I could have done much more. But I give thanks for what I had. Thanks to my nature for helping me survive, not break, and not give up.

Chapter Forty-Two

My Ballets

We have a dance combination called "Ivan Averyanovich." A Moscow ballet legend explains the name: Once upon a time there lived a certain dancer who worked at the Bolshoi Theater. His name was Ivan Averyanovich (his family name is also preserved—Sidorov). He danced. He rehearsed. At one rehearsal Ivan Averyanovich was executing a big jeté, that is, a jump. Just as he got aloft, strained, and put a smile on his face, and while he was admiring himself in a mirror, someone behind him abruptly called out: "Ivan Averyanovich!"

Ivan Averyanovich managed adroitly to make a 180-degree turn up in the air, yell "Huh?" in response, turn around again, and land successfully in an arabesque. That's how this trick named in honor of its creator got into everyday use in dance. Our Ivan Averyanovich became a choreographer by circumstance.

Something similar happened to me, too. I was never dying to get into choreography. I was never racked with burning passion for it, although I've always had an abundance of fantasies and ideas. By nature I'm more of a performer. My choreographic experiments appeared in the world by dint of circumstance. For example, I've already written about staging Dvořák's "Melody" for my Czech tour. I had to dance something Slavic and there was no choreographer on hand, so I got down to business myself. It didn't turn out to be a masterpiece, but it's no worse than other works by other people — the audience watched it and applauded.

It was on the set, during the shoot of the dramatic film *Anna Karenina,* in which I performed the role of Princess Betsy Tverskaya, that the idea of a choreographic embodiment of Tolstoy's novel began to hover in the air. I steadfastly cherished the memory of the questions Ingrid Bergman and Jacqueline Kennedy had asked me long ago. The music Shchedrin wrote for the film was theatrical and adaptable. One could dance to it. This also stimulated me. I was fascinated as I watched Tanya Samoilova move toward Tolstoy's figure scene after scene. Director Zarkhi's speeches to Samoilova before the camera rolled often angered me. It would have been better to focus the actress's attention on something else, even the exact opposite. My inner dispute with the director went on nearly throughout the entire filming. To top it off, Shchedrin also had a knock-down, drag-out quarrel with Zarkhi: the director cut up his music carelessly and shamelessly.

"We'll do the ballet differently. Completely the way we want to."

Who would choreograph it? I went through names alphabetically, as if they were telephone directory listings. This one could do it, but he wouldn't be allowed into the Bolshoi. This one would do it, but no one wants him. That's why he'd be accepted, because he's ordinary. This other one is weak as a dramatist, and if you're going to take on a famous novel — things won't work without strong libretto.

The first name I seriously settled on was Igor Belsky. I love his *Leningrad Symphony,* which he based on Shostakovich's music, and his staging of Shchedrin's *Little Humpbacked Horse* at the Leningrad Maly Opera Theater. We talked on the phone. Igor immediately came to Moscow from Leningrad. And we talked, fantasized, argued. Belsky agreed — "I have some ideas" — as long as the Bolshoi accepted him. We saw the Red Arrow off at 23:59 from the Leningrad Terminal. Looking out from behind the implacable obese mass of a female conductor, Igor yelled from the railcar platform as the train pulled out, "We'll talk on the phone tomorrow."

But the next day, instead of the phone call, a telegram arrived. Rejection. Belsky refused. The arguments were formal ones. I presumed that an unavoidable conflict with the head of the Bolshoi was what stopped him. Then we met with Kasatkina and Vasilyov. They agreed immediately, too. They said they would also do the libretto themselves. During the next conversation Vasilyov explained to us that the set would resemble a glass tumbler from which Anna cannot extricate herself for the duration of the performance. *Anna* in a glass is the idea," Vasilyov explained maliciously. It would be a thirty- to forty-minute, one-act ballet. The entire conflict in the love triangle would be repeated by the children — a girl and two boys.

I thought, No, I don't want such a modernist style. And in desperation I brazenly declared, "I'm going to stage the ballet myself."

The next step was a meeting with the dramatic director, Valentin Pluchek. Pluchek had formerly been an actor in Meyerhold's theater. He had been friendly with him and had performed in his sensational productions of Mayakovsky's plays. After the theater was destroyed, Pluchek got a job in a semiprofessional navy troupe in Murmansk. That was where he waited out all those long, terrible years. And he survived, dammit. His cousin was Peter Brook, the English director (in perceptive parents, Peter Brook took the lead), but more important, the Lord God gave Pluchek talent.

We spent several evenings throwing out ideas in the office of the chief director of the Theater of Satire — V. N. Pluchek's office. One of Pluchek's ideas was to bring more intelligent people together into a team. "Start with good ingredients. The soup will cook itself."

He named Lvov-Anokhin — "He will be able to set out what we decide in a literary way." He recommended the artist Valery Levental: "Valery is a playwright by nature."

"Maya, both staging an entire ballet by yourself as well as dancing in it won't work. Creating a feature-length performance piece is a diabolical expenditure of energy. And you want to dance Anna, too. You must, without fail, get yourself some assistants. Give them all the crowd scenes. Strictly speaking, for you the figure of Anna is most important. Well, and Vronsky and Karenin, too. Their plot lines."

I made note of the couple Ryzhenko and Smirnova-Golovanova — both dancers at the Bolshoi. They have choreographic experience in television films. *Daring Ditties* with Vladimirov and Sorokina in the title roles was a successful, mature work. Besides which, Ryzhenko is from my *Carmen* team. We understand each another without strain. And the artist Valery Levental. That was our team.

We had a team. But was there a playing field? I wrote a substantiated letter of request addressed to Furtseva. I set forth my arguments for putting Anna Arkadyevna Karenina on the Bolshoi ballet stage. We would need space for two orchestras (winds onstage and a symphony in the pit). Seven operas have been written based on the plot of Tolstoy's novel, but there's not a single ballet based on it. We would be the "first in space." The troupe would have an opening next season; we could fit it into the two empty months.

But after *Carmen Suite*, trust in me was decidedly undermined, and Furtseva asked the logical question: "Do you have the music? When Shchedrin writes the ballet, then we'll talk. That's when we'll also have to set up a preliminary hearing in the theater. Let the specialists sort it out. Express their educated opinions. You can present your ideas there in the company of enlightened people; it's premature for me to listen to you today. Let the collective decide. Comrades, we must trust the opinion of the collective." Shchedrin finished the score by the end of the summer. That was also when my niece, who was baptized Anna in honor of the completion of the composition, was born. But her patronymic is Alexandrovna not Arkadyevna, since she is my brother Alexander's daughter.

Yuri Muromtsev, then-director of the Bolshoi, arranged the preview at the Ministry of Culture's instructions. A mass of people crowded into the Bolshoi's Beethoven Hall. Before it began, I presented the general design of the ballet, referring constantly to a summary prepared at home (we had worked on it as a team the night before until the roosters crowed). Gesturing gently, Lvov-Anokhin impressively discoursed in his well-trained actor's voice on Stanislavsky and Nemirovich-Danchenko's ideas about Tolstoy's creation. That scholarly speech was also part of our homework. Essential color. We had to convince the audience that Lev Nikolayevich Tolstoy was intuitively thinking about ballet primarily as he was writing the novel. The audience became interested.

Lvov-Anokhin's flowery speech had its effect. The sentimental reminiscence about the genesis of Tolstoy's work particularly got to the audience: how, in postprandial drowsiness, Tolstoy saw a black curl of hair on Countess Hartung's (Pushkin's daughter) snow-white neck. The memoirist swore that this dream vision of the curl gave the writer his initial stimulus to write *Anna Karenina*. Several ladies took out their handkerchiefs. Even a preview has to be staged.

We persistently and unabashedly emphasized those lines from Tolstoy where the novelist speaks about the heroine's movements, light gait, the way she behaved at the Moscow ball. And naturally about the figure of the station *muzhik*, forging iron and condemning her with the menacing augury in French: "You'll die giving birth, ma'am, giving birth." This figure is truly strange, frightful, and inexplicable. I am still completely convinced that only the art of movement truly has the power to embody the mystery, the enigma of Tolstoy's fantasies.

Then Rodion talked about Tolstoy's reverence for Tchaikovsky and vice versa. He told how Lev Nikolayevich cried while listening to Pyotr Ilyich's string quartet with variations on the theme "Vanya, Sitting on the Couch Smoking Tobacco in a Pipe." He explained that he himself used micro-quotes in the fabric of his own composition from the works of Tchaikovsky that were written during the years that Tolstoy was writing the novel. The aroma of those times, their connections!

Next Rodion sat down at the piano and played the entire ballet. From beginning to end . . . That very same ending where the clattering of iron wheels against the joints of the rails melts into oblivion. He produced these sounds by rapping his knuckles on the wood of the instrument's lid.

We were well prepared. We were serious about this hearing and won the round. Not with a knockout but on points, which was sufficient. The majority of those present, especially the musicians, supported our venture, praised the music, and spoke in favor of the ballet's speedy inclusion into the theater schedule. The singer Irina Arkhipova, who possessed considerable authority in the theater — she was a deputy in the Supreme Soviet of the USSR from the Sverdlovsk district of Moscow where the Bolshoi Theater and the Kremlin itself were located — passionately advocated the immediate start of rehearsals. "This is so interesting. We could use something like this in the opera."

Director Muromtsev tried to lead the discussion into the thickets of vagueness — that, apparently, was how the agenda for the day had been planned — but he was not supported by those who spoke. The reins of party authority in art weakened with each year. Not everyone was obedient anymore.

I sat next to Ulanova and explained to her in a whisper what was going on onstage during this music and that . . . Galina Sergeyevna remained silent during the discussion. But since she didn't object, did that mean "for"?

And now the first production rehearsal. Both the date and the number of the rehearsal hall are written down in my journal. October 25, 1971, Hall 3. There were two of us — the pianist Irina Zaitseva and me. My first try was Anna's solo mazurka at the Moscow ball. With a bouquet of pansies in her hair, as my heroine was portrayed by Tolstoy's pen. It's not hard to stage a mazurka. It's just a mazurka. But this was Anna Karenina's mazurka. That's why I was in agony, torn up, endlessly redoing it, sifting through variations. The first number took me four days.

Then I sketched out my variation — The Snowstorm, an echo of Tolstoy's scene on the snow-covered platform in Bologoe. The unforeseen meeting with Count Vronsky. Then I tackled the final scenes of the third act. My monologues. And then rushed off to Leningrad to show my work to Yakobson. I've already written about this.

The production of any ballet is a tentative affair. A rehearsal time is scheduled. But suddenly someone has to replace an indisposed performer that night. The rehearsal is wrecked. Everyone is twitchy and irritable. Some other dancer implacably goes off on a trip, even though half the part was made on him. Teaching a new dancer when you're pressed for time is a waste of time. The corps de ballet has forgotten everything it worked on yesterday. Muddles things. The days fly away so quickly that the vile feeling of panic begins to creep into you.

But finally we had the ballet staged in its rough form. I couldn't believe it myself. The rehearsals were brought from the studios out onstage. At first by acts with piano accompaniment. Then with the orchestra . . .

But the most difficult part was just beginning . . .

A ministerial committee descended upon us during the first orchestral run-through of *Anna*. Furtseva herself was with them. The familiar faces of members of the Artistic Council of the Bolshoi flashed by. All the judges seated themselves at their leisure in the orchestra seats of the auditorium. I was dressed and in makeup — I was warming up on the stage. I was tuning myself up, as if I were an orchestra. Panting, people suddenly began to nervously overtake me — some from the wardrobe department, some members of the my second cast: "Maya Mikhailovna, the doors to the auditorium are closed. They're not letting anyone in the main door."

"Get seats in the boxes."

"What boxes! They're also locked."

"Go up to the dress circle."

"It's closed up there, too."

"What, have they gone off their rockers?"

"The theater is full of ushers, they've been herded in as if for an evening performance."

"Wait for me. I'm going to the director."

But the door from the stage to the director's box was also securely locked. I pressed the bell button, banged on the door, I yelled. Useless. What, had they all croaked behind that damn door? I was at a loss. Maybe I should run to the theater manager's office.

Sasha Sokolov, who was leading the rehearsal today, caught up with me: "Mayechka, the conductor's in the orchestra. We're starting." I heard the first plaintive sounds of the ballet already, coming from behind the closed brocade curtain. We had to dance. We would sort it out during intermission.

We ended the duet, which we called Anna's Fall, with Maris Liepa (he was Vronsky). The first act ends there, too. I saw Shchedrin on the stage.

"How was it?" Then, without waiting for a reply, I asked, "Are the doors really locked? How did you get into the auditorium?"

Rodion grinned: "I crawled through the orchestra barrier."

"You're kidding?"

"Wish I were."

"But what's going on? How can they not allow the second cast in? It's essential that they see this."

"They say it's Kukharsky's instructions."

"They've truly gone mad."

Right after it was over, there was a discussion of the piece in Director Muromtsev's office. The general tone of the voices was grim. The attempt is not successful, Tolstoy's novel cannot be danced, everything is raw, unconvincing, the music is noisy. Anna Karenina drops down onto Vronsky in her negligee: eroticism again (Furtseva was the one concerned about this, as usual).

"But after all, that's one of the methods, Ekaterina Alexeyevna," Shchedrin joked, trying to turn the sexophobia into humor.

The minister started to get angry: "The ballet still needs a lot of work. There will be no premiere this season. As for the future—we'll see," Furtseva said.

Nevertheless we did not give up. I launched into an attack: "Why were the house doors locked? I cannot in all my life remember a case when the second cast couldn't see the run-through of a production."

"Yes, it's the ministry's orders," Kukharsky, Furtseva's hitherto silent deputy, hissed at me. "There's no point in spreading rumors around Moscow."

"What rumors? But this is merely *Anna Karenina*. It's not political. What are you afraid of? What rumors?"

"We're afraid of discrediting Tolstoy's great name, Maya Mikhailovna." Tolstoy would have not only left Yasnaya Polyana on foot to get away from defenders like these, he would have set out on his way from Russia.

Sofia Golovkina, who was a virtuoso at winning the trust and friendship of generations of the cream of Soviet *nomenklatura* elite ("dancing granddaughters" bound Golovkina closer than blood ties), tugged at Furtseva's sleeve; time to leave. They had discussed the matter, given their advice, and that was sufficient; high time to stop. Matters of far greater importance awaited them. She whispered something right into her ear. Furtseva's granddaughter Marina was also studying with Golovkina at the Choreographic School (incidentally, this girl was talented in ballet, but after Furtseva's suicide, Golovkina expelled her).

Suddenly Furtseva addressed Ulanova. Ulanova was there, too, but hadn't uttered a word yet. "Galina Sergeyevna, tell us your opinion."

Her address was unexpected, and Ulanova quailed. "It's difficult for me to reply. I haven't grasped it. Assessing it from a first look."

"We're all doing it 'from a first look.' But then, you're a professional."

"I am. But no, I can't presume."

Furtseva was a direct person and could speak straight from the hip. "Galina Sergeyevna, would you at least repeat what you told me during the intermission?" Furtseva needed authoritative support in rejecting my *Anna*.

Ulanova shrank as if huddling from the cold: "At one time we also tried to create a ballet based on Balzac's *Lost Illusions* . . . but it didn't work out then either," G. S. whispered in a meek voice.

I was silent, but the word *also* crushed me.

A monstrous trial had been organized at the first — take note, first! — orchestral run-through of a ballet. The committee dropped in completely without warning. People couldn't get into the auditorium. It was locked. There were usher-sentries at the locked doors. The dancers were hearing the orchestral version for the first time. The echoing emptiness of the five-tier, two thousand–seat auditorium spoiled the artistic atmosphere. And the orchestra members — following the ancient habit of musicians — craned their necks out of the orchestra pit to see what was going on onstage. Conductor Simonov kept drowning out the music with his shouts, appealing to the conscience of the players: "Play, don't look at the stage, you'll get your fill."

The sets were up, but not illuminated. A dirty gray service light flooded the stage. The servants' candelabras — and they are a constructive part of the choreography — were not lit, the batteries hadn't been readied yet. The servants moved what looked like three-fingered phalluses in the semi-darkness. Some danced in unfinished costumes, one in a worn-out Adidas track suit. The fur coats of the passengers on the platforms of the Nikolayevsky Station (sewn by the wardrobe workshops following Levental's sketches) were completely authentic. They were so heavy and cumbersome that Ryzhenko cut out their linings and shortened the hems with scissors right there in front of everyone. In the theater, the first full rehearsal is called the one from hell. We had so many components, so many performers. To pass judgment after such a rehearsal was a blow below the belt.

How inconsistent authorities are! At first they gave us permission to create the ballet — now they were destroying it before it was born, on the vine.

Rodion told me that when *Anna Karenina* was staged in Belgrade a year later, he kept waiting from one rehearsal to the next for the committee to show up. Would they allow it, approve it, would they find fault with it? He would twist his neck around at the slightest noise in the auditorium, thinking that the committee had finally arrived. And at the final rehearsal, the night before the premiere, he couldn't restrain himself and asked the conductor Dusan Miladinovic, "When is the show going to be approved, when is the committee?"

"We are the committee — you, me, and the choreographer Parlic."

That's how they had deformed us in our native homeland.

While people left, I lingered near the director's office door. And he was back — he had accompanied Furtseva to her black limousine — climbing the stairs to his office.

Dejectedly staring at the floor, I asked the director, "Yuri Vladimirovich, won't I get to rehearse *Anna* any more?"

"Why not? You can continue rehearsing."

"Will they give me an orchestra? And a stage?"

"The orchestra and stage are taken. Rehearse in the classrooms with a piano."

I looked up at Muromtsev.

"But the ballet will not be performed, Maya Mikhailovna."

"This season?"

"There's no room for *Anna Karenina* next season."

"Does that mean never?"

Muromtsev wanted to get through to his office without saying anything in response. I held his arm. "So what's the point of rehearsing, Yuri Vladimirovich?" The director freed his arm and disappeared beyond the dull whiteness of the tall door.

The subdued Karenina team met at our place on Gorky Street. Gulping down gallons of tea with Katya's sandwiches, we wondered, Should we rehearse? Or stop? Everyone was so troubled and devastated that conversation was difficult. We would discuss it tomorrow. Those who enjoy a drink opened a bottle of Stolichnaya to ease their tension.

The next morning I was called to the theater house phone during class. It was the director's secretary, Nina Georgievna. "Maya Mikhailovna, after class call Kukharsky at the ministry from our phone. As soon as possible."

What else lay ahead for me? What unpleasantness? Vasily Kukharsky, like a black demon, had always brought our family dismal troubles and burdens. He joined the militia during the first days of the war and been seriously wounded. His leg had been amputated. Naturally, his disability had made him irritable and unkind.

When I, along with a number of other members of the intelligentsia, signed an anti-Stalinist letter addressed to Brezhnev in which we demanded that the creeping process of Stalin's rehabilitation after Khrushchev's ouster be stopped, the letter received wide publicity. The Voice of America repeated it hourly. Kukharsky took a dislike to me. He went on the attack for Stalin, for the Homeland; the fist raised against his idol Stalin was hateful to him. I fell into disfavor. It was Kukharsky who made up trite arrangements of well-known names for collective letters of support-condemnation-protest, inserting my name many times in this sewage, without even thinking of asking my permission, without even informing or calling me. There was always something shameful in these letters, as if you were being undressed in front of people, and Kukharsky, sensing this internally, would invariably include in the alphabetical cartridge clip of "protesters and supporters" those whom he didn't like. His own pals he protected and would unintentionally forget their names when managing the servile work of fulfilling the next order from the highest party level. Troops were sent into Afghanistan — the intelligentsia had to instantly support the "wisdom" of the criminal decision. To wallow around in crap. Czechoslovakia was being strangled — again — Intelligentsia, applaud your government. I am completely certain that the majority of the collective letters never really existed. They were composed in Kukharsky's office, and the signatures on them were added there, too . . .

I call from the director's box. Kukharsky's secretary is keenly interested: "Are you calling from the theater, Maya Mikhailovna?"

"Yes, from Nina Georgievna's."

"Vasily Feodosievich will get on the line right now."

I see myself in the mirror in passing, how bristled up and tense I have gotten at Kukharsky's friendly, cordial voice: "Maya Mikhailovna, thank you for calling. Would you be able to drive over here to my office at two o'clock? But come alone. Don't let your husband, Rodion, know about our meeting. I insist."

Not a chance, I say to myself out loud, already dialing our telephone number so I can catch him at home.

"Well, what's come down? Are you calling from the director's box?" I relate the conversation with Kukharsky in one breath.

"I'll be at the first entrance in twenty minutes."

We'll enter Kukharsky's lair together. When we walk into the office of Deputy Minister of Soviet Culture V. F. Kukharsky, he tries to turn his dirty trick into a joke: "I wanted to tell you that I loved you without your husband present, but I'll have to postpone it until next time."

We don't smile.

"Here's what I have to tell you. Ekaterina Alexeyevna flew to Vietnam today. And she asked me to explain to Maya Mikhailovna that rehearsals of *Anna* in the theater should be stopped this season. You can continue the studio work with your assistants, but we won't be able to give you the troupe, the orchestra, and the stage."

I won't recount our nervous, highly charged conversation. Reader, you've already guessed that *Anna Karenina* was banned . . .

At the evening council at the annex on Gorky Street again, we decided to appeal to P. N. Demichev, to the Central Committee, where he was in charge of science and art in those years — actually a minister of culture, too, but of a higher order. Suppose he helped out . . . You couldn't overlook Kukharsky, he was as stubborn as Gogol's Head, while Furtseva, we heard, was leaving Vietnam to travel either to Singapore or to Malaysia. How long could we wait for her to return?

All of human life consists of accidents and of luck, good and bad. If Furtseva hadn't flown to Vietnam, we probably wouldn't have gone over her head to try to see Demichev. For that would mean giving offense and starting a feud. Forever. We would have stepped on Furtseva's toes. And here was fate itself taking care of things. But would we get to Pyotr Nilovich? He was so high up on the totem pole. His title was secretary of the Central Committee of the Communist Party of the Soviet Union.

Future generations, let me advise you. Listen to me. Don't submit, don't submit until the very end. *Do not submit.* Even then — fight, shoot back, blow your horns, beat your drums, make phone calls, and send telegrams from the post office, don't give up, struggle, fight until the very last moment. It has happened — even totalitarian regimes have backed down in the face of obsession, conviction, and drive. My victories rested only on this. Nothing else! Character is indeed destiny.

Demichev saw us quickly. Rodion and I explained to him the disastrous nature of the situation. The soloists, the corps de ballet, the orchestra, the workshops had accomplished an enormous amount of work. We had to get our show ready. It was absolutely imperative to get it ready. The court's verdict — the death penalty! — couldn't be pronounced at the first, "hell" rehearsal. Even if the show were allowed to return next season, it would be too late, everything would be forgotten! We'd have to start all over again. And people would cool off, become indifferent. There was no sex, no politics in *Anna* — all the dresses in it were long, everyone's thighs were covered. We were just dying to create a new ballet. All we wanted was creativity, that's all . . .

Demichev listened to us cordially. We were seeing him up close for the first time. Up close, he was simpler and gentler than his image in the portraits that participants carry in May Day rallies. Demichev spoke softly, unhurriedly, liltingly. Everything *piano,* everything in the same intonation. At times his voice grew so quiet that it was impossible to make out what he was saying. We strained, we stretched our necks and, at times, we guessed the meaning of his words only by reading his lips.

A heavily starched waitress brought in fragrant tea with crackers.

"I share your anxiety. Even if the attempt to embody *Anna Karenina* in ballet form will not turn out to be very successful, the ministry should support you for your daring. It has to be seen through to the end. I'll deal with it."

We left, encouraged. Was this really salvation?

In those years, people in Russia hadn't forgotten how to obey their superiors. Director Muromtsev summoned me to his office. This time he was courtesy itself. How easy life must be for people without convictions. Should the wind blow from the heavens, you speak in direct contradiction to what you said yesterday.

"Maya Mikhailovna, work on *Anna* must be seen through to the end. The ballet has memorable scenes. 'The Horse Race' seems to me a definite success. I gave instructions to find the time for stage rehearsals for you."

The wheel turned backward. The orchestra also found time, as did the lighting people, and the stage was suddenly empty . . .

Performing in *Anna* was a joy and a success for the excellent soloists.

My good friends, my marvelous kindred spirits, who shared my views, my kindred ballet folk, subjugated tribe of dancers! How you helped me in the days of battle for my unwanted *Anna.*

Maris Liepa, Sasha Godunov were ardent Vronskys. Kolya Fadeyechev, Volodya Tikhonov were gloomy, graphic Karenins. Marina Kondratieva was the second Anna. Yura Vladimirov was the menacing station *muzhik,* soaring in the air and condemning Anna. Nina Sorokina, Natasha Sedykh danced Kitty. Allochka Boguslavskaya was a restrained, arrogant Betsy. (I am mentioning those who performed in the premiere performances). Thank you for not losing faith, not retreating, not dropping or slipping out of the game that the bosses finally lost.

But I'm running ahead. Everything is better in order . . .

The rehearsals started up again. The ballet was beginning to take shape. The dress rehearsal. The committee was back again. Furtseva with her deputies again. But this time there was an audience in the house — people from the workshops, pensioners, relatives, friends of the performers, musicians, critics, and Moscow theater-goers. It was much easier for those of us onstage to dance when there was breathing in the auditorium, and it wasn't dead and icy. Everything went better than that first, "hellish" time.

Another discussion in Director Muromtsev's office. But this time the speeches were not so hopeless: no need to wear black, mourning at a requiem. Word that Demichev had lent a hand to save our creation spread in a flash. In Russia no news, either good or bad, stands still. The chief choreographer* of the theater had not shown up. There was no need to push the previous discussion off a cliff — we were falling down like cast-iron weights. The best way was for the chief choreographer not to attend.

But we had lost too much time. It was already June. The season at the Bolshoi ended in a week and a half. If we could have only rehearsed more, given the alternate cast a dress rehearsal, but then we would have had to postpone the premiere to the fall. Extremely dangerous. We would have had to survive until the fall. What if something had happened?

Everybody became so sweet. Compliant. They said, "Decide for yourselves. It's up to you."

We — the entire "Karenina brotherhood" — met in the deserted auditorium. I put a stop the arguments: "Let Shchedrin decide. How he feels is the way it will be." Everyone froze in anticipation. Rodion said nothing. He was silent for an entire minute. He weighed the pros and cons.

"We'll open the day after tomorrow. We shouldn't postpone or reschedule." We informed Director Muromtsev of our decision.

On a glass plaque, near the main doors of the Bolshoi, behind the columns, where people who didn't buy their tickets in advance try one last time, is a list of the performances in the coming days: *The Tsar's Bride*, opera, music by N. Rimsky-Korsakov; *Traviata*, opera, music by G. Verdi; *Eugene Onegin*, opera, music by P. Tchaikovsky; *Madame Butterfly*, opera, music by G. Puccini. In the slot for the date June 10: "There will a special announcement about the performance."

Shura Krasnogorova's voice, choking and breaking up in the telephone receiver: "Maya Mikhailovna, *Anna* has been announced. They changed 'special announcement' to *Anna Karenina*, ballet, music by R. Shchedrin, premiere . . ."

"When did they change it? Did you see it yourself?"

"Five minutes ago. I'm calling from the pay phone on Theater Square."

"Is that for sure?"

"Couldn't be more exact. I just read it. I'm calling from the box office — it's directly opposite."

That was normal. That was the way it should be. But joy was literally choking

---

*A reference to Yuri Grigorovich. See chapter 47.

me. Happiness stopped my breath. I had to live another two days, only two days and . . .

We were like small children, squealing and pushing about as we got into the car. Into our Volga. Rodion raced at illegal speed over to the Bolshoi.

A warm June evening. It was still light. We noisily ran to the columns. Passersby looked back at us with disapproval. Who were those characters? The Stone Apollo winked conspiratorially at me from his chariot. Can you go crazy from happiness?

Everything was exactly as Shura said, except it said "mus. by R. Shchedrin," not "music by R. Shchedrin." But then, that was the same thing. I just had to live another two days!

I usually come to a performance two and a half hours early. The day of *Anna*'s premiere I came four hours early. Pierre Cardin and his Japanese traveling companion and secretary Yushi Takata managed to fly in from Paris that day. He came to the theater straight from the airport. I had to model his great costumes for him, before the audience saw them. But would Pierre be upset that his name wasn't in the playbill? Director Muromtsev didn't even want to hear about it: the ministry refused outright.

The violins and flutes began to sing their sad melody. The performance started. Help us, oh Lord!

I stood in the second wing in Cardin's black fur coat, with its luxurious bow at the waist. On my head was a tiny hat with a thin veil. The hat really was very similar to the one I wore when I met Jacqueline Kennedy at the White House. Yoo-hoo, fate. My hands were wrapped in a muff by Cardin, velvet with a black rose. I saw that the projection of snow falling on the stooping lampposts of the terminal of the Nikolayevsky rail line was switched on . . . Flakes, snowflakes . . . I stepped into a bourrée.

Shchedrin watched the performance in the light room in the dress circle. The ballet was still tacked together loosely. Rodion prompted the light artist Boris Lelyukhin about the changes in positions in the musical score as it was being played. Valery Levental was also right there.

My assistants Ryzhenko and Smirnov—also because of the loose tacking— rushed around in the wings: safeguarding the entrances of the dancers and arranging the set changes. Ryzhenko had the piano reduction of the ballet in her hands; she reads music fluently.

The Train Terminal seemed to go well . . . The first meeting with Vronsky took place. The station *muzhik* with the dead body . . .

The Ball was successful. The heavy chandeliers were lowered on cue, in time with the music. The servants' candelabras lit up in unison. My solo mazurka with the lilac pansies was fine. I did all the turns well . . .

Now the Snowstorm. I danced a headlong variation in the darkness, in a blizzard of snowy gusts. The rays of the front floodlights mercilessly blinded me. Just so I didn't screw it up. No, everything went smoothly.

Betsy's Salon was not difficult. As long as they rolled out the white piano in time. How about it? Excellent. They weren't late.

I heard the music of Karenin's Office. The hoarse solo of the bass. How was Fadeyechev executing his chess moves?

The flute yearned. It was now my cue. Our scene. Everything was successful. Now my long, rapid exit in bourrée from the proscenium to the extreme back of the stage. I enclosed my face with my hands: "Too late, it's too late."

Anna's Dream with my four understudies. A break for me. I stared from the wings on the right side. Makeup artist Nina Nestratova dabbed my face with a state-issue towel. My face was damp. I waved it off: "Nina, get away from me, don't block my view." Well done, girls, they didn't forget anything, didn't get mixed up.

A new light position. Maris-Vronsky is alone in his bedroom.

And most difficult for me in the first act—Anna's Fall. To have enough strength. You have to reveal yourself, turn yourself inside out. All the lifts were successful. Not a single one fell through. After an outburst of emotions—relaxed, dying away. I swayed in Liepa's arms like a pendulum on the clock of eternity.

The hushed audience exploded into applause. That audience was a difficult one. All of Moscow. Those who believed in our project and evil-tongued skeptics, cold cynics who know everything and everyone ahead of time. Carefree, sweet foreigners who read the plot of the ballet in the playbill with their translators: how will this little story end? And my close, dear, beloved Moscow audience. My audience. An audience that stood at the Bolshoi box office all through the night in order to get into the top balcony for my premiere.

Act Two. The Races . . . Anna's Confession . . . The Wrede Garden . . . Illness . . . Dreams . . . Departure to Italy.

Act Three. The Ceremony at the Palace . . . Meeting Her Son (After Vrubel's Drawing) . . . The Italian Opera . . . Rejection by Society . . . Argument with Vronsky . . . The Obiralovka Station . . . My Tormenting Conscience—The Station Railroad Trackman.

The performance has gone well right up to the last scene. We are on the edge. Everyone has danced better than at rehearsals. Only the finale remains. I am alone. The pre-death monologue. Now everything depends on nobody but me. I have to gather up all my strength. How I perform the epilogue will decide the fate of the ballet.

The stroboscopes . . . And there are people, people everywhere. There are so many of them, no end to them, and they all despise one another. What are these churches for, this bell ringing? Everything is untruth, everything is lies, everything is deceit, everything is evil. Where am I? What am I doing? Why? Lord God, forgive me.

Making the sign of the cross.

Collapsing on my knees.

The solar flare of the locomotive's headlight.

The lights of the train that crushed me receding in the distance.

The clattering of wheels.

The music of the track ties.

The performance happened.

We—I think—won!

Chapter Forty-Three

My Ballets (Continued)

I am dancing in the French city of Rennes. It's in Brittany. I'm dancing *The Madwoman of Chaillot*. Two evenings in a row.

What's today's date? The 2nd. The month? April. The year — I won't be mistaken — is 1993. Which means that I have been dancing exactly fifty years today. Dancing with the title of ballerina. Which means that exactly fifty years ago today I was accepted into the Bolshoi Ballet troupe. Actually that isn't a bad record — dancing before the public for exactly fifty years. Fifty to the day. Then again, I can dance, but is my dancing worth watching? Since I'm still being invited to do so — then it is.

Here in Rennes, I continue my work on this book. I've already spoken about *Anna Karenina*. I'll add only that the future of this ballet on the stage was quite successful. It ran at the Bolshoi more than a hundred times. It went on tour and was staged in other countries. It was made into a film, and shot successfully. Is it not the best cinematographic attempt to show ballet on the screen?

Margarita Pilikhina, who produced the ballet film, also worked behind the camera. This was her final work. Cancer was implacably devouring her body and soul. During the shoot, assistants carried Margarita in an armchair, brought her up to the viewfinder of the camera on crossed arms, and carefully picked her up off the floor when, in her weakened state, she collapsed flat on her back. Pilikhina was a strong individual and bore her pre-death cross stoically. Her creative power did not diminish in spite of her physical torment. Her genes helped here — Margarita was Marshal Zhukov's niece. Nonetheless, she didn't get to shoot the last two scenes. Death showed her no mercy. Clips from the roughs were included in the film. But even these small flaws did not damage the film.

Godunov was filmed in the part of Vronsky with me. When the film was already in the last stages of editing, we left on a scheduled American tour without waiting for the finish. Sasha told me in the plane that he was not planning to return to the USSR again.

"But then our filming of *Anna* will go to waste. Wait until the film comes out on the screen. And then . . . Next time you can stay."

Sasha Godunov was a man of his word. "Fine. I'll wait. Maybe, next time — together?" And Godunov kept his word. He stayed. But I didn't have a "next time" with him.

The "next time" was Chekhov's *The Seagull*.

Anton Pavlovich's play is all enigma. Why was its premiere at St. Petersburg's Alexandrovsky Theater such a stunning flop? A failure with the great Komissarzhevskaya as Nina. Why was it such an ecstatic success two years later in the Moscow Art Theater with Roksanova as an unremarkable Nina? Why is *The Seagull* a comedy? The main character shoots himself. What's funny about that? And what is the play about? Love? Art? Boring life at a dacha?

This is perhaps the only play in the Russian theater in whose productions directors have managed to make each of the characters in turn — there are thirteen in the play — the main character of their "bold, innovative interpretation." Nina Zarechnaya, Treplev, Arkadina — that makes sense, but the writer Trigorin, Masha, Dorn, Polina Andreyevna, and Medvedenko the teacher?

But now here's what hasn't been tried yet. Chekhov has a fourteenth character, which the play is named after. The seagull. A bird, a victim of a bored hunter. How can you portray a seagull in a dramatic performance? A stuffed prop — a dummy. A realistically or crudely made one. And that's about it.

I have danced so many birds myself in ballet. There's no counting the number. A swan, the prophetic bird Syuimbike, the Firebird . . . And there are the parts that are not mine: the male Bluebird in *Sleeping Beauty,* the Sad Bird . . . There are so many birds in ballet because it is a tasty morsel for every choreographer. Fairies and birds — they're our bread and butter.

But they can be made interesting. Several flights of the seagull, breaking the flow of the action. The flight of the wounded seagull. The dead seagull on the ripples of the magical lake. Dancing with the support of an invisible partner. Or partners? Maybe white arm-wings and the neck in space, clothed in black velvet?

Of course, this was merely the first stimulating motif. Nina's hopeless love story, the loves of Treplev, Masha, and Medvedenko. "Two *poods** of love," as Anton Pavlovich himself defined it. Everyone loves, everyone is unloved. Arkadina's jealousy. Arrivals, departures. Kostya's decadent play on the boards of the dacha's theater stage. A theater within the theater. The melancholy game of bingo during long autumn evenings. Croquet. Nina's arrival during the stormy night. The old semi-dilapidated dacha stage with its theater curtain, torn by wind and rain. The poet's suicide. All of this can be embodied in the art of movement. And if we succeed, done convincingly.

This time, I decided to stage the ballet alone. I had gained a little experience with *Anna Karenina*. And there weren't any crowd scenes here at all. Only thirteen Chekhovian characters. Only the cackling public, mocking the author, and swarming against the backdrop of Valery Levental's panels with idiotic reviews by critics of that time. That episode was very short. Every interlude was two to three minutes long. The set would change, but the little folk would continue to flit annoyingly back and forth. As in the first film experiments of the Lumière brothers.

But . . . my usual story. What obstacles did I have to overcome before *The Seagull* received permission to be produced on the Bolshoi stage? The prehistory is long. Tedious. I'll spare the reader. Its last stage was the hearing in Demichev's office. By then, Pyotr Nilovich was the minister of culture. Fursteva had voluntarily exited from life. And Demichev was demoted for some Party offense from Central Committee secretary to minister. Of culture, to boot. The last thing you'd think of. That made him our direct boss. And, remembering *Anna Karenina* and his sympathetic participation in it, it did not seem like a bad thing to me.

We didn't succeed in showing the music and script of *The Seagull* at the Bolshoi. There was an implacable enemy camp there. You couldn't get near it. The personality cult of the chief choreographer was at a peak. Anything that didn't fit into the category of courtly eulogies and toasts didn't exist. There were no other choreographers, and there could be no others. There was only one genius.

---

* A unit of weight.

One, like the sun. Our system, having nurtured Stalin, also spawned little tyrants, mini-Stalins. In the most diverse fields. In biology, aviation construction, and even conducting.

In addition, Georgy Ivanov, the director of the Bolshoi, took to zealously protecting our choreographic sun. Even a mouse couldn't squeeze through a barrier like that. I began negotiations with the Stanislavsky Theater but stopped. Well, I do have some pride, don't I? I didn't want to bow my head. We'd do battle. The Bolshoi Theater was my alma mater.

At that time Demichev was fresh, an outsider (he was educated as a chemist), lacking experience in theater confrontations. They whispered to him, explaining to him, no doubt, why he should not allow me to produce my new ballet. But we hadn't let Demichev down with *Anna Karenina,* and he expressed his belief in my new creative project as well. That's why the hearing was organized at the ministry, not the theater. In neutral waters, so to speak. God help us!

Not many ballet people came. Only desperate, bold spirits as well as informer-sponger types, whose objective was to bring the latest news, like a dog with a bone in his mouth. Diligence and smarts were always valued in the royal court. Maybe I'd be taken on a tour abroad once more?

Mostly, it was musicians, opera singers, and soloists from the Bolshoi orchestra who came to hear us. (Being summoned to spend some time in Demichev's office was not an everyday occurrence—maybe they'd treat us to ministry tea or remember my face?) And also several independent critics (independent of the chief choreographer).

Shchedrin played the entire ballet score on the piano. I elucidated the choreographic design.

The speeches were full of goodwill, in support of us. The ballet should be produced. But not a single one of the small number of ballet people opened his or her mouth. This seemed to Demichev, in his naïveté, strange.

"Why is the ballet silent? I'd like to hear your opinion, too."

"The poor, frightened ballet," Shchedrin said to himself after the longest agonizing pause.

Demichev understood the remark. "Is that true?"

And suddenly Sasha Bogatyrev, whom I didn't even notice in my agitation, impulsively rose from his chair. "I want to speak. May I?"

Compelling interest flooded the faces of those present.

"I liked it very much. I would like to dance the part of Treplev."

The set designer Levental, who was sitting next to me, whispered right into my ear: "Sasha is a suicide. Now they'll do him in. A Moscow kamikaze."

(Alexander Bogatyrev danced Treplev with me. He was amazingly good on opening night. Authentic. His appearance reminded me of Alexander Blok— nobility, an aristocratic air, and spirituality. This made the conflict in the piece even more exposed, more highly charged. But he paid an unbelievable price!)

I began the production from the very first number of the score. All the characters appear at the same time except Nina, Arkadina, and Trigorin. They are but a step away from each other, but alienated, tragically alone. Is this not one of the main themes of this mysterious play by Chekhov?

Usually, in ballet, tribute is paid to symmetry. Duet, quartet, octet, thirty-two swans. You have, dear ones, no doubt seen this many times? The dancers' achievement of absolute synchrony becomes one more sign of high art (not to mention the class of the troupe—it's obvious).

In my *Seagull*, I did the opposite. It wasn't symmetry of movement but music alone that was to unite my characters. It was their inner worlds, their secrets. Each one danced his own dance, told his own unhappy life story. All of Chekhov's characters are unhappy in their own way. All of them are in love. But their love goes unrequited. Indeed, perhaps the Russian nobility and intelligentsia's ultra-inability to relate to others was the main reason for the bloody revolution that turned the country to ashes? Or have I gone too far in my assumptions?

The seagull's cry. It's in the music. Almost a moan. Treplev freezes at the proscenium. Shudders. Is the seagull real? Or is it his poetic imagination? The characters dissolve into the darkness doing a lemur-like step. The seagull soars high in the sky over the magical lake. It's me. I'm dressed in a leotard, which whitens my torso and arms. My legs are dark. An ink-black color. Four invisible partners carry me in a closed black cube. A piercing light from the side. I break free from their arms, soar over the lake, throw myself like a stone down into the abyss, rocking rhythmically, carried by the wind on the lake.

Every time—and I danced *The Seagull* around sixty times—I sense in this first flight my kinship with nature, with eternity, with water and the sky.

The Moscow audience received the premiere with kindness. But those who judged in the old-fashioned way—how many turns were twirled, how many chaînées were spun—were repelled and disappointed. There's very little dance in Plisetskaya's new ballet. And what is dance, venerable sirs? I saw a brilliant, motionless dance of a Japanese dancer from Kyoto, Inoue Yatsiyo. She would magically freeze in one spot for an entire hour, even longer than an hour. Only her fingers, eyebrows, cheekbones, finally her eyes, were expressive and danced. I would give all the chaînées and fouettés in the world for such a "nondance," venerable sirs. But capture me, thrill me, enchant me. Then we'll talk.

The ballet *The Seagull* enjoyed serious appreciation from Chekhov scholars and dramatic actors. Chekhov's niece Yevgenia Mikhailovna Chekhova attended performance after performance. And every time, she would call me late at night after the performance, revealing newer and newer hidden meanings of her uncle's play which she had divined . . . through the ballet. Through my wordless ballet! The famous Chekhov scholar Z. Paperny became another fan. His articles and letters to me explained to me after the fact many connections, combinations, and deductions that were invisible to the lazy mind.

Chekhov again. *Lady with the Dog.*

When *The Seagull* was performed in the Swedish city of Göteborg, local journalists pestered me with various interviews. Your favorite beverage, what dish do you prefer, where do you spend your summer vacation? One of the music journalists — his name was Borg — interviewed Shchedrin. Suddenly Borg pressed the "stop" button on his Sony and interrupted the talk: "Why haven't any of the Russian composers, Mr. Shchedrin, addressed Chekhov's *Lady with the Dog?* In my opinion, it's a splendid story for both an opera and a ballet."

"Really, why haven't they? I don't know. I'll have to reread the short story," Shchedrin pondered.

Our *Seagull* was successful in Göteborg. The Swedes know how to work in theater. Nothing had to be repeated twice. Everything was remembered, everything was executed without a hitch. There were only a few from the Bolshoi involved in the production: a few soloists, the set designer Valery Levental, and one of my loyal rehearsal directors, Boris Myagkov.

Victor Barykin danced with me in Sweden. Later he was also both Karenin and José in my ballets. His Treplev was different from Bogatyrev's. Sasha brought Treplev's drama closer to the Blok epoch and the aspirations of early twentieth-century Russian decadent art. Whereas Barykin played the modern, the recent. Barykin had Mayakovsky, not Blok. Or was it Esenin?

The Swedish public took a liking to *The Seagull* — Chekhov's plays are always highly valued there. The number of announced performances was even increased. After our departure the work was placed at the complete disposal of the Göteborg Ballet troupe.

But the road to *Lady with the Dog* was not short. Between the two premieres lay two thousand days. More precisely, 2,003 days. *The Seagull* opened on May 27, 1980. *Lady with the Dog* on November 20, 1985. Right on my birthday.

On my sixtieth birthday I danced two ballets on the Bolshoi stage. The premiere of *Lady with the Dog* and *Carmen Suite,* after the intermission. I never rehearsed so assiduously and fanatically in all my creative life. I wanted to make it exactly for my birthday. The festive occasion furnished me with the opportunity this time of undisturbed work. For the first time in my life I didn't have to spend an ocean of energy on overcoming all sorts of obstacles and barriers. The only problems were of a creative sort.

The work was also easier because only two of us from the ballet troupe were performing in *Lady:* I (Anna Sergeyevna) and Boris Efimov (Dmitri Dmitrievich Gurov). I got the rest of the participants from the extras of the Bolshoi. On the one hand, I didn't have to beg in the ballet office. On the other, I was making a point. People who love soar above the mundane and the pettiness of life. Lovers always live in different dimension.

This hint came to me from Chagall. His lovers always soar in the heavens above the settlements and cities. As if they'd grown wings. And dance is akin to flight. That is why the formal construction of the ballet was subordinated to the goal of structuring all the action in the form of five major pas de deux (Duet-Prologue, Strolls, Love, Vision, and Meeting). The rest is merely background, accompaniment, bursts of consciousness. The Yalta public promenading along the seashore are extras. Anna Sergeyevna with a spitz on the Black Sea pier is an extra with understudies. The night watchman observing the heroes is an extra. The scenes of winter Moscow life, again, extras. The many-faced, seemingly waltzing crowd of residents and fellow citizens whom neither Anna Sergeyevna nor Gurov notice — extras. This is good contrast, atmosphere. And for Efimov and me it's a rest, too. This has to be taken into account as well. We're dancers, not gods.

Chekhov wrote his magnificent story in the dizzying state of being in love with Olga Knipper, a young actress of the Art Theater. That is why, perhaps, the passion is so pervasive, so turbulent, so frankly sensual in the relationship between Anna Sergeyevna and Gurov, who are trapped by banal marital ties, in which the love is long gone. Or had never existed?

An involuntary spasm tightens my throat every time I read Chekhov's lines: "Anna Sergeyevna and Gurov love each other like very close, related people, like a husband and a wife, like tender friends . . . and just as if they were two migratory birds" (do you hear, it's birds again!) . . I can recite by heart, almost sing,

Chekhov out loud. "Lady with the Dog" — this is my impression — is written in verse, not prose. Everyone is educated, everyone knows everything, but please, listen a bit more: "Anna Sergeyevna, this 'Lady with the dog,' regarded what had happened very seriously, as though it were her own fall. . . . She grew pensive, in a downcast pose, like a sinner in an old-fashioned painting."

" 'May God forgive me!' " she said, and her eyes filled with tears. 'That's horrible.' She hid her face in his chest and pressed into him. . . . He was looking into her motionless, frightened eyes, kissed her, spoke quietly and affectionately, and she calmed down a little."

And here's another thing. Every moment of this story is permeated with sadness. How I dreamt and raved about conveying through dance the boundlessness of Chekhov's nuances, the unique atmosphere of the story, its tone, its poetry, its subtext, its sad melancholy, the mysteries and the simplicity of Chekhov's music: Gurov "drew Anna Sergeyevna to himself and began to kiss her face, cheeks, hands. . . . She cried from agitation, from the sad realization that their lives had turned out so sadly; they . . . hid from people like thieves! Were not their lives destroyed?"

Efimov and I began rehearsing in the Operetta Theater building (Zimin's Theater, the former Second Stage of the Bolshoi). We met in the middle of the day when there was no one in class. Boris would come into the auditorium, efficiently eating his lunchtime sandwich — the dancer was still warmed up after morning rehearsals at the Bolshoi. I would work at the barre for a time while waiting for him, and we immediately plunged into in our duets.

We worked to exhaustion, stupefaction. A duet means lifts. I am in Efimov's arms the greater part of our time onstage. Sometimes Boris would get so exhausted that he would lie down in his black-and-red running suit flat on the floor for several minutes. And when he got up, there would be a damp outline of his powerful body left on the floor. Even rivulets of his tousled hair left their wet trace: a new trend in painting. He was drenched in sweat.

"Are you completely exhausted, Boris?" I was sympathetically alarmed and worried — would he endure it, not break?

"I'm fine, Maya Mikhailovna," Efimov would always mutter. "Let's rehearse further."

When we had already moved the rehearsals to the Bolshoi Theater on the fifth tier, and it was a stone's throw to the premiere, I unintentionally came down clumsily from a high lift, the force of the fall crashing down on the nape of Efimov's neck. The ever most patient, imperturbable Boris gave out a piercing cry.

His cheekbones stood out and turned white in an instant. He hung onto the ballet barre limply. Something inside him bubbled up, began moving.

"Does it hurt a lot, Boris? Forgive me." I've wrenched Efimov's back, flashed through my brain automatically. There won't be any premiere. My Anna Sergeyevna is lost . . . In confusion, I tried to ease his pain with massage. Boris freed himself from beneath my fingers: "It'll let up now, Maya Mikhailovna. It'll pass."

"Forgive me, Borya, my hand slipped."

Efimov slowly, slowly straightened up. "It's not your fault. My back got chilled. Yesterday all the tires on my Zhiguli were punctured near the theater. I had to tinker for a long time. I got a chill."

I found out the details. There are vile people on this earth. My theater had thought of a way to sabotage the premiere of *Lady*. Efimov wore a light jacket no matter what the season. His overworked body would get chilled and . . . Did they do it on their own initiative or by command? And here I thought I was creating without obstacles for the first time.

Nonetheless, we rehearsed again the next day. Boris miraculously restored himself overnight after his severe breakdown. An iron organism! Or the will of Heaven? The Lord God was with us. With us at the rehearsals of *Lady with the Dog*. We both worked without understudies; the slightest trauma would be the end of a bold dream.

I danced in all the rehearsals in a leotard, adding, however, a worn-out *Karenina* skirt for its silhouette and for my partner's skill. Of course, I asked Cardin to design Anna Sergeyevna's dresses. Cardin had spoiled me with the regal generosity of the clothes he created for *Anna Karenina* and *The Seagull*. Pierre had firmly promised. But time was passing, and there were no costumes. Not wishing to annoy him, I didn't pester Cardin with reminders. Only once, unable to restrain myself, I called Yushi Takata and, in my barbaric English, repeated the date of the premiere: "November 20." From Yushi's answers, I knew that Cardin had not forgotten about either my dreams or the date.

"Don't worry, Maya, the costume will be on time. Pierre is working."

Late in the evening on November 18, on the eve of the last rehearsal (I was in total despair, racking my brains to cope with the situation), a certain gentleman who knew only three words in Russian—*big, comrade,* and *blini*—knocked on our apartment door. Just like Santa Claus. How did the Frenchman who knew no Russian find our Moscow refuge in the dark city?

A box from Cardin.

A note in the box and a translation attached with a pin (Natasha Yanushevskaya, an employee of Cardin's boutique, was fluent in Russian). Cardin wrote that Anna Sergeyevna had to have only one costume. But that it would be different with different belts. Depending on the plot, I had a choice of three variations. A straight severe belt stitched on the top and bottom with a silver thread. The second one was slightly wider, more fanciful, with a giant yard-long bow and long ethereal bell shapes to the floor. The third possibility — to withdraw into abstraction, as Cardin put it — beltless, like a tunic.

I tried on my Paris Santa Claus's gift in front of the mirror. Now it was clear why there was only one costume. It had to be worn with a leotard, like a cosmonaut's spacesuit. In order to change again, I'd have to strip down to the nude. I tried on the dresses as suggested by the production. I would dance the first duet — the epigraph to the ballet — without a belt. It was also easier for Efimov, since there were dozens of lifts in the epigraph. I would wear the bow in the Strolls, which was quieter. The Love pas de deux was ecstatic passion. Here, of course, the tunic. "Vision" with the strict belt. The line of the waist had to be visible. The meeting in city S. (did Chekhov have Saratov in mind?) and the finale were a return to the beginning. Form. Reprise.

I marked my fiftieth birthday with the premiere of Béjart's *Bolero* in Brussels. My sixtieth birthday with the premiere of *Lady with the Dog*.

Customarily, ballerinas celebrate this dastardly age proudly sitting in the floodlights in a draped box near the stage. And each of the dancers performing during the evening of dance in honor of the birthday girl, Lady X, decorously presents her with a lavish bouquet. By the end of the evening the eminent Lady X is covered over with flowers up to the chin, like a corpse.

Instead, what lay ahead for me at my birthday evening was a good workout: *Lady* was fifty minutes long, and *Carmen Suite* was forty-six. I was onstage almost all the time. But I endured it. I won. And I want to write about it without banal modesty. For future collectors of theatrical chronicles.

Through the stage radio I heard the director's customary yet fiery announcement: "Attention, the conductor is in the orchestra, we're beginning." Alexander Lazarev gave the upbeat to the violins. Shchedrin had entrusted him with the fate of *Lady*, just as he had with the fate of *The Seagull*. The first aching phrase sounded. For me it personifies Anton Pavlovich's words: "Anna Sergeyevna and Gurov were like two migratory birds, a male and female, caught and forced to live in separate cages."

Efimov and I stood opposite each other a meter from the curtain, which was still closed. I faced the audience. His back was to it. Not moving a muscle. Listening to the music. The sigh of the violins. The drops of pizzicato. Not to make a mistake! In a bar the curtain will slowly part. Gurov lifts Anna Sergeyevna, pressing her legs to his chest. How happy I am that I am dancing this most lyrical, superlative Chekhov story. The white spitz, which is soon to stroll with Anna Sergeyevna along the Yalta pier, whimpered softly in the wings. Shchedrin's music had an effect even on the dog, as it alarms, grates, and affects the nerve endings.

The performance ends with the very same lift. I extend my arms toward the Crimean sky, to the Black Sea, to the billowing clouds, to all the people who inhabit our divine, incomparable earth. Aren't the lives of Anna Sergeyevna and Gurov "destroyed?" How are they to go on living?

All the performers come out in a row for bows: Efimov and I, the conductor Lazarev, the set designer Levental, the rehearsal coaches Boris Myagkov and Tatiana Legat, and the composer who created this crystalline, sensual score.

Shchedrin embraces me onstage, in front of everyone and, smiling, says conspiratorially, "This music is your birthday gift. I wasn't going to give you a diamond ring, now, was I?"

Chapter Forty-Four

I Want Justice

My name is inscribed on the title pages of four of Rodion Shchedrin's ballets:

The Little Humpbacked Horse — to Maya Plisetskaya.

Anna Karenina — to Maya Plisetskaya, faithfully.

The Seagull — to Maya Plisetskaya, always.

Lady with the Dog — to Maya Plisetskaya, eternally.

False modesty will not stop me from telling everything I perceive, what I feel, about my husband's music.

Shchedrin was always in the shadow of the spotlight of my riotous success. But to my joy, he never suffered from it. Otherwise we couldn't have lived serenely for so many long years together. This is because of both his happy nature, which is incapable of envy, and his quiet conviction in the power of his great and primary creativity. And his constant immersion in music as well.

When I first married Shchedrin, Elena Mikhailovna Ilyushchenko once asked me, "How is it possible to get into bed with a man who's got music in his head all the time?" It's possible, Elena Mikhailovna, and it's not bad at all! But, really and truly, it is complicated when two artists live side by side. One of them has to give in on a daily basis. If you do this continuously, clenching your teeth and forcing yourself — finally the imaginary equilibrium will inevitably be affected and . . . that's the end of the union.

And what about his music for my ballets?

The philistines gossiped: the husband is a "ballet composer," composing ballets at the bidding of his unpredictable prima donna, who's advancing her career. But in reality, everything was just the opposite. I'm not afraid to say that maybe there was self-sacrifice involved. Shchedrin was a professional of the highest order. He could create a superb ballet or an opera—anything you like. And he wrote ballets to help me directly. To assist against advancing age: a new repertoire undoubtedly leads to the next step in art, for only a new repertoire can save you from theater intrigues, from repeating yourself, from getting dragged down and sinking into inertness, into idleness.

Naturally, each new goal absorbed him; the obstacles spurred him to rise to the occasion. But there was also genuine concern about me, support, empathy, and anxiety. But maybe—more simply—love? . . . As I write these lines I'm flooded with tenderness.

My book would be incomplete if I remained silent about all this.

Shchedrin's name is sufficiently well known in the music world. But it pains me that his name is better known than his music. Rodion Shchedrin? Yes, of course, *Carmen Suite,* the ballet *Carmen.* Variations on Bizet.

Carmen Suite is a great success. A virtuoso piece! But if Shchedrin was able to do so well with motifs that are familiar to absolutely everyone, aren't you gentlemen conductors also interested in taking a look at his real work? You would discover much that is remarkable in them! *Carmen Suite* is a mere snippet of what Shchedrin has composed.

It is simply amazing that the ballet *Lady with the Dog* has escaped the attention of choreographers: A truly balletic theme. The magic of Chekhov. The marvelous heroine. Compactness: one act. Duration: three-quarters of an hour. A minimal number of musicians: winds plus three or four instruments. And most of all, that penetrating music, exciting to the heart, as fresh and succulent as an Antonov apple. Why do you ignore it, dammit? How can I wake you up, sleeping beauties? Wherever I have danced my production of this ballet, it has earned an instant response from the auditorium. At some point, Madame. But why not now?

I was at the premiere of Shchedrin's *The Old-Time Music of Russian Circuses* in Chicago. The famous Chicago Symphony Orchestra, conducted that evening by the dazzling Loren Maazel, was literally swimming in the score's delicacies and delights. Why, every self-respecting orchestra ought to play this piece! Again, people are asleep . . .

The premiere of the Fourth Piano Concerto at the Kennedy Center with Niko-lai Petrov and Slava Rostropovich. Recognition. Praise all around. Positive criti-cal acclaim. And then what? Have many admirers turned up to play the new concerto?

The choral liturgy *The Sealed Angel*. What pure, crystalline music! What a ballet could be created based on *Angel!* (Don't berate me for my constant refer-ences to the ballet; after all . . .)

True, Shchedrin has compositions to which I listen with difficulty. I try not to be prejudiced. Take, for example, *A Musical Offering* for organ and winds. It has been at times excruciatingly difficult to listen to this composition through to the end. And it is more than two hours long. Only my wifely obedience has kept me in my concert seat to the last bar of the finale. I desperately felt like rushing after the refugees fleeing the auditorium, the floorboards creaking in protest. I would begin to feel that I was, in taste, joining our dachshund Bati (a gift from Maria Schell), who suddenly howled impatiently when the first bars sounded on the television tape of this composition.

I am writing this chapter secretly, in strict secrecy from Shchedrin. I know that he's going to get angry, exhort me to cross it out and delete it from the book. But I won't obey him. I won't obey him, not for anything. I so desperately want to restore justice.

It would also be just if Shchedrin's music were judged solely on the basis of the music itself. If his Salieri-type colleagues did not hang all their envious baggage around his neck. (Besides, I don't believe that Salieri really did poison Mozart. His own personal Salieri-types slandered the old gent. All because of envy, meanness, all because of what is, in essence, utterly human. But Pushkin so exhaustively revealed the workings of one artist's envy of another that not a single lawyer in the world will ever be able to whitewash the villainous reputation of the real Salieri.)

People were extremely envious of Shchedrin. And there really was something to envy. They were right! A brilliant man, marked by God and the Muses of music, irresistibly charming, emanating luminescence all around him. A man of rare generosity, more than exactly corresponding to the meaning of his name, for the Russian word *shchedry* means generous. How could he not draw atten-tion to himself? He was accepted in absentia into the Union of Composers as a twenty-year-old student of the conservatory, without his personal request, without formal procedures and applications.

He didn't clamber up the ladder of recognition. Recognition came to him all by itself. How our "experts on Russia" simplify the life we live: black-white, black-white . . . No, gentlemen, life in the raw is far more complex.

In the early 1960s, on the last wave of Khrushchev's "thaw," Dmitri Shostakovich founded the Union of Composers of Russia as an alternative to the Union of Composers of the USSR and became its first chairman. He spoke to Rodion several times about carrying on the tradition of this good work. Incidentally, Shostakovich and Shchedrin had had their fill of being dragged around to all the high Central Committee offices. The legend and the promising young musician, gripped in a gentle but iron stranglehold, temptation and threats alternating to make them join the Communist Party. This pressure continued for a long time, and Dmitri Dmitrievich finally gave in and put in an application. Whereas Shchedrin held out and remained, just as he had been, a nonmember. Do you think it was easy?

But I can understand Shostakovich perfectly! How much torture did he have to endure from Soviet authority? When in the recent past, Stalin organized edifying public lashings, only a quarter of a step separated his victims from physical annihilation. Shostakovich feared for his children and for his creations. Could the sense of fear vanish without leaving a trace? Other splendid musicians of Shostakovich's generation did not avoid this fate, either. Oistrakh, Khachaturian, Gilels, Flier, and Kogan were also Party members. Our younger generation sometimes dared to take bold action. The bacillus of fear was no longer as all-encompassingly powerful. But only sometimes.

In 1973, after a two-hour persuasion session in Moscow's Hall of Columns, Shchedrin agreed not to withdraw his candidacy for head of the union. Only two out of several hundred members voted against him. The rest were for him. And Rodion became the chairman of the Union of Composers of Russia. Now he was in "Shostakovich's chair." Incidentally, the office of the Composers of Russia was only three floors below Shostakovich's Moscow apartment, in the same building, the same entrance. It was convenient for D. D.: he was already having difficulty walking.

I know the main reason for Shchedrin's agonized acquiescence. It was me.

Things were growing more difficult for me in the theater. I had to fight for a place in the theatrical sun. And what trumps did I have in this battle? A wide stride, flexibility, and all that? Or artistry? An obsession with ballet? Or the public's favor?

I needed Shchedrin's honorary post in the Union of Composers as a warning to people to wipe their feet on me less frequently, step on my soul less often. Is it really difficult to understand this? Making a vitally important compromise for a

$100 bill is one thing. But what if it's for the sake of creativity, for someone close to you? Does that make a difference?

"The men of the 1960s" — the *Shestidesyatniki* — in Russia (and Shchedrin was one of them) all walked toward truth in creativity and truth in life by circuitous paths — Yevgeny Yevtushenko, Andrei Voznesensky, each one walked toward this truth following his own path. They did not escape compromise — the system was cruel. You had to survive, not allow them to step on your throat and crush your song, "skid out of the way" — this verb was in vogue with the *Shestidesyatniki* — and yet remain a decent person. The *Shestidesyatniki* also naively endeavored to change the world, to destroy the system, to shake people up and appeal to their consciences. Today we see how naive they were. The Don Quixotes of the 1960s!

During the years of his chairmanship Shchedrin was able to do much good for people. Truly, much good. But who is capable of remembering good? A few individuals. Fortunately, noble people still exist. They haven't disappeared from the earth, like dinosaurs and mammoths. Nonetheless, it is those for whom he did the most good, whom he helped, stood up for, who say without batting an eye: What is Shchedrin? Establishment.

What establishment? — when our apartment was bought with our own money, whereas the "persecuted composers" (such is their reputation, now repeated like an echo with a momentum of its own) were given apartments and other privileges gratis from the Union of Composers (the now cursed Union of Composers). Now that's the truth for you.

Shchedrin always held to a position.

In 1968 he dared refuse to sign letters in support of the invasion by Soviet troops into Czechoslovakia. The radio station Voice of America included him with others who refused, bold spirits, the writers Alexander Tvardovsky and Konstantin Simonov.

Shchedrin was a member of the Moscow Tribune and the Interregional Group of Deputies from the first days of their formation, that tiny group of brave people presided over by academicians Andrei Sakharov and Boris Yeltsin. That was Shchedrin's political position, his political conviction, his political face. Shchedrin was among those who openly resisted the regime. That's the truth. Establishment, indeed!

And what were the "persecuted composers" doing? Also visiting the rebel platform? No, they were regaling foreigners from the press with blini and caviar and transporting them in their own cars instead of taxis to the sights outside Moscow. Kolomenskoye, Arkhangelskoye, Zagorsk . . . And whispering, whispering that they were persecuted, saying that they were unrecognized, unnoticed, uncelebrated.

Now, incidentally, it has somehow suddenly been discovered that half the people in the country were dissidents. And those who used to answer the interviewer's standard question, "What book is on your bedside?" with "Lenin, of course," now repeat in unison "The Bible, the Bible." Oh, those chameleons! But this is just temporary. For as long as it is in fashion, while power is on its side. But this is just . . . an observation.

There are several simple and merry fairy tales by brilliant creators, written for humanity as edification. These fairy tales are far more profound than the wise tomes of philosophers. Alexander Pushkin's "Tale of the Golden Fish" and "About the Priest and His Worker Balda." Hans Christian Andersen's "The Emperor's New Clothes." Something similar to the story of the new clothes is occurring now, but in the music world. Or am I imagining things?

However, it's not my place to judge how it's better for music to be. Blue or Violet. Eunuch or Ecstatic. There are enough places under the sun for everyone. Both those writing and those listening. But prove you're right in an open battle — with music. Don't whisper, as if in passing, incidentally, that "Shchedrin was a Soviet boss," so that people with no conscience or the gullible ones with politicized brains can reproduce the slander. Judge by the music, you people who do not wish to think independently — only by the music. Not by the labels (if that's what you do) pasted on by your waning colleagues, envious folks, subtle connoisseurs of Rossini's brilliant aria about slander. Truly, no one throws stones at an apple tree with no apples.

Another from that lot is the "persecuted director" Yuri Lyubimov, who cultivated friendships with Communist leaders, who was a Party member and served in the NKVD club himself, who received all kinds of Communist honors and played the buffoon in Stalin's beloved film *Cossacks of the Kuban*. But now he ardently cuffs others around the ears left and right. Saying that he alone was a warrior for the bitter truth. That others were all stooges.

Shchedrin has an original symphonic composition called "Self-Portrait." He dedicated it to himself (that's what the first page says). It was written in 1984. Before perestroika! Before the awakening from the lethargic seventy-year sleep began — it's just recently that everyone's become bold and independent. I want you to hear this score. Because it is a confession. A musical confession. And if you're not deaf, then you'll judge and understand for yourself who Shchedrin is, what he believed in then, what he despised. It's so simple — listen to it!

It saddens me that today some have deliberately confused truth with falsehood. That the emphasis on truth has been displaced from people's minds today. Within a generation or two, there can be no doubt about it, everything will be sorted out—what was allotted to whom by God. According to their talent and not their politics. As the poet said:

> To open but one eye
> To look but once and know,
> To see who after us will be. . . .
> To know what dresses they will sew,
> For whom they'll clap, for whom they'll sigh.

Chapter Forty-Five

Work in Italy

The elevator operator on duty at our building on Gorky Street (the French have the lovely word *concierge*) has such a round face that every time I see her I think that nature must have used a compass to draw it. One day the friendly and ingratiating Vera Dmitrievna rose in agitation from her desk to greet me. "While you were out, Maya Mikhailovna, the mail carrier brought a telegram. From abroad. From Rome. I accepted it. Here." Vera Dmitrievna was the most diligent of our concierges and always became visibly agitated, breaking out in red splotches, when something involving foreigners came up on her shift.

Shutting the apartment door, I looked at the foreign missive. The telegram seemed to be in Italian, and except for the city and the signature, I couldn't make out a thing. The signature, as I read it, was impressive: Antonioni. Could the famous filmmaker need me? Wow! Only later, with the whole household helping, could we read, Antignani, director of the Rome Opera. But how could the Roman director have learned my address in Moscow?

The text, translated by friends, was an invitation "to come to the city of Rome to discuss the possibility of taking the post of artistic director of the ballet troupe of the Rome opera. . . . A copy of the invitation has been sent to Gosconcert USSR."

A telephone call from Paola Belli, a soloist of the Rome Ballet who was interning in Moscow, cleared it up. She had given them my address.

"Accept. Come to Rome. It'll be interesting."

"But Gosconcert?"

"Antignani already talked to parliamentary deputy Corghi, who is chairman of the Italy-USSR Society. He sent an invitation, too. Your Gosconcert won't turn down our Corghi."

Paola, despite her youth, was wise and clever beyond her years. Later she married our virtuoso dancer Volodya Dereyanko and managed to whisk him away to the West.

The year was 1983. An invitation like that was a rarity then. Without the Ministry of Culture, you couldn't go anywhere. So I started wearing out the carpets of official offices. At the top of the pyramid of my obstacles sat deputy minister Georgy Alexandrovich Ivanov. The one had had recently been director of the Bolshoi and knew how to push my buttons.

I had promised to tell you about him. Well, here goes.

Ivanov was a machine, an evil machine, that had no reverse gear. Mulish stubbornness, ambition, infallibility, and smugness were clearly evident in his face. I've never met a person in my entire life whose appearance did not correspond to his character! The face blabs everything about its owner. Nose, ears, brows, nostrils, cheekbones, line of the mouth, birthmarks, teeth, wrinkles — they're all informers about their owner. And the eyes, the crystals of the pupils — they are simply treacherous snitches. If there's ever a plan to erect a monument to a bureaucrat — here's your model, Messieurs Rodin, Comrades Shadra.

Someone might reproach me and say, Why so much about people who hurt you in the past? Don't hold a grudge, forgive them like a Christian. And why did Michelangelo depict — with prejudice — his foes and enemies in the frescoes of the Sistine Chapel? Wounds may heal with time, but the scars remain. My eighteen-month romance with the Rome opera was a duel between a ballerina and a high-placed official. Which is why I'm starting my Italian chapter with Ivanov.

After Mr. Corghi convinced Lunkov, the Soviet ambassador to Italy, to support the Roman proposal unwaveringly (which he did energetically) Ivanov decided to push me into a financial corner. No problem, he'd make Plisetskaya turn it down herself.

And there were reasons to turn it down. The ministry made my per diem $18 — for everything. Everything else that the opera paid according to the contract went straight to the Soviet treasury. The theater had to make the payments to the Soviet Embassy in Italy, according to Ivanov's contract. And they would hand me $18 a day (to be totally objective, I must note that by the end of my Roman epic, after many written protests, the per diem for ballerina Plisetskaya was doubled to $36).

The Italians had to pay the Soviets for me for all twelve months of the year. And I had the right to receive my per diem only on the days when I was at the Rome opera. Good conditions, no? And at the time the ninety-day rule was strictly enforced. A Soviet artist could not be abroad more than ninety days a year. Otherwise, we might get used to the free winds of the West. The number of days abroad were added up and the sum could never be more than ninety. In going to Rome, I had to limit my other trips. Now, how could I not refuse?

But I didn't refuse. Running my own troupe was so interesting, so new, so enticing.

I lived at Paola's house, and she drove me around in her tiny, bug-shaped car, to the theater and back, to the theater and back.

For the summer festival in the Baths of Caracalla I took on *Raymonda*. The Baths are an immense theater space, bleached white by the sun, for Romans and — more important — the tourists who clog up the city. A vast stage space eighteen centuries old lies under the velvety night sky, under the stars made pale by the lights of the Eternal City, under the Milky Way, clear and bright, like a page in an astronomy atlas.

I've managed to get used to almost everything in sorrowful Russia. I've managed to accept a lot. But I've never gotten used to the cold, the chill of Moscow nights. What luxury — hot nights, when warmth enters every pore and flows throughout your body, filling you with joy, delight, and pleasure. That's the Baths of Caracalla! The three champion tenors of bel canto — Luciano Pavarotti, Plácido Domingo, and José Carreras — did their supershow for the world there. The climate here for tenors is the best.

But how was I going to fill the ancient arena with the naive yet completely murky plot of *Raymonda?* Play it for real? My concept was to bring the plot outside the page, so to speak. Before each act I gave the contours, hints of the plot in silent pictures: the knight Jean de Brienne sets off, the farewell to Raymonda, the invasion of the Saracens, prison, Abderakhman's demands, the messenger, the lady in white, the return of de Brienne, the duel, the wedding, the joyful apotheosis.

They say that in the café opposite La Scala there's an unopened bottle of wine that has been waiting for more than a century, promised by a former owner to the person who could give a sensible resumé of Verdi's *Trovatore*. Perhaps someone should promise a dozen bottles of our vodka to the wise man who can explain the plot of *Raymonda?*

Glazunov's music is so pure, lyrical, and danceable; you simply want to dance and dance. Dance without thinking too much about the consistency of the confused libretto offered by the brilliant composer.

Perhaps not everything was perfect, but my troupe danced its head off in *Raymonda*. I had given some of the solo variations to groups of two, three, and four soloists, so that everyone would be involved. There were three interpreters of Raymonda herself. Margarita Parilla was particularly absorbed in the role, with good technique and grace. Clearly, my interpretation suited her. After the premiere (which was on August 20, 1984) I embraced her and praised her sincerely. She was so touched that she unexpectedly gave me her raincoat. (Why Margarita had been wearing a coat in that incredible heat, no one could say.)

For my final bow to the audience, I wore an evening dress made and given to me for the occasion by Princess Irina Golitsyna. The dress was fantastic, luxuriant, made up of gauzy pinkish gold scarves and shawls. Toward evening a gentle breeze always picks up in Caracalla. And Irina knew that. And my scarf dress came alive. Perhaps Princess Golitsyna knew the words of Marian Tsvetaeva, that only things that fly in the wind look good on a woman.

I truly didn't want to put on Margarita's raincoat over my breathing dress. It got passed from person to person and finally left behind, as if accidentally, in the dressing room. Nevertheless, Margarita's raincoat reached me in the morning at Paola's. Italians are like Georgians!

I brought in other choreographers, too. *Petrushka* was staged by Nikolai Berezov, father of Svetlana, in whose London apartment I first met secretly with Rudi Nureyev after his flight to the West. Berezov was known for his extraordinary memory. He was like an animate VCR. He did not simply show the troupe the Fokine version of the Stravinsky ballet; he gave fascinating commentaries on many of the moves: so-and-so added a soubresaut here, that one liked to hold the passé en tournant. His advanced age did not limit Berezov's desire or ability to do each pas himself. There, that's the old school for you. The troupe liked Berezov.

Jean Sarelli transported *Phèdre* to the Rome opera. He had worked for many years with Serge Lifar, and he knew almost his entire repertoire by heart. In the ballet world Sarelli was considered Lifar's closest confidant. The canonic text of *Phèdre* was preserved untouched. However, at our next meeting Lifar greeted me with a marked coolness. What was that about?

"Maya, why didn't you invite me to stage my own *Phèdre?* I know the ballet as well as Sarelli."

"But I thought you wouldn't have time. You're a busy man."

"For my favorite child I always have time. Remember that in the future."

The ballet *Les Biches* (music by Poulenc) which made Bronislava Nijinska (sister of the legendary Vaslav) famous in the 1920s, was staged by her daughter, Irina. She had devoted her life to her mother's creations. I was astonished yet again by how contemporary and bold the ballet, created back in 1924, was. Russia had squandered her Columbuses and Magellans.

Other productions that season were created by Dmitri Briantsev and Alberto Alonso. I also brought Béjart's *Isadora* to the opera. The Roman company didn't pass a lazy year with me.

Next in my plans was *The Nutcracker.* In the West, it's customarily performed at Christmas. It's a Christmas story — tree, guests, gifts, dreams. I arranged with Irina Kolpakova to stage the production. The Vainonen *Nutcracker* was a fixture at the Maryinsky, and Kolpakova had danced it many times. I was saving the fall for the premiere of *Lady with the Dog.* And I had used up my ninety days. The Italians agreed. Kolpakova did, too. The timetable suited everyone. It was going well.

There was a long time before Christmas, but I had a scary dream. It was the long-awaited premiere of *Nutcracker* on the stage of the Rome opera. I was in a box in a new Golitsyna dress. Next to me Ira Kolpakova. Also in a chic dress, also from Golitsyna. Sparkling snowflakes were in her hair. Masha — I think it was Margarita Parilla — was dancing beautifully. She gets her nutcracker as a present. The audience is charmed. The music turns anxious. A devilish tremolo, then a crescendo. The tree grows to gigantic heights. I am afraid. The Mouse King's entrance. Who is dancing the role? Oh, horrors, leaping onto the stage in a big jeté is Georgy Alexandrovich Ivanov. He is in tights, ballet slippers with pink ribbons. But he is not wearing the usual mouse mask. His head is bald, round, serious, and completely without makeup. Just the way it is in his office at the Ministry of Culture. The audience is outraged. They jump up from their seats. There are protesting cries in Italian. Ivanov stops dancing and comes to the footlights. He makes a megaphone with his fingers.

"Signori, I am here to keep the corrupting influences of the West from our great Russian Soviet ballet."

Someone deftly throws a rotten tomato at him. Ivanov is too slow. I can hear the sound of the vegetable bursting against the comrade deputy minister's clean-shaven cheek. The sound awakens me. I woke up. Shchedrin lifted his head from the pillow.

"Are you having a bad dream?"

"Ivanov is going to ruin the *Nutcracker* for me."

The dream was right. A vile and dragged-out hassle began over Kolpakova's trip to Rome.

What was there to complain about? What didn't suit? Tchaikovsky. *The Nutcracker.* Vainonen's classic production. Kolpakova was a Hero of Socialist Labor, a People's Artist of the USSR. A prima at the Maryinsky Theater. She had travel days in reserve. The treasury would get hard currency from the Rome opera. Was it simply revenge? Revenge against me? Because I wouldn't kowtow?

There was a long history to our unpleasant relationship. A bad history. My personal story about Captain Kopeikin.* The sharpest battle had been in 1978. My jubilee night at the Bolshoi. Thirty-five years of dancing there.

It is customary for the celebrant to choose the program. The best from the past and something new; that's the way it's done. Here was my plan: Act 2 of *Swan Lake* and Béjart's *Isadora* and *Bolero.* Moscow — in fact, the whole Soviet Union — had not seen my *Bolero,* even though the Moscow dancers knew the "accompaniment" parts because for a recent tour in Australia impresario Michael Edgley had flown Peter Nardelli, a soloist with the Béjart troupe, into Sydney. In a few days, he had taught our men the entire part. We did *Bolero* six times in Australia. Edgley had calculated properly — it was a success.

However, we did *Bolero* secretly in Australia, without Moscow's permission. It was not hard to guess that Ivanov, director of the Bolshoi, was not going to allow *Bolero* on his stage.

"Dance something else."

"Why something else?"

"It's not familiar to Muscovites."

"It's my night. In my honor."

"The theater doesn't have a table."

"I'll pay for the construction of a table for my dance out of my own pocket."

"Béjart's *Bolero* may not be performed on the stage of the Bolshoi Theater."

"Why not?"

"Do *Carmen Suite* instead. I believe you like it?"

*In Gogol's *Dead Souls,* the postmaster describes the efforts of Captain Kopeikin, wounded in the war of 1812, to get a pension.

"But I want to dance something new for my jubilee. Something that I want to dance."

"*Isadora* is enough."

"Moscow has seen *Isadora*."

"Béjart's *Bolero* may not be performed at the Bolshoi. And it will not!"

There isn't enough paper for our dialogue. When Ivanov says no, he means no. The reverse gear doesn't work in his round, serious head. It's broken. Comrade Ivanov is stubborn, pathologically stubborn.

From Pyotr Khomutov, now director of our ballet (he's a former dancer), I learned the real reason of the categorical ban on *Bolero*. "That loose pornographic ballet by the modernist Béjart cannot be shown to the public from the Bolshoi stage. A half-naked woman on a table with ogling men around her. It's a strip-tease! *Bolero* is for the Folies-Bergères or the Moulin Rouge, not for the Bolshoi. As long as I am director, I will not allow our temple of art to be violated." This was Ivanov's approximate argument in Khomutov's confidential version.

"Has Ivanov ever seen *Bolero?*" I asked.

"I doubt it. But someone who was in Australia with you sent him a report. And added photos."

"Who had so much zeal? One of the dancers? Who accompanied me?"

"Don't ask, Maya. I can't tell you that," Khomutov said.

I banged on many doors. But the answer was always negative. Later I learned that Ivanov had gotten the support of Mikhail Zimyanin, ideology secretary of the Central Committee. That meant that all roads were barred to me. Dead end. I had to either take a stand and cancel the jubilee night, or replace *Bolero* with *Carmen Suite*. I hesitated. The days raced by. The date of the concert fast approached. The theater was poised in tension—how would Plisetskaya's jubilee end?

But I found a way out. Who in the system was higher up than Zimyanin? Only Brezhnev. I had to get to him, or to one of his close aides. Through inconceivable efforts I managed to meet with Andrei Mikhailovich Alexandrov. He was Brezhnev's right hand. A professional politician. A man who was educated and spoke foreign languages. I did not need to explain, for a change, what *Bolero* was, who Maurice Ravel was, and what Maurice Béjart had to do with it.

I was also helped—Igor Moiseyev's formula came into play here—by foreign journalists. The aroma of "something cooking" came from the doors of the theater, and reporters kept asking for interviews. The telephones were tapped, of course. That was pure politics.

But the main force that beat the Ivanov-Zimyanin tandem was, I repeat, Alexandrov. He told me that he had told Brezhnev about my despair, and the leader mumbled something kindly in response, which gave Alexandrov the right to refer to the opinion of the country's chief official person.

I danced *Bolero!* And my tormentor Ivanov walked around the theater with the ashen violet face of a drowning victim. Catastrophe. The burial of Pompeii. The sinking of the *Titanic*. Plisetskaya was undermining the pillars of the Soviet state. How could Comrade Ivanov forget his ignominious defeat, his shame? Our battle had been waged in full view of the entire theater.

And so this was the grudge match. That was the trouble with *The Nutcracker*. That's what was wrong with Pyotr Ilyich Tchaikovsky. That's why Irina Kolpakova was not acceptable. That was the explanation, the hidden meaning of it all.

Alas. Ivanov won that time. I lost. He ruined *The Nutcracker*. Kolpakova did not go to Rome.

And what about the theater in Rome? They had advertised it. It was too late to change the announced repertoire. The tickets for the Christmas shows had been sold. Roman mothers had promised their children a fairy tale at the opera in Rome. Will-nilly, Signor Antignani had to dredge up a *Nutcracker*. They brought in a choreographer from Prague, like a fireman to a fire. Not from St. Petersburg.

And another loss. Ivanov told the television people (and he had been in charge there before the Bolshoi) to erase the tape of my successful *Bolero*. So it vanished into oblivion. Too bad! Otherwise, some silly staffers could have put my concert on T.V., destroying the Soviet Union with Béjart's pornographic fantasies.

The theater in Rome got tired of me. Of the uncertainty, vagueness: Will I come or not, will they let me go or not, yes or no? Might as well pluck daisy petals. But my contract with Rome was never broken. Things just quieted down and stopped. Even the financial arrangements came to an end. And, as long as we're on the subject, when I danced Isadora or Phèdre, the theater paid me a separate honorarium as a performer. But still through Gosconcert. Three years later, when I was working in Madrid, the perestroika and glasnost-era magazine *Ogonyok* came to my defense rather clumsily. From Ivanov? The slave system? It printed a large article by M. Korchagin, "Plisetskaya's Millions" (July 1988). Readers who did not know the facts would understand nothing. All that was clear was the desire to defend me and the crackling headline about millions. When Misha Baryshnikov read the article, he said with heavy grimness, "How lucky that I'm not there anymore."

The appearance of the sensational article in *Ogonyok* was completely unexpected for me, but I certainly wasn't pleased by its content. I immediately wrote a letter to the editor-in-chief, Vitaly Korotich. Like a true child of perestroika, he tried to straddle two chairs like a rubber man and never to dot any "i"s. Let me make it plainer: Korotich was a bold coward.

They didn't publish my letter. They were afraid—Ivanov was still throwing his devilish ball in the culture ministry. They limited themselves, once again, to opaque summarizing comments from the editors about the readers' letters. I kept a copy of my letter of Korotich, and I want to show it to you, my readers. Its authenticity is the best way to clarify the twisted past. Let's go back just a few years. Here is the letter. Perhaps the smaller type will help you get through its length:

Esteemed Comrade Editor:

M. Korchagin's article in issue no. 31, "Plisetskaya's Millions," omits details that constitute the point.

1. We are talking about my salary—payment for my work—and the extortion, I can't find a better word, by Gosconcert. For the long period of my tours abroad, I gave the Soviet state more than $2 million. That's where the millions are. I continue doing it today: my salary as artistic director of the National Ballet of Spain is $7,500 American a month. Gosconcert "lends me" per diems—day of arrival, day of departure, crossing borders, and so on. A medieval cabala is what it is. Or look at this proportion. For a three-minute performance on television I was paid $10,000 net. Gosconcert generously allows me to keep $160. And to do that I must bring a mountain of papers, copies, notarized bills, and receipts, including a note from a bank in Madrid attesting to the exchange rate of the American dollar the day I was paid my salary. Just getting those papers together would make a normal person crazy! And I'm not talking about carrying traveling bags full of cash across foreign borders to turn in to Gosconcert, which is punishable by law in such places as France, Italy, and Spain . . .

There is no attempt to establish stability in my quitrent. Each time the amount to be turned in varies (and for some artists, for instance, the pianist Andrei Gavrilov, the rule does not apply at all). That's what happened this "Italian" time. A few months after I did my accounts with the accounting department of Gosconcert, the sum was changed retroactively to a larger one. I reacted violently. Then the sum began to take on a "punitive" and threatening size—we'll twist her into a knot, grind her into a powder. The mailman started bringing notices.

For six performances in one year Gosconcert set six different sums—

from $2,000 to $9,000 and back again. There. I personally had seen in quite recent times thieving directors and their numerous deputies sign two different contracts for me with the same impresario, one official, the other secret, and pocket the difference of thousands of dollars before my eyes. Of course, to be fair, I must note that they shared their bounty with their higher-ups. (When I brought this up to anyone who would listen, including deputy ministers of culture, they all lowered their eyes and did not react.) What possible reason could I have to trust their accuracy, decency, or honesty?

2. Italian millions sounds impressive. But . . . $1, i.e., 67 kopecks, today is equal to 1,200 Italian lira. Today's Italian millions are like the millions back in the days of NEP*—just noise. But it's easy to dupe trusting people.

3. The history of the issue. My three-year contract with the Rome opera was not officially broken until almost two years of work had passed. Simply, the former deputy minister of culture of the USSR, Comrade G. A. Ivanov, in charge of Gosconcert, did not wish to "approve" (he had his "state considerations") a Christmas production of *The Nutcracker* in Rome by Irina Kolpakova, Hero of Socialist Labor, People's Artist of the USSR, as agreed on and included in the opera's schedule. (I was busy in Moscow with the production of *Lady with the Dog.*) Neither dozens of telephone calls nor appeals to common sense nor eleven panicked telegrams from the Romans, nor a conversation between I. Kolpakova and P. N. Demichev had any effect; master of our fates Ivanov was implacable. Time was passing. Getting no response from the Ministry of Culture and Gosconcert, the Romans were forced to get a choreographer from another country to stage *The Nutcracker.* Contacts faded away. By the way, I always got "approval" with difficulty (and with scandals and nervous tension up until the last minute), a problem that always left the large Roman troupe hanging, wondering whether I would be able to come or not.

If there really had been a problem with the accounts—which I doubt to this day, for facts are like a wax nose, whichever way you turn it is the way it points—then it was caused by Comrade Ivanov. He is the creator of the situation; let him deal with it now and be sorry. Why shouldn't a high-placed bureaucrat be responsible for his actions?

4. Finally; if you plan to print a sensational article, I think ethically you should show it to the lead character first. The journalist was an outsider

---

*New Economic Policy, Lenin's unsuccessful 1921 attempt to reorganize the economy of the Soviet Union.

and did not understand the complicated subtleties of our long-suffering Gosconcert casuistry. I am grateful to your magazine for its willingness to defend me, but it would have been better done not as a fast-paced mystery, but as a thoroughly researched document in the solemn style of a chronicle of times past.

Respectfully yours,

Maya Plisetskaya

28 August 1988.

But the Italians had not forgotten my brief work with the Rome opera. In 1989 they awarded me and Lenny Bernstein the Via Condotti, a prestigious arts prize. They kindly praised my short labor with the Italian dancers. Probably, as usual, they exaggerated and sweetened my achievements. Or perhaps I really had managed to give something to the people of the Eternal City?

I was back on the swirling streets, raising my face to the hot Roman sun. The crowns of pines etched wild shadows on the warm earth. It was June. I followed familiar alleyways to the tubby building of my opera house. I was about to go in. But something deep inside, a sense of bitterness to come, stopped me. I had had so many hopes and plans, so many plans and hopes. But I had wasted my energy on stupid, ridiculous battles with the Moscow monster. Nothing had seemed more serious or important at that moment. What idiocy!

Then I looked in at a familiar little restaurant, just a few steps from my theater. The owner recognized me instantly: Oh, Signora Maya. A torrent of words followed, accompanied by heated Italian gestures. Magical language. I sat down — there were almost no other clients — at a window table, where I had eaten mozzarella with tomatoes during breaks in rehearsals. A minute later, the owner had brought my favorite dish, without even asking what I wanted. Or maybe there had been a question in the torrent of words? The sharp fragrance of fresh basil came from the plate.

"A Campari, please."

"Just a moment, Signora Maya."

A sip of the bittersweet, grenadine-colored drink. Oh, how good.

Isn't life wonderful, people?

Chapter Forty-Six

Work in Spain

In my youth and even later, Spain did not exist for citizens of the land of the Soviets. There was no such country. Sometimes in the last page of the newspaper *Pravda*, the Kukryniksys, the famous artists, would paint a tiny Spanish Lilliputian with a huge hooked nose and curly hair messily pushing out from behind his cap, wearing a military uniform and holding a big ax that dripped the blood of innocent proletarian workers. The Lilliputian man was usually standing knee-deep in blood on the innumerable corpses of his victims. It was, you've guessed by now, Franco the warmonger. From the generalissimo's mouth there always came some misanthropic, cannibalistic remark. That's all we were allowed to know about Spain.

Nowadays, belief in reincarnation has become popular. Those who try hard can remember living as a Chinese coolie, a borzoi hound, a lily of the valley, or an escaped Australian convict. I have a good friend, a famous Hollywood star, who assures me that she was once a Russian princess and then later a Japanese geisha. I don't argue. Maybe she really was. But I can't remember myself in the distant past at all. However . . . Where then did I get this passion for Spain? For everything Spanish—flamenco, the corrida, combs and flowers in my hair, mantillas? Nothing specific. But there is a hidden connection between us. There is . . .

I adored dancing Lope de Vega's Laurencia, Cervantes's Dulcinea-Kitri, and Kasyan Goleizovsky's Spanish dances. I pushed to do my Carmen. Coincidence or fate? When the outline of Spain began to reappear, as if on tracing paper, on the map for the eyes of the citizens of the land of the Soviets, I began being invited there occasionally. But I usually learned about the invitations sent to me through Gosconcert either with unforgivable, hopeless lateness or not at all. Only now with great bitterness do I read the faded copies of those old telexes. And yet I did have two meetings with Spain and the Spanish audiences. I took my *Anna* and *Carmen* there with the Odessa Theater and then with a splinter group — more about that later — of the Bolshoi. With the Bolshoi, I performed *Seagull, Lady with the Dog* (these were complete performances), and solo numbers: *La Rose Malade, Isadora, The Swan*. And again, a second time, I did *Carmen Suite*. My Spanish ballet went very well in Spain and was, I want to note proudly, the main reason for the second invitation.

Showing our idea of Spain to the Spaniards was terrifying. When I think of all the times we made faces and swore when foreigners showed us their idea of Russian life on the stage. Before the first *Carmen* I was so worried that I asked my dresser for an herbal tea — not typical of me. But when at the end of my final bows, the Madrid audience stood and chanted "Olé," my eyes welled up.

And then José Manuel Garrido, deputy minister of culture of Spain, came to Moscow. The classical troupe of the National Ballet of Madrid was without a leader that year, and they decided to offer the post to me. Maybe I would accept (wouldn't it be interesting)?

Garrido came to our house on Gorky Street, accompanied by the honest and helpful Seryozha Selivanov, who was then in charge of Spanish-language countries at Gosconcert. Perestroika was in its second year. The business was done quickly. The contract was signed. Gosconcert handed me a memo with its conditions (everything to Gosconcert, a crummy nothing per diem for me). I had to leave for Madrid in a few a days.

The Barajas Airport. I had seen it in travelogues and photographs. But how can you convey the taste of the saunalike hot, dry air of Madrid, which, almost burning, bursts into your air-conditioned lungs? The well-trained chauffeur Carlos opened the door of the dark-blue Mercedes. We headed for the Palace Hotel.

It was a stone's throw from the ancient Zarzuela Theater. Under one roof with mutual respect abide the opera, the old Spanish classical operetta, the Ballet National de España (a fantastic flamenco troupe), and the National Lyric Ballet. That was me. It is a classical ballet troupe. The Spaniards did not have a very good classical ballet before, nor any ballet traditions. The troupe is quite young, but very promising. I could tell right away that the dancers wanted to work seriously. They listened attentively, engrossed in my every remark and comment. Where would it be best to start?

I used to say, without thinking about it, when someone would tell me something confused and filled with intrigue, "Oh, that's a mystery of the court of Madrid." Where does that phrase come from? Why Madrid? The court of Madrid kept inviting me to receptions and parties. Eating bubbling oxtail soup and crunching on aromatic salads with pine nuts, I didn't notice any mysteries — to myself. All the people around me were just people. Nice people. But at the theater . . .

From the very first I was being pulled into a frangible state of permanent, twenty-four-hour intrigue. Gently, softly, loyally, with disarming frankness, they would bring me to an apparently independent decision that soloist A was totally wrong for role B. But soloist B had been born just to dance the part. He would dance, stun the world, and then die happy. Humanity would remember him. And ballerina D was too old and totally unsuitable for part E (D being only nineteen), and our demanding critics, who loved the truth and only the truth, would be shocked to the end of their days. Only ballerina F, only F, no one else, should dance the part (and F, by the way, was twenty-seven, I went to the trouble of checking). Each of my assistants, and I had quite a few, would quietly but firmly tug the blanket toward himself. I would be tossed and jounced. But I held on, resisting. Even though I soon found myself totally confused — who was sleeping with whom, who was under whose boot, who was related to whom and was therefore such a genius? . . . The web of intrigue extended to the coming repertoire. I was uncomfortable. Maybe all that was the court of Madrid?

My assistants were killing me with intrigues. The troupe itself took to their new director warmly, and I had few problems. They understood me. However, as a famous conductor once said — I think it was Bruno Walter — the most a chief conductor can hope for from the orchestra is benign neutrality. I definitely had benign neutrality.

We learned and danced ballets by Fokine, Balanchine, Béjart, Mendez, and Alberto Alonso. And the old classics — acts from *Swan Lake, Raymonda, Paquita.* And of course, several ballets by contemporary Spanish choreographers.

I was attracted by the works of José Granero. I had seen his brilliant *Medea* back in Moscow, when the Ballet National de España performed it at the Stanislavsky Theater. Using the language of flamenco, Granero could recount fascinating tales of ancient drama and delineate tragic characters. I decided to invite

Granero to work with our troupe. He could create something unusual, fresh, based on classical dance.

Granero and I were sitting in our theater cantina sipping coffee as black as a raven's wing and chasing it with icy, soft Madrid water—the water in Madrid is so tasty. Totally off the subject, I brought up Mary Stuart. I was reading Stefan Zweig's book about the executed Scottish queen, and I was full of her life and death on the scaffold. But not only that; I had long pondered a crazy thought—was Mary Stuart the real author of the plays attributed to Shakespeare?

Granero was interested but demanded proof.

"Here you are. Stuart was interested in literature, theater, played musical instruments, and in her long imprisonment wrote divine sonnets, poetic letters, diaries—why not plays?"

"But not *Othello* and *Romeo and Juliet*."

"Why not? Stuart had been to Italy; she knew Italian, she read Bandello's novels in the original. And their plots are the plays of Shakespeare."

"But Shakespeare knew them in English."

"Nope. Bandello's novels were not translated into English in his lifetime. I've been in Verona, and no one can convince me that *Romeo* was written by someone who had never been there. Moreover, a person who had never set foot in Italy. Everyone knows that Shakespeare had never traveled abroad and did not know foreign languages, including Italian."

Granero chuckled skeptically.

"José, let's do a ballet about Mary Stuart."

"Well, a ballet—that's another matter. But only if you dance Stuart. That's my condition."

"Why not? But will there be a scene with the theft of the plays?"

"If you insist."

The next day I was in the office of Campos, director of the theater. It's torture for me to put things off. Campos agreed to change the Zarzuela's plans, if I got additional funding from the Ministry of Culture. He believed in Granero, too.

Garrido helped us. And soon we began work.

I think it turned out to be an interesting ballet. The music was created on computer by Granero's collaborators, Emilio de Diego and Victor Rubio; and the sets and costumes were created with absolute taste by Hugo de Ana, an artist celebrated in Spain for his productions of Wagner operas.

And what was the choreography like? A woman's dance in laced sandals. Granero doesn't do pointe work. A lot of attention to arm movements. Mary Stuart has four shadows, four Marys. We take turns, we repeat each other's dance phrases, we seem to be in competition. I can't say just who the shadows are. They are messengers of tragic events. At times, a small Greek chorus, accompanying the action. The shadows are ladies-in-waiting, and finally, spinners and weavers. By the end of the ballet their wool reaches the size of a human head, the lopped-off head of Mary. To the sound of electronic lutes, one of the shadows tosses the bloody ball of wool at my feet. I trip on my own head. Now the executioner's blade.

What I loved most was Granero's sense of drama. He combined the colorful cubes of action so cleverly, lining up the accents. Elizabeth, naturally, was danced by another ballerina (Mabel Cabrera), but I would suddenly appear in her image for an instant. All the duet dances and the big pas de trois were good. Mary Stuart had quite a few husbands and lovers, and following historical truth the troupe's best dancers divided up their roles among them: Ricardo Franco, Hans Tino, Manuel Armas, Antonio Fernandez, and Raúl Tino.

But I was not completely happy with my solo episodes. I thought that in trying to get a complete picture of my capabilities, Granero had watched too many videos of my dancing. And then he either deliberately tried to fit it into his vocabulary or else did it subconsciously. Granero did not remove the quotes "from Plisetskaya," which brought in a slightly jarring note. But on the whole, I'd like to think that it worked.

The austere duchess of Alba came to my dressing room after the performance with a huge orchid and said very sternly, "Señora, Mary Stuart is a relative, and if you had twirled around or jumped on pointe, I would have gone to court to ban lightweight ballet experiments. But you touched my heart. It was so beautiful and tragic."

Mary Stuart. It was 1988.

At the end of November 1991, my Spanish friend Ricardo Cue took us outside Madrid for the premiere of Granero's new ballet theater. We wandered around for a long time, getting lost, on the crooked streets of small towns. Finally, in the evening mist, we saw the illuminated facade of a small municipal theater. In the USSR we call them regional palaces of culture. Parking at some distance, for there were quite a few cars with Madrid plates, we hurried to the theater. It was rainy and cold. Almost December.

"It's impossible to live in Madrid in summer and winter. It's too hot in summer, and in winter it's the wet cold that seeps into your bones," Ricardo grumbled, pulling his raincoat tighter around him.

Granero had put together his new troupe on his own funds. He not only spent his savings but got into a spider web of bank credits.

"If José doesn't succeed, he's a pauper," Ricardo said, worried.

What other choreographer would do that? Granero comes from a line of fanatics. His new work was, as usual, unexpected. He managed to get so much that was new from the flamenco style. *Hamlet* set in modern day, in the language of flamenco, to Ravel's *Bolero*. Granero created a sermon about the end of the world. I liked his new theater. But what about the audiences, the critics? I don't want José Granero to be a pauper.

Of my own works, I remember two. *La Fille Mal Gardée* and dances for the opera-ballet *Le Villi* by Puccini. The second work was interesting for me because it meant working with Montserrat Caballé. Montserrat had dug up a youthful score by Giacomo Puccini, who had termed his composition an opera-ballet. With a hyphen. That meant we were equal.

The name in Russian sounds like Wilis. It's like Act 2 of *Giselle* without the first. But much longer. All kinds of nonsense in a kingdom of women. But the men are pretty active, too. And they are — have you guessed? — the cause of all the problems. This plot could easily rate a second bottle of wine in the café near La Scala.

While we, the ballet, depicted the torments of unrequited love, jealousy, and compassion in pale-blue tunics, the singers, headed by the brilliant Caballé, sang about the same on the second floor of the structure onstage, in wonderfully made concert costumes to the music of a marvelous orchestra. And, by the way, they sang loudly, but . . . wonderfully.

I heard that the Diaghilev company did *Le Coq d'Or* in the same opera-ballet manner. I can't judge how it was. But there truly is something about the close synthesis of the two arts.

We prepared the Wilis for the summer festival in Perelada. Perelada is an hour's drive from Barcelona. Old castles, well-maintained parks, the sea nearby, and hot nights. The egg-shaped, rich Salvador Dalí museum is not far, in Figueras. The place is crammed with tourists. The audience for the open-air theater was dressed in black-and-white tuxedos and ballgowns. Perfume filled the air, reaching the stage. They applauded generously.

I may have joked a bit about the Wilis, but working with Caballé was a joy. As a sign of our friendship, Montserrat recorded Saint-Saëns's *Dying Swan* for me. I've danced it to a solo violin, an ensemble of cellos, and a flute, but now I could "die" to the enchanting voice of Montserrat Caballé.

After the premiere Montserrat and her brother Carlos, who produced *Le Villi*, took me to a seafood restaurant to celebrate the birth of the show. Several of the soloists of the performance went with us.

In Spain the day goes like this: work in the morning, then food, followed by a blissful three-hour nap, a siesta. After that, work again, but not for long. Performances start late; by Central European standards, very late. And afterward, food again, tasty and abundant. Restaurants are busy almost all night. That's why they need the siesta. And the summer heat is exhausting. The merry nocturnal Spanish life!

That night our menu was all fish. From tiny ones, half the size of your pinky, fried bones and all in fragrant olive oil that burned the roof of your mouth, to bigger ones, the size of your index finger, your hand, a third of your arm, all the way up to a piece of the special fish San Pietro, cooked on a spit, which melts in the mouth like crème brulée. Your appetite, fueled by noble wines, gets so stimulated that you wonder, Maybe we should do the fish menu again, this time in descending order? Spaniards love to eat well. And nighttime is the best time for their stomachs. But for a ballerina's regimen, it's awful.

With the troupe, I traveled all over the country. And we had far-ranging tours, as well—Italy, Japan, Israel, and Taiwan. But for me those were more familiar than performing in Mursia, San Sebastian, Alremia, Alicante, Malaga, Valencia, Seville, Granada, Zamora, Oviedo, and Santader.

Every Spanish city made an impression on me. Like coins falling into a piggy bank. Of course, there is the architecture. Of course, the mountainous horizons. Of course, the vast pastures for bulls for the corridas. Of course, the monasteries. The olive trees. The lemon groves. The observation towers built by Arabs on the Mediterranean coast. The last home of El Greco in Toledo. Mysterious canvases by Velázquez in the Prado. A copy of Columbus's frigate docked in Barcelona. The deadly serpentine of a mountain road between Granada and Almunequer. And of course, the genius of flamenco.

I was so taken with that dance! A few times flamenco stars, knowing that I was in the audience, invited me up onstage to join in. Refusal was impossible. I was in Spain. I accepted the challenge. Lucera Tena, whom I had met on the concert stage of the Palais des Sports in Paris—we were in a jubilee night for Picasso—invited me with her dance to come up. I rose and went up the steps. There was music—guitar, violin, castanets, voice. Lucera performed her monologue. She froze. It was my turn. Flamenco is always a competition, a duel. I began improvising. My feet tapped out the rhythm. My arms bent into a Spanish port de bras—I had watched Lucera's movements closely and remembered a bit. My spine stretched, trying to reach my navel. A haughty expression on my face. Circle. Turn. Accents. I had no castanets, but my fingers behaved as if they were there. The soloist's high notes. What was he singing about? The music speeded up. A whirlwind of movement. The audience, along with the dancers onstage, supported my rhythm by clapping. The final pose. Oof! Wild applause.

(In 1964 in the windy mountains of Armenia, in a roadside snack bar near Lake Sevan, a truck driver who had wet his whistle with a bottle of beer started doing the figures of an Armenian folk dance near our table. We were there with Shchedrin and his friend Arno Babadzhanyan. I was the only woman in the smoky café, lost in the cliffs of a valley, full of truck drivers and other travelers. No choice. I got up, watching the movements of my unexpected date, and began my dance response. The chatter of the diners and the clatter of dishes and forks ended. Someone started singing a sorrowful Armenian melody. The dance, I don't know how, worked. My little roadside triumph! Friendly shouts of approval. The tipsy drivers praised me in Armenian. Arno, surprised, asked, "Maya-dzhan, where did you learn our Armenian dances?")

And in 1992 Lucera Tena had asked Shchedrin to write a concert for castanets. She didn't know that he was my husband. God, the world is so small! But Shchedrin had turned it down. He had too much other work.

In general, ritual, music, and dramatic processions are in the Spanish blood. I remember how everyone in the tiny Andalusian town of Malaga Veles celebrated Holy Week in the spring. To the hypnotic rhythm of low drums, carrying heavy—full-sized—painted wooden sculptures of Christ and the Madonna on their shoulders, the male population, divided up like centurions, ten to a row, either strangely marched or danced a choreographic text in unison. And behind them, in dancing waves, wearing monastic robes with eye slits and being showered by rose petals from the balconies by children and the elderly, came the rest of the residents of the town. Men and women. They were redeeming their sins, past and future. Some were barefoot on the cold pavement, and they had to walk in circles around the town, a good three or four hours, some with chains, others with burning candles.

Our friend José Anderica, who had invited us to this festival, is a kind, good, and shy man, and he dragged a huge wooden cross along the stones, its top on his back. When the procession stopped—the men carrying sculptures needed breaks—the band in the procession deafened the local streets with the brass notes of a march. But this march was in a minor key, a sad one. I had never heard a sorrowful march before.

The next evening Jose Anderica and his lovely wife, Carmen (once again Carmen + Jose = love), visited us in the village of Maro above Nerja, where we were staying.

"Well, Pepe, was the cross heavy?" Rodion asked. (All his friends call José Pepe.)

"Yes, it was."

"You mean you had a lot of sins?"

"Are you without sin?"

"Maybe they were the sins of your festival?"

José Anderica was director of an annual festival in the stalactite caves of Nerja — Cueva de Nerja. I danced in that underground miracle of nature, turned into a roomy but cozy theater, several times. Stalactites frozen centuries ago in incredible abstract designs, the vault of the cave carved by Mother Nature in filigree designs, and the steady drip with its hollow resonance in the unearthly space create a sense of mystery in the participants and the audience. Rostropovich and Menuhin played here, and the most prestigious companies of Europe sang and danced here. Being in Nerja is a joy.

But I have bad memories of Spain, as well.

A performance in Bilbao. After the last one, a long voyage that I had been anticipating impatiently. In a few days there was to be a fundraiser for the Martha Graham Dance Company. I had a round-trip ticket from Madrid to New York in my pocket and an American visa in my passport. I had been invited by Martha Graham herself. She had sent me a videocassette of a small solo ballet, *Fimiam*, created by her colleague Ruth St. Denis in 1916. Two others from Russia would be dancing Graham choreography that night, two refugees from Russia — Nureyev and Baryshnikov. It would be their first performance together.

I spent the whole summer learning the new ballet from the video. I always preferred a live demonstration to a tape. But Graham promised to polish the number in America, when I got there.

Telephone call. From Madrid. A man's voice in Russian: "Hello, Maya Mikhailovna. This is the cultural attaché of the Soviet Embassy in Spain. My name is Pichugin."

This is about America, I thought with a shudder.

"Hello."

"Are you busy?"

"No. Is something wrong?"

"I need to see you."

"If you want to talk to me about my appearance in America, don't waste your time. I'm going."

"We still have to meet."

I was still going to go. No matter what. But what if they tied me up, or drugged me? Why worry—these were different times. Perestroika. But you could expect just about anything from embassy people. After the performance, which ended at midnight, the local impresario offered to drive me to the Barajas Airport. The flight was in the morning. It was a long trip to Madrid. The whole night. What if they scared off the impresario? There wasn't a train or local flight that connected. I felt panicked. I had to insure myself. To whom could I turn? I quickly went through my list of local friends who spoke Russian. I needed both Russian and a car.

"The Spanish children of 1937" is what they called the children of Republicans during the Civil War who were sent to Russia by boat and who hurried back home once the political weather cleared up. They had them in Bilbao, too. But my first call on one of them bewildered me. The answer was, Don't do stupid things, don't even think of going, it's dangerous, the embassy people will hunt you down, just accept it, I won't help you, I don't want to get involved.

The second conversation was a repeat. Where was the famous Spanish bravery, the hidalgos? Had it all dissolved in Soviet shit and fear?

I had to find scions of the first wave of émigrés. They had to be bolder. But I made one more try among the "Spanish children." A ballet lover called Garvine (to my shame, I've forgotten her surname, and I left the address book with all this in a taxi in Madrid). Before I finished my first sentence, she accepted with determination the job of helping me disobey the authorities.

"My nephew has a car, Maya, and he is a good driver; he'll take you to Barajas. Don't worry."

The last day in Bilbao. No one from the embassy had come. They must have given up. I was safe. Whew. But no. Exactly at noon the clerk from reception called with Pichugin. "Good day. I'm downstairs in the lobby. May I come up, Maya Mikhailovna?"

A fine, good day, indeed.

It's always harder for me to keep my mouth shut, to keep quiet, than to speak straight out. It may be stupid but I can't change my personality. Pichugin was a confused, pale man of medium height and age. I could see that he was not enjoying this conversation. Or this assignment.

"You've come to talk me out of going to America?"

"Yes."

"Is it forbidden?"

"Yes."

"But why? Because Baryshnikov and Nureyev are with me?"

"Yes."

"But who gave you the orders?"

"A telegram came to the embassy from Yuri Dubinin, the ambassador in the United States, and from Moscow. From the Ministry of Culture. And our ambassador in Spain, Comrade Romanovsky, is also categorically against it."

"And where are these telegrams?"

"I left them in Madrid."

"Then I don't believe you."

"And what then, you'll go?"

"Definitely. I hope you won't tie me up or give me a shot?"

Pichugin was completely lost. I was beginning to feel sorry for him.

"But what shall I tell the ambassador?"

"Tell him that I am for perestroika and he's against it."

"Just like that?"

"Just like that."

Pichugin's ashen face began to show signs of life. He looked around my hotel room cautiously. He glanced up at the ceiling. And spoke very low, "You're right, Maya Mikhailovna. But . . ."

My disobedience cost me several months of a ban on my name in the Soviet press and television. I even had to write a letter to Gorbachev. But Pichugin, innocent Pichugin, was fired because he could not stop "Plisetskaya's ideological diversion." They took advantage of his vacation in Moscow and sent all his Spanish belongings after him to Moscow by cargo freight. But I learned of this only much later.

I've given my conversation with Pichugin accurately, based on my diaries. I seem a rather heroic person. But I have to admit that I was so nervous, with a throbbing headache, my legs trembling. I kept calling Shchedrin in Trakai — he was spending the month there — for advice. I called to hear the hearkening words, "Hold on, make sure you have a car, but go. These are different times, no one will dare use force against you. They'll be afraid."

And my impresario was great. Or maybe no one even tried to influence him? I didn't need the driving skills of Garvine's nephew. My impresario's chauffeur drove me in the night from Bilbao to Madrid. I made the plane on time.

And the wise and all-seeing journalists in American newspapers wrote about how smoothly perestroika was going in the Soviet Union. Plisetskaya was dancing at Martha Graham's with the refugees Baryshnikov and Nureyev. At last the sunny kingdom of liberty and glasnost had come to the Evil Empire. Oh, how naive! When I think of all the nerve cells I lost for that advertisement for perestroika! Before the premiere and after. I hate thinking about it.

I looked at the white cotton T-shirts on sale in the theater lobby with four profiles—Martha, Rudy, Misha, and me, just like Marx-Engels-Lenin-Stalin—and I thought about how you could never explain to the Americans that behind a reckless individual action there's usually no general political line or liberal directive from above. Risk takers make changes.

From New York I returned to Spain.

In the meantime, my court of Madrid of assistants—painful as it is for me to write about this—used my every absence from Spain to increase and complicate the internal intrigues and machinations. Each of them, apparently, was waiting for me to leave the Zarzuela, then planned to take over the ballet. My lack of Spanish made it easier for them. Like all rulers on the earth—big and small—I was told only what they considered necessary for me to know. Without keeping me informed, they used my name when someone had to be removed from a part or punished or not given a raise, so that all bad things were blamed on me: Plisetskaya's orders, Plisetskaya wants it this way, Plisetskaya told me to tell you . . . Plisetskaya, Plisetskaya. And I knew nothing about it. Sometimes, by accident, the truth would surface, revealing the mechanism of the intrigue, but more often these schemes worked, and they worked against me. I should have rolled up my sleeves and entered combat, fought back, won allies, and played up to them. But it was too hard to deal with the mysteries of the court of Madrid.

I was getting tired. I couldn't take being alone, without Shchedrin. The telephone alone was not enough. Life was bringing me to the point where I would part with Spain. Well then, that was what fate wanted.

My contract was expiring. Two years had come to an end. The extra six months the Ministry of Culture had requested were also running out. Time to pack.

But leaving Spain was hard. It was my country. My Carmen!

It was sad leaving my Madrid friends. Unbearably hard.

My faithful Ricardo Cue, a pure man, too embarrassed to discuss money, fees, expenses, even though being a manager means measuring all of life by money . . . and nothing else.

My caring and agitated Felipe Quaisedo, a first-rate cellist, and his charming wife, the Russian pianist Zhenya. You helped me thousands of times with advice, negotiations, complicated Spanish circulars, instructions, and forms. And as interpreters — what would I have done without your Russian? It was my luck that you had studied in Leningrad and had mastered our complicated but marvelous language. I loved you ever since you once said to Rodion and me that when you played *Madame Butterfly* in the Zarzuela orchestra, you kept waiting throughout the entire opera for Puccini's final chord, not resolving but requesting . . .

My Madrid savior, masseur and chiropractor Jesús Abadia, who pulled me out of the many daily problems our fragile ballet legs are prone to.

Quiet, big-eyed Tore Canavate, who treated me with injections and drove me, like a professional driver, through convoluted Madrid routes.

Dr. Xavier de la Cerna, surgeon at the Ramona hospital, who gracefully and with virtuoso hands, like Horowitz, did healing nerve blocks without charging a single peseta. He grew angry when I brought up money. He knew about injuries because his son was a famous torero.

The beautiful *bruja* sorceress Esperanza Gracia, who told my fortune in a darkened room with only a red candle burning. Who read my future with horrifying accuracy. Who protected me in Spanish from the evil eye, objects under the spell of demons, and black magic.

The manager of the dancing school where I could work day and night, Angela Santos, who revealed to me the boundless horizons of immortal flamenco.

My sympathetic Madrid girlfriends — Julia Milans del Bosch de Cavestani, Mercedes Olmo, Africa Guzman (your names are like music) — what will I do without you?

Señor José Manuel Garrido, who had always believed in me as a choreographer, who came to my aid in decisive moments of my work at the Zarzuela. How you embarrassed me once, getting on one knee with a bouquet of flowers after my performance in the open air in the small town of San Xavier (Murcia Province). So there is one hidalgo left on the Pyrenean peninsula.

And Your Majesty, Queen of Spain Sofia, you were always very kind and attentive.

I say to you all, Farewell. Thank you. Remember me.

But perhaps we will meet again?

So the fortune-teller said.

Chapter Forty-Seven

Untitled

What should I call this chapter?

I discuss it out loud (I always speak to myself loudly — people who don't know me recoil).

"Not My Bolshoi Theater"? Or, "How the Bolshoi Ballet Was Destroyed"? Or maybe this long title, "Gentlemen Leaders, Don't Send Your Grandchildren to Study at the Bolshoi Ballet"?

The predecessor of the present artistic director, or chief choreographer, which-ever you prefer, at the Bolshoi Ballet was Leonid Mikhailovich Lavrovsky. Twice. Once he was charged with something political and removed. The second time, they said, "You must make way for the young. Young talent!" The present one (a former young talent) will cede his position only when he dies. And that won't be soon, since his cardiogram, as he tells us, is good.

But my sin here is great, too. I was one of those who spoke out and got upset; how long can Lavrovsky run the Bolshoi Ballet? I demanded. Only now have I found out. Eternally, as it happens.

Lavrovsky's peak — the Prokofiev *Romeo and Juliet* — I danced many times. And while the choreography of the ballet always seemed monotonous and not very interesting, the dramatic side of the performance was brilliant. They say now that the theater director Sergei Radlov had lent a hand to the dramaturgy. But Radlov was a victim of the Stalinist Terror, and his name could not be mentioned. However, other works by Lavrovsky are not forgotten. *Walpurgisnacht*— dances for the Gounod opera *Faust*—are performed successfully around the world to this day. I loved dancing that ballet, and I danced it innumerable times. On my first American tour, my bacchanal received, perhaps, the highest acclaim from the critics and the ballet audiences.

I mention all this in order to look back: what did we have that did not satisfy us? We wanted—I can't speak for everyone, but I am certain about myself— new ideas, new movements, new horizons.

The Stone Flower in Moscow was not a success. Moscow ballet-goers were unanimous in their opinion. But then a rumor reached Moscow that at the Kirov a young choreographer, himself a dancer (he had danced the leaping role of Pan in Lavrovsky's *Walpurgisnacht*), had staged *Flower* in his own way, very danceable and unexpected. Lovers of the new made trips to Leningrad and returned full of delighted tales: this is the kind of ballet Moscow needs. A new name always ignites enthusiasm, and people who hadn't seen and those who had seen Grigorovich's production started a campaign to bring the ballet from to the Kirov to the Bolshoi. I helped, too. For many years this practice—the same performance in Moscow and Leningrad, in Leningrad and Moscow—was popular.

Thus, the Leningrad production of *Stone Flower* premiered at last in Moscow. It could not have been pleasant for Lavrovsky, just four years after his lack of success with *Flower*, to have on the same stage, in the same theater, with the same troupe, his troupe (for he was in charge here), working on the same ballet choreographed by a beginner, a still-unknown choreographer. But Lavrovsky—I can only imagine how he felt—behaved with dignity, with gracious loyalty.

I took part in the premieres of both *Flowers*. In both, I danced the Mistress of Copper Mountain. I will also try to be loyal but perhaps without the same degree of graciousness. Forgive me. The Mistress by the second Leningrader was much more interesting for me. The freshness of the dance combination, the clear resonance with Bazhov's image of a nimble lizard, and the multiplicity of moods. I was much more taken by the second version. The new ballet went abroad to America and went well there. I even sent a letter to Leningrad, to the author of the production, congratulating him on his success.

It took another few years before the author of the second *Flower* would come to the Bolshoi as chief choreographer, replacing Leonid Lavrovsky. It was in 1964. And in that capacity Yuri Grigorovich transported yet another successful production from Leningrad. *Legend of Love*, which I also enjoyed dancing and loved. Our relationship was shaping up in a friendly and cloudless way. And to this day I have not changed my opinion of *Stone Flower* and *Legend of Love*. They are the peak of his work. All his subsequent works — this is my opinion — went downhill. Fast.

What was the main cause — I ask myself — of our disagreement? The old banal theater story: his wife was a solo ballerina and the "boss" didn't need any others? Or wanted only the very young? Perhaps I, and even the soloists of the generation after me, were already "veterans," the past, theatrical ballast? That's another banal explanation.

No. It was something else.

In my lifetime I have often seen what a trial life creates by handing a person power. Only a very few pass the test. I will capitalize Power. How it transforms, disfigures, and ruins people. How it plunges them into the swampy morass of grudges and vengefulness, how gladly they listen to flunkies. The love of Power dries up the creator, taking away drop by drop the talent for creation, makes the person petty. That's what happened to Grigorovich!

And multiply that by Power in a totalitarian system. Our servile, and later semi-servile, life gave rise to many a little Stalin. The mortar of Soviet society was fear. It was the cement that held the system together. And there were plenty of reasons for fear at the Bolshoi.

Our whole life in the theater from the late 1950s was reduced to travel abroad. Even the miserable hard currency per diems, if the dancer was clever and bold, made it possible to buy a car, video technology, to dress better and feed the family well. To break out of a communal flat into a private coop apartment. The difference between the ruble and the dollar was always astronomical. And if you couldn't go on a tour and had to stay in Moscow, you might as well put your teeth on a shelf, curse yourself, be jostled in a bus filled with sweaty people, and listen to your wife's weeping rebukes.

If the KGB won't let you out, it's an incurable disease from which you'll never recover. But what if it's only the chief choreographer who doesn't need you? If he "doesn't see you" in certain roles and has crossed your name off the list on a tour? Then try giving him a major compliment, be thrilled by last night's rehearsal. And be sure to say nasty things about his enemies. There are many ways. And what if you can help him live more comfortably? Move some furniture, take his car to be serviced, prepare dinner for guests, wash up afterward? Maybe then the chief will condescend, change his anger to sweetness, and include you on a trip? So if you're willing to ignore the truth, if you're suicidal, if you're willing to kill yourself, then . . . Well, I'd rather let whoever wants to do that, do it, but as for myself . . .

That's why our chief choreographer was suddenly such a great artist, with no equal in the solar system. Before him there was only a blank spot and after him there will be nothing. Everyone dreamed of dancing only his immortal ballets. Only from them could they learn, could they move forward.

I've noticed a strange thing. Our midget Stalins were the most susceptible to flattery. Open, blatant, obvious flattery. Not because they were stupid—a child could see that people were lying, sucking up, being toadies. But it worked anyway. Hearing flattery must be so sweet.

I maintain with deep conviction that the mainstay of life at the Bolshoi Ballet had become foreign touring. It had corrupted the dancers. Western troupes also have travel and guest tours. But their whole lives, their very existence, does not depend on them. For a dancer from Béjart's troupe, it doesn't matter where she buys boots, pantyhose, and bras—Brussels, Lausanne, or Detroit. But try to buy them in Moscow, especially on your pathetic salary in rubles. Then you'll want to fly to Detroit or Brussels. Even the worth of a new premiere was judged by its participants by its potential to tour. That was the most important factor. If the new production would travel, you had to be in it. An interesting premiere. If they wouldn't take it abroad, it was a doomed production.

So once again, damn it, it all boiled down to politics. But it was our Soviet system that gave Grigorovich the ability to make the entire troupe of the Bolshoi Theater totally dependent on him. To put it on its knees. Keep it in fear. And, intoxicated by his unlimited power, he took full advantage of it. Grigorovich was a direct product of the Soviet system, and that's why he was remade from a creator of ballets into a dictator, a tiny Stalin. That's why he changed the good old classical ballets, adding just a slight retouching but not forgetting to add his name. And then he took on Petipa, Perrot, Ivanov, Gorsky. In the last ten years he didn't even bother making changes. He did nothing. He took his old works around the world. Bowing to the audience, reigning at receptions in his tuxedo. And greedily, implacably gathering more monarchial power. A ballet encyclopedia is published. Who's the editor-in-chief? Grigorovich. An anniversary book about the Bolshoi Ballet comes out. Who's the editor-in-chief? Grigorovich. A ballet competition in Moscow. Who's chairman of the jury? Grigorovich . . .

The critic Gaevsky dared to criticize Grigorovich in his book *Divertissement*. How could he? The sun may have spots but not Grigorovich, who emits only a divine radiance. Immediately, the newspaper *Sovetskaya kultura*, published by the Central Committee of the Communist Party, printed two thunderbolts (just as in Stalinist times) by Grigorovich's court biographer Vanslov (the one who cooked up the book *Principles of Marxist-Leninist Aesthetics*), decrying it as diversion, slander, and libel. Gaevsky's books was banned. The book's editor, Nikulin, was fired. The publisher, Vishnyakov, lectured severely. And this was not 1937, mind you, but 1981. That's why I call Grigorovich a petty Stalin.

Grigorovich would whine on national television, "I haven't produced anything in a long time? The troupe is inactive? It's the opposition in ballet that's keeping me from working. They won't let me do anything creative." Listen, Yura, you have complete rule of a troupe of more than two hundred people. If you need a thousand rehearsals—take them, just put on something new. Two thousand, a year of work, two, three, four years—the Soviet state will pay for it all. Do whatever you want. You're absolute monarch!

He would announce one work, then another. Then silence. Quiet. As if people had misheard him.

There were those who were not allowed to work—and not by five or six "opposition" people in ballet who refused to burn incense before Grigorovich but by the entire Soviet state—and they include Shostakovich, Akhmatova, Goleizovsky, Yakobson, Zoshchenko, and Prokofiev. But they did work. They created. Yet you have a superpower behind you, supporting you. A superpower armed to teeth with missiles, tanks, and aircraft carriers. What more do you want?

When all your energy is focused not on creativity but on punishing people who disagree with you, on self-assertion, then of course you don't have time to make ballets!

There used to be an administrator in the Writers' Union called Stavsky. He would call around to Soviet writers, asking who needed what. One complained about his apartment, it was too noisy, hard to work. Another that his dacha was cramped. A third needed a car. And no one, not one, ever complained that he lacked talent. It's just something that came to mind. An aside.

And then another very Soviet thing; it's useful to always have a letter of resignation on you. At the slightest provocation, put it on the minister's table and say, "I'm leaving." Or else, "Shape up those people, they're keeping me from my work." And the Soviet hounds like the latest minister, Zakharov, would attack to save their poor, sensitive, and irreplaceable Grigorovich. But he never did leave, no matter how much he threatened.

It's totally unconscionable the way Grigorovich tries to make people believe that the Bolshoi Theater is him, Grigorovich (like Mayakovsky's line "The Party and Lenin are twins" or Louis XIV's "L'état c'est moi"). Nothing can be taken on foreign tours except the sacred works of Himself. Festivals of Grigorovich.

Béjart conceived, bore, fed, and brought up his Ballet of the Twentieth Century. From zero. He has the right to call his troupe the Béjart Ballet. But before Grigorovich the Bolshoi Ballet had existed for two hundred years. There had been Ivanov, Gorsky, Tikhomirov, Moiseyev, Vainonen, Zakharov, Lavrovsky. But now it seems they didn't exist! Only Grigorovich for two hundred years.

Some years after the fact, Sam Newfold, from the New York office of Columbia Artists, told me how they had wanted to bring the Bolshoi with a few ballets by Grigorovich and my *Anna Karenina*. "I didn't dare tell you before, what happened to Grigorovich when we told him. He became hysterical."

I wasn't surprised.

"He turned as white as a corpse and shouted, 'Either me or Plisetskaya.' We barely got him back to normal. 'Of course, you, maestro.' After all, he was the director of the troupe. But it was too bad. It would have been a beautiful season. The Americans wanted to see *Anna*."

Another Soviet trick is to create the illusion of democracy. This is the procedure: a "sign-up sheet" is placed next to the ballet calendar (the troupe members have to sign up for the ballets). Whoever signs next to his printed name is for Grigorovich. Whoever doesn't sign is therefore against. This is a microscopic examination of your opinions. "And now let's see the results, dear comrades, of the ballots." Everyone, of course, is for. Only a few suicidal truth-seekers and a few of the theater's crazies are against. The "overwhelming majority" certainly want and desire only Grigorovich: just try to wish for anyone else.

And you have to know how to show your delight. Learn! It's dangerous to praise wanly or stingily. The dictator's head will remember it all. Quite a few talented young people were ruined just because of their attitude. For still retaining a few shreds of human dignity, for normal instead of brown-nosing behavior. A slave is supposed to fall flat before the dictator.

And what supported this dictatorial regime at the Bolshoi? A few years ago, the editor of the liberal and truly bold newspaper of the perestroika period, *Moskovskie Novosti*, nevertheless refused to publish an open letter to Grigorovich from a few artists from the ballet. The editor wanted to know something. "I know little about ballet. But please tell me, who is behind Grigorovich? Not the operetta minister Zakharov? Without super support, even a genius wouldn't last if he didn't do anything for years. Tell me, does Gorbachev's granddaughter study ballet?"

"You are clairvoyant, editor. Gorbachev's granddaughter does study ballet."

Granddaughters of the Politburo members were the impregnable defense of Yuri Nikolayevich Grigorovich and Sofia Nikolayevna Golovkina (director of the Moscow Ballet School (or academy or whatever). Golovkina started a special preparatory class just for Gorbachev's six-year-old granddaughter, Ksyusha. With our boundless talent for toadying, they might have started teaching the president's granddaughter sooner. Why not in the crib?

But what if Anna Pavlova or Olga Spessivtzeva had been granddaughters—one of Gorbachev, the other of Andropov? What then, don't teach them ballet? In a country where Grandfather is the president, please, don't teach them. In a country where the state pays for the school and the theater, finances them completely, please, don't teach them. And if the county is Soviet, belongs to the Party, and is deformed, then I entreat you, don't teach them!

One simple visit from the modestly smiling Raisa Maximovna in a black armored limousine, with a dozen bodyguards, gives the director such capital, such unlimited power, brings such fear to the teachers and classmates of little Ksyusha—what if we get kicked out?—such an imbalance in their relations, that common sense and any similarity to objectivity goes out the window. And then whenever possible Sofia Nikolayevna slips into her conversation, "Yesterday, Raisa Maximovna and I were at the steambaths, and she really wants . . ." And Grigorovich does the same thing (he and Golovkina are a pair): "I was at Gorbachev's, and he said—do whatever you think necessary, Yuri Nikolayevich, fire people, make them retire—he gave me carte blanche." Talk like that makes Soviet officials of all levels tremble. Stand at attention. After all, there's a heritage of seventy years of malicious deeds and toadying. That's what elite granddaughters can do.

I write this with quiet heart. Little Ksyusha—she must be grown now, and may God grant her success and luck in ballet if she's still dancing—said in a recent interview in Germany that Anna Pavlova and Maya Plisetskaya were her idols. Thank you, Ksyusha. But I hold firm to my position. The interference of the president and his wife in our ballet affairs was harmful and destructive. It would have been better, Mikhail Sergeyevich, if you had spent more time dealing with the economy, instead of sticking your nose in ballet affairs, or at least keeping a better eye on weapons warehouses. Perhaps there would have been less bloodshed in the outlying regions of the former Soviet Union.

The powers that be in the Soviet world always seemed to think that since they were high up, they understood everything better than anyone else: advice and suggestions were showered right and left. And the Party toadies nodded and said yes, feigning astonishment and awe — what an outstanding leader. Gorbachev managed to overcome a lot of his natural Soviet mentality. But he tripped up there — Raisa Maximovna and I are experts in ballet. Bolshoi, eyes right!

And here's something quite curious. Friends translated a sensational report from the German newspaper *Bild* about how the director Golovkina saved Ksyusha from being kidnapped (just like the *Abduction from the Seraglio*). She had come out from her dance school and saw a car by the curb with three suspicious thugs in it. Sofia Nikolayevna figured out instantly that these were three bandits after Ksyusha. Bravely, she approached the perpetrators and sounded the alarm. Naturally, they beat it. Those boys were terrified of Golovkina. And Golovkina ran back into the school. She clasped Ksyusha to her breast, patting her head, holding back her tears, sobbing, "I won't let anyone take you, dearest." And here Raisa Maximovna pulls up in the black limo. They saved Ksyusha. Glory to Golovkina, hurrah!

I'm writing this chapter in Lithuania. The pope is here now. I watched his Lithuanian trip every day. Today he was on the Hill of Crosses near Shyaulia. The place where forty-five thousand crosses were hammered into the ground. Not on anyone's orders. Just people following their hearts during the Stalin years, secretly, at night. The pope says noble words. About kindness. Pure thoughts. Forgiveness. And suddenly I compare what the pope has to say with the object of my thoughts in this chapter. There is no kindness, no purity of thought, no forgiveness. Grigorovich is engrossed in revenge, in settling scores. That's the vessel into which all his creative energy has flowed.

His vengefulness was even more visible after several premieres done by Vladimir Vasiliev and me at the Bolshoi. Done against the wishes of the monopolist who did not want new dramatis personae among the choreographers in his "private theater." Everyone and everything had to be his alone.

The soloists we employed were later punished. The way back into Grigorovich's troupe was blocked. And so three groups formed in the theater: the huge main one, which was Grigorovich's, and two small ones, only semi-authorized, that were Vasiliev's and Plisetskaya's. But many impresarios were interested in showing Western audiences works by other choreographers. Especially since critics were getting really sick of the endless *Spartacus* and the refigured *Lake* and then later *Ivan the Terrible*. Our dictator started getting slap after slap from the pages of Western newspapers (take the American headline "IVAN IS TERRIBLE").

The blows of the Western press enraged the already furious Grigorovich, and like any dictator, he redoubled his efforts to crush ballet dissidents. First among them were the soloists in ballets by Vasiliev and Plisetskaya. Here's an example.

The very young dancer Victor Barykin, whom Vasiliev had given one of the main parts in his *Icarus,* was ostracized by Grigorovich forever. Once on the blacklist, Barykin could dance only in other people's productions, that is "enemy" ballets: *Anna Karenina, Macbeth, Seagull, Anyuta, Carmen Suite.* Revenge struck the heads and ballet careers of Alexander Bogatyrev (I've already written about him), Sergei Radchenko, Butskova, Lagunova, and Nesterova . . . Clearly, Grigorovich did not listen to the pope's sermon.

I am not indifferent to the fate of the Bolshoi Ballet. The Bolshoi is my whole life. The whole without the part remaining. My heart truly aches over the fact that power in the theater and in the school has been taken by people for whom Power is the most important, most precious, and most beautiful thing in the world. Not creativity, not ballet, but Power. And they are clinging to it tenaciously, like bulldogs. It's been a very long time. As I write, thirty years have passed.

Maris Liepa, who did not have a sweet time of it with that power, once tried to joke about it. "Why get upset, Maya? You should be happy that our Moscow school teaches so badly. At least there won't be any good ballerinas for the next twenty years."

And there truly won't be any for a very long time, with this degeneration of spirit, this cynicism, this leveling of course work to the standards of important parents. Liepa himself was not helped by joking. After the guards refused to allow him into the theater on Grigorovich's orders (Yuri Nikolayevich had a talent for using other people to deal with his foes) — allegedly because his pass had expired — Liepa burst into tears and had a heart attack. A man with a trained, well-exercised heart! Liepa died soon afterward. He died of another heart attack. At the funeral several orators named the guilty party.

And it does not make me happy in the least that there won't be any good ballerinas for a long time. I can see clearly that their backs are not placed properly, their knees don't work, their uncontrolled arms get in the way instead of helping turn pirouettes. And whatever happened to musicality, artistry, style? It's a disaster. This doesn't mean that there are no professional teachers in the school. It means that there is a dictatorship there. The dictatorship of Golovkina, who cannot be argued with. Golovkina, whose alleged pedagogical gifts are constantly praised and celebrated. Since she goes to the steambaths with Raisa Maximovna, she must be a great pedagogue.

Times are changing. New leaders are coming in. But they have grandchildren and great nephews and nieces. They're human. They multiply. And the recipes for friendship are the same: the baths with Furtseva, the baths with Raisa Maximovna. Who's the next to have a steam? Naina Yeltsin? . . . And so untrained artists join the theater. And the fame of the Bolshoi Ballet dwindles and pales. And the ballet stands in one place for years.

Now wherever you go, whatever troupe you meet, there will be refugees from the Bolshoi. From the fetid air, the creative boredom, the claws of Grigorovich — they're here.

I'm afraid to ask myself this question: Was it really better before Grigorovich? Or am I turning into an old fogey who believes that things were always better in her day?

No, there's something rotten now in the state of Denmark.

How long will the vultures have to circle?

Chapter Forty-Eight

Years of Wandering

And now — Germany.

I moved with all my stuff to Munich, to be with Rodion. He has settled here. He has contracts. That means visas, too. In Moscow there is still perestroika, and such things are possible. But anxiety about the future of our homeland keeps me awake at night. Persistent horror fills my every morning. There has to an explosion. And soon. It won't end well. The Communists won't leave the stage without blood. That's not like them. A dictatorship is in the future, logic suggests. Some unknown general with a persuasive face will shout a speech on television. He'll arrest Gorbachev. Rescind all the innovations of perestroika. Shut down the airports. And you'll be stuck in Moscow to the end of the century. The second coming of the Bolsheviks will be for a long time. And then you'll have to listen to ideological nonsense until you die. I don't have the strength for that. Not at all. The limit for idiocy is used up. That's why we're here. In Munich.

The city is marvelous. All in green. Washed. Cleaned up as if for a parade. I like the German preference for order and coziness. For hard work. We have rented a two-room apartment on Thereseinstrasse. It's right in the center of town. Everything is handy. Everything is nearby. Everything is convenient.

I like Munich on Sundays. Even though every city is lovelier on a Sunday, reducing its nervous pitch, emptying out. But the Bavarian capital rings bells festively. German families head off for a treat of white sausages with sweet mustard and some amber beer. For ballet folk, beer is better than any medicine. It relaxes the muscles and gives them rest.

I'm less well known in Germany than in France, America, Spain. Less than in Japan and Argentina. And much less than in Russia. Of course, not many people know that I'm in Germany, in Munich. Maybe I'll be needed yet. Only balletomanes ask for my autograph. Life is easier. But it's unusual. There are many trips. Here all I need is my willingness and a visa. When you have an invitation, they give you a visa.

I danced a new ballet in Argentina. At the Colon theater. It's called *El Renidero* (Cock Fight). It's based on the book by Sergio de Checco, but it's basically a paraphrase of *Electra*. The characters are dressed in flashy forties dress — zoot suits, ties, and hats. Hats like the ones Gary Cooper and Humphrey Bogart wore in films. When they take them off, we see that the men's hair is brilliantined. Blindingly. The dancers wear patent-leather shoes. The women are in stiletto heels or sandals. I am unlike the rest, in toe shoes. They distinguish me from the stage crowd.

Many times the action is interrupted by characters, in masks with huge faces. These big-headed monsters are lame jesters. There are fourteen of them. Sometimes half (seven) also dress in modern clothes. At the same time, the other seven depict something from ancient Greece, a tragedy.

There is a strong Argentine accent. It is seen mostly in the music. It was written by Astor Piazzola, who brilliantly plays the solo accordion. The spirit of Argentine tango rules. It is clear in the music and in the choreography.

The plot comes from *Electra:* the murdered husband, the cruel mother (that's my role: in the ballet my name is Nelida Morales), the vampire lover (he wears a red-currant-colored suit), the grieving children who punish the mother and lover in the end, the daughter who loses her mind. The ballet was choreographed by Julio Lopez. He is the most modest, most quiet person, and yet marvelously talented. But being quiet in our day is suicidal. You have to make a lot of noise, perform extravagant deeds, and be brazen. Then people will notice you and remember you. What a strange tribe, people.

My first appearance was on a bull, from which I looked down the line of all the members of the cast. And my first dance was a tango. A tango on toe. That was the choreographic language of the entire ballet. Piazzola's music urged me on with nervous cries of the accordion. Throughout the ballet it never weakened the pressure of the swiftly developing action. I was comfortable dancing to it.

The muscles of my legs, arms, and back hear the music on their own, without me. They accepted it.

The performance was to taped music. But every time I listened closely for where the sound director's hand would stop that day. Even the volume — louder or softer — colored my behavior in dance. The recording was the same. The tempo didn't change. Just the final mix. That was all. But I would be different from the night before. You can imagine when there's a new conductor or new musicians, I dance a completely different ballet.

Astor Piazzola did not make it to the premiere. He was dying in a private clinic in Buenos Aires. A long, hopeless coma. Only his wife saw the performance — a beautiful, full-breasted peroxide blonde, her luxuriant hair in a black velvet net. The television cameras dispassionately captured the tears on her suffering face.

It was my first meeting with the Argentine audience and the Colon Theater since my terrible back injury a decade earlier, in the same place.* Unconsciously I was holding back, doing some things almost at half-leg, well, three-quarter. The body would not listen to the brain. It remembered the blinding, inhuman pain and did not wish to obey the order of the mind: everything was over, the wound had healed, everything was Okay.

Dastoli, director of the Colón Theater, who had once conveniently conducted *Carmen Suite* and *Swan Lake* for me, dropped by my dressing room. "It's a miracle, Maya, that you are here again, dancing again. I was afraid that you would never walk."

I flew to Japan from Munich several times. I was invited to perform in major ballet galas. I've been there nineteen times in my life. It's also my country. Japanese audiences like me. At least, so it seems to me. The Japanese have seen almost my entire repertoire. From *Swan Lake* to *Mary Stuart*. And now they've seen *The Madwoman of Chaillot*. Impresario Tokishi Takada was at the Paris premiere and immediately brought the new ballet, while it was still hot, to Tokyo and Osaka. And the roomy Bunka Kaikan Theater was full. The curious Japanese all buy the colorful, elegant programs. Bending their dark heads, with marvelous seriousness, they study the ballet's story before the start of the performance. They want to know who Jean Girodoux was and what neighborhood of Paris is called Chaillot.

Japanese food is the ideal diet for a ballerina. Sushimi, sushi, shabu-shabu,

---

*See chapter 18.

sukiyaki, and tempura fill you up and give the body energy. But you don't feel heavy or sleepy. You can go straight from the table to the stage. It was in Japan that I set my personal record, doing *The Dying Swan* four times for an encore. Of course, I later repeated that in Lisbon, New York, and Paris.

A lovely ritual awaited me when I came out the stage door. In a neat line, ballet lovers waited for my autograph. Asking permission, they had their pictures taken with me, flashbulbs blinking. They gave me scarves, shawls, bell dolls, and their drawings. The most daring asked me for my worn ballet slippers. If I promised to bring them the next night, you can be sure that the collector would be at the stage door early.

And in Moscow the pressure kept building. On short trips into the country, as soon as you cross the threshold at Sheremetyevo, you sense the fear and terror all around you. When you saw any of the friends who had not left Moscow yet, you heard the same advice: "Go away, don't stick around. The mousetrap will snap shut any day now." And everyone was tired of anticipating the explosion, the catastrophe, the counterblow. If only it would happen and we'd get it over with. I whistled in the dark. The uncertainty was exhausting.

I flew back to Munich.

With a Chicago troupe, quite impromptu—I am in Chicago just as my husband's wife—I appeared in a production of the local ballet. *By Django*, staged by Gordon Schmidt. A genre I've wanted to do for a long time: dancing to jazz. Django Reinhardt was a star of the jazz world in the 1930s to 1950s. A three-fingered virtuoso guitarist, the idol of Paris. A Belgian gypsy. A man who created an amusing legend about himself. Our good friend, conductor Mario di Buonaventura, told me about him. Mario was a student in Paris then and had often attended concerts by the legendary Django. Virtuoso, drug addict, fighter, drunkard, bohemian, genius, he had bought himself his first suit just a few days before his death. He had lost two of his five golden fingers in a fire. And he managed wonderfully well with three on the neck of his incomparable guitar.

My part was small—how could you learn a longer one in just two days?— but vivid and effective. At last I was dancing in high-heeled white satin slippers. Floor-length dress, with deep slits to the waist. Streams of crystal drops in my hair. A huge concert boa: I was dancing a singing star. Dancing. But I danced as if I were singing. An interesting task. Four partners, like a jazz quartet, accompanied me, conveying me gently. The singer's part was created by the choreographer with humor, conviction, and believability. The authentic recording by Django filled me with electric energy.

Rodion and I spent the summer of 1991 in America. He was Composer in Residence at the festival in Lancaster, Ohio. And then we went to Florida. It was the first visit to that hot state for both of us. The Atlantic Arts Center had invited Rodion to work with young composers. I had no professional engagements in that period, so I turned into an accompanying figure.

Of course there were problems with American visas. We were supposed to leave the next day, but the visas in our Soviet passports would be ready, as we were told coldly and formally, only in a few days. Desperately worried that everything would be ruined, that the tickets would be wasted, and the opening concert canceled, I suddenly thought to call Shirley MacLaine in California. Later I tried several times to thank my dear old friend. And there was never any answer. Silence ... But that day after a long ring, I heard her familiar, friendly voice from the other side of the ocean.

"Hello, Maya. They won't give you your visas? Where are you calling from? I'll call our ambassador, then I'll call you back. I'll try to help."

Five minutes later, the totally inaccessible (for holders of Soviet passports) Mr. Josef Sapala, American ambassador to Spain (our wanderings had brought us there again), was on the line. "This is a misunderstanding. Of course, you'll go. I'll be waiting for you with your passports."

Another small miracle happened in my life. The long-awaited American visas were stamped into our red passports. And we made it on time everywhere. We were really flying there. To America. Thank you, Shirley.

Lancaster, and especially Florida, brought new impressions. In New Smyrna Beach, we met the granddaughter of Leo Tolstoy, Vera Ilyinichna, who despite her almost ninety years boldly drove her cigar-shaped car and did not refuse an extra shot of vodka at dinner. I showed her photographs of *Anna Karenina* at the Bolshoi, and Vera Ilyinichna recalled that her aunt Alexandra Lvovna had told her about my ballet. Both Tolstoy relatives, as if they had planned it, at first seemed extremely surprised that the famous novel could be turned into choreographic action. But then they talked about the ballet as something long assumed and understood.

We made some very good friends, the Chelishchevs. Marina's ancestors on her mother's side went back to the Goncharovs, right to Natalia Nikolayevna Pushkin. And Victor Chelishchev, in addition to all the writers, vintners, and military leaders, had in his ancient, noble line the Bavarian monarch Wilhelm Lunebourg. But having famous ancestors was not the only fine attribute of this hospitable and charming couple.

The frivolous Florida days came to an end. We had to go back. Home. But where was that?

We arrived in Munich in the morning and got into a taxi. The driver had his radio on full blast. I saw Rodion's expression change. What were they saying in German? I didn't understand.

A coup in Russia. Tanks on the streets. Gorbachev was — allegedly — sick and could not run the country. Well, there it was. What we had expected and feared all these months. The chances of a good outcome were nil. The coup leaders had the army, the police, the KGB. That meant that those who in fact had power wanted it. In Russia, everything is always done the opposite way.

Reporters from several American newspapers found us in Munich. We cursed and swore at the coup leaders. But how could that help? We stayed glued to the radio, waiting for the latest news from Moscow. Things were bad. And suddenly — this was providence, nothing else — the coup leaders flew to the Crimea to see Gorbachev. Yeltsin signed orders for their arrest. The army refused to defend the Communists. However, if someone tougher had been in the place of those political impotents, we would all have been in trouble.

Two evenings with the Vienna Opera. December 1991. I was invited by Lena Tchernichova, who was appointed director not long before. Once again, my trusty *Swan*.

At some point I had lost something in it. The last few *Dying Swans* (Los Angeles, London, New York) had been more boring. I sensed that the audience wasn't totally captivated by the danced story. Four minutes did not pass as an instant, as a single whole, but fell apart into components, into sections. The same held for the choreography: what surfaced were simply movements, simply an arabesque, a turn.

Then, before Vienna, I watched the videotape of one of my recent unsuccessful performances. I had to find a rational explanation for what was happening to me. At least for myself. Or give up dancing forever. You can have one unsuccessful performance. But a whole series of failures?

I thought I found the reason. I had gotten bored with faithfully repeating the canonic text over and over. And then the "swan imitations of Plisetskaya" that I had seen innumerable times live and on tape had ruined my appetite and provoked spontaneous changes. How I understand Claude Debussy's exclamation, "God spare me from the debussyists."

Even earlier, when I danced the *Swan* for an encore, I intentionally tried to do the number differently, to contradict myself. I would come out from the other side, shift some accents. The final pose I often did in mirror image or just completely different. And if being not the same had become a goal in itself, then it was easy to lose the essence of what I was doing. And I had. So, in Vienna I was going to return to my beginnings. I would add a slightly Picasso-esque break in the line, the sharp scribble of his pencil in his enchanting, magical drawings. But the rest would be the old way, everything the way it used to be.

Mid-December. It was very cold. Evenings and icy mornings, Vienna was deep in fog. Rodion in his rented Opel barely made it from Munich in time for my performance. I had realized my intention and felt triumphantly that the audience of the Vienna Opera that night was in my power. I guessed I could dance a bit more. As long as people asked.

On December 16, we decided to celebrate Rodion's birthday just the two of us, as well as my victory over myself. To celebrate it in Eisenstadt, the city of Haydn. He was also born in '32. But two hundred years before Rodion. And December 16 was the birthday of several composers. Good ones at that. Well, for instance, Beethoven.

Armed with a map of the area around Vienna, heroically overcoming the enveloping fog, we tried to find the road to Haydn as indicated in the guidebooks. In vain. Three times we ended up back at the crossroads from where we set out. Oh well, it wasn't meant to be. We walked to a Japanese restaurant instead. As I mentioned, Japanese cuisine is the ideal food for a ballerina.

And so those years passed. Interestingly. Busily. Strangely. Not at all boring. Complete. Sometimes extraordinarily interestingly. But sometimes in all that bustle you want to go home. To rest. To have a breather. But where was my home? Our home?

Moscow was moving farther and father away. I wasn't invited to dance there. The Bolshoi was an enemy camp. A cult of personality! All my ballets were taken out of the repertoire. The sets were rotting in the snow. The costumes were sold. My desire to stage a new ballet was met with deadly silence. The administration of the Bolshoi pretended not to have received my proposal.

I sent a worried letter to Gorbachev. I explained that my home theater had deprived me of all work. Silence. No reply. In a forty-minute talk with Raisa Maximovna Gorbachev, Shchedrin was met with disdain and stubbornness. She did not wish to discuss President Gorbachev's dictatorial participation in the ballet conflict at the Bolshoi. Payment of my salary was stopped. No pension was given.

So where was my home? Not there. Then where?

Perhaps in Lithuania, on the farm Kozelkiskes, on the shore of a lake, where our beloved dacha lies? In spring and summer months it is like paradise. And we are surrounded by kind and warm people. But once the landscape grows grim, and the winds, fogs, and rains come, the days grow shorter, and the wind creeps into every crack, we have to move to winter quarters. To stave off depression. So, not there.

Perhaps in Munich? In comfortable Thereseinstrasse? In a furnished flat? Where I don't even have a desk to write this book? Where after lunch I clear someone else's German dishes and wipe dry the bright yellow tablecloth — not mine — and sit down at the kitchen table and write these lines?

For the third day in a row I stopped at a store window nearby. On Turkenstrasse. What a lovely chest of light Mediterranean wood. And relatively inexpensive. I wanted it so badly. It would be so useful every morning for my makeup. But where would I keep it? I asked myself. Maybe tomorrow we'll set off traveling again? As it was, half my wardrobe, which wouldn't fit in the apartment, was hanging in the closets of my most loyal friends, Luda and Erik Zorin (the first auditors of the chapters in this book) and getting crumpled in suitcases in the basement. We were afraid to rent a place — what if the Germans didn't extend our visas?

Or perhaps, a person doesn't need a home at all? Doesn't need his own roof over his head? The writer Vladimir Nabokov and the artist David Burlyuk never had their own homes. And they didn't live badly, homeless. They wrote and painted so much.

So I must be an old-fashioned, unmodern person. Not a Futurist. I needed my own home, my own roof. I needed a roomy closet for my dresses. And I needed the light chest. And a desk . . . Of course, I remembered Shostakovich saying that you can write in a doghouse if you have the thoughts.

I don't know, I don't know . . .

I do know that it was hard for everyone who was born in the former land of the Soviets. The evil colossus on clay feet dressed in army boots was tumbling down. An earthquake. And the earthquake would affect everyone.

I know that. But I still wanted my own roof over my head.

In very early January 1993, on the 3rd, actually, a Sunday, Rodion and I came to Sheremetyevo Airport. We were going back to Munich. There was a small festival on his music in Moscow and St. Petersburg to mark his sixtieth birthday. And he received the State Prize of Russia. The New Russia! It was a very solemn occasion, in the Kremlin.

We were in an elevated mood. Friends were seeing me off with flowers. We handed our passports to the young, good-looking border guard. Recognizing us, he smiled and bent over our passports in his glassed-in booth. "You I'll let out," he said to Shchedrin. "But you, Maya Mikhailovna, I can't. Your passport is invalid as of January 1."

"Why is it invalid?" I was getting nervous. "How can that be? It expires in November 1996. Look at it. And I'm allowed to exit. There's the multi-entry stamp until November 1, 1993. It's still valid."

But the border guard returned the passport to me. "I see all that. But I repeat, your passport is invalid as of January 1, 1993."

"How can that be? You're not getting something wrong?'

"On December 31, my last shift, I would have let you out. The passport would have been valid. But today I can't. The passport is invalid."

"What am I supposed to do?"

"Try to appeal to the duty consul at the airport. His number is . . ."

Rodion wrote down the numbers on his boarding pass. He was furious. "Now do you see why everyone is getting out of here?"

"Don't shout at me. I am following orders."

We called the consul. This was the dialogue:

"Yes."

"Hello. This is Plisetskaya."

Silence.

I continued. "They're not letting me out. My ticket will be lost. I have a concert in Brussels the day after tomorrow. What should I do?"

"I can't help you."

The receiver was replaced on the other end.

It had been a long time since anyone had talked to me in such an icy, unfriendly tone in this country. It had been a long time since I had not gotten a response to a greeting.

We feverishly began searching for a way out. Whom should we call? Whose phone number did we remember by heart? And the real question was — whom would we find on a Sunday?

I heard them announce the boarding of our flight. In a half-hour the plane would be in the sky. Well then, let Rodion go without me. In the morning I would make the rounds of the ministries to change my passport. They might be willing to help. Not drag things out. But how would I get my German visa in the new passport? It was impossible to get into the German Embassy. Thousands of people were lined up.

Finally, through an acquaintance, who reached another, who called a third, we got the telephone number of the duty officer at the Ministry of Foreign Affairs. The voice was friendly.

"Yes, it's true. Yes. Your type of passport, Maya Mikhailovna, is no longer valid. It will have to be changed."

"Can that be done tomorrow?"

"No, not tomorrow?"

"Why not?"

"The new passports won't be ready until April."

What rubbish! Nothing had changed in our lives. The same servile dependence on abrupt whims of the Powers. O land of absurdity! O Mother Russia!

But a middle-aged border guard in major's uniform appeared opposite me while I was on the phone. He shuffled his feet, waiting for me to finish. "I just heard, Maya Mikhailovna. Did you speak with the consul? What did he say? I'll take the responsibility to let you out. Please, don't worry. I'm the senior man on the shift. I really liked your *Lady with the Dog*, I saw it on television."

We went down the aluminum intestine to the Lufthansa plane. We made it.

One more stress. One more humiliation. One more idiotic hassle.

But also one more kind person in my life. I didn't even get a chance to ask the helpful major's name.

We wanted so little — to come and go from Moscow as we pleased. That's all! Would we need another — foreign — passport to do that?

What if they took me off the plane? The familiar cowardly thought. But no. The German jet, bumping along the seams in the concrete, moved away from the building in Sheremetyevo. The engines revved. There was the runway. We took off.

So where was my home then?

Chapter Forty-Nine

Curfew

Time to sum up. This is the last chapter.

Yesterday I got to talking with the woman who cleans our apartment on Thereseinstrasse. Frau Steinbeisser. A silly, women's dreamy conversation. Would you want to be twenty again? And the frau said, "No, I don't want to be twenty. Just to work all over again? All I've seen in this life was work. I never noticed springtime. I never saw the world."

And do I need to be twenty?

For ballet twenty is the best time. But twenty, when your life has been set? When you're already in the Bolshoi? When your ballet study is behind you? When *Nutcracker* and *Raymonda* have been danced? When you've had a few lessons with Vaganova? If so, then give me twenty. I'll take it. I'll try to live differently and more wisely. I'll try — promise — to avoid a whole mountain of mistakes that I made over my life. But won't I make new ones? My character won't have changed.

And if I were to take twenty, then, probably, I wouldn't have Kutuzovsky Prospect, or meeting Shchedrin, or *Carmen Suite* or *Lady with the Dog*.

No, I don't accept. Then the hell with being twenty. Let things be the way they are. Then I'll say, like Frau Steinbeisser, "No, I don't want to be twenty."

Of course, twenty is a magical age for any woman, because at twenty she looks good round the clock. By thirty, alas, she's good for about three hours a day. And then, even less. By fifty she has five or seven minutes. And that only in good lighting, with careful makeup.

I am at an anniversary concert for the return of Galina Vishnevskaya to Moscow, where I greeted her with my *Dying Swan*. Afterward, at the party in Choral Hall of the Bolshoi, Anatoli Sobchak, the mayor of St. Petersburg, half-jokingly suggested I celebrate my coming stage anniversary in the city on the Neva. I half-jokingly accepted. Why not? Fifty years on the ballet stage deserves celebrating. I remembered what Igor Stravinsky, whom I was visiting in Los Angeles with my American friend, the lovely Lena Atlas (I had brought Stravinsky an entire herbarium of dried herbs from Moscow at the request of his wife, Vera Arturovna), said wryly about artists' jubilees: "They praise their comrade to the skies. And yet, they wish their colleague nothing but death in fiery Gehenna." (Stravinsky used the word *comrade* in the old sense, not at all in the Soviet; I noted that in my diary.)

But if we did have the celebration, couldn't we do it without insincere speeches? Celebrate without any talk. Just dancing.

Sobchak asked that I sketch out a program for the evening and send it to him. Back in Munich, I did that and sent it with a reliable person to St. Petersburg. But, typically for Russia, my letter was not given to Sobchak. Nothing happened. Then the Lithuanians wanted to do my jubilee, but that got hung up, too. The French impresario Albert Sarfati wanted to do my evening on the stages of the Paris Opera and the Metropolitan. But Sarfati died suddenly.

Well then, we'll managed without a jubilee.

But on a June day in my Lithuanian summer of 1993 came a phone call from Moscow. It was Vladimir Panchenko. "Maya Mikhailovna, how would you feel if the new GosCo together with the Bolshoi had your jubilee at the Bolshoi in October?"

"I doubt the Bolshoi would want to celebrate me. Plisetskaya hasn't been welcome there for a long time."

"And what if they do? What would the program be like?"

"I have a program ready. Will the theater give us the stage?"

"That's our problem, Maya Mikhailovna. I have a preliminary agreement already."

I took out the draft of my lost letter to Sobchak and reread the proposed program for my evening. Three acts. Act 1: Orchestral overture; *Dying Swan* (four ballerinas, one after the other); *Dying Swan* (now me); two or three classical pas de deux (it would be good to invite guests, from the Paris Opera, for instance); flamenco (Spaniards); *Isadora* (me). Act 2: *Carmen Suite*. (Not the whole thing, but a twenty-minute resumé of the ballet. A digest, as the Americans day. I need an assistant—that way I'll save my strength for the third act and amuse the audience: two Carmens means two Josés, a small duel.) Act 3: *Madwoman of Chaillot*. My last work. Muscovites were always eager to see something new. They'll be interested. For that we need to bring the Gigi Caciuleanu Company from Rennes. The entire troupe, with sets.

Would I be able to take that load? It wouldn't have been easy for a twenty-year-old. Panchenko accepted the program.

"Will there be speeches?"

"Not a single word, Vladimir Vsevolodovich, please. Only dancing."

"All right, Maya Mikhailovna, we'll get to work."

I hadn't danced Carmen or Isadora in a long time. I started remembering. I remembered it. Completely. My memory holds good choreography well. When logic ties the movements, like links on a necklace, one combination prompts the body to the next. But still, I should get to Moscow early. Give myself plenty of time.

And what, by the way, was going on there now?

We dutifully watched every broadcast of Moscow news. Both main Russian channels were available in Lithuania. But the news was bad. The crazed Supreme Soviet, which for some reason calls itself a parliament, and its brazen, huffy shepherd under the Russian tricolor spouted speeches that made you sick. The speeches were familiar: obnoxiousness and obscurantism. They wanted communism again. So, I was wrong in one of the preceding chapters, when I said that communism was dead. Not at all. It was doing fine.

Sometimes you watch the parliamentary chaos and can barely keep from throwing something at the screen. Every word's subtext is: give us power. And direct threats to those who do not want a return to the past. And people who are that brazen often win.

This spring, for instance, our Supreme Soviet introduced a new law. Soviet citizens had to change their foreign passports yet again. The old ones were invalid again—you couldn't go anywhere. The new ones are the same familiar passports, with a hammer and sickle and the abbreviation USSR in the middle. You can't tell them apart from the old ones. The whole secret is in the numbers (a different series). And the stamp of a different ministry on your face. That's the innovation! But all the hassle, the worry! Shchedrin and I filled out our applications. A month went by. Now the second is almost over. They won't give us our new passport. What's going on? The official response: We are checking you." They are checking Plisetskaya for two months. Checking Shchedrin for two months. What's new about us, what's to understand? It's just mockery and humiliation. Communism isn't dead. It's fine and dandy.

The sense of danger was growing. Was there going to be a new civil war in Russia? The day for my departure for Moscow was approaching. The ticket was bought for September 29. What if the turmoil started before then? That would be the end of my jubilee. And what if it happened while I was in Moscow? That would be bad, too. No point in guessing. I was going.

I entered my familiar, but now alien and no longer my Bolshoi Theater. My hand had not touched the doors of entrance Number 1 in a long time. More precisely, January 4, 1990, was my last performance here. *The Seagull*. And then in March 1992, *The Swan* at the Vishnevskaya gala. And now it was September 30, 1993. A long time.

My pass for the theater had long expired, and I didn't even have it with me; it was at home somewhere. What if they wouldn't let me in, like Maris Liepa? Or maybe they had some new rules? An unfamiliar watchman took half a questioning step forward. His face was stern. I don't like admitting it, but my heart quivered. They weren't gong to let me in. I would have to explain myself. There used to be a table, and next to it a watchman, always someone I knew. And now they had built something like a low partition (a thought flashed: like a gate in a sheep pen). But a voice behind him said, "It's Plisetskaya." The unfamiliar watchman smiled sincerely and said, "Come in, please."

Through the stage — where the opera folk were vocalizing — I went to my dressing room. The one where Valya Lopukhina settled me in fifty years ago. Ballerina generations. The brevity of ballet life. But I've lingered on alone.

Rehearsals and classes began. My first priority was to go over *Isadora* with the pianist Natasha Gavrilova. She remembered my tempos. She played comfortably. The next day I would rehearse with the children. Children who were not from the Moscow Choreographic School. As Misha Krapivin, who had met with them before my arrival, explained to me, they were from "the choreographic school of the Foundation for the Support of Ballet Art." And I hadn't even known that such a foundation and school existed in Moscow. The children were good. Well-behaved and touching. Just what I needed. Béjart would have been pleased.

Misha Krapivin, in the recent past the brilliant premier dancer of the Stanislavsky Theater, was a great help in realizing my concept of the concert. Besides preparing the children, he coached the four soloists of the "collective *Swan*." The soloists (Ryzhova, Popova, Makarova, and Krapivina) were also from the Stanislavsky. I didn't want to borrow from the Bolshoi. The hurt still rankled. Would it ever heal?

What date were the French coming? With a little time to spare? Or right before the performance? Besides the Ballet du Rennes, I was also expecting two first-class couples from the Paris Opera. It looked like the evening was coming together.

And then came October 2. I had rehearsed hard all morning. It was moving along. And that evening the T.V. news showed revolting shots of a rally of neo-Bolsheviks on Smolenskaya Square. Some of the demonstrators had pictures of Stalin's mug. The lovers of equality and fraternity blocked the Ring Road with all kinds of garbage and set fire to it. The flames blazed. The red-browns (Communist fascists) attacked police with iron pipes. I think that was the first time in my life that I was completely on the side of the police. The cameras captured enraged, savage faces, blows, blood, the flinching wounded. Was this serious turmoil? Then that was the end of my jubilee. Or would it end with this?

October 3. Once again I worked all morning at the Bolshoi. Things were moving well. That evening I felt an anxiety that was no joke. Police barricades were knocked down. A militant, clamoring, enraged crowd took the mayor's office and headed for Ostankino television tower. Channel 1's broadcast stopped in midword. What was going on? Had my forebodings been right? Damn the jubilee! What would happen to the country?

The way events developed is well known. Today's ideal chronicler is the television camera. The many hours of CNN reporting on the coup told the smallest details of the bloody events to the whole world. What if we had had a tape of Ivan the Terrible taking Kazan or Suvorov storming the fortress of Izmail? How will the world go on under the fixed eye of television?

They imposed a curfew. The attack on the T.V. tower was beaten back. A sleepless night in front of the television set. Shots heard from the street. The red glow of fires in the distance was clearly visible from the balcony of our sixth-floor apartment. Crowds of Muscovites came down Tverskaya right under my windows, on their way to defend democracy at the Mossoviet. I could hear footsteps in the middle of the road.

The exhausting morning, when the White House was stormed. After watching the battle and the arrest of the leaders of the rebellion, I walked to the theater.

Classes had been canceled. But I couldn't miss a day of work. Of course, who knew if my evening would be held at all?

Rodion called from Stockholm (he was negotiating with the Royal Opera over his *Lolita*) to find out whether he should come to Moscow. Would my evening take place? Or should he go back to Munich? But I couldn't tell him. No one knew anything. There was a curfew.

I walked down Pushkinskaya. It is parallel to my Tverskaya Street. There were fewer pedestrians, and it was quieter. The barricades from the night before had not been taken apart. The barriers by the buildings were lower, and I got over them easily. But it was very difficult to go down the middle of the street. However, as an obstacle for a tank — what a joke! — they were merely symbolic. On the corner of Stoleshnikova a grim group of people were drinking tea from a metal thermos. Munching on sandwiches. They were seated in circle right on the asphalt. Not too cold, gentlemen comrades, for October?

They let me into the theater. The same watchman who had been on duty that first day. Now he knew me. "Have you come to work? Do you live far from the White House?"

Without waiting for a response, he continued, "I'm on Dorogomilovskaya. We could see everything from there. Like the palm of my hand. The smoke poured out. There was shooting." Everyone wanted to be part of the action. At least geographically.

I didn't meet anyone at the theater. No one at all. The Bolshoi was a ghost town. So I was the only one so diligent. It had never felt it so empty in all my fifty years in the theater. The class was over. Then a shower. Time to go home.

I took the same route back. The tea party on Stoleshnikova was over. Pushkinskaya Street was cleared a bit more. Easier to walk. I went past the Stanislavsky Theater, which sent help for my jubilee concert. And I stopped myself: what if there wasn't any concert?

However, on Pushkin Square, close to the poet's statue, a very hopeful sign. Once again, as they were before the second putsch, bananas were on sale. Banana merchants had multiplied all over Moscow. But I didn't like buying them. They said that the dealers kept the bananas in Moscow's morgues. The refrigeration was just right for the exotic fruit.

The next day I took a taxi to the theater. The streets were clear. The ordinary bustle of Moscow life was slowly coming back. But the police patrols wore armored vests and carried automatic weapons. And there was the burning smell carried by the wind from the Krasnopresnenskaya Embankment of the Moskva

River. From the White — until recently — House. There were panicked stories of snipers firing from rooftops.

That night, just before bed, I had an unpleasant phone call from GosCo. From Vladimir Panchenko. His assistant said that the Paris stars were afraid to fly to Moscow. During the storming of Ostankino a correspondent from a French newspaper had been killed. There was a lot written about it in the French press. And so my colleagues from the Paris Opera chickened out. Some weren't allowed by their parents to go. I had to think about replacements. I would take young people from Moscow. But what if the Rennes company didn't come? Then I would have to change the entire line-up. The Spaniards had already arrived. They were first. Only one singer from the flamenco group imitated the Parisians and stayed home. But that was all right, Joaquín Cortez could dance without him. But then, I still didn't know for sure whether the evening would take place or not.

The artists of the Caciuleanu were braver than the Parisians. They were arriving the next day. That meant that Moscow would see *Chaillot*. If the concert took place, of course.

Shchedrin flew in from Stockholm. I went to meet him at Sheremetyevo right after the first rehearsal with Gigi. Now that *Madwoman of Chaillot* was on, the program with two intermissions would take more than three hours. And then the bows and applause. The audience wouldn't get home before curfew. Curfew was 11 P.M. What if we were to start at 6? We had to find a way to let the ticket holders know.

The final confirmation that my jubilee at the Bolshoi Theater would take place on October 6 came the day before it was due to take place. So, the 10th at 6.

Dress rehearsal.

We went through the entire concert in order. The orchestra rehearsed the Entr'acte to Act 3 of *Raymonda*. I had selected that episode myself. *Raymonda* is my ballet. Glazunov's music is festive and exhilarating. And the coda of the Entr'acte ends in ellipses. The attention of the audience will naturally switch from the orchestra to the stage.

Rostropovich showed up. He decided to give me a present and play the *Swan*. Slava came to Moscow just for that. Today the *Swan* will sound the way Saint-Saëns wrote it. In the original, no additions: cello and piano. Slava hadn't played the piece in a very long time. And I could tell that he was a bit worried. Concentrated. On demi-pointe, at half-leg, I went through the entire number. Wonderfully conformable. How significant Saint-Saëns's melody became under the bow of a great musician. No one could be better!

Later, as soon as the theater orchestra stopped, I heard through the slightly open door of the opera class, which is near the stage, Rostropovich repeating the Saint-Saëns over and over. There's the difference between a master and the merely good. A good artist would have long been gone, cello case slammed shut. But even perfection doesn't satisfy a master.

The young dancers replacing the cowardly stars of the Paris Opera that evening went through their paces with the orchestra. Then the brilliant Japanese dancer Morihiro Iwata. And then another gift from the musician's guild: Vladimir Spivakov (who was in Spain) recorded Massenet's "Melody" in my honor. And using that marvelous recording, choreographer Andrei Petrov staged a poetic pas de deux.

A lot of time was spent working out the lighting for the flamenco. Ricardo Cue — who was there in Moscow with us — prompted the Russian light men with all the changes.

Then I danced *Isadora*. From beginning to the very end, without letting myself relax. I read Esenin's poetry. I checked my breathing.

Then we tackled *Carmen Suite*. That was going to take more work. Arancha Arguelez, a young Spanish prima ballerina whom I have always liked, was to be the second Carmen that night. Arancha was not frightened of the coup. She was truly a Spaniard. She came ahead of time during the risky days of sniper shooting; she fearlessly traversed the entire city in curiosity.

When I created my digest of the ballet, the idea seemed amusing. But now, on the stage of the Bolshoi, my imagination went wild. Two Carmens. Two Josés — Victor Barykin and Gediminas Taranda. The unchanging Sergei Radchenko as the torero. We got carried away, improvised, added details, rejected others. It was working out wonderfully! What joy to be immersed in creative work with people who think like you.

My eye fell on the clock and the inquiring face of Gigi Caciuleanu in the wings. My God, it was 2. And we hadn't gone over *Madwoman* yet. I had arranged for the car from the theater to pick me up at home at 3:30. Maybe I should just stay at the theater? Go over *Madwoman*? Not go home?

No, I would take a break. I didn't want to lose my small treat of arriving at the theater for an evening performance. That sensation always brought me such sweetness.

And I would give my legs a rest for an hour! To tell the truth, just before leaving for Moscow I strained a hip muscle in class. Our marvelous Bavarian friend, the genius healer Rudolf Englert, gave me an injection in the painful spot. It helped, but the Moscow rehearsals and the walking over the barricades strained it again. Dammed imperfection of our muscles! The eternal preamble about traumas, of which you must be sick by now. But how can you avoid them in fifty years on the stage? Two days earlier, Moscow surgeon Efstifeyev gave me a shot. And today, about twenty minutes before coming onstage, I would freeze my hip right through the leotard with chlorethelyne. Insurance against pain. The canister of anesthesia was waiting for me on my dressing-room table.

I've been asked so many times in my life, What is your regimen like, your schedule on the day of a performance? Well, it's like this—dress rehearsal, an hour's rest, anesthesia. But it's not always like that, of course. Please, don't be afraid. Only once every fifty years—that's for sure.

Time to go. The car was waiting.

At the theater I realized that I had forgotten my white tights and the swan feathers. They were at home. I forgot. Quickly to the telephone to ask them to bring it to the theater. Was everything else there? Had I forgotten anything else?

Well, I would begin the routine I had developed over fifty years: makeup, hair, tights, leotard, slippers, legwarmers, you have to start by warming up.

I worried that we might mess up the evening because of the curfew. You could start hurrying, worrying, shortening the intermissions.

But then I got yet another gift. This one from the military: curfew in Moscow starting tonight would be at midnight instead of eleven. In that case, we would manage. There would even be time for the postperformance banquet.

I was ready. I stood in the wings on the men's side. The fanfare and joyous sounds of *Raymonda* fill the theater. Behind me, one of my swans got on pointe for the fortieth time, loosening up her feet before the bourée.

For an instant of fifty years, for a long-long-long fifty years, I waited for my entrance in the last wing on the men's side.

Would this be my lucky night?